87 - rel. has greater perceived influence on pornography than on economic development. So, ~~rel. auth another way to investigate~~ ~~rel auth is over most~~ rel. auth's scope over other parts of society may vary as to content of activities -- more influence over TV industries than over economic development industries. Perhaps more influence over areas the cultural elites are indifferent ab. to. Or residual influence over cultural production (TV, art, movies, books) remains ~~because there~~ ~~sphere~~ at least <u>contested</u>. That is where rel. continues to try to have influence, tho rarely (I suspect) with any success.. Rel. auth. influence can be (a) direct or (b) indirect via influence on individuals that can lead to votes or boycotts.

* [So secularization at ind. level can lead to sec. at
     societal level.

1266b . MA ballots on which ch. ~~the~~ attempted mobilizate show has rel. auth tries to mob. but seems unable ~~a situation~~ to deliver. Would expect ~~most~~ ~~attempt~~ rel. ~~to~~ to move into "cultural" realm, since no longer able to move people. Cf. this with earlier stories of Cath. bishop killing a piece of local ~~legislation~~ ~~practice~~ by his ability to credibly threaten boycott.

164 - raise issue of kinds of resources rel. can mobilize
170. notion of "cultural power" - I can put this is rel. auth context: "rel. has cult. power" when its auth is longer exists ~~ever~~ on societal/ind. level. That is ater cultural power comes to fore. Cf. rel. influence on Springfield cy. plate of black churches in CR or fund. in 1980s. Very different. Cultural resources of ~~religion~~ are g variable depending on ~~the~~ nature of rel. authority.

26 3 - shift fr. "bishop as boss → bishop as lobbyist"

279, - explicit mention of declining rel. auth.

282 - offering mobilization potential.

288 - of 60% of Cath. attend & accord. to survey!

292 - good e.g.'s for spe. as dec. rel. auth.

A Bridging of Faiths

—————————————

STUDIES IN CHURCH AND STATE

JOHN F. WILSON, EDITOR

A Bridging of Faiths

RELIGION AND POLITICS
IN A NEW ENGLAND CITY

N. J. Demerath III
and
Rhys H. Williams

PRINCETON UNIVERSITY PRESS

PRINCETON, NEW JERSEY

Library of Congress Cataloging-in-Publication Data

Demerath, N. J. (Nicholas Jay), 1936–
A bridging of faiths : religion and politics in a New England city
/ N.J. Demerath, III and Rhys H. Williams.
p.   cm. -- (Studies in church and state)
Includes bibliographical references and index.
ISBN 0-691-07413-5 (alk. paper)
1. Church and state—Massachusetts—Springfield—History.
2. Christianity and politics. 3. Springfield (Mass.)—Church
history. 4. Springfield (Mass.)—Politics and government.
I. Williams, Rhys H. II. Title. III. series.
BR560.S7D45   1992   91-39181
261.7¿9744›6--dc20   CIP

To our academic fathers

Nicholas J. Demerath and Reese M. Williams (1922–1991)

CONTENTS

ILLUSTRATIONS

All photos courtesy of the Springfield Republican Company
(*Union-News* and *Sunday Republican* newspapers)

TABLES

FOREWORD

THIS DETAILED STUDY of the interactions among religious, political, economic, ethnic, and legal factors in one city's past and present is the sixth volume published by the Princeton University Press in its series "Studies in Church and State." The series is funded by the Lilly Endowment and is located at Princeton University. Two objectives define the work of the Project. The first is to commission scholarly publications concerned with the interaction of religion and politics giving special—but not exclusive—attention to United States history. The second is to broaden scholarship concerned with church-state issues, in part by identifying authors whose competencies and interests lead them to view the subject in engaging ways. The current publication takes its place among others that admirably fulfill these objectives.

To date two of the volumes have concerned American society. Robert T. Handy's study, *Undermined Establishment: Church-State Relations in America, 1880–1920,* explores the reduced influence of Protestant Christianity in the society at the beginning of this century, while Robert Wuthnow's *The Restructuring of American Religion* analyzes the religious changes in the culture of the last half-century. The three other published studies have suggested comparative dimensions of our work. Helen Hardacre reviews Shintō as a Japanese religion in its relationship to the state. Peter I. Kaufman focuses on a range of case studies in the interaction of religious and political authority from the post-Constantinian era to the early modern west. The most recently published study by Daniel Levine concerns *Popular Voices in Latin American Catholicism.* Additional volumes will continue these emphases. Two will analyze decisive periods of U.S. history, the revolutionary and the Jacksonian eras, while others will explore dimensions of the subject in India and modern Europe. A final volume will explore these issues as they have evolved throughout our history as a nation.

The Project on Church and State has also sponsored several other publications. One is a two-volume bibliographical guide to literature on church-state issues in American history, edited by John F. Wilson. A second is a casebook on church-state law compiled by John T. Noonan, Jr. Most recently, the summer 1991 issue of *Daedalus: Journal of the American Academy of Arts and Sciences*, devoted to "Religion and Politics," developed out of collaboration with the Project.[1]

---

[1] John F. Wilson, ed., *Church and State in America: A Bibliographical Guide*, vol. 1, *The*

The steering committee members believe that many additional topics deserve scholarly attention. While unable to commission studies beyond those noted above, we hope that their existence will broaden discussion of these fundamental issues, stimulate students and scholars to frame further inquiries, and eventually lead to a fuller understanding of the dynamics present in the interaction of religion and politics.

A Bridging of Faiths adds an important element to the work of the Project. Through close and imaginative study of a multi-ethnic, medium-scale industrial city in the northeast, Jay Demerath and Rhys Williams invite us to recognize the complex and shifting relationships among religion, politics, law, economy—to name only the most obvious factors—in the actual society and culture in the United States. What they discover through their research on Springfield, Massachussetts might be demonstrated with minor variations in other locations as well. They help us to recognize, as only the study of a single community can, the interaction of dimensions of our society that we separate for analytical convenience. In this sense, *A Bridging of Faiths* very much requires us to observe church-state issues not as lofty abstractions but as questions in everyday life.

The Project on Church and State was originally proposed by Robert Wood Lynn, who offered resources from the Lilly Endowment to make it possible. We have depended on Vice President Lynn and his successor, Craig Dykstra, not only for their advocacy of the Project but more importantly for their confidence in its worth. The Project also depended upon the skills of its coordinator, Yoma Ullman, who helped to shape and direct its course. We warmly thank Princeton University Press, and especially its director, Walter H. Lippincott; the current religion editor, Ann Wald; and the former history editor, Gail Ullman. The working relationships involving the Project, numerous authors, and the publisher have been exemplary.

John F. Wilson
Robert T. Handy
Stanley N. Katz
Albert J. Raboteau

Colonial and Early National Periods; vol. 2, *The Civil War to the Present Day* (Westport, CT: Greenwood Press, 1986, 1987). John T. Noonan, Jr., *The Believer and the Powers That Are* (New York: Macmillan, 1987).

ACKNOWLEDGMENTS

THIS STUDY owes its inception to one of the country's great intellectual brokers, Stanley N. Katz, then professor of history at Princeton University and currently president of the American Council of Learned Societies. On the basis of a previous colleagueship at the University of Wisconsin, Katz suggested that Demerath be included as sociological ballast among a distinguished group of historians and legal scholars at a two-day conference concerning the desirability and feasibility of a major reexamination of church and state in American life. The conference was jointly convened by Robert Wood Lynn of the Lilly Endowment and John F. Wilson, professor of history and religion at Princeton. It was held at Dunwalke—Princeton's elegant mansion retreat in the rolling hills of central New Jersey.

It will come as no surprise that the conference responded positively to the idea and that the project was soon under way with Lilly's funding and Wilson's direction. What seemed more surprising was an inquiry from Lynn concerning Demerath's interest in serving as Lilly's outside "evaluator" of the enterprise. After a series of exchanges concerning what evaluation might entail for a foundation anxious to secure sound assessments of its scholarly ventures, Demerath agreed. Indeed, he has continued in that role, even after he responded positively to yet another invitation from Lynn and Lilly to submit a proposal for a church-state project of his own. That, of course, became the study on which this book reports. It was funded just in time to provide a research assistantship for Rhys Williams, then a second-year graduate student in sociology at the University of Massachusetts.

Bob Lynn has been a patron, a colleague, and a friend throughout. As many others have noted, Lynn is an exemplar of the successful foundation official, and it was not just Lilly's financial resources that enabled him to mount perhaps the single most successful portfolio of scholarly research on religion in the nation's history. He is gifted both in stimulating projects and in nurturing them. Certainly, his support of this study has transcended the generous funding that Lilly provided. During most of Demerath's many trips to Lilly headquarters in Indianapolis, time was set aside for a two-person seminar in which the sociologist and the church historian could trade responses to a reading agreed upon in advance. Characteristically, Lynn conveyed a consistent concern for one's person that went far beyond his concern for one's project.

The "Springfield project" has benefited from an unusually wide array of wise counsel. Demerath's four coevaluators for Lilly's larger church-state program have been invaluable sources of advice and support in the Springfield venture. John Demos, William Gamson, Gillian Lindt, and John Mansfield have all shared their special expertise in history, political sociology, religion, and constitutional law, respectively. Whether meeting in Boston, New York, or western Massachusetts, we have all gained from the challenge of trying to understand a city in its terms as well as our own.

John Wilson has been a particular boon to the study, and perhaps only two academics could have thrived within the nested relationships that Wilson and Demerath developed for themselves. On the one hand, Demerath looked over Wilson's shoulder as an outside evaluator of his various undertakings, which have included not only editing a legal casebook, a two-volume bibliography, and a substantial monograph series but also authoring a forthcoming capstone work on American church-state history. On the other hand, adding this volume to the monograph series has given Wilson editorial license to look over Demerath's shoulder. He has done so with the utmost discretion, gently insinuating astute suggestions within messages of enthusiastic support. This same combination has characterized the comradeship of a number of others also stomping in the church-state vineyard, especially Katz, Robert Handy, Bruce Nichols, and Albert Raboteau.

Of course, the study has been greatly assisted by a number of local colleagues, students, and staff. We received various kinds of support and assistance from "Five College" faculty, including Joseph Ellis of Mount Holyoke, who read the entire manuscript in a penultimate draft. Early on we convened several dinner seminars to elicit the advice of pertinent scholars from Amherst, Hampshire, Mount Holyoke, and Smith colleges and the University of Massachusetts. We held the first of these meetings serendipitously in the nearby hilltown of Ashfield, Massachusetts, which we later discovered to have been the site of the country's first church-state litigation in 1768, when local Baptists objected to paying taxes in support of the town's established Congregationalism.

Meanwhile, the university community was helpful in various ways. Journalism's Howard Ziff introduced us to the local world of newspaper archives and editors. Within sociology, Clark Roof provided valuable assistance with our questionnaire survey. Michael Lewis and Tim Black gave penetrating responses to a late draft, drawing upon their own research in Springfield. Sr. Mary Johnson, S.N.D., did the same, combining her expertise as a sociologist of religion with her personal background in Springfield's Irish neighborhood, Hungry Hill. We are especially grateful for the research assistance of Gretchen Stiers, the omnicompetent fiscal administration of Sally Ives, and the sunny clerical help of Cathy Sanderson.

Certainly, we are indebted to the citizens of Springfield, many of whom shared their time and their candor despite what must have been considerable reservations. We have pledged not to identify our informants individually, and so can only thank them collectively. However, several Springfielders do deserve special recognition for facilitating particular aspects of the research. Richard Garvey is the doyen of Springfield's newpapers, and one who richly deserves his mantle as the city's historian laureate. He provided a wealth of anecdote and perspective while acquainting us with various file sources. Ellen Kristoferson was especially helpful in seeking out pertinent photographs from the files. Joseph Carvalho and the staff of the Springfield Library's "local history" room were a constant source of good counsel and good cheer. James Sullivan and Jim Controvitch of City Hall provided a superb introduction to the local demographic scene and rendered a signal service in drawing a sample from the city rolls for our small survey. Of course, they are no more responsible for the survey itself than those who pretested it; these included the always helpful Andrew Searle and a group of his young professional friends, the First Congregational Board of Deacons, and the Third Baptist Church Choir. The choir's generosity even included an opportunity to sing with them in a gospel rehearsal.

Finally, Princeton University Press has been a model of professionalism throughout. We are especially indebted to Jane Low, Ann Himmelberger Wald, and Christine Benincasa for their can-do editorial management. As a copy editor, Joan Hunter is a dulcet exception to the compulsive scolds of publishing lore. She is in no way responsible for our occasional spasms of stylistic idiosyncrasy and self-indulgence.

It is perhaps especially appropriate that a community study should rely upon so many communities of support and assistance. But of course, every community has its incorrigibles and recalcitrants. Insofar as we have failed to do justice to either Springfield or the larger topic of religion and politics, the problems are most assuredly not attributable to the many who have sought to steer us clear of them.

July 1991   *Jay Demerath (Amherst, Massachusetts)*
                               Rhys Williams (Carbondale, Illinois)

A Bridging of Faiths

Chapter One

APPROACHING SPRINGFIELD

In 1986, Springfield, Massachusetts, celebrated its 350th birthday. Still a youngster by European standards, it is a municipal Methuselah for the United States. Celebratory events dotted the annual calendar, as the anniversary gave added legitimacy to any city occasion for good food, good music, good fund-raising, and good civic piety. Finally, the year climaxed with a solemn ceremony held not in the city's own auditorium—its Symphony Hall—nor in the place of all previous birthday gatherings—Old First (Congregational) Church on Court Square; this time the city's past, present, and future were consecrated by the mayor, the bishop, and attending dignitaries in St. Michael's, the cathedral of Springfield's Catholic diocese.

Clearly, much had changed over the city's three-and-a-half-century history. Never quite a Puritan "city on a hill"—so extolled by Governor Winthrop—it was in fact founded in a swamp on the banks of the Connecticut River. While growing from twelve original families to a city population of more than 150,000 at the hub of a metropolitan area of some half-million, it has also undergone massive changes in every sphere of civic life.

This study focuses particularly on twentieth-century developments in two of these spheres: religion and politics. And yet it can hardly avoid other aspects of the city, and indeed is part of a long but recently lapsed tradition of "community studies" in the social sciences. This tradition has spawned such distinguished works as those of Robert and Helen Lynd on "Middletown"—Muncie, Indiana (1929 and 1937); W. Lloyd Warner on "Yankee City"—Newburyport, Massachusetts (1963); Liston Pope on "Millhands and Preachers" in Gastonia, North Carolina (1942); Floyd Hunter on the "Community Power Structure" of Atlanta, Georgia (1953); Robert Dahl on "Who Governs?" in New Haven, Connecticut (1961); and Arthur Vidich and Joseph Bensman on "Small Town in Mass Society"—"Springdale," of upper New York State (1968).

And yet our interest was not in the genre for its own sake, and our approach to cities and to Springfield was more oblique. Like most contemporary scholars and many citizens, we tend to think of issues in national and sometimes cross-national terms. With the exception of the country's major metropolitan leviathans, American cities and towns have receded into the backwaters of our social consciousness and compel little attention for their own sake. In fact, we had driven by Springfield countless times without even considering it as a possible research site until we became involved with a problem for which it offered a case study. It quickly became more than that. Like all cities, Springfield offered a sense of urgent social theater. Once we began to understand its plot lines and its cast of characters, we became a rapt audience for its serial drama.

This chapter is an introduction in several senses. First, we shall introduce the problem that led us to Springfield in the first place. Second, we shall introduce Springfield itself in somewhat more detail. Third, we shall introduce the research procedure, noting both aspirations and disclaimers, and describing its several methods and sources of information. Finally, we shall introduce the book itself by previewing the chapters to follow and commenting briefly on the volume's title and its multiple meanings.

APPROACHING THE PROBLEM

Few topics are more characteristically "American" than the relations between church and state. Indeed, the shibboleth concerning the "separation of church and state" is for many Americans probably one of the most familiar parts of the U.S. Constitution, notwithstanding the fact that it nowhere appears in that document but comes instead from a private letter of 1802 in which Thomas Jefferson referred to a desirable "wall of separation" between the two domains. The error is understandable. After all the Constitution is our political Bible, and it is seen as the probable source for many high-flown social principles. Recently 23 percent of a national sample even saw it as the source of "From each according to his ability; to each according to his needs"—Karl Marx's formula for communism. The original Constitution mentions religion only once, in Article VI, which stipulates that "no religious test shall ever be required as a qualification to any office or public trust under [the authority of] the United States." But of course, the subsequent First Amendment includes the sometimes nettlesome nub of the matter in its statement that "Congress shall make no law respecting an establishment of religion, or prohibiting the free exercise thereof."

The second clause concerning free exercise seems clear enough as a general principle, and it may be worth noting that now some 90 percent of the world's nation-states make similar provisions (Van Moorseven and Van der Tan 1978). It is the first clause concerning "establishment" that has proved more elusive. Whatever it may mean, a "wall of separation" is no more accurate as a historical fact than a constitutional citation. For the nation's first one hundred and fifty years, it endured more as an article of faith than as a statement of reality. The Protestants' domination of the country's political and cultural life was always implicit and sometimes explicit. But since roughly World War II, the topic has become increasingly contested as religion has been implicated in a widening range of social issues and as various new religious groups have vied for influence. No longer just a cue for superficial self-congratulation, our church-state legacy has become a source of burgeoning controversy and litigation. Whether the specifics involve prayer in the public schools, aid to parochial schools, abortion rights, or tax exemption for religious groups, frequent murmurs occasionally give way to raucous dins.

Through all of this, scholars have hardly been idle, as the voluminous literature on church-state issues attests. And yet Winnifred Sullivan (1987) deplores two characteristics of this work in her recent bibliographic assessment:

> [Scholarship concerning] questions of religion and the law since 1870 have been increasingly dominated by the Supreme Court. The result has been both a nationalization and a constitutionalization of the issues. (p. 339)

By "nationalization," Sullivan means a tendency to confront the issue at the federal rather than the local level, with an overwhelming emphasis on events in Washington rather than in the provinces. Scholars have been far more attentive to opinions of the U.S. Supreme Court than to decisions elsewhere in the federal judiciary, let alone state, county, and municipal courts. They have been much more compelled by the actions of the U.S. Congress than those of state legislatures, city councils, or town meetings.

This is certainly understandable within a federal system. However, while there is much at the local level that reflects the national, the emulation is by no means slavish, even with respect to the law. Although American cities and towns share at least an abstract reverence for the nation's legal system and founding documents, a good deal is lost in local translation. Dolbeare and Hammond (1971) provide important illustration in their analysis of the poor compliance of Wisconsin communities to the Supreme Court's school prayer decisions of the early 1960s. This is less a matter of willful nose-thumbing than a combination of ignorance, diffidence, and allegiance to local priorities. In many communities, even formally prohibited practices may endure in the absence of some messianic misanthrope with the resolve and the resources to challenge the consensus and make an issue of them. Finally, quite apart from the letter of church-state law, its spirit is also haunting. A wide range of customs and developments lurk around the edges of civic politics and religion like ghosts from the past and harbingers of the future. Finding them requires a search that goes beyond the law books themselves.

This leads back to Sullivan's second point concerning the "constitutionalization" of the matter. Sometimes the mere mention of church and state among scholars prompts a stuffy emulation of the prose and postures of the great jurists of the courts and their current heirs. The rhetoric alternates between the lofty language of rights and the sometimes specious precision of legalese. The Constitution is invoked as Holy Writ on the basic premise that this document and its judicial interpretations have had a dominating impact on the nation at large. Of course, much of our status as a democratic society depends upon this assumption. But it is not merely academic pedantry or sheer cantankerousness to insert some qualifications.

For example, consider the phrase "Ours is a government of laws, not men." Few refrains are more common in times of political crisis, and the chorus crescendoed in the aftermath of both Watergate and Irangate. As a motto of American constitutionalism, it has been clutched to the bosom of "constructionists" everywhere; in suggesting that the rule of law ultimately transcends our human foibles, it offers warm reassurance in chilling circumstances. However, as a theorem of social behavior, it is likely to set any social scientist's teeth on edge—not to mention its offense against women. The point is not that the law is idle or that the Constitution and Bill of Rights should be consigned to the archives as historical curiosa. But as important and prophetic as the law may be, its effects are inevitably filtered through other institutions. The shibboleth's distinction between laws and men not only sets up a false dichotomy but, if anything, also places its faith on the wrong party. From the First Amendment forward, church-state law and judicial decisions have been unevenly implemented, and their effects have been blunted or distorted by other considerations.

John F. Wilson (1987) makes the point more eloquently in introducing the first of two recently edited volumes of church-state bibliography:

> behind and beyond the narrow institutions denominated "church" and "state" lurk enduring questions such as where authority within a culture is to be found, and what form it takes. . . . How does religious power establish its authority against governmental claims to legitimacy? And how much scope do governments permit to actions taken in the name of religion? Understood in terms of this wider definition, the concept of church and state has a continuing relevance to American social experience. But it is a relevance obscured by beguiling metaphors ("the wall") that substitute for thought, or constraining doctrines ("strict separation") that fail to take account for social variety and change. (pp. viii–ix)

Wilson points toward a different approach to the "church-state problem," one that goes beyond a narrowly legalistic framework to a broader range of interactions with a broader set of causes and consequences. A concern over church and state must be placed within an expanded perspective on religion and politics.

We have tried to bring this perspective to a single city in order to cross the grain of both nationalization and constitutionalization. Rather than attempt another recapitulation of the national experience, we have focused instead on the local level, as represented by Springfield, Massachusetts. Rather than a courtside view of how church and state ought to interact, we have asked the citizens and leaders of this midsized city for their judgments. And rather than concentrate primarily on the world of "ought," we have aimed for a more empirical assessment of how church and state actually relate and how these relations have evolved historically. Indeed, rather than restrict our attention to only those church-state relations mentioned in constitutional legacy, we have sought out broader issues not only of religion and politics but of culture and power.

In fact, the book may be seen as an answer to a basic question that attends the reversal of a fundamental power relationship in Springfield. For almost three hundred years, the city was dominated by its Yankee and largely Congregationalist elders. For the first one hundred and fifty years, this dominance involved the virtual exclusion of outsiders; for the last one hundred and fifty years, it was fundamentally a matter of keeping the newcomers in their place. While the newcomers represented a variety of religious faiths and denominations, it was primarily Catholics who were cast in the familiar drama of immigrants mired in the hostile muck of class and ethnicity as well as religion. But especially over the past half-century, this has changed dramatically. Catholics have undergone a major transformation from the victims of power to its wielders. This began demographically as a matter of sheer numbers; it then moved into the arena of municipal politics, only to culminate much more recently with developments in the civic economy.

Without suggesting that the city's Yankee Protestants have been relegated to the miserable lot of the nineteenth-century Catholics, there is no question that where power is concerned, the Catholics have considerably more than the Protestants. But what are the consequences? Actually, several possible scenarios suggest themselves. A first might entail consolidating dominance by making today's Springfield as thoroughly Catholic as yesterday's was Protestant—a new form of religious establishment. A second might involve redressing grievances as contemporary Catholics "stick it to" the Protestants as retaliation for past oppression—a new set of restraints on religious free exercise.

In fact, neither of these scenarios is accurate, and much of the book is devoted to explaining why. In assessing Springfield from a constitutional standpoint, not surprisingly we have confronted a wider set of social, political, and cultural forces. Issues of both establishment and free exercise bleed into other questions, including how civic policy is made and

Approaching Springfield—and its bridges—from the south.

influenced in the first place, how various religious groups can affect the process, and how all of this has changed over the city's history. These all relate to still broader matters such as religious pluralism and secularization; cultural versus structural power; the impact of size, differentiation, and de-differentiation in an urban setting; and the place of religion within the warp of class, race, and ethnicity.

APPROACHING THE CITY

For most visitors, Springfield is glimpsed first from the south as the Connecticut River, Interstate 91, and the Amtrak lines all swing wide to the east before resuming their northward line on the city's west flank. The city's skyline is dominated by the conspicuous successes of its recent downtown development—though not as spectacularly as Hartford some thirty miles downriver. As one draws closer, the new Basketball Hall of Fame passes in a blur of fast-breaking multicolored panels on the left; to the right, the steeple of the First Congregational Church and the classical campanile of the municipal complex seem hunkered at the feet of the hotel and business high rises just beyond.

The distinct neighborhoods of this "city of homes" (a label the city applied to itself in the 1890s) occupy the hills rising away from the river and the former swampland now straddled by the city's power center. The central uphill sweep to the east moves from the municipal Court Square up through a museum and library complex and the Catholic diocesan cathedral to a national park on the site of the decommissioned Springfield Armory. For almost one hundred and fifty years, this armory was the chief source of American military arms and the hub of the city's long-standing economic concentration of machine industry. Since World War II, however, this has largely given way to insurance and finance. At the same time, the city's population declined from a high of 174,473 in the 1960 U.S. census to 163,905 by 1970 and 152,319 in 1980, although the preliminary 1990 count shows a slight rise again to 154,528. Meanwhile, suburbanization has grown apace. While the "larger Springfield area" population now approaches three quarters of a million, its formal size as a "standard metropolitan statistical area" stood at 523,000 in 1988.

We would like to report that Springfield's selection as our research site was the result of an exhaustive national search. Alas, we cannot. The visitor who goes twenty miles farther upriver will come upon our own base of operations at the University of Massachusetts in Amherst. Proximity was clearly a chief criterion in the site selection. And yet the choice does have some redeeming characteristics.

The largest of the forty-nine "Springfields" across the nation, this one is a fair demographic representative of the country's "middle-sized cities."

Nor is this a trifling category. Although we tend to equate "urban America" with giant centers such as New York, Chicago, and Los Angeles, smaller cities account for almost as large a population segment in the aggregate. As of 1988, our urban behemoths of over one million accounted for 12.6 percent of the U.S. population; cities like Springfield with populations between 100,000 and 250,000 accounted for 12.1 percent and were part of almost half of the population (47.5 percent) living in middle-sized communities of between 50,000 and 500,000 people (U.S. Bureau of the Census, *Statistical Abstract of the United States, 1990*, 110th ed., Washington, D.C.).

Students of community life have generated a series of dichotomies that have been simplistically interpreted. Whether "*gemeinschaft* versus *gesellschaft*," "folk versus urban," or "local versus cosmopolitan," it is tempting to infer that societies are divided into villagers and metropolites, country bumpkins and city slickers. The more common situation is, of course, a bit of both. While this is even true of residents of the megalopolis (cf. Herbert Gans' *The Urban Villagers*, 1962), it certainly describes the scene in cities such as Springfield. Here one not only has personal access to one's neighbors, but often to one's leaders. Springfield abandoned the quintessentially New England "town meeting" in the middle of the nineteenth century when it was incorporated as a city; but its subsequent political forms and processes combine machine and bureaucratic qualities with more personal and particularistic attributes. The combination may be more typical of the urban scene than many of the impersonal and satanic images we have inherited as part of a pastoral and antiurban legacy.

Many of our respondents shared the sentiment of one of the community's elite: "Springfield is small enough to manage but large enough to matter" (interview). The basic trade-off underscores the appeal of the midsized city, and it recurred in interviews with business entrepreneurs, politicians, social reformers, and residents in search of urban attractions with small-town accessibility.

The sentiment also applies to our own situation as researchers. From the standpoint of urban ethnography, neither small nor large is necessarily beautiful since both have pros and cons, as described especially in Appendix A. However, Springfield is a far more negotiable environment for a variety of research strategies than the country's metropolitan goliaths. At the same time, it is considerably larger than the country's "Middletowns" and "Yankee Cities." Later, we shall explore the political and cultural implications of Springfield's size and its standing midway between the stereotypic town and city. Meanwhile, we can paraphrase our respondent's quote by noting that the community is large enough to reflect virtually all of the major tensions and dynamics of the American urban scene but small enough to allow an intimate acquaintance with them.

Springfield was a recent finalist in a national All-America City competition, and it can take pride in a number of all-American characteristics. These range from its own witch trial in 1651 to the invention of basketball in 1891 and the development of the M–1 rifle to replace the Army's "Springfield" by 1936. In fact, the town earned its first national notoriety in 1777 when its federal armory was personally approved by Gen. George Washington following a brief stopover. The resulting machine-tooling capacity was subsequently shared by other industries, especially in transportation. In 1896, Springfield was the site of the first mass-produced car, the Duryea, to be followed by the Atlas, the Bailey, the Knox, and, from 1920 to 1935, the Rolls-Royce. The original Indian Motocycle (*sic*) plant has recently been made into condominiums following a lengthy dispute over urban renewal. But the city has done more than keep the nation moving and equip the military. A source of both guns and butterfat, it has also been a home to ice cream (Friendly's), as well as toys (Milton Bradley's), children's literature (by Dr. Seuss as well as Thornton Burgess), and literature more broadly (Webster's dictionary).

The city has had a distinguished collection of political critics, ranging from Daniel Shays and his rebellious farmers, who stayed briefly in the city on the afternoon of January 26, 1787, before they were scattered, to the antislavery crusader John Brown, who spent several years in the late 1840s as the respected proprietor of a wool business that served as a cover for an Underground Railway stop. Springfield can also bask in the considerable intellectual light of such nineteenth-century national figures as the newspaper founder and publisher, Samuel Bowles; the newspaper editor turned utopian novelist, Edward Bellamy; and the well-known preacher of Protestant social reform, Washington Gladden.

During the twentieth century, the city has tended more to celebrate American values than to fault their implementation. This is exemplified by such contributions as *Good Housekeeping* magazine (actually begun in 1885), the Junior Achievement awards in business and industry, and the Springfield Plan for multiracial education and citizenship, which was celebrated in "March of Times" newsreels and mass-market periodicals during World War II, only to founder shortly thereafter. The city's most recent distinction is perhaps its most difficult one to interpret; according to a recent survey, Springfielders "walk faster than the residents of thirty-six other U.S. cities" (*Psychology Today*, October 1989).

Meanwhile, Springfield has an all-American flavor from a religious standpoint. Certainly, its religious history mirrors that of the nation at large. It was first founded as a Puritan trading post in 1636, and for almost two centuries it was an almost exclusive enclave of Yankee Congregation-

alism. Beginning in the early nineteenth century, however, religious homogeneity began to give way to a growing pluralism. The need for a
greater labor supply overcame opposition to Episcopalians, Baptists, and
finally Catholics. Throughout the nineteenth century and well into the
twentieth, Springfield was a reluctant host to successive waves of immigrants from Ireland and both Western and Eastern Europe. By the late
1920s, Catholics had attained a demographic plurality; by the 1950s, they
had a majority of elected political officials; and by the 1980s, they had
achieved proportional representation among the city's major business
leaders. But, of course, lay representation within a city's secular ranks
does not necessarily entail ecclesiastical power over them, as we shall see.

The relative decline of "mainstream" Protestantism and the corresponding rise of Catholicism are important parts of the American historical experience, especially in the Northeast and in urban centers across the
country. But the nation has also resembled Springfield in retaining a basic
pluralism. The city's Catholicism may be preponderant, but it is not exclusive; liberal Protestantism may be down, but it is not out. In fact, Springfield also has a significant representation of Evangelicals and Pentecostals,
a small but influential Jewish community, and at least a smidgen of virtually every other religious faction or trend that has surfaced in the nation at
large.

All of this reflects its general representativeness across ethnic, racial,
and class lines. While the Irish are the city's largest white ethnic group,
there are substantial French-Canadian, Italian, and Polish communities,
not to ignore the longtime Yankees who remain in the city or populate its
suburbs. Springfield's African-American community has roots in the early
nineteenth century, but since the 1930s it has increased in numbers to
almost one fifth of the population. The Hispanic—largely Puerto Rican—
population has arrived more recently and constitutes over one tenth of the
city proper. Again there is a sense of pluralism. The classic New England
mill towns, such as nearby Holyoke, were socially dichotomized between
the ethnic millworkers of the flats and the Yankee mill owners and managers on the hill—workers and managers. But today, Springfield's more diversified economy has led to a more complex social structure, one that is
further fractured by recent patterns of social, economic, and geographical
mobility within the city and its environs.

In all of this justification of Springfield as a research site, our reasoning
is very similar to that of the historian Michael Frisch (1972), who used the
city as a locus for an examination of early patterns of municipal incorporation and urbanization in the nineteenth century:

> But why Springfield, Massachusetts? As must often be the case, the subject
> was bold enough to suggest itself long before any rigorous search for the
> perfect specimen could be launched, or even before the framework for inves-

tigation had been fully developed. Fortunately, as the study progressed to a more serious level, Springfield proved extremely well suited to the task at hand. It was and still is a small city, which made feasible the comprehensive study of an adequate span of years. Its roots are deep, providing a background of cultural and institutional identity against which nineteenth-century change could be seen in sharp relief. Because change was never sudden or substantial enough to completely overwhelm tradition, the more subtle and interesting interactions between old and new proved visible. No claim will be advanced here that Springfield is "representative," but at least it can be noted that there is nothing in the city's structure or experience to disqualify it as a guide to more general patterns. (p. 5)

Finally, however, it is as difficult to justify the selection of any one city as it is to justify the selection of Springfield as the one city in particular. In some sense, this project is rendered implausible from the start by trying to produce a nationally meaningful study by looking at a single local case. Of course, this is methodologically impossible in any strict sense, and we have no delusions of having stumbled upon the perfectly representative American city. On the other hand, Springfield does have microcosmic qualities for our purposes, and beyond its specific all-Americanisms, the city has hosted a series of political and religious processes that have recurred in other communities across the country. The details surely vary— e.g., from Catholic to Southern Baptist or even Mormon hegemony, and among a variety of political forms from strong mayors to oligarchical city councils, city managers, and county governments. But many of the basic tensions, conflicts, trends, and transformations we discuss are also muttered over elsewhere. Throughout, we shall bear in mind a responsibility to move beyond the Springfield city line through cautious conceptualization and generalization. While we agree that an analyst only earns the right to generalize following a deep immersion in the historically specific, we also feel that such immersion can lead to intellectual drowning unless one resurfaces to breathe both out and in.

So much, then, for a broad description of the study site and our intentions concerning it. But if these are the ends of the study, what are the means or the methods—or the "methodology," as we social scientists are perhaps too inclined to call it?

APPROACHING THE RESEARCH

In introducing any study, it is as important to note what it eschews as what it attempts. This is not a "history" of Springfield in the comprehensive sense, though it is certainly grounded in that history, particularly that of the last century, and most particularly the period since World War II. It is not a fully nuanced examination of Springfield's political life and "power structure," though they will be crucial in relation to religion. Nor is it a conventional study of Springfield's "churches" or its larger religious community, although this too is a critical component of the whole. In providing a sociological account of Springfield's recent history of religion and power, we have tried to stress the shifting relations and "bridges" between spheres and sectors rather than provide inventories of each for its own sake.

Because the book focuses especially on relatively recent—and, in some cases, still unresolved—developments within the city, another sort of caveat is necessary: This is not a journalistic account of facts for their own sake. Of course, we have tried to get the facts as straight as possible, but we have also included putative occurrences and interactions even where hard documentation is unavailable. As scholars more interested in the culture of politics than in political events *per se*, we have found that what is believed to be true can be as important as the truth itself. A consensually validated opinion may be more revealing than an empirically authenticated incident.

There are two additional respects in which we have strayed from common journalistic practice. First, we do not divulge our sources or quote by attribution; second, while we mention the names of public personages in our early chapters on the city's history, our accounts of more recent events only identify individuals by their roles, not their names. After all, what is important here are not the persons peculiar to Springfield but the processes that Springfield shares with other social settings. In fact, in probing many phenomena, it was sometimes more difficult to know when to stop—a problem compounded in a case study where details themselves can become criteria of worth. As compelling as Springfield has become to us, we recognize that it will be far less so to others unless it informs more generalizable issues.

Appendix A provides a more thorough account of the study's methods and data, along with our ruminations and misgivings concerning them. Here, however, we want to describe the essentials. Basically, we have used *three* sources of data or information; namely, historical records, personal interviews, and a small questionnaire survey. Although the three are certainly compatible, even complementary, they each present quite different problems and prospects.

Historical materials are as varied as they are elusive. They include demographic data from both federal and Massachusetts censuses, election statistics, publications by religious and community groups, the personal papers and biographies of prominent citizens, minutes and records from city agencies and the local courts, scholarly histories, and newspapers. As we have already noted, Springfield has a proud newspaper tradition reaching back into the nineteenth century to the great publisher, Samuel Bowles, and looking forward into the twentieth through the family of Edward Bellamy. In addition to the city's several daily papers, there have been a number of subcommunity weeklies, especially around the turn of the century. Much of this heritage is available on microfilm, and both the newspapers themselves and the local library maintain clipping files on various subjects.

Although we have been trained as sociologists rather than historians, our respect for the latter has grown throughout this project. Historical records are often buried beneath both dust and gloss; they are frequently disorganized and contain equal numbers of false starts and false conclusions. As noted in Appendix A, we suspect that such problems increase with the decreasing size and bureaucratization of the venue. The historical files of the federal experience are likely to be far more codified and comprehensive than those of any city; and the larger the city, the better the quality of information available. Springfield occupies a midpoint on this implied continuum. Our search for nuggets of historical gold was only occasionally rewarded; more often it involved futile panning in barren creek beds.

We sought evidence and insight at several different levels. Of course, we were broadly concerned with the grand sweep of the city's more than three hundred and fifty years. But our interest quickened over the past century and the years that have elapsed since the focus of Michael Frisch's work (1972) on the period of incorporation, *Town into City: Springfield, MA, and the Meaning of Community, 1840–1880*. Developments over the past fifty years have been especially revealing of fundamental shifts in the character of both religion and politics.

In order to sharpen the focus, we isolated three ongoing matters of community controversy for particular attention, not only through historical materials but in our interviews and questionnaires. These involved, first, the response of the city and various religious groups to the problem of homelessness; second, conflicting priorities and actions concerning the economic development of a largely black neighborhood during a major surge of downtown development; and third, controversy surrounding abortion, contraception, and sex education—domains made more urgent by the rising tide of AIDS. Religion has been involved in each of these matters, but in different ways and with different outcomes. Each amounts to a case study within a case study.

Meanwhile, our second research method entailed *personal interviews*, and these present a different set of methodological issues. Overall, we interviewed some 104 persons. Some of the respondents were informed observers; others, major participants. Some were valuable for the light they shed on the past; others are vital actors in the present. The interviewees included both reputed members of the city's elite and influentials behind the scenes. We talked with clergy, politicians, educators, city employees, community activists, social workers, reporters and editors, and members of the business community. Rather than use a strict sampling procedure for this varied population, we followed a kind of "snowball" strategy by asking each of our interviewees who else might be appropriate and building the list as the study rolled on.

The interviews themselves averaged one and a half hours. For the great majority, both of us were present, one as the primary interviewer and the other as scribe and supplemental prodder. We promised each subject anonymity, and following Dexter (1970), the sessions were only minimally structured to allow open-ended coverage of a range of topics that varied from one interviewee to another. Our goal was more to sustain a conversation than to administer an instrument, since it was more important to pick up new leads and insights than to dwell on what we already knew enough to ask. But of course, there is an important distinction between one person's hunch or recollection and a consensually validated observation. We used the interviews to explore this boundary through a series of checks and cross-checks.

With very few exceptions, our interviewees were extraordinarily gracious in opening up themselves and their community to two outside academics—one in Ivy League livery and the other in cowboy boots. This was all the more remarkable since our questions concerned a potentially explosive subject about which the city—and many of the individual respondents—might have much to lose and little to gain. Violations of church-state law and unwarranted relations between religion and politics were not matters to be taken lightly. Still, only two persons declined to be interviewed, neither one a member of the city's central cast of characters. There may have been frequent instances of purposeful distortion or dissimulation, but they were rarely apparent. While this might suggest an unusual talent for prevarication, we prefer to interpret it as a combination of their cooperativeness and our growing command of the issues. In any interview session, interviewers have power to the extent that they have knowledge, and as the study progressed we no doubt became more efficient in both generating and assessing information. By and large, respondents seemed to warm to the subject rather quickly, following an understandable initial reticence. Rapport grew as our obvious fascination with their city gave credence to our beginning comment that we were there to learn from Springfield rather than to expose it.

Finally, as a third source of information, we used a small *mailed questionnaire survey* as a way of reaching more extensively into the community for a broader gauge of its sentiments, perceptions, and pertinent characteristics. If interviews tend to provide depth at the expense of representativeness, questionnaires offer the reverse prospect. In fact, we used two quite different sampling strategies. First, we sought a random sample of city residents (using the city's own census of the voting-age population); second, we focused on several specific subpopulations, including clergy, political and business leaders, and public school teachers and administrators. All samples received the same questionnaire, with the exception of a few additional questions for the educators concerning religion in the schools. The instrument is reproduced in Appendix B.

Once again, we faced a problem as outsiders asking for an individual's responses to highly controversial issues. And unlike an interview, mailed questionnaires afford no personal contact for conveying bona fides or the sincerity of a pledge of anonymity and confidentiality. We knew we could anticipate real difficulties after two early pretest sessions—one in a black Baptist church and the other in a white Congregationalist parish. In each setting, a respondent reacted to the same critical question in the very same words: "Whew! I wouldn't touch that one with a ten-foot pole." Forewarned, we did our best to provide appropriate assurances, and to delete gratuitous complexity and controversy without diluting the instrument unduly. We also followed up our initial questionnaire with three reminder mailings and a final phone call.

Despite such efforts, we achieved a disappointingly low response rate of only 47 percent for the general sample, yielding 256 actual questionnaires for analysis. There are a number of possible explanations for this shortfall, but the basic difficulty and volatility of the issues themselves seem uppermost. Several questionnaires were returned with such comments as "The answers to these questions are private," or "My husband said there was no way I should answer this." Our telephone contacts revealed a number of persons who were skeptical about the confidentiality of the results. And despite our insistence that there were no "right" answers to the questions, a number of respondents saw the instrument as a kind of civics test and were embarrassed by their problems in reaching any answer. One respondent may have spoken for the sample as a whole when she wrote with strained politeness at the end of her completed questionnaire: "Thank you for considering me for this questionnaire. Don't send any more!"

In the world of survey research, it is axiomatic that both politics and religion rank high among topics difficult to probe. Here, of course, we have joined the two and added a series of controversial questions concerning the community itself—its ethnic tensions, the role of organized crime, corruption in city hall, and so forth. The resulting response rates provide a serendipitous measure of the sensitivity of our concerns, and not just in Springfield. Cities and citizens alike have a good deal invested in idealized public images. It is only slightly less popular to ask about the emperor's clothes than to remark upon them.

APPROACHING THE BOOK

The conventional format for examining church-state relations is that of a court proceeding, where, of course, arguments are offered and probed on both sides of a case, and justice is weighed before it is wrapped. Certainly a book could be organized in a similar fashion, building from one bit of evidence to the next and culminating in a final magisterial verdict. And yet the model is not appropriate here. This is not an exercise in the law, and we are more interested in broadening issues for deeper understanding than narrowing them for specific judgment. Because we want to examine church-state relations as part of a larger city fabric, the book is organized to give a cumulative sense of its texture and color.

Given the centrality of religion in what follows, we begin with an overview of its historical development in Springfield. Chapter Two describes the transformation of Springfield from a Puritan trading outpost in 1636 to a dominantly Catholic city by the mid-1950s. In one sense, this would seem a tale of two establishments—from the early Yankee Protestant to the later ethnic Catholic. However, the evidence for and against a current Catholic establishment frames the instructive mystery that occupies the remainder of the book. As a historical sprint through more than three hundred years, this chapter can only introduce the question without supplying the answer.

Chapter Three concerns events of the last thirty years as new high-rise buildings and a new city elite both produced and reflected a new civic spirit. This was a period in which Catholics secured their political hold on the city and began to gain an upper hand in the local economy. It was also a time in which Catholicism itself began to change, along with the configuration of civic power. Here, we use our questionnaire data for the first time in describing how the city thinks of itself and its governance.

With this as background, the next four chapters turn more specifically to recent matters of church and state, and religion and politics. Chapter Four provides a sense of how Springfielders themselves view the issues, including the constitutional concerns over a religious establishment and religious free exercise. In addition, the chapter describes a series of specific church-state episodes and entanglements that have occurred in Springfield's more recent history.

The three succeeding chapters each deal with a particularly prominent facet of recent city politics in which religion has played a role. Chapter Five concerns homelessness in the "city of homes." The controversy is relevant to church and state because clergy were active in different camps pushing toward a solution. But in addition to describing an important episode at the interface of religion and politics, the chapter also provides an introduction to several important conceptual issues and frameworks that recur in subsequent chapters. It briefly reviews several judicial tests and precedents for church-state cooperation; it notes that the social science literatures on religion and power have tended to pass each other like ships in the night; and it describes recent developments in the study of both social movements and cultural power that help to locate religion in the city political scene.

Chapter Six focuses on the conflict surrounding the economic development of the city's most prominent African-American neighborhood, and the degree to which the neighborhood was slighted by the priority assigned to the downtown area. The conflict's religious pertinence stems from a small ecumenical group of predominantly black clergy who served to keep the wound open and raw. Known as "the Covenant," this group used its religious standing and moral authority in the service of its political activism. While the results were mixed, they are also instructive. On the one hand, they reveal more of the boundaries concerning church and state in Springfield; on the other hand, they also illustrate the prospects and frustrations of social movements more generally.

Perhaps the most volatile question on the Springfield agenda—and one not yet resolved—is the focus, in Chapter Seven, on sexuality and sectarianism. Abortion, contraception, teenage pregnancy, and AIDS all underscore the controversy surrounding sex education in the Springfield public schools. There is no question of religion's involvement both behind the scenes and very much out in front. But there is also no question that the issue has produced strange alliances, especially among a small group of activist parents that included both Catholics and Evangelical Protestants. The public policy dimensions of sexuality reflect the considerable changes under way within the city's various religious communities, and the communities' various relations to the civic power centers. The issue also reflects the interaction between short-term and long-range factors in what we have called politics' "temporal dialectic."

Finally, the book concludes by "bridging the gaps" in Chapter Eight. After looking inward to Springfield and offering several layers of summary, we then try to look outward from Springfield in hazarding several more generalizable and conceptual ruminations. The general problem concerns the conditions and constraints for religious influence in the power relationships of the civic arena. Here, we begin by exploring several key variables concerning civic power itself. We end by returning to a consideration of religion, especially the various meanings of the term "secularization" and its seeming opposite, "sacralization."

In none of this do we have delusions of offering final answers. After all, the very people we consulted for clues are still available for second guessing. This book is written for them in more than the usual sense. Throughout we have tried to make it accessible to the general reader by avoiding some of the common characteristics of the scholarly tome. In addition to relegating a good deal of methodological and statistical detail to the appendixes, we have dispensed with footnotes altogether—incorporating what is valuable within the text itself and jettisoning the rest. Moreover, although we do indulge in several sections of theoretical broodings, we have tried to set these off at the end of their respective chapters to allow the non–conceptually inclined reader to skim them quickly or not at all. Unlike some authors who assume their every word is of equal high value, we welcome such skimming as the price to be paid for reading at all in a busy world.

APPROACHING THE TITLE

Authors seldom divulge their experiences in selecting titles. But perhaps there is something to be gained in making this private process public. We suspect that few book titles materialize in a sudden burst of intuitive lyricism. Even those that later seem most apt may reflect as much calculation as inspiration. Frequently there are a number of options to select among, each of which captures part of the project's essence. Sometimes there is a struggle over just what is to be conveyed, and on occasion there is a tension between titles that are wonderfully stylish and those that are, if nothing else, modestly faithful to the project's substance. Finally, titles are among the few legitimate outlets for the wordplay which has made scholars infamous. If patriotism is the last refuge of scoundrels, titles may be the last sanctuary for punsters.

All of the above applies here. Of course, we wanted a phrase that not only captured something of the city and the basic issues but was also distinctively beckoning. For a long while we worked under a series of whimsical rubrics. These included "Springfield Rifled" (which we thought suggested not only the well-known product of its federal armory but also our own roles as researchers ransacking the city's past and present); "Of Crooks and Mace" (which appealed to us solely because both terms carried quite different sacred and secular connotations); "Cross and Double-Cross" (a phrase that leapt from the mouth of a cynical colleague in political science upon learning that the book concerned religion and politics); "Full Court Press" (to honor both the law and Springfield as the birthplace of basketball); and finally "Critical Mass" (an all-purpose cliché in Massachusetts that at least had the merit of pointing to crucial developments within Springfield's Catholicism).

Our final choice may seem only marginally preferable to these perverse alternatives. However, "A Bridging of Faiths" appealed to us on several grounds. First, it alludes to Springfield's status as a city of bridges over the Connecticut River that forms its western border and has played such an important part in its economic history. Second, and more obviously, the movement between faiths and faith communities is a very large part of what the book is about. As we shall begin to make clear in the next chapter, Springfield has undergone a major historical transformation from Congregationalism to Catholicism. There are other religious transitions too, including bridges between historical and contemporary Yankee Protestantism and between older and more traditional Catholicism on the one hand, and its several current variants among the newly middle-class Irish, French, Italians, Germans, and Poles, as well as the more recently arrived Hispanics.

But we also intend a broader sense of faith. In addition to the conventional religious connotation of faith, there are a series of other belief systems that sometimes approach sacred status. The book offers another kind of bridging between the faiths of religion, on the one hand, and the faiths of politics, on the other. In the wake of Jean-Jacques Rousseau, Alexis de Tocqueville, Emile Durkheim, and most recently Robert Bellah (cf. Demerath and Williams 1985), scholars often speak of a nation's "civil religion" as its near-reverential sense of a collective identity and a noble purpose. Correspondingly, we discuss Springfield's civic religion at the municipal level and explore its relation to other faiths based upon ethnicity, race, class, gender, and generation.

In all of this, the bridge itself is an important symbolic representation. For us, it signifies a city's overarching cultural span, which all faiths must traverse in their relations with each other and with the community at large. From some perspectives, the civic bridge has become a more significant—and perhaps more transcendent—reality than that which it crosses or joins. On the other hand, no bridge floats entirely free, just as no political or legal system can be fully divorced from the faiths that surround and sustain it.

Finally, we confess to some wordplay of our own. Read aloud, the title conveys another important theme from the book; namely, the extent to which many of the faiths above have been "abridged" in the sense of being lessened, curtailed, or, more sociologically, secularized. This does not hold true for all of the adherents of any faith, much less portend an end to faith itself; nor does it deny the very real bursts of faithful vitality that run counter to the trend. Still, the tendency toward religious change and attenuation is central to an understanding of both church and state and religion and power. The dynamics are as important for the country as a whole as they are for Springfield, as each nears the end of yet another bridge— this one into the mists of the twenty-first century.

Chapter Two

FROM MEETINGHOUSE TO CATHEDRAL

FEW COUNTRIES have been more preoccupied with change and progress than the United States. And yet many observers have seen New England as an exception. Its very name conjures lingering ties to a bygone era and another country altogether. Widely regarded as the country's historical bedrock and wellspring, its attractiveness to tourists depends upon a quaintness that borders on the fusty. In a nation sometimes embarrassed by the sheer brevity of its conventional history, New England is a plum of antiquity buried deep within the pudding.

But, of course, this is also misleading. In fact, few regions of the country have hosted more dramatic change. The shift is not only between whole economies—from trading through agrarian, industrial, and commercial—but between two quite different social fabrics. Once fiercely and rigidly cloistered in its homogeneity, the area was later besieged by pluralism. In the process, many of its jurisdictions experienced transformations of both "ins and outs" and "tops and bottoms" within their social structures. Tables have been turned demographically, politically, economically, and, of course, religiously. Indeed, perhaps no change prefigured more than that between Puritan and Catholic.

Springfield provides as firm a purchase on these changes as any locality, as this chapter and the next attest. However, ours is by no means a complete rendering of the city's history. In focusing not only on religion but even more specifically on religion's relationship with governance and power, we have been more selective than exhaustive. Certainly this is not an exercise in history for its own important sake. At the same time, we can scarcely deny the press of the past upon the present, or history's continuing salience even for those thoroughly preoccupied with the here and now. As much as Springfielders themselves are mired in their past, it would be foolish for us not to seek a grounding of our own.

Like the history itself, this review of it is apportioned between two "establishments." The first, of course, was Puritan, Congregational, colonial, and Yankee; the second is immigrant, ethnic, upwardly mobile, and Catholic. We realize that "establishment" is a loaded term in any work on church and state, and we use it here less as a legal judgment and more for sensitizing purposes. There is no doubt that the first establishment would have been in flagrant violation of the First Amendment had it not run much of its course in the one hundred and fifty years before the Constitution and the Bill of Rights were adopted. While violations continued afterwards, this was a period of the decline of one establishment and the stirrings of another. But to speak of the two under the same establishment rubric is certainly an overstatement in constitutional terms. As much as the new Catholic dominance may seem an establishment—especially to older Yankees—it is at best a pale and quite different imitation. Like its Protestant predecessor, it too has followed a trajectory—one that may even now be in descent.

PROTESTANT DOMINION AND DECLINE

The Native American history of Springfield is lamentably beyond our ken. But to the early settlers in the Connecticut River valley, the Indians were anything but dismissable. In 1634, Plymouth's Governor Bradford noted a providential intercession that made the push westward more feasible: "It pleased God to visit us with an infectious fever. The disease also swept away many Indians" (Bauer 1975, p. 3). Two years later, twelve families from Roxbury, who had found the tilling poor and the taxes high, sailed from Boston south and east, then up the Connecticut River to establish a "plantation." They were organized and led by one William Pynchon, who had earlier moved from his native Springfield in England to Roxbury in the Bay Colony and now refused to pay his Roxbury taxes. Upon arriving at what was not named Springfield until four years later, Pynchon bought land on both sides of the river from the agreeable Agawam Indians for a total price of "18 fathoms of wampum, 18 coats, 12 hatchets, 18 howes, 18 knifes" (Green 1888, pp. 12–13). The community's first cottage industry was the stringing of wampam, derived from collected seashells, by the women and children. Trade with the Indians—especially for beaver pelts—was lucrative from the start.

The Articles of Agreement around which the town compacted in 1636 stressed religion in both its preamble—"We whose names are underwritten, being by God's providence engaged together to make a plantation . . ."—and its first resolve—"We Intend by God's grace, as soon as we can, with all convenient speed, to procure some Godly and faithful minister with whom we purpose to join in church covenant to walk in all the ways of Christ" (Innis 1983, p. 124). The Rev. George Moxon arrived shortly thereafter in 1637, and although the first meetinghouse was not completed until 1645, there is ample record of early piety. Church attendance was, of course, mandatory, and in 1644 Mr. Pynchon wrote to then Governor Winthrop:

> I praise God we are all in good health and peace in our plantation; & the Lord
> hath added some 3 or 4 yonge men out of the River that are godly, to us lately:

& the Lord has greatly blessed Mr. Moxon's ministry, to the conversion of many soules that are lately added to our church, & hitherto the Lord hath preserved us in peace from enimies. (Green 1888, pp. 74–75)

Developing Tensions in the First Establishment

Actually there is reason to question the religious character of early Springfield. In fact, the city has figured in a generational dispute among historians. Whereas older scholars have followed the august historian, Perry Miller (1939), in depicting New England's early towns as "covenant communities," a new breed has emerged to challenge this emphasis on religious consensus and centrality, some from a more Marxian perspective. Stephen Innes (1983) argues that Springfield was more a "company town" than a "covenant community," a point reinforced by John Martin's (1991) account of "Profits in the Wilderness." Innes notes that all but the first of the thirteen Articles of Agreement were concerned with practical matters; he might have noted that even the first, as quoted above concerning a minister and church, is cushioned with concerns of convenience. Innes' conclusion disputes the received historical wisdom for colonial New England this way:

> As the pragmatic nature of its founding articles suggests, early Springfield bore little resemblance to the subsistence-oriented covenanted communities. It was not a "peasant utopia" or a "Christian Utopian Closed Corporate Community." Nor was it a "peaceable kingdom," a "one-class society," a "homogeneous communal unit" or a "nucleated, open-field village." The inhabitants of early Springfield would have looked with wonder on such characterizations of their society. Their community was founded not as a peasant utopia but as a fur-trading post. Although composed of believing Christians, Springfield failed to make rigorous efforts to distinguish the unregenerate from the Visible Saints. (p. 124)

Although Innes casts cold water on the more religious depictions of New England communities, he does not drown them completely. Instead, he argues that there were three different settlement zones: first, the urban coastal area of Boston and Salem; second, an area of subsistence farming, as in Andover and Dedham; third, "highly commercialized agricultural towns," such as Springfield. The covenant model may be useful for the second zone, but it is misleading for the first and third.

Certainly there is much to sustain this view of Springfield. In his book and subsequent article, Innes notes that, even in its earliest days, the town was far from homogeneous and included both "distinguished and obscure men" (1987). He describes several of the latter in detail, including one John Woodcock, who was called before the magistrate for slandering

the Reverend Mr. Moxon and "laughinge in Sermon tyme." Innes suggests that the rough and tumble demands of frontier life were conducive
to greater moral tolerance of such idiosyncrasies. Still, "The minister's
position and authority in the town [were of a] fragile and problematic
nature" (Innes 1983, p. 147). In fact, this might have described the sense
of religious solidarity generally by the mid-seventeenth century. Paul
Lucas (1976) depicts the Connecticut River society of the time as a "valley
of discord," and he centers the strife within the church congregations
themselves:

> The collapse of clerical authority and the continuing struggle between lay-
> men and clergy kept the church system in continual disarray, curbing its
> ability to carry out tasks assigned by brethren, ministers, or society in gen-
> eral. The instability of the system infected the entire institutional structure
> of . . . the Connecticut Valley. Mechanisms intended to curb dissension
> failed to perform. The locus of authority became as blurred in the civil realm
> as it was in the ecclesiastical. Consequently, [the area] emerged not as the
> tightly knit, carefully structured, harmonious society so often described by
> New England's historians but as one troubled by drift, dissension, and a
> search for both order and purpose. (p. xiii)

In 1648, Springfield discovered a witch in its midst. Mr. Hugh Parsons
was finally convicted in 1651 on the testimony of his disturbed wife, who
later recanted on her deathbed and confessed to witchcraft herself. Ultimately, Mr. Parsons was allowed to depart rather than remain for hanging.
Meanwhile, the community's very pillar was salted with charges of heresy
by the Puritan elders in Boston. Mr. Pynchon had published his religious
convictions under the title "The Meritorious Price of Our Redemption,"
arguing that Christ had been killed by the devil incarnate rather than
suffered God's own judgment against our sins. The verdict was reached
before the book was read, and it was quickly burned and banned in Boston. Mr. Pynchon made a partial retraction and returned to England in
1652 at the age of 62 to manage the plantation's interests there, leaving
the local community in the hands of his son, John. It was understood that
the General Court had Springfield uppermost in mind in proclaiming:

> This Court, takeing into consideracon how farre Sathan pvayles amongst us in
> respect of witchcraft, as also by drawing away some from the truth to the
> pfession & practise of straung opinions . . . conceive it necessary that there
> be a day of humiliation throughout our jurisdiction in all the churches.
> (Green 1888, p. 119)

Humiliated or not, Springfield struggled forth. Although the Reverend
Mr. Moxon also returned to England in 1652, and the town's two succeeding ministers lasted only months each, John Pynchon provided authority

The southwest corner of Court Square, featuring the statue of Puritan Miles
Morgan, the fourth First Church structure on the original site, and the former
Hampden County Courthouse (designed by H. H. Richardson).

and stability. Known to his fellows and lessers alike as the "Worshipful
Major Pynchon," his substantial home, the "old fort," was the town's primary defense against King Philip's Indians in 1675. According to Innes,
"in Springfield the class structure was essentially two-tiered: John Pynchon and everyone else." Certainly, he presided over Springfield's transition from a plantation settlement to a colonial town. And at his death in
1703, the famed Rev. Solomon Stoddard of Northampton preached the

funeral sermon for this "Father of our country" under the title "God's Frown at the Death of a Useful Man."

Not even Pynchon was able to able to maintain Springfield as a single seamless and always seemly whole. By the late seventeenth century, there was already a sense of looming heterogeneity. Following the spirited debate between the liberal Stoddard and Boston's conservative Increase Mather, the "half-way covenant" extended church membership on the basis of birthright alone without requiring a full-fledged conversion experience. Edmund Morgan (1963) has argued that this was more an adaptation to demographic change than a decline of piety, but impiety was far from unknown in Springfield. In 1673, one George Filer admitted "entertaining Quaykers" [and] was reprimanded for his "heritical opinions." His sentence was a fine of five pounds or to be "well-whipped" for his "speaking against the ministry" (Green 1888, p. 143). Quakers and Baptists both were to become more severe threats in the years ahead for their often obstreperous separatism. In fact, a mild version of separation was enacted by the Crown when, in 1684, it suspended the first Massachusetts Charter and, in 1691, enacted a consolidated "Dominion of New England," one provision of which rescinded church membership as the condition of political participation.

Diluting the Establishment Brew

Springfield's local government continued to operate in and through its First Church Meetinghouse until 1734. But by the turn of the eighteenth century, First Church lost its exclusive religious franchise after a considerable struggle. In 1695, thirty-two families on the west bank of "the River" petitioned the General Court to allow them to construct a church of their own. The required state approval in such matters is itself noteworthy, and it was granted in the following year as the First Church community was assessed fifty pounds to help with the expenses. This created considerable ill will, and as late as 1711 the money had not all been paid. Meanwhile, another group of early suburbanites to the south in Longmeadow filed a petition of separation in 1703 and had a church of their own by 1713. These depleting developments saddled the members of the original First Church with the heavier burden of paying their minister's salary and church expenses; some refused to pay and were taken to court by the town itself.

Still darker clouds gathered ahead. By the 1740s, religious revivalism was gaining sway in the Great Awakening. This often unruly enthusiasm for the spirit swept over all of New England but was particularly strong in the Connecticut River valley under the kinetic but controversial prodding of the Rev. Jonathan Edwards of Northampton. As Gregory Nobles (1983) points out in his recent history of "divisions throughout the whole" in neighboring Hampshire County, the call to awaken was no respecter of status. Indeed, the greater the pedigree the greater the vulnerability, as a number of Harvard and Yale graduates discovered in encountering pulpit sentiments like the following:

> I make no Doubt but the Colleges pour forth Swarms of young Men, who have spent their days in diverse Lusts and Vanities; —and these unhappy Men come forth to serve the Churches (but really to serve *themselves*) and after a Life spent in Pleasure, Pomp, and Worldly-mindedness, go down to the dead, and to the *Damned*, and *their People with them*. (p. 49)

It was in this context that Springfield experienced its second case of heresy. In 1735, First Church invited as its pastor the young Rev. Robert Breck of Marlborough, Massachusetts, and Harvard College, where his high academic achievements had been marred by an allegation of petty book theft. This coupled with his liberal opposition to "antinomianism" provoked a stern reaction from a major faction of the church and a major imbroglio. Breck was finally exonerated by a committee of outsiders—and went on to a distinguished tenure of almost a half-century in the Springfield pulpit. Local historian Mason Green (1888) observed the irony that his more celebrated age-mate, Jonathan Edwards, had offered little assistance during Breck's early trials, only to suffer later (if unintended) retribution when Breck himself cast the deciding vote in Edwards' own dismissal from Northampton in 1750, an event that dramatically punctuated the end of the Awakening itself. Green's comparison between the two men elucidates a developing contrast between two quite different traditions within Protestantism overall:

> The two rising young men of this valley—Breck and Edwards—set at work at about the same time to examine the portals of the orthodox faith, —one with doubt and the other with herculean faith. One held up the shield of the love of God, and the other brandished the sword of the glory of God; one had the heart and the other the intellect of theology, and both felt the demoralization of Christian society in New England. They and their respective partisans— for that is the word to use—met in open combat, and the results were as dramatic as the immediate conflict was terrible. Breck brought the religion of Springfield into the revolutionary period, and opened the way to modern ideas; while poor Mr. Edwards, after establishing his metaphysical scheme, was forced to retire to [be a schoolteacher to] the Stockbridge Indians under a cloud. Scholars have since bowed to the genius of Edwards, but people live the principles of Breck. (p. 229)

Clearly, changes were afoot in New England society and culture. By 1750 Puritan authority and austerity were giving way to new forms of thought, morality, speech, and dress. All of this was apparent in Springfield. In fact, Green's description anticipates our own view of the city as a microcosm:

> In dealing with Springfield, we are, in a large sense, writing the history of a hundred plantations. Townships were growing out of the gardens planted by the churches, and in these townships was the spirit of democracy. The American Declaration of Independence was written early in the eighteenth century, when out of a dismal religious reaction, and a healthy counter revival, and a hundred confusing things, political and social, came a common faith in self-government. One can find ground high enough in Springfield during the first quarter of the eighteenth century to look straight into the revolutionary war. But it would be uncandid to neglect to say that many in Springfield in Breck's time deplored the liberality he encouraged. . . . When we say that not a third of the Springfield inhabitants were full communicants, we do not say that the churches were empty on the Sabbath. Everybody went to church, as a rule. . . . The routine of their daily life was indeed correct, but the spirit of the pioneers had gone, and the new life dawning upon the people was destined to be as pure, and at the same time unburdened by coercive political machinery. (Green 1888, pp. 257–259)

The imperfect relationship between full church membership and church attendance is as pertinent to recent historical scholarship (cf. Finke and Stark 1990) as are the weakening ties between church and state. In both areas, the literature's focus on "structural" aspects of religion cues our own counterbalancing emphasis on more "cultural" phenomena, a distinction to be elaborated in Chapter Five.

Meanwhile, centrifugal tendencies accelerated. Within church circles, the pressure from Baptist and Quaker separatists continued to increase throughout the surrounding countryside. Whether on economic or theological grounds, they sought to avoid paying local taxes that would support the Congregationalist minister and meetinghouse. In order to maintain the peace, the General Court had offered formal exemption in 1728 to

> persons commonly called Anabaptists [and] those commonly called Quakers . . . who allege a scruple of conscience as the reason of their refusal to pay . . . *provided* that such persons do usually attend the meetings of their respective societys . . . and that they live within five miles of the place of such meetings." (McLoughlin 1971, vol. 1, pp. 225–226)

Somewhat surprisingly, the broad reference to "a scruple of conscience" anticipates U.S. Supreme Court decisions on military conscientious status in the early 1970s, almost two hundred and fifty years later. And yet the exemption remained a consistent source of problems and required continual adjustment, culminating in a new tax adjustment act of 1771. Among other things, this changed the pejorative term Anabaptists to the more civil but more cumbersome "antipedobaptists." Actually, Springfield itself

was spared the issue until the very end of the eighteenth century, maintaining its Congregationalist exclusivity by using its local magistrates to
threaten any migrating Baptists or other religious undesirables with pros-
ecution as vagrants or worse should they choose to stay.

However, the town faced fissures of its own. As early as 1749, the parishes of Chicopee and West Springfield began to move toward separation,
and by 1773 an outside committee was required to pass judgment on what
many Springfielders saw as an incipient dismemberment. Although the
committee failed to prevent the branching off of a number of satellite communities, its sentiments on the sanctity of a township are worth citing
nonetheless. In Nobles' summary:

> A town represented not just a place to live, but a source of identity and pride
> to its people. Its people could experience the "General Benefit and Advan-
> tages accruing to the Community from that Constant and Unavoidable Inter-
> course occasioned by the Public Business of every town,: not the least of
> which were the "greater Sociability and more generous Sentiments among
> the Inhabitants" created by their shared participation in the life of the town,
> and especially in its political affairs. . . . "Nothing but Absolute Necessity
> Can ever Justify the lessening of Dividing a town," they argued; "nothing but
> oppression or Injustice or the evident want of Harmony and peace in the joint
> Management of the common Concerns of a town Consisting of Divers parts
> or parishes Can create that Necessity." (Nobles 1983, p. 146)

But the new spirit of civic independence predominated—and prefigured the larger move toward national independence that was gathering
momentum. On August 30, 1774, a "mob" of several thousand convened
at the Springfield courthouse and forced the members of the Court to bow
to the collective will and sign a renunciation of royal authority. While
some conservative observers were fearful of the impending anarchy, the
concerns proved overblown despite a series of such incidents down the
revolutionary path. Springfield had its small share of Tory holdouts, but
overall the town fell easily into step in the War for Independence. In fact,
one such British loyalist was the senior Pastor Williams of Longmeadow
who, nonetheless, on August 11, 1776, read the Declaration of Independence to his congregation, as was required of him by the Provincial
Congress. Springfield's primary role during the war itself was as a federal
arsenal. With the surrender of Cornwallis in 1781, Pastor Williams' diary
reported "great rejoicing in town and prayers and hymn-singing in First
Church" (Bauer 1975, p. 26).

Casting the Postcolonial Die

Not all was rejoicing in the years immediately after independence. As the
young nation struggled with old debts and new burdens, the load was

passed to an increasingly restless populous. In January 1786, the Springfield arsenal was the primary target of the nation's first antigovernment insurrection. Organized by Daniel Shays, a former army captain from nearby Pelham, "Shay's Rebellion" drew disgruntled men from all over western Massachusetts in an assault that was nipped in the bud by troops largely financed by the alarmed Boston business community. However, the rebellion did wrest tax concessions from the government, which combined with an economic upturn to alleviate the crisis.

As rural capitalism began elsewhere in western Massachusetts (cf. Clark 1990), Springfield took a more industrial path. Perhaps the single most critical decision in Springfield's middle years involved the arsenal once again. General Washington had been well pleased with its performance during the war, and was further impressed with its condition during a brief stopover in the town in 1789. On his recommendation, Springfield was selected as the site of the new federal armory, devoted not just to the storage of weapons but to their manufacture as well. The decision set a pattern of heavy industrial manufacturing that was to last for the next one hundred and fifty years. It was this pattern that distinguished Springfield from New England's textile centers, and caused it to leap ahead of its neighboring towns in every dimension of civic dynamism.

Not every Springfielder approved of taking on the armory, however. A number were concerned that it would not only change the town's economic face, but its social and religious complexion as well. There is no question that these Cassandras were correct. At the start of the nineteenth century, according to one local observer,

> there were about 2500 inhabitants, a dozen stores and shops, two or three public houses, two printing firms, a church and several schools in nine school districts. Armory jobs were held by about 100 workmen, and there were mills of several varieties. (Bauer 1975, p. 31)

All of this was to change quickly as the need for an armory work force opened the gates to a stream of new and different residents that was to become a torrent over the next century.

As originally interpreted, the First Amendment to the U.S. Constitution did not apply to state governments. But well before Massachusetts became the last state to officially abandon an established religion in 1833, Congregationalism had lost its exclusive franchise in cities and towns all across the commonwealth, including Springfield. By 1811, the Baptists had a "lodgement" for their nineteen members, and in 1815, eleven Methodists began holding services—both in the watershops connected to the armory. In 1817, Episcopalians began to meet within the armory itself, and in 1818 a group successfully petitioned the state legislature to break away from Old First Church to form a Unitarian church of their own. Over the next decade, five new Protestant churches were built, although the

continuing Protestant hegemony was best symbolized by the Episcopal
services held in City Hall as late as 1838. By 1843 Springfield had eighteen houses of worship: six Congregationalist, four Methodist, two Unitarian, three Baptist, and one each for the Episcopalians, Universalists, and
Roman Catholics (Springfield *Republican*, as cited in the parish *History of
South Congregational Church*, 1942, p. 12).

By midcentury Springfield's religion was booming, if not from the single old cannon of Congregationalism, at least from the gleaming new shot-
gun of a more diffuse Protestantism. Michael Frisch (1972) described the
scene this way:

> Religion, the original source of the communal orientation in New England,
> continued to bear most of the institutional responsibility for community val-
> ues even after the denominational uniformity began to dissolve. All the
> churches, taken together, had a social function hardly separable from the
> purely religious, and few in town had more influence in general matters than
> the leading ministers. . . . The churches distributed Bibles to workingmen,
> and sponsored reading rooms, lecture series, and social events for nonmem-
> bers in an attempt to bring them more securely within the framework of
> community life and values. . . . But it was the battle against rum, lasting
> through the century in varying degrees of clamorous engagement, that illus-
> trates the meaning of community social control more precisely. (p. 36)

Between 1840 and 1860, the number of churches in the community
doubled. But if temperance galvanized the religious community, other
issues were surging to the top of the civic agenda. The economy flourished
with the building of dams, canals, and railroads, as well as the burgeoning
armory. This increasingly diversified industrial base protected Springfield
from the business swings that damaged mill towns such as its upriver
neighbor, Holyoke. However, Springfield was every bit as dependent as
the other towns on an expanding immigrant labor force. In 1852, having
amassed the necessary 12,000 inhabitants, the town became a city by formally incorporating under Massachusetts state law (Frisch 1972). Caleb
Rice, the president of Massachusetts Mutual Insurance Company, was
elected its first mayor, joining a slate of Common Council members
united in their Protestantism.

The growth of an urban economy and physical infrastructure became a
civic preoccupation. Gradually schools, then streets, sewers, drinking
water, and finally zoning all fell under the purview of public officials and
local government. But the most consistent source of political tension during the town-to-city transition concerned the extent of the municipal government's responsibilities for public life and public welfare, or as Frisch
(1987) puts it: "the emergence of the overarching, abstract notion of 'public interest' " (p. 113). David G. Hackett (1990) describes a similar prob-

lem of defining "social order" in his recent account of Albany, New York, and its transition from an early-seventeenth-century Dutch Reformed church and trading outpost to a mid-nineteenth-century city that was far larger and more heterogeneous. Hackett notes that, from the standpoint of a civic culture, Albany moved from a "Geertzian" to a "Swidlerian" mode; that is, from the kind of tightly bound culture defined by the anthropologist Clifford Geertz (1973) to the conception of culture defined by sociologist Ann Swidler (1986) as a much more problematic process involving an ever-changing and strategically selective "tool kit" of options. The description is equally apt for Springfield's transition across the same two-and-a-half-century span.

Not surprisingly, the Civil War was a culminating economic and moral event. A financial boon to an economy dominated by an armory, the war also served as a cultural gathering point for a city that had resonated to the antislavery cause for some time. Several churches had participated in the Underground Railway; John Brown alone is credited with passing through more than two hundred and fifty former slaves during his several years as a respected citizen and churchman in the 1850s. When war came, the city was prepared to respond. Indeed, the Rev. J. N. Mars helped organize blacks to fight for the Union Army, and he later went south as a chaplain for a black brigade. He explained his position: "We see the rebels slaughtering our white friends and destroying their property; must we stand and look on quietly?" (Bauer 1975, p. 52).

In the years after the war, the city succumbed to a general edifice complex that was especially pronounced within religion. According to Frisch (1972), there was a "dramatic, almost hectic rush to raise elaborate new churches. . . . Within a decade of the war . . . and mostly within six years, twelve major church buildings arose, almost all of them elegant stone and brick structures on a scale of elegance and design previously rare in Springfield" (pp. 145–146). This was Springfield's architectural zenith, and it featured the early work of a major figure in American design, H. H. Richardson.

Religion quickened throughout the latter nineteenth century. This involved not only church buildings but church men such as the conservative evangelist, Dwight Moody, and the liberal "Social Gospel" leader, Washington Gladden, who exerted major local influence in the 1870s from his pulpit at North Congregational Church. Between these two extremes, institutional Protestantism continued to grow and prosper. Indeed, Trinity Methodist Church proudly proclaimed itself the area's leader of the "institutional church movement," featuring parish houses, a boys club, a swimming pool, and the general features of what a later observer (Page 1952) was to dub the "basketballization of American religion"—a phrase peculiarly appropriate to Springfield where the game was invented in 1891.

The Springfield municipal complex (*left to right*, the Civic Auditorium, the campanile, and City Hall), with the northwest edge of First Church and Court
Square in the lower left corner and Memorial Bridge visible at the top.

By the beginning of the twentieth century, Springfield's population had
exceeded 70,000, and according to a Special Report of the U.S. Census on
"Religious Bodies," Springfield had forty-five churches in 1906, not to
mention two Protestant colleges, both founded in 1885. Springfield College was established by the YMCA—and with the now-lapsed proviso that
neither Catholics nor Unitarians could sit on its boards (Garvey 1987).
American International College was begun as a school for French Protestant workers.

The city itself was experiencing a sense of manifest urban destiny. Its
city hall was destroyed by a fire in 1905, reportedly started when a fair-
booth monkey knocked over a kerosene lamp (Garvey 1987, p. 155). Such

was the community's sense of its growth, prosperity, and promise that a replacement group of municipal buildings was planned to dominate the entire north side of Court Square, flanking the First (Congregational) Church. Even the projected cost of two million dollars did not deter the usually thrifty city leadership. The city was in tune with the spirit of the Progressive era and saw itself on the threshold of civic greatness, perhaps as another Boston. Thus, the municipal group took on grand proportions, with two classically columned buildings, one for City Hall and the other for Symphony Hall, flanking a 300-foot clock tower whose carillon chimes eschewed the traditional Westminster tones for sixteen triumphant notes from Handel's "Messiah" (Garvey 1987, p. 156). During construction in 1911, the campanile was shaken by a dynamite blast set by anarchists. Although the incident was interpreted as a symbolic attack upon the city, it succeeded only in cementing the community's commitment to the project. The finished complex was finally dedicated in 1913, with extensive remarks from the expansive former president of the United States, William Howard Taft. From this vantage point, the twentieth century looked promising indeed.

And yet there were political and social tensions beneath these flaunted civic achievements. Even the dedication ceremonies had a controversial subtext. Leaders of the Swedish community complained that they were snubbed in the distribution of announcements and invitations to various opening events (Garvey 1987, p. 157). More ominous was the slighting of Henry Lasker, the city's first Jewish lawyer and elected official who was president of the Board of Aldermen and acting mayor at the time, since Mayor John Denison was away on family business. Before leaving, however, Denison had designated the city solicitor to represent him at all dedication ceremonies and social events. Accordingly, the city's most prominent Jewish citizen and its official leader went without a seat in any of the honorary boxes and without an invitation to any of the attendant social occasions. Springfield was still a Protestant city, though perhaps now with a vengeance.

An Establishment in Eclipse

The first two decades of the twentieth century witnessed the beginning of another phase of Protestant disestablishmentism. Quite apart from continued immigration and the looming challenge of Catholicism, which we shall describe shortly, Protestants themselves were experiencing both the costs and benefits of social and geographic mobility. This led many out of the teeming city and into the verdant suburbs; for some, it also involved a shrinking from public religion into more private pieties and a growing restlessness under the moralistic thumb of the clergy. Old First Church once again faced a crisis of authority in 1908 when its pastor was moved to resign and delivered a parting sermon that echoed widely:

> If we are going to have a "boss" in the church, why not have an educated boss, not one who is vulgar and common? . . . The Congregational Church is supposed to be a pure democracy . . . but some churches [have] bosses who are worse than ward heelers in politics and there is as a result a Tammany church, ruled by a ring or clique. (Springfield *Republican*, April 28, 1908)

Of course, the ethnic slur was unmistakable and by no means uncharacteristic of the times.

By the 1920s, a number of Protestant leaders saw the problems at hand and others in the offing. They asked the distinguished religious sociologist, H. Paul Douglass, to take the churchly pulse and provide both diagnosis and prescription. Douglass focused more on the churches themselves than on the contextual factors conspiring against them. The resulting *Springfield Church Survey* (1926) was a tough-minded assault against institutional indolence:

> The worst interpretation that can be put upon . . . Protestantism in Springfield [is that it is] an organized religious movement of doubtful success, with incoherent and inefficient units working with poor command of the facts, and deficient in the moral qualities that lie under institutional strength; that the churches are illogically related to the city geographically, have only one common principle consistently followed, namely, to get as far off as possible from the socially undesirable areas. (Douglass 1926, p. 40)

Although Douglass's tone suggests that Protestantism's day was virtually over, any such obituary would have been vastly premature. Whether because or in spite of Douglass's strictures, Protestantism persisted as Springfield's dominant religious community for almost a half-century—at least if dominance is measured by status and prestige rather than sheer numbers.

Meanwhile, like many midsized industrial cities, Springfield was hurt badly by the Great Depression, although the city's relatively diversified economy and the armory provided some cushion. World War II brought only moderate relief, as the armory had gone from large-scale production to research and development functions. During the immediate postwar years, it became clear that the Protestants' days were numbered in the corridors of civic power. They had retained disproportionate political influence for several decades after the turning of the demographic tide, but they were soon to lose their prominence, first in city hall and later in the chambers of commerce as well. Although the mainline Protestant churches enjoyed a final spasm of institutional growth during the 1950s, they began to fulfill Douglass's dark prophecy in the 1960s and 1970s.

The fates of the city's various Congregational churches illustrate how the mighty have fallen. Old First Church now occupies the fourth building to be erected on the site of the original settlement meetinghouse. It has begun to live off its endowment capital as an increasingly empty symbol of years past, and although its membership has occasional growth spurts, the long-term trend is downward. Perhaps more important, the church is a ghostly imitation of the power center it was during the seventeenth and eighteenth centuries. Not long ago, a newcomer to the church did an informal survey of passers-by on the square beyond, asking with a tourist's innocence what went on in the building:

> A number said it was a historic structure, kind of like a museum where they sometimes had concerts. But not one mentioned that it was a still a church or that it still conducted religious services. (interview)

And according to a recent staff member:

> Almost half of our members live outside of Springfield proper—all but one or two of the lay leaders. But then we're not really part of the Protestant establishment either. In fact, we're very blue-collar and ethnic without many professionals or upper-management types. They're mostly over at South Congregational or out at the Longmeadow Congo where they have about 1,600 members compared to our 700. (interview)

South Congregational was founded as an "evangelical" offshoot of First Church in 1842. Gradually it became the denomination's most prestigious church in the city. It combined a high-status membership with a series of highly visible clergy, including one—the prolific James Gordon Gilkey—of whom a possibly envious successor commented in a later church history: "[His] eleven volumes were in no sense profound, but they reached and possibly helped great numbers of people" (*History of South Congregational Church*, 1942, p. 76). South Church was more than just a place for worship; as an early "institutional church," it ministered to the broadest needs of its distinguished flock. By the late 1970s, however, it had become a citadel of comfort for an aging, middle-class congregation concerned about its hostile urban context. Entrance into the locked church now requires identifying oneself on the intercom by the door.

Several Congregational churches have been abandoned altogether. As early as 1920, Olivet Congregational merged with South Church, having found even then that its neighborhood had changed to the point where it was "unable to support a Protestant Church (ibid., p. 66). South Church also absorbed Memorial Congregational in 1940. Much more recently, Emmanuel Congregational's membership plummeted from 770 to 220 in twenty years. When the church property was sold in 1982, only 44 people attended the final Sunday service.

But the most dramatic example of Protestant reversal is—or rather was—Hope Congregational Church. Begun as a South Church mission to the black community in the 1870s, it was poised to benefit from the rapid growth of a nearby white neighborhood that began to flourish by the turn of the century. The growth continued, and by 1950 Hope was the largest Congregational church in Massachusetts, and the fifth largest in the nation, with a membership peak of 2,838. Rapid decline began in the 1960s as the surrounding neighborhood quickly became predominantly black. By the time of the church's centennial in 1976, there was an ominous beat to the festivities. Just six months later, the congregation voted to disband. At the time it had a membership of 400 people, 65 percent of whom were over sixty years of age and 70 percent of whom lived outside the neighborhood. Roland Holstead has drawn an instructive comparison between Hope and St. Peter's Episcopal Church, only a few blocks away. Whereas St. Peter's had the support of a bishop and managed a relatively smooth transition from a largely white to a principally black parish, Hope was left struggling as an autonomous polity that had little outside support and refused to make the switch.

> Hope Church entered the early nineteen seventies with the same basic orientation it had in the forties, fifties, and sixties. It continued to think of itself as a theologically liberal congregation. It served the community in traditional ways such as parishioner involvement in local community activities like the Symphony Association, the Museum Association, and YMCA and YWCA activities. Hope Church continued to own rental property on the Square, but there is no evidence that the church involved . . . the people living right around it. The leaders . . . never seemed to understand that there may have been a contradiction between their roles as Christians to spread the Gospel and their lack of activity on behalf of the people living in Winchester Square. (Holstead 1982, p. 133)

By 1978, Hope had closed its doors, sold its property to a Seventh-day Adventist group, and merged with Faith Congregational Church in the Forest Park area on the city's prosperous southern edge. Faith continues to reflect this prosperity. One staff member described it as "the local Republican party at prayer," some of whom indulge the clergy's occasional forays into civic controversies "because they embarrass the Democrats in charge" (interview). But a clergyman from the past took a somewhat broader view:

> When the UCC [United Church of Christ] lost about half of its membership in Springfield between 1965 and 1975, I think we also lost a lot of our willingness to get involved politically. We became cooperators, not adversaries, and we just began to follow the policies of the Democrat party. I guess the parishioners just as sooned that the clergy kept quiet. But I

do think we bought religious peace at the price of political withdrawal. Nothing seemed to bother us anymore; we just stayed home through it all. (interview)

Finally, the most politically vibrant of the city's current UCC congregations is St. John's, founded in 1844 by a group of free blacks and white abolitionist Methodists. This was John Brown's church in the early 1850s when he and his family lived in Springfield (*History of St. John's Congregational*, 1962). However, for most of its history, St. John's has been virtually all black, with a basically lower-middle-class membership, and a succession of notably prophetic voices from its pulpit.

It is, of course, ironic in this saga of Protestant marginalization that the most vital of the city's Congregational churches represents a disadvantaged minority. But then, as one observer noted of the white Protestants themselves: "I guess you could say that Protestants are now a minority group, except I don't think Protestants even feel like they're a group at all" (interview). The comment is appropriate to mark the end of one establishment and the entrance of another.

THE CATHOLIC PRESENCE

On June 1, 1897—a day of warm spring promise—the cornerstone was laid for Springfield's new Central High School. The building was to be a massive statement of the city's educational and democratic philosophy; its plain but classical proportions well reflected the city's sense of itself as a growing economic and cultural center. And yet there was a discordance to the ceremonies that was portentous. Because the festivities were entrusted to the city's Protestant Masons, Catholics moved to boycott the occasion. The word went out not only in the lay Catholic newspaper but also from several Catholic pulpits. The pastor of the predominantly Irish North End parish, Sacred Heart, Fr. Thomas Smyth, argued: "On no account should any church or society be given the privilege of laying the cornerstone of a building paid for by the citizens of all shades of belief" (*Springfield Republican*, May 25, 1897).

Catholic clergy received invitations to the ceremonies, but several of them formally declined and "it is generally understood that none of the clergymen will be present" (*Republican*, May 27, 1897). The *Republican*, a thoroughly Yankee paper in which, it was said, an Irishman could only get his name in print if he died or got arrested, noted that Father Smyth's argument carried weight and that it would probably be better to have the mayor perform such duties in the future. However, the paper concluded that it was too late to change the existing plans, and it urged everyone to attend because "the good and glory of Springfield is the large matter involved" (*Republican*, May 26, 1897).

Despite its clouded initiation, Central High School endured for some ninety years as the cornerstone of Springfield's growing public secondary school system. But on May 22, 1987, its successor school was dedicated. Again, there was a crowd and a ceremony, but this time no boycott—certainly not by Catholics. Indeed, the major speaker was the Catholic bishop, whose political intercession had been crucial in breaking a political stalemate in the protracted planning process. There is no record of Masons being present, and although the rostrum did include both Protestant and Jewish clergy, they were invited only as an eleventh-hour afterthought at the suggestion of a school official who felt their absence might be unseemly.

The ninety years separating these two events embrace the greatest ethnic, religious, and political change in Springfield's three and a half centuries. And yet the change itself began earlier. Having broadly chronicled the history of the city's Protestant establishment, it is time to do the same for its Catholic successor.

Establishing a Beachhead

According to informed local lore, Springfield's first Catholic visitors were the French-influenced Native Americans whose tour through western Massachusetts involved not only an attack on Springfield itself but the upriver massacre at Deerfield in 1704, followed by a trek back to Canada with more than one hundred captured settlers in tow, twenty-eight of whom elected to remain when a truce was later negotiated in 1706. The episode was a perverse harbinger of subsequent Yankee-Catholic contacts, which were not to begin on a significant scale for another century and a half. However, even by the mid-seventeenth century, there were isolated Irish of low status in New England. These included several in Springfield, whose coerced Congregationalism belied their Catholic background. There was also the infamous Goodwife Glover of Boston, who as an outsider was convicted of witchcraft in 1688 following an examination by Cotton Mather (Burns 1976b, pp. 5–7).

As we have already noted, Springfield guarded its gates closely against religious outsiders. If Baptists and Quakers were the bane of the eighteenth century, Catholics assumed this dubious mantle in the early nineteenth. Springfield's first Mass was observed on St. Patrick's day in 1834, when Fr. John Brady of Hartford traveled north to perform the ceremony at the home of armory worker John Sullivan. But the first major influx of Catholics did not enter the area until the late 1830s, when Irish laborers took up work on the canals and on the railroad, which reached the city in 1839. In fact, Charles Dickens described the living conditions of the railroad builders during a trip to the American Northeast (and Springfield) in 1841–42:

with means of hand in building decent cabins, it was wonderful to see how clumsy, rough, and wretched its hovels were . . . of sod and grass . . . walls of mud . . . neither doors nor windows; some had nearly fallen down . . . all were ruinous and filthy. Hideously ugly old women and very buxom young ones, pigs, dogs, men, children, babies, pots, kettles, dung hills, vile refuse, rank straw and standing water, all wallowing together in an inseparable heap, composed the furniture of every dark and dirty hut. (Greeley, *The Irish Americans* [New York: Harper and Row, 1981], p. 76, as quoted in Anne Halley, "Afterword," to M. D. Curran 1986, pp. 230–231)

Only a confirmed romanticist would apply the term "wonderful" to such conditions. Certainly, this did not describe Samuel Bowles' newspaper, the *Republican*, which only a few years later laid an outbreak of cholera at the Irish doorstep:

They work in a leisurely way all day, and dance and drink all night—then crawl into their close, filthy holes to sleep awhile, and wake up with the cholera, or something like it. [The solution is] a thorough cleaning and white-washing. (Burns 1976b, p. 13)

By this time, the Protestant establishment was more generic than denominational, and more de facto than de jure. Still, it closed ranks against the blue-collar and no-collar immigrants. For example, in 1846 the commandant of the armory, Maj. James Ripley, was taken to court by a citizen's petition accusing him of firing "good workers" and replacing them with Irish. Fights at the armory between Irish employees and Protestant nonworkers were common (Burns 1976b, p. 11). For most of the next century, "N.I.N.A." ("No Irish Need Apply") notices were common in employers' windows and newspaper classifieds. And although we have found only haphazard and anecdotal recollections of its religious equivalent ("No Catholics Need Apply"), there was as much concern about the Irish's Roman Catholicism as their immigrant status, and the terms "Irish" and "Catholic" were synonymous.

This not only accounted for their difficulty in finding good jobs but also in establishing a church. In 1843 a Yankee contractor sold land to a group of his Irish workers for this purpose. However, it was located next to the armory, and if Major Ripley was not averse to hiring Catholics, he refused to have them as worshiping neighbors. The dispute between the sympathetic contractor and the obdurate major made the rounds of both the Massachusetts courts and the government in Washington—but with no resolution. Four years later, the Catholics sold the contested lot and used the money to purchase and remodel a former Baptist meetinghouse. St. Benedict's opened in 1847 as Springfield's first Catholic church.

Meanwhile, Catholic immigration continued, and the local reception remained begrudging. In 1854, just two years after Springfield's incorpo-

St. Michael's Cathedral, consecrated in 1866.

ration as a city, a local variant of the national Know-Nothing party ran a basically anti-Catholic slate in the city elections. After receiving the *Republican's* endorsement, its candidate for mayor, Eliphalet Trask, won with 900 of the 1,400 votes cast. Shortly thereafter, the accumulating national crisis surrounding slavery and the Civil War transcended local religious and ethnic tensions. While tensions persisted, immigrants and Catholics began to move from the position of threatening outsiders to accepted insiders—albeit at arm's length.

A Diocesan See and a Democratic Wave

In the years following the Civil War, Protestants were not alone in building new churches. In 1866, many of the city's leading Protestants were guests at the Catholic consecration of St. Michael's Cathedral—the first Catholic church in New England to be debt-free and eligible for the ceremony. Then as now, it was one of the city's largest and most impressive structures. The attitude of sophisticated Protestants toward their Catholic townspeople is reflected in Samuel Bowles' editorial concerning the church:

> If Catholics exist in our midst, it is better that they should have a place of worship of their own peculiar preference than that they should remain without any of the ordinance of religion as they otherwise would. The only true and, in the end, effective engine against Popery is enlightened education. For the education of a well-balanced mind cannot be satisfied with the senseless forms, which go to make up all that Popery is. It is useless, therefore, to indulge in denunciations or persecutions of such a religion; they will only enkindle its flame and increase its power. Rather should its influences be counteracted by the great work of education. (*Springfield Republican*, as quoted by Burns 1976b, p. 12)

By this time, the Catholic population had swollen considerably as the Irish continued to arrive in large numbers and were joined by increasing numbers of French Canadians. In fact, Springfield had become such an important center of New England Catholicism that, in 1870, it was made the episcopal see of a new diocese broken away from Boston and including all of Massachusetts from Worcester west. The new bishop was Patrick T. O'Reilly of Worcester—at age 36, the second-youngest bishop in the country, whose move into a twenty-seven-room mansion next to the cathedral set local tongues wagging—though the mansion also accommodated the cathedral's staff.

At the beginning of the new diocese, its broad geographical expanse included some 100,000 Catholics served by forty-three priests with thirty-eight parish churches and fourteen mission chapels (Garvey, *Springfield Daily News*, October 31, 1977). Already, however, Springfield could claim a disproportionate and growing share. In fact, while the city's Catholics continued to be second-class citizens and the victims of discrimination in virtually every civic sphere, things were worse elsewhere, and Springfield's Catholicism was marked by a certain buoyancy. Local Catholic historian, Richard Garvey, notes that by this time

> residents did not fully equate the Catholic Church with poor Irish immigrants living in ghettos. Although there were still colonies of poor Irish . . .

many of the Irish Americans were already upward bound. Irish Americans in Springfield included a lawyer who had been a Civil War officer, a stone quarry owner, two building contractors and a Civil War veteran who ran a Catholic bookstore and foreign exchange office. (Garvey, ibid.)

Predictably, the move upward included a move into politics. In fact, Springfield's Catholics were led by their bishop who, fourteen months after arriving in the city, ran for a seat on the School Committee—a position he had held in Worcester, where Catholics had been granted seats as a way of warding off Know-Nothing divisiveness. The bishop ran on a reformist ticket, which also included Protestants and Republicans. Although he did better than many of his running mates, he did not do well enough to win. Still, as Garvey notes, his candidacy served as a political stimulant to Springfield's Irish Catholic community:

> The best available statistics indicate that only about 500 male immigrants were registered to vote in Springfield in 1870, which means that, even if they all voted and voted for the Bishop, still more than half of his total votes came from native born voters. Interest in the vote so intensified that the Hackson Naturalization Club, formed about a year after the election, could boast by 1875 that it had tripled the Irish vote in Springfield. (Garvey, ibid.)

The results were rapidly apparent. In 1862, John Mulligan became the first Irish Catholic elected to city office; though this was to the ward-based City Council, and Mulligan was a loyal Republican. In 1874, the lawyer Hugh Donnelly was elected to the at-large Board of Aldermen as the first of many Irish-Catholic Democrats to come. Catholics were beginning to make their move both economically and politically, although it is instructive that as late as 1888, they could be ignored almost totally by Mason Green's officially commissioned but nonetheless magisterial account of Springfield's first two hundred and fifty years.

Bishop O'Reilly served until his death in 1892 and was credited with confirming some 75,000 adherents, dedicating forty-five churches, and laying another one hundred cornerstones. The eulogist at his funeral credited him with transforming the diocese "from wood to stone," though perhaps his greatest legacy was bringing in the Sisters of Providence to staff the diocesan hospitals and the Sisters of St. Joseph to run a new parochial school system. Although these became the two largest orders in the diocese, they were joined by a number of others, some of which were specifically based within Springfield's emerging ethnic parishes.

Immigration continued to swell. The Irish and French-Canadian influx persisted, and the first of two great Italian waves occurred between 1885 and 1893, with the second to come later between 1897 and 1903. The first Catholic weekly paper began publishing in 1889, although its editor,

Daniel Mullaley, commented that other papers had also begun covering the beat: "Judging from the way other Springfield papers have been doing up the news this past week, one would think they were Catholic papers. But they will all be Catholic papers by and by" (*Springfield Tribune Anniversary Collection*, p. 10). In fact, one of these papers, the *Springfield Homestead*, already served a primarily Irish working-class readership. It had a tendency to rail against immigrants as immigrants but then champion them later as residents—and potential readers. Certainly, the paper was sensitive to the Protestant-Catholic difference. Its front-page column, "Among the Churches," was devoted exclusively to Protestant doings, while Catholic church activities were relegated to a separate space entitled "In Town and Out." There was no question that the Irish were first among unequals, and given its predominantly Irish readership, it is not surprising that the paper vented the Irish antipathy to other ethnic groups below them:

> To have a swarm of half-civilized Poles, Huns, Italians, and Bohemians always in hand ready to stone and burn and pillage wherever there is a conflict between labor and capital, is an experience which ought to teach the United States a lesson. (*Springfield Homestead*, July, 14, 1894, p. 6)

During the 1890s, this ethnic divisiveness continued as an accompaniment of increasing immigration. The new bishop of this fractured empire was Thomas Beaven, a Springfield native whose appointment was described enthusiastically (if somewhat unfortunately) by another local newspaper:

> It may be questioned whether an appointment that would please all classes and sects in the diocese more . . . could have been made. . . . [His many attributes] will make him a worthy successor to the dead prelate whom he resembles in many points (*sic*). (*Springfield Graphic*, August 20, 1892, p. 4)

Bishop Beaven served for twenty-eight years until his death in 1920. The son of a local railroad worker of some accumulated means, he used both his city contacts and his private inheritance to good political advantage, distributing the latter widely among local schools and charities. The bishop's "day-book" survives as a largely unilluminating appointment record only rarely given to elaboration. However, at one point it suggests evidence of a dawning pluralism in a concert of sacred music performed by the Hampden County Catholic Church Choirs in the city hall in 1896. Since Catholics had yet to make city hall a home, this use of public space is notable. Equally surprising is that the concert raised five hundred dollars for the St. Vincent de Paul charitable societies. But then, the day-book may hint at the bishop's sense of the ironic: "4/11/97—Palm Sunday—did not officiate on account of sore thumb."

By all accounts, Bishop Beaven was a strong and popular leader with wide-ranging interests and a taste for the political fray. Early in his tenure, he supported the Catholics' first major show of citywide economic force in an action organized by a parish priest against Springfield's leading department store. The issue concerned a Christmas Day work requirement. In the early years of Massachusetts and as legacy of the Puritans, the celebration of Christmas was a criminal offense, and the law forbade anyone from withholding their labor on December 25. Long after the state law was repealed, many Springfield businesses continued the practice of firing those absent. Generally interpreted as an anti-Catholic position, several of our older Catholic respondents recalled childhood Christmas dinners always in the late evening, after the adults had returned from work.

However, in 1896, a group of Catholic clergy, led by Fr. Thomas Symth of Sacred Heart parish, lobbied many Springfield businesses to discontinue their Christmas work schedules. After receiving little cooperation, the priests organized a Catholic boycott of the offending merchants. By the next year all but two of the city's businesses were closed on Christmas, but the city's finest department store, Smith and Murray's, remained not only unchanging but openly contemptuous. By the following year, this store too had altered its practice, but its early arrogance and the continuing bad blood between Mr. Murray and Father Smyth led many Catholics to continue a boycott, which is generally credited with forcing the eventual bankruptcy of the enterprise (Garvey 1987, 152–153). Smyth was a swashbuckling hero in the battle for Catholic rights, who later had a falling out with the bishop. The Beaven day-book comments that this man once "thought to be of episcopal timber" was banished to a corner in southeastern Massachusetts and told, "You'll be able to look over part of the diocese that might have been yours."

As the boycott demonstrated, Catholic muscle was not restricted to the workstation; it was becoming an increasing factor in local politics. Although the terms "Catholic" and "Democrat" were not yet coterminous, in 1895 the Democrats won both the mayoral race and a majority on the Board of Aldermen, and the century ended with the 1899 election of Springfield's first Catholic mayor, William P. Hayes.

More recent local Catholic historians tend to credit this event with more religious significance than did the accounts of the day. Actually it is not clear whether Hayes was elected because or in spite of his religion. A product of a relatively affluent Irish family, he was a very young but very successful lawyer who, after attending the Springfield public schools and (Protestant) Boston University, might well have passed for a Yankee. Hayes's candidacy made no overt mention of his Catholicism; nor was his election trumpeted on religious grounds. Although a Democrat, he ran well ahead of his ticket and benefited from the help of a number of prominent Republican endorsements in upsetting the incumbent Republican, Dwight Gilmore, by 192 votes out of 7,908 cast. There was surprise at Hayes's showing, "even by the most ardent Hayes men" (*Republican*, December 8, 1899). However, the Republicans swept the Board of Aldermen and the School Committee, and retained an 11–7 majority on the Common Council. Hayes's victory was primarily personal, and while the next day's newspapers saw it as a win for the Democrats, there were only two oblique references to an Irish-Catholic ethnoreligious subtext. The *Republican* observed that "The liquor men were apparently with Mr. Hayes yesterday," recalling the long political feud between temperant Protestants and "wet" ethnics. It also noted that the North End had elected a mayor for the first time in a quarter century. By the 1890s, Springfield's North End had become an ethnic enclave dominated by Irish and French-Canadian Catholics, though it also included a substantial Russian Jewish community and developing parishes of both the Russian and Greek Orthodox churches.

Hayes's victory was a harbinger of political changes to come, although the period of "Catholic politics" in Springfield was still several decades in the future. In fact, when we asked present-day respondents to name the first Catholic mayor, by far the most common response was Daniel Brunton, who held the post from 1946 to 1957. Meanwhile, Hayes was reelected by a landslide in 1900, after which he declined a third term and served briefly in the Massachusetts Senate and several statewide appointed posts before moving back to his law practice and an influential position behind the political lines.

The Tide and the Century Turn

In the decade after the turn of the century, Springfield and its various ethnic communities flourished. James Gelin (1984) described the ethnic turf and turnover as part of his history of the city's early Jewish community. Although the first synagogue services had been held in a third-floor room in November 1887, the next twenty years witnessed a proliferation of Jewish congregations and an expansiveness within the community at large:

> In the decades before the turn of the century immigrants tended to congregate in neighborhoods already settled by their fellow countrymen; consequently, by 1905 there existed in Springfield several ethnic communities, each with its own churches, associations, and stores which catered to ethnic needs, and each dominating a certain area in the city. . . . [By] the turn of the century the Irish had moved into the neighborhoods in the extreme west

and north ends of Ward Two and on into Ward One. . . . The [Jews] moved
into the area vacated by the Irish in Ward Two. . . . Ferry Street was the hub
of this Jewish community . . . just as on [New York's] Hester Street on any
given Friday morning, the narrow dirt road just north of Union [Railroad]
station was packed with Jews doing last-minute shopping before the Sabbath
began at sunset. . . . To be (there) was to encounter noise, crowds, and the
smells of the many types of produce sold there. From the butcher shops came
the subtle smell of raw meats, from the bakery the sweet scent of breads and
pastries, from the delicatessen came the smell of pickles and baking meats,
especially chicken, and from the fish market, whose odors were already
strong, came the powerful smell of whitefish being smoked in the backyard.
(pp. 5–6)

The process was the same for other ethnic groups. The French parish of
St. Joseph's had been organized as early as 1873, but the first Italian parish, Our Lady of Mt. Carmel, was not established until 1907, at which
time Springfield had eleven Catholic churches, many of them ethnically
defined.

All of these ethnic communities were to undergo the same sort of internal differentiation that had already begun to characterize the Irish. Immigration was greatly affected by networks of family and friends, and American Irish communities were known by their Irish county origins. Whereas
the Irish in nearby Holyoke were preponderantly from County Mayo,
Springfield's Irish came overwhelmingly from County Kerry. However,
there was an important subdistinction among the Kerry-ites that persists
today. Even now it is said that the "real elite" of the Springfield Irish come
from the specific part of Kerry known as the Dingle Peninsula. These
were the controlling denizens of Ward 2's Hungry Hill who later became
the controlling figures in the city's Democratic party.

But, of course, internal class differences also began to surface early
within the various ethnic communities. The very title of Mary Doyle
Curran's novel concerning Holyoke, *The Parish and the Hill* (1948),
provides a topographical description of the difference between the so-
called "shanty" Irish, on the one hand, and the upwardly mobile "lace
curtain" or "two toilet" Irish, on the other. Curran describes the change
this way:

> None of us who were used to the fresh shining air of the sea and the green
> grass of (Ireland) liked the dark mill, but there it was and a man could earn a
> living for himself and his family in it. . . . There was no dissension then. . . .
> You will never see those days again, for they are gone, all of them, and it's the
> Hill did it, the Hill with its pot of gold and Irishmen fighting Irishmen to get
> at it. Irish parish was full of peace till the time came when the serpent got into
> the garden and none content after—all of them making the gold rush to the
> Hill and trying to outdo the Yankees at their own game. (p. 49)

In many ethnic families, status and status aspirations were tied up with gender and religion. Curran noted the difference between her father and mother's religion:

My father's Catholicism suffered, as well as everything else he believed in, for being touched with lace-curtain refinement. It was tinged, as is almost all lace-curtain Catholicism, with the Protestantism of the Yankees they imitated. Catholicism for my father held none of the joy it did for my Mother. It was a grim, respectable business requiring monthly confession and Communion and a get-to-Mass-on-Sunday-or-die-in-a-state-of-mortal-sin attitude. Going to church was the respectable thing to do. We went in a body at a slow pace, gloved and gloomy at the prospect of a long dreary sermon. My mother preferred the High Mass with the elaborate ceremony and singing; but the nine o'clock Mass, stripped and bare of all but the most essential part of the ritual, with its homely sermons and its raspy boys' choir, was the family Mass and the one we attended. (ibid., pp. 106–107)

William Hartford provides a historian's complement to Curran's novelistic treatment. His book *Working People of Holyoke* (1989) provides a penetrating account of life among working-class Catholics at the turn of the century, and he cites the special efforts of clergy to frustrate the activities of union organizers whom they regarded as competing agents for a competing set of priorities. A somewhat different tension is described by Roy Rosenzweig (1983) in his study of working-class leisure time in nearby Worcester, Massachusetts. While the bulk of his analysis concerns the shift from the saloon to the cinema as a leisure outlet, he also describes how the Catholic Church paled in comparison to both in the eyes of many working-class men.

It is likely that sometime during the 1920s, Catholics attained demographic dominance with the city. Although census talleys eschew religion and no precise figures are available, continuing immigration and traditionally high birth rates made Catholicism an accumulating force. Certainly the local media reflected its influence. Shortly before his death in 1920, Bishop Beaven was impressed with the Knights of Columbus newspaper and its successful campaigns to depose the head of the state education commission and prevent the reelection of an incumbent state senator. Beaven bought the paper and converted it into a diocesan monthly, *The Catholic Mirror*. The paper was a success financially as well as politically, carrying periodic reminders to patronize its good Catholic advertisers— presumably including "Father John's Medicine,"which featured a drawing of the Father in clerical collar touting a potion "scientifically designed to build up the flesh [and] keep one free from colds" (*The Catholic Mirror*, February 1921, p. 43).

Following Bishop Beaven's death in 1920, his successor was the Right Rev. Thomas Mary O'Leary whose twenty-nine-year tenure was marked more by endurance than by efficacy. A New Hampshire native educated in Ireland and Canada, Bishop O'Leary was by nature a shy and diffident man who was in poor health for much of his term. Neither a charismatic nor a compelling force among the city's Catholics, he was remembered by some of our older interviewees as follows:

> O'Leary really had no relationship to city politics. If he would have said, "I'm against that," it didn't stand a chance. But I don't remember him ever taking a strong position on his own. Maybe he didn't have to because the issues in those days were more clear-cut. (interview)

> O'Leary let many priests keep a lot of money they collected and took care of the priests he liked. I don't want to say he bought their loyalty, but . . . (interview)

> When O'Leary was in control, there were a number of financial irregularities, including some that made his brother-in-law rich. But he swept them under the rug. He was a kind of Irish atavist. You couldn't run the church that way today. (interview)

> In those days the priests often owned the land the church buildings stood on, and they could will it to anyone—not always the bishop. I remember a priest left a cemetery in Holyoke to a nephew, and it took a land court to get it back to the parish many years later. (interview)

> Bishop O'Leary wasn't very gracious, and a lot of people were anxious to see him go. But back then you couldn't retire without being suspected of wrongdoing, so he hung on while ailing in his later years. However, he finally got the message in July 1949 when Cardinal Spellman came to Springfield and made an unannounced call at his house when he was napping. The cardinal rang at several of the doors and finally got the bishop up. But the bishop never did invite him in, and they had just a brief formal exchange on the stoop. Spellman got his revenge not long after when a member of his staff was appointed as O'Leary's successor. (interview)

The early decades of the twentieth century saw the mayoralty revert to Protestants, but in the midst of a lively competition between Democrats and Republicans, Springfield's politics were being redefined. Slowly the Republican party was becoming the lair of Protestants, while the Democrats were aligned with Catholics—especially Irish Catholics. And yet there remained important exceptions on both sides. On the one hand, Protestant denominations such as the Baptists and the Methodists had working-class Democratic legacies that extended back into the Jacksonian era. On the other hand, the Catholic political coalescence was also inhibited by several factors, including the invidious distinctions between the ethnic communities themselves.

Among Democrats, the Irish had an upper hand that was sometimes a clenched fist. Two of our interviewees, both gnarled pols from the past, might just as well have been talking to each other, although their respective ethnic groups, Irish and Italian, talked past one another for years:

> Of course, we Irish lorded it over the other ethnic groups in those days. But religion was the deeper issue, and it was much more disciplined in those days. The first question was always, "Is he Catholic?" And I remember a "No Catholics Need Apply" sign as late as the 1940s in a notice for telephone operators. (interview)

> Sure, the Irish blazed the trail. They had the best political names—easy to remember, attractive to voters. Whenever the Democrats won, the Irish considered it their victory. I remember once when I was running for office back then, an old Irish pol took me aside and said, "Smarten up. The Yankees have been running this thing; now it's our turn." (interview)

The city's second-largest ethnic group, the French, remained substantially nonpoliticized until well into the twentieth century. Many retained their Canadian citizenship and remained locally uninterested or unregistered; most who did become involved in Springfield's politics were Republicans despite their Catholicism and, as one of our interviewees noted, to the "wonderment of the Irish." But, of course, the Irish were part of the reason. There was long-standing French-Irish tension in the church, and repeated French requests to the chancery for more support fell on deaf and hostile ears (cf. Burns 1976b). A 1901 newspaper reported that four fifths of the French Canadians in the city were Republicans, "because the Irish are Democrats" (quoted in Burns 1976a, p. 25). As late as 1953, the French political organization, L'Avant Garde, estimated that 10,000 of Springfield's 17,000 Franco-Americans were registered as Republicans or Independents (ibid., p. 40).

The French were not alone in being driven into the arms of the Republicans. As the phrase "Irish Democrat" became a redundancy, a number of middle-class Italian Catholics and a smattering of black Protestants also found Republicanism a more encouraging path upward in local politics. These were more the exceptions than the rule since, as a whole, both groups remained largely Democratic. But newspaper accounts of Republican party activities from the late 1920s into the 1950s are dotted with names such as St. Germane, Calderigi, Francesconi, and Gibbs (an African American). With this legacy, it is not surprising that Springfield's only Republican mayor since World War II was also its only non-Catholic mayor—a Jew.

Meanwhile, Al Smith's 1928 candidacy for the U.S. presidency played a major role in shoring up and mobilizing the city's Catholic Democrats.

Not only was Smith a nationally prominent Catholic from nearby New York, but since this was the first presidential campaign in which women were allowed to vote, he was among the first national politicians to actively recruit their support. The "Irish style" of politicking, with its personalized, church-sponsored, and neighborhood appeals, was well calculated to reach and enlist females, and few groups have voted in higher or more loyal numbers since than Irish Catholic women.

The Smith campaign may also have had a significant indirect effect by stimulating anti-Catholic and anti-ethnic Ku Klux Klan activity in the Northeast. Here firm numbers are elusive. One local interviewee recalls an estimate of more than 12,000 members in Springfield's Hampden County by the early 1930s. But according to Kenneth Jackson's authoritative *The Klan and the City: 1915–1930* (1967), there were only 2,000 in the Springfield area and no more than 10,000–12,000 statewide—the number kept down by J. M. Curley's formidable opposition in Boston, the Klan headquarters. Although Klan rallies were largely outside Springfield proper, there is no question that the city quivered to their strains, and many Catholics saw political unity as a meaningful response. By then the Great Depression had hit, and as it hit Catholics harder than most, they began to fight back by using the Church itself. As one interviewee recalled:

A big issue in the 1930s was employment discrimination against Catholics. The real hero wasn't Bishop O'Leary but Monsignor John O'Connoll over at Holy Name. He went to employer after employer and told them if they didn't start hiring Catholics—and the Irish Catholics were especially discriminated against—he'd issue encyclicals against them and post them in every parish in western Massachusetts, saying: "They won't hire us; we won't trade with them." That brought a lot of them around real quick. (interview)

By 1930 the city's population had more than doubled since the turn of the century and was listed at 149,900. But by the mid-1930s, there was concern that the magic number of 150,000 would never be reached. Suburbanization had long since begun. Immigration had slowed as a result of new laws and bad times; in fact, in 1930 the percentage of first-generation Irish was half that of the previous decade.

Certainly the Depression went far to discredit the Republicans nationally; now they began to lose local favor as well. In 1930 the Republican hold on the mayor's office was finally broken by Dwight Winter. Although Winter was a Protestant and part of that diminishing breed, the Yankee Democrats, our older Catholic interviewees recalled him as a "great friend to Catholics," and one even went so far as to remember him as a Catholic in his own right—perhaps because his "kitchen cabinet" included several Catholic businessmen. Meanwhile in the next year's elections,

William Granfield was elected Springfield's first Irish-Catholic U.S. congressman, running on a straight repeal-of-Prohibition platform. But the biggest Catholic-Democrat triumph came in 1932 with the carrying of seven of the city's eight ward-based city council seats. Coupled with Winter's reelection, this amounted to a major political coup. Several interviewees recall the joy in Catholic households at the time, although wise heads were cautioning that Winter's place at the head of the ticket no doubt kept many Protestants in the fold. The election was an exciting taste of what was yet to come, and if it was not precisely a Catholic mandate, one interviewee remembers, "It had a striking effect as people began to realize what could be done if everybody got together."

Dwight Winter left the mayor's office in 1934 and was replaced by Henry Martens, a Republican alderman who defeated the Irish-Catholic Democrat, Quinlen. When Martens in turn prepared to step down in 1938, the Democrats were split on who to run. Charles Redmon had the backing of most of the Irish, but the remainder of the party supported Roger L. Putnam—like Winter, a Yankee Protestant, albeit with a wife from a distinguished Catholic family in Maryland. The impending intraparty conflict threatened to hand the mayoralty to the Republicans, until a young state representative whose district encompassed the Irish stronghold, Hungry Hill, declared for Putnam.

This was Edward P. Boland, who was later to serve thirty-six years as Springfield's U.S. congressman and leading political practitioner. At the time, however, his greatest assets were his family and his neighbors, one of whom described the situation this way:

> I was born on Hungry Hill in 1919, and both of my parents were from County Kerry. Eddie Boland was a neighbor, and both his mother and mine were from Dingle. I remember they used to speak Gaelic with other women on the Hill, and until recently, three of these women formed a kind of "Irish Mafia." If you were politicking on the Hill, you had to go and talk to them first. If you got their approval, you were in; if not, forget it. Your neighborhood was the four blocks around your house—the whole world. You didn't need money to run for office; you just got some volunteers and went door-to-door.
>
> Anyway, Eddie really rescued the Democrats from a mess of religious and ethnic conflict when he decided to back Putnam. He just personally took him door-to-door, and this young Catholic kid with this handsome Yankee Brahmin went all over the Hill. Putnam's primary opponent had a lot of backing from Irish Democrats, but after this it was all over. If you had Ward 2, you were a winner. (interview)

Whether the representative realized that Putnam had a better chance at winning citywide, or was himself angling to take control of the party from Redmon, remains open to speculation. In any event, Putnam won the primary and the mayoralty, including Ward 2, thus ushering in a period of Democratic dominance that has not yet receded. Interestingly, Putnam himself converted to Catholicism in 1941 while in the navy in England. Although the conversion was not a significant event in the life of Springfield's Democrats or its Catholics, it does stand as an eloquent symbol of transition.

Turning Sand Castles into Cement

The religious and political changes that began in the 1930s were solidified by the mid-1950s. The decade following World War II pushed Springfield further toward a second establishment. Protestants began to recede into the shadows and the suburbs; Catholics became less divided and more entrenched. While still dominated by the Irish, Catholicism's interethnic tensions were beginning to subside. The Church experienced a new surge of institutional expansiveness in its schools and medical facilities. And the press toward citywide political control continued.

As noted earlier, Bishop O'Leary was in poor health toward the end of his lengthy administration, and he died on October 10, 1949, to be replaced in April 1950 by Cardinal Spellman's personal choice, Christopher J. Weldon. Once a young parish priest in the New York area, the Irish-American Weldon had served as a navy chaplain during World War II, after which he served the New York archdiocese as director of Catholic Charities. If O'Leary had come to Springfield from small-town New Hampshire, Weldon was fresh from the nation's largest city, and Springfield felt the difference quickly. Three different members of his church staff described him in three different but obviously related ways:

> He was a two-fisted "mick" from New York who was tough, blunt, and autocratic. Actually he really tried to change after Vatican II. I think he was the first Catholic bishop in the country to set up a priests' senate, and then he also set up a priests' personnel group and a senior-priest consulting group. But, of course, there was no liaison between them, and the truth is they were kept pretty confused and powerless. (interview)

> Weldon didn't like fence-sitters. He wanted you to take your stand. He came in with a mandate for building and for change. . . . His major achievement was building a Catholic community. He got all the successful Irish involved and had a good relationship with the mayor. They didn't visit each other regularly, but they spoke often enough. Weldon was not one to actively campaign, but he could drop a word. In fact, he could be tough and sarcastic, and he wasn't always well liked. Although he grew more relaxed and friendly after his hepatitis in 1956, every now and then he'd choose the proper circumstances and show the iron fist was still there. (interview)

Bishop Weldon arrived as a breath of fresh air. He was seen as open, accessible, willing to change—whereas his predecessor wasn't seen at all except in the back seat of a speeding black limousine. Whereas O'Leary ruled through Catholicism's old-fashioned emotional grip, Weldon used power with real political skill. That's what encouraged the alliance between the Irish-Catholic politicians and the Yankee business leaders that succeeded where Putnam had failed. . . . But after a while, Weldon changed from a promising new source of change to an old-guard authoritarian. I remember the furor when a . . . man wanted to see the diocesan books. . . . Weldon treated the educated, cosmopolitan lay leaders of the church as if they were all immigrants. (interview)

A different man for a different time, or perhaps a different man made by a different time, Bishop Weldon did indeed energize a new sense of Catholic community that was already manifest in politics.

In 1946, the city elected its second Catholic mayor, and the first since the somewhat closeted William Hayes in 1900. Daniel Brunton was the son of an Irish immigrant and coal heaver in Ward 2. Brunton himself was an electrician whose avocational interest in politics had led to an appointment to an unexpired City Council seat in 1935, where he served until being elected at-large to the Board of Aldermen in 1942. A reporter of the day described his own sense of Brunton's religious significance this way:

As time wore on, we became aware that Danny felt that he had a mission in life. He was acutely aware that he was the first Catholic mayor since . . . Hayes almost a half-century before, and that not only was he on trial but so was his church. (Burns 1976b, p. 41)

Brunton certainly worked closely with the Church, as noted by a close observer of his administration:

He was a clean-looking guy who convinced people that he was doing all that could be done. He was always on good terms with the bishop, and his secretary had been a nun, who later became an official of a local civic organization. Her religious background was not well known. (interview)

Brunton must have passed muster within the Church, for he was reelected six times during his twelve-year tenure.

The elections of the 1950s marked the coming of age of a political machine. In 1953, not only did Mayor Brunton enjoy his largest victory margin, but nine of the eighteen Common Council members and all eight aldermen were Democrats. The latter was a first for the city, as was the bishop's appearance at the Brunton reinaugural the following January, an honor customarily left to the mayor's parish or congregational clergyman. And just as there was no mistaking the Catholic significance of these developments, their Irish meaning was not lost either. A *Morning Union* article of October 11, 1954, reported on the music at a preelection open house sponsored by the Democratic City Committee: "McNamara's Band," "The Irish Washerwoman," and "When Irish Eyes Are Smiling."

Apparently the open house was successful, because in 1955 the Democrats repeated their feats of the previous election and added a complete sweep of the School Board. By the fall 1959 election, the Democrats won the mayoralty, the Board of Aldermen (7–1), the School Board (9–1), and the Common Council (15–3). The two-party system was basically dead in Springfield even before the change to a nonpartisan system was even discussed. In 1949, the Republican party enjoyed an enrolled-voter majority of 2,892 members; by 1959, the Democrats had turned the tables and had a majority of 14,593. Only Ward 5 had a GOP edge—and only by 58 votes (*Daily News*, July 18, 1959).

Mayor Brunton was finally defeated in the 1957 Democratic primary by another Irish Catholic, the young Thomas J. O'Connor. Bishop Weldon tried unsuccessfully to persuade Brunton not to stand for reelection, and having been out of the country for much of the campaign, the bishop returned just in time to pay a public visit to city hall in order to convey a gift from abroad and his obligatory symbolic support. It was to no avail. And when Brunton tried to come back in 1959, O'Connor won even more resoundingly.

But it was not simply among elected officials that Catholics were taking over. Catholics were also sweeping the appointive posts. It was said, especially among the new outsiders, that the city's snow-clearing crew now consisted of any Catholic with a pickup truck and a relative in city hall. The School Department quickly gained a reputation as the employer of first and last resort for the products of the nearby College of Our Lady of the Elms (now Elms College), a Catholic women's school. In fact, it was during the 1950s that the first Catholic superintendent of schools was appointed. However, his situation was doubly ironic, first, because he was a Yale graduate with the name Saunders, many no doubt thought of him as another Yankee, and second, because after only six years, he left "partly done in by some local Catholics who wanted more for the parochial schools than he was willing to give" (interview).

SUMMARY

Springfield's three-and-a-half-century history defies any quick recounting, but certainly one theme involves the gradual marginalization of mainline Protestantism and the corresponding move to the center on the part of a growing Catholic community. In the story's most dramatic version, Catholics wrested control of the city out of the hands of the Yankee estab-

but not of a
Cath. Church.

lishment. But there is also a sense in which the Yankees merely relinquished their positions. As the immigrants move in, they moved out, and this applies to the political arena as well as to residential locations.

And yet Protestants retained their hold on the city's economy long after they retreated to the suburbs and bowed out of city hall. In 1891, the paper *Progressive Springfield* ran biographical sketches of the officers of the city's leading business concern, the Massachusetts Mutual Insurance Company. There was not a single mention of religion or church affiliation, but of course that was unnecessary, since there was not a single Irish or ethnic surname, and the hegemony was understood (vol. 1, no. 3, February, 1891). That understanding was to persist for another three-fourths of a century. Indeed, it was not until 1968 that Springfield had its first Catholic bank president, and not until the 1980s that two of the city's largest corporations could each have Catholic CEOs, neither of whom knew it of the other.

At this point, then, it is misleading and premature to call this last section a "summary." It is more accurately a pause before moving ahead to events in Springfield since the 1950s. Clearly there is another shoe to drop in the development of the Catholic establishment, and this is described in the next chapter along with important changes in the city's political and economic structure. But, as we shall see, there is also a lurking irony in this development that will become more apparent as we proceed. Once Catholicism had attained the structural standing necessary to function as an establishment, it had lost much of the cultural wherewithal needed to fulfill the mission.

not "structural"?

Chapter Three

HIGH ROLLERS AND HIGH RISES

IN HISTORY'S HINDSIGHT, the America of the 1950s seems a collective sigh following the desperate days of the Great Depression and World War II. As Nelson Algren once remarked, "The Eisenhower years melted like cotton candy in the mouth of history." For many, it was a time of almost resolute innocence, an invitation to idealistic visions rather than another round of flinty challenges. But, of course, not all was dreamy beneficence. In the midst of this day at the beach, undercurrents of change were already sucking at the nation's ankles. Many were especially apparent in urban America. On almost every conceivable front—economic, political, racial, cultural—cities were facing incipient crises and radical alterations. By the 1960s, "downtown" was no longer a term of excitement but a synonym for despair.

As was so often the case, Springfield's fortunes were tied to and symbolized by its federal armory. Largely because of the armory, the city was spared the depths of the depression trough and experienced a lift during World War II. But by the 1950s, the lift had subsided, and in 1968 the armory itself was decommissioned—its sprawling grounds ultimately divided between a national park with a museum of weapons, an assembly plant for a leading computer manufacturer, and a campus for Springfield's two-year technical college. Meanwhile, the city's population reached an all-time high of 174,463 in 1960, only to embark on a steady decline in the two decades following.

Clearly the inner city was losing in its competition with the outer suburbs. A city whose early growth and momentum depended heavily on its role as a transportation nexus for river barges and railroads, Springfield was now at the mercy of the automobile, and federal monies flowed plentifully for highways and interstates. In 1958, Springfield began work on Interstate 91, a major north-south throughway that was laid out between the city's Main Street and the Connecticut River, dissecting and destroying several residential and business areas in the process. During the dozen years required to complete the project and its linkage to the Massachusetts Turnpike through the east-west I-291, the city had thrown in its lot with federally funded urban renewal more generally. The results were described in an extensive brochure to promote subsequent redevelopment in the 1980s:

Hard times. These two words sum up conditions in Downtown Springfield over the last generation. Main Street was once termed: "the industrial, commercial, and financial spine of Western New England." But [more recently] Main Street has been characterized by vacant lots, empty storefronts, and dilapidated buildings. Worse yet, the street has been devoid of people, particularly after the business day. . . .

With much fanfare, the federal government undertook to save the cities in the 1950s and 1960s. Urban renewal—rip down the old and build up the new. If suburbia is the answer, bring suburbia to the cities. In Springfield, urban renewal gave us the New North. Low, wide buildings, plenty of room for expansion, huge parking lots, just like the suburbs. Urban renewal cleared many blighted areas in the central city, and we still have the vacant lots to prove it. (*TIME for Springfield*, p. 5)

This was a wrenching period of economic change, which later required a court-contested doubling and tripling of local property taxes to keep up with expenses. Changes in the downtown scene cost the city several of the old ethnic neighborhoods on the near north side and in the Italian south end. And physical dislocation was followed by social unrest, as each of the three mayors (Ryan, Freedman, and Sullivan) who served the city from 1962 to 1977 had to contend with major incidents of black (and later Puerto Rican) protest, which whites perceived as reaching near "riot" proportions. Meanwhile, the city lost some of its major landmarks and historic buildings, including H. H. Richardson's nineteenth-century Church of Unity. In fact, this site now stands as a mocking symbol of the era's frenzied futility; after having been cleared for an apartment complex that was never built, it remains a parking lot. Sarcastic references to the city's "urban re*mov*al" program contained more than a soupçon of truth.

Springfield's experience with urban renewal was a double pivot-point in the city's political development. It involved two specific alterations in city politics, one early and one late. First, urban renewal itself was contingent on a major change in the structure of city politics and city hall. This was the shift to a wholly new form of city government under the Massachusetts Code of Municipalities, one that involved nonpartisan elections, a unicameral City Council, and most important of all, a strong mayor with new powers of personnel appointment and policy initiative. The change occurred despite considerable Democratic (and synonymously Catholic) opposition, though ironically it later secured a Democratic (and largely Irish-Catholic) hegemony. The revamped city government was in place by 1961.

A second major response to the urban renewal debacle did not occur until the late 1970s. Springfield Central, Inc., was an organization of business leaders devoted to working with the established political structure in an effort to rebuild the downtown area and the city's economic infrastructure more generally. Like the shift to a new city charter, the rise of Springfield Central offers a revealing window onto both power and religion in the city. This was no longer Yankee money dictating to ethnic wage-earners. It represented not only a new ecumenism in the ranks of the powerful but the attainment of full class and status parity by the community's Catholics.

This chapter's first two sections complete the overview of the city's political and social history begun in Chapter Two. However, the third section marks a departure of both substance and method. Here, the question is how Springfield's political system of the 1980s measures up in the eyes of its citizens. The answer involves our small community survey of the general population and several of its elite groups. Questionnaire responses range from estimates of corruption to assessments of community influences, from a profile of power to a sense of an overarching "civic idealism."

In all of this, Springfield is again both a microcosm of the country as a whole and a representative of the changes affecting other cities and towns. Indeed, while we may seem to be stretching the point in generalizing to *both* cities and towns, both sets of attributes remain important within Springfield, and their interaction is critical to an understanding of the changing face of community power and the city's overriding sense of itself. The chapter's last section discusses these issues by way of placing power in Springfield in a somewhat broader and more conceptual perspective.

A NEW POLITICS OF EFFICIENCY

When we left the local political scene in the preceding chapter, the preponderantly Irish Catholics had achieved firm control of the Democratic party, which in turn had solidified its dominance of city politics and city hall. By 1959, the Democrats were dominantly Catholic, and Irish Catholic at that. That autumn they converted their enrolled-voter majority of 14,593 into a virtual sweep of the city's political board. Democrats not only carried the mayoral race, but also earned overwhelming majorities on the Board of Aldermen (7–1), the Common Council (15–3), and the School Board (9–1).

But winning elections is one thing; effective governance is quite another. Despite its heavily Democratic composition and solid voter majorities, the system involved a weak mayor with no structural basis for exercising strong leadership. For many years, Springfield's city government had been a house divided. In fact, it resembled more a fragile association of condominium owners who disputed everything from the parking to the garbage. A 1953 report from a political science class at the University of Massachusetts described the setting this way:

> The city has an old fashioned form of municipal government, there being only eight other cities in the country with bicameral legislatures. The weak-mayor charter was adopted in 1852 and has been changed very little during its 102 years of existence. The mayor is chosen by biennial, partisan elections. He appoints some of the members of the city's thirteen boards and commissions, these appointments being subject to the confirmation of the city council, and he exercises a rather general supervision over the subordinate officers in the government.
>
> The eight members of the Board of Aldermen are elected at large, but each alderman represents one of the eight wards of the city. Members of the Common Council, the lower chamber, are elected by wards—two from each of six wards and three from wards three and four. There are a total of thirty-eight who are directly elected by the people: the mayor, clerk, treasurer, eight aldermen, eighteen councilmen and nine school committee members. (Prof. J. Fenton, "The 1953 Springfield Municipal Election," class report, p. 1)

The system of ward representation, coupled with Springfield's ethnic-based residential patterns, meant that city government was often little more than formalized ethnic squabbling. Weak executive authority meant that even basic city services were inefficient; at one point there were almost two hundred and fifty different subcontractors responsible for garbage collection, some of whom collected refuse with horse-drawn vehicles until 1950 (Kaynor 1962, p. 30). Indeed, through the 1940s and 1950s the mayor was not the city official with the most political power. As one interviewee put it:

> The city kind of cried out for a "boss," and for while it was the chairman of the Board of Water Commissioners. When the mayor needed something, that's who he went to and regardless of the issue. (interview)

The byzantine formal structure of city government descended by default into a system of informal networks and patronage. Springfield had more firemen per thousand population in 1956 than any city in the country and the highest per capita spending of any city in its population class. As one commentator noted, Springfield's government was a "picture of stagnation, patronage and inefficiency" (Kaynor 1962, p. 31).

Dissatisfaction with this state of affairs had been building since shortly after World War II. In fact, two less radical efforts to change the charter to a city manager system were defeated at the polls in 1949 and 1953, and a 1954 attempt at charter change was blocked from the ballot by the City Council itself. All three of these setbacks occurred despite—or perhaps because of—strong support from the predominantly Yankee business community. As was the case in many urban centers during this period (see, for example, P. H. Rossi 1970), "good government" movements sponsored by the Protestant business class met with resistance and resentment from ethnic politicians who viewed them as devices to shut off their access to political and economic resources. One of our respondents, eventually active in the successful effort in 1959, referred to these early charter proposals as "Yankee plans."

By the late 1950s several new developments converged to make a change more likely. First, petty political rivalries among the city's various elected bodies and officials had become an obvious obstacle to much needed actions. Even the city's Democratic newspaper accused the City Council of an "ineptly-planned, clumsily-conducted, inadequately-rehearsed farce" in subverting the antigambling initiatives of the mayor's appointed Police Commission (*Daily News*, December 9, 1958). The city's superintendent for streets and engineering was accused of purposely mangling a needed public works program, and he publicly opposed the reelection of the mayor—a fellow Catholic and Democrat.

Second, the city's need for more effective management was becoming more pressing. As economic problems mounted, city hall seemed in disarray. In one sense, Springfield was well positioned to take advantage of federal largess for urban renewal; after all, its U.S. congressman had become a member of the House Appropriations Committee, where he chaired its subcommittee for the Department of Housing and Urban Development. But even under these conditions, successful grants require coordinated planning and execution. The city's decision making had become confused and stalemated at precisely the time when new clarity and purpose were required; Springfield was one of the last New England cities to file for preliminary planning grants for urban renewal.

This simmering crisis led to a *third* development in the form of a new strategy and coalition for change. Rather than push for a city manager while retaining bicameral city chambers and partisan elections, a new group formed to pursue a bolder change that would exchange a bicameral for a unicameral City Council, at-large and nonpartisan elections for ward- and party-based contests, and a strong centralized mayor for a weak and largely symbolic position often at the mercy of other city officials elected independently. Known as the "Plan A Charter" under the state's municipal code, this would greatly alter both the rules and the stakes of city politics. But even more important than the new objective was the new group behind it. Whereas previous reform efforts had pitted the old Yankee business establishment against the new Catholic political order, the reform lineup had changed significantly by 1959.

This was especially clear in the choice of a new chairman to spearhead the effort. Charles V. Ryan, Jr., was a young lawyer and a member of a prominent Irish-Catholic family with mid-nineteenth-century Springfield roots. In fact, his background was far more "lace curtain" than "shanty" Irish, as he had grown up not in Hungry Hill's Ward 2 with most of the town's Irish-Catholic politicians, but in the more affluent East Forest Park neighborhood in the city's southeastern Ward 6. He graduated from the best public high school ("Classical") rather than its parochial counterpart ("Cathedral"). He then left the state for his undergraduate education, albeit "with the Jesuits" at Georgetown University, before returning to law school at Catholic Boston College. When Ryan came home, he joined a highly respected Catholic law firm in which his father was a senior partner. Clearly, this was not the conventional background for a Democrat in Springfield. As one political veteran put it: "Charlie was the wrong kind of Irish. He wasn't a street-corner kind of guy; his family had money and lived across town" (interview). But if Ryan's background would have made a direct entry into electoral politics difficult, it helped him become a reform leader working between elites. Here was a man ideally suited to bridge the several gaps at issue—ethnic, religious, and economic. He was a man with whom both the business and political communities had something in common.

Ryan took hold quickly and led a spirited charge at the head of a large "New Springfield Committee," which combined Democrats and Republicans as well as diverse ethnic and religious groups. However, the opposition was neither idle nor insignificant. Although the sitting mayor and his popular predecessor—both Catholic Democrats—cleaved to the sidelines, a number of other Democratic politicians and city-office holders defended the status quo that they now dominated. Many were concerned on two fronts. First, a strong mayor would reduce their own political access and influence around city hall; second, a shift to nonpartisan, at-large elections seemed an invitation for Republicans to reenter the political fray through a newly opened back door. As it developed, only the first concern was justified. Fear of the Republicans was an outdated political reflex. There was a gnashing of Democratic teeth when nominal Republicans won some three of the ten seats in the first formally nonpartisan postchange City Council. However, it was the Republicans who had more reasons to fear such nonparty open elections, as subsequent history attests. Within a decade, the city's Republican party was virtually dead.

The change to a Plan A Charter carried by an affirmative vote of 29,636, compared to 11,965 who voted to retain the old system and 12,361 "blanks", which endorsed neither alternative. The vote occurred in the fall of 1959, and the change was first implemented in the elections of 1960 for the new city administration of 1961. In a single stroke, Springfield's city hall was changed from an arena for competing political fiefdoms to the garage for a strong political machine with the mayor very much in the driver's seat. In addition to chairing the important School Committee, the mayor now had the power over municipal appointments and control over the entire city budget. While the unicameral City Council had to approve the budget and could cut from it, the council lacked the capacity to initiate personnel changes or appropriate funds on its own. The words of one observer expressed the sentiments of many:

> Charlie Ryan and the Plan A Charter took politics out of the gutter and put them on a high plane with an emphasis on standards, educational background, and the issues. City government is just more professional now. There's less part-time, "good-ole-boy" type of involvement and more competency. (interview)

But it is easy to overstate both the extent and degree of change. City hall was not professionalized overnight, and there was a considerable difference between the procedures of government and the practice of politics.

Politics was altered significantly once the mayor commanded a clear pecking order. Aspiring politicians learned to find their places in the queue and realized that any forward advance would be controlled more by backstage influentials than the voters at large. The trick was not so much getting on the ballot as doing so with the appropriate sponsorship. This became especially true of the mayoral race itself. At this level, nonpartisan elections often translated into noncontested elections. Since the charter change, there have been fifteen mayoral elections, of which less than a third were sufficiently contested to deny the winner 65 percent of the vote in either the primary or the final. Not since 1957 has an elected incumbent mayor lost. Indeed, while most incumbents have amassed considerable campaign funds by professing to "run scared," it is rumored that in at least one instance funds were quietly donated to an opponent's campaign to provide for more active—hence more legitimating—opposition. As several of our informants noted, "These days, Springfield leaders aren't so much elected as anointed."

Two local politicians elaborated the process in different ways, one concerning the elites at the top and the other concerning the grassroots in the wards:

> It's pretty much a matter of culling. I mean you have to pay your dues and earn it—work your way through like a journeyman. The business community and the newspaper support who they think can win—they don't just reach down and grab someone. Besides business support is not very influential at

the polls. It really matters afterwards in terms of the dollars they put up for projects, and that sort of thing. (interview)

As early as the thirties and as late as the sixties, anyone wanting to run for office as a Democrat had to carry the Hill, and to do that you had to first go and see three women who really controlled it. I remember my courtesy call. We chatted, and I could tell that at first they were reluctant. But finally they were persuaded, and I was taken around the Hungry Hill fair, and contacts opened up to all sorts of organizations. Today the media's so important, that kind of politics is gone. But, no, come to think of it, it's still there. You still have to push the informal networks, make the calls, and develop the contacts. (interview)

For the most part, then, the city's nonpartisan, at-large elections have encouraged an oligarchical system that protects the leaders on top from the pretenders below. Certainly it has rewarded Springfield's Irish-Catholic Democrats. Despite the apprehensions that many felt on the eve of the charter change, there have been only two exceptions to their control of the mayor's office in the almost thirty years that have elapsed since, and both exceptions were included in the anointment process—one a Republican Jew in the early 1970s, and the other an Italian Democrat later in the same decade. Two political insiders accounted for the aberrations this way:

There just weren't any good Irish candidates ready at the time; besides, those were both good men. (interview)

Freedman was elected when there was no Irish on the launching pad, and Grimaldi and Dimauro split the Italian vote. Later, there were no Irish on the pad when Dimauro was elected either, but it didn't hurt that his wife was Irish. (interview)

There have been other exceptions to prove the rule. In Chapter Six we shall describe in some detail a recent contest for state representative that involved unpredictable candidates with predictable consequences. Meanwhile the 1968 congressional primary deserves recounting as the most infamous instance of political bloodletting in Springfield's postcharter change era.

Here the incumbent was Edward P. Boland, the eight-term lord of the political manor—an immensely popular Democrat first sent to Washington in 1952. The challenger was none other than Charles Ryan, the young Democratic lawyer who had chaired the charter-change campaign, gone on to three highly successful terms as mayor, and hoped to take advantage of the city's continuing economical travails as symbolized by his opponent's inability to save the federal armory with its 17,000 jobs.

The race seemed to confirm the dialectical axiom that every new establishment contains the seeds of its own opposition. Both candidates were Irish Catholics, but the incumbent came from a working-class background in Ward 2 on Hungry Hill, and we have already described his rival's middle-class roots in Ward 6 on the city's southeast side. Not surprisingly, sides split largely on the basis of social class. The challenger sought a new coalition that spanned the city's business sector as well as its French-Canadian and Italian communities, who had often felt so excluded by the Irish Democrats as to vote Republican. In fact, Ryan had succeeded in replacing some of the long-time members of the Democratic city committee with his non-Irish allies, and his campaign manager was an Italian-Democrat lawyer.

Meanwhile, the incumbent was hardly idle. As one city pol described the race, "We let Ryan take all the bankers, and we took all the depositors." Boland laid successful claim to the old Irish political machine, but he also made forays into other communities:

> Poor Charlie. The congressman saw quickly he couldn't make it with the Irish alone, so he made it his business to attend all sorts of affairs—Polish, French, Italian. He still attends everything he can possibly get to, and, of course, he has always had good relations with the bishop. (interview)

Boland retained control of his old constituencies and reactivated old loyalties. Although Ryan had hoped to capitalize on the city's recent economic downturn and its loss of the armory, Boland was equal to the challenge:

> Charlie just miscalculated. Labor really did a job for Boland, and people came out of the woodwork to vote for him. There was tremendous sentiment that we had an Irish Catholic doing a good job, and you just don't run against him. Boland also bridged the generations. I remember one elderly woman in a wheelchair who hadn't voted since his first city race in the 1930s. She said, "I won't let them do this to Eddie." (interview)

The results still evoke winces. Overall, Boland won 42,100 votes to Ryan's 25,058, and in Springfield proper the contest was a better than two-to-one rout (19,711 to 8,594) as the incumbent swept every ward in the city, save one. The king was crowned again, and the betraying prince was badly chastened for poor form even more than poor politics. As one person said:

> Ryan was a safe lace-curtain Irish and had the support of a lot of people like himself—Republicans pretending to be Democrats. But he betrayed the old Irish, and that hasn't healed yet. When the Irish hate; they hate. (interview)

The basic lessons were clear: in Springfield, public political struggles are unseemly; power is better conferred than fought over; and any changing of the guard tends to occur on the guard's own schedule and terms. This is not only the politics of efficiency but efficient politics.

So much for an introduction to recent dynamics in Springfield politics and the culture that envelops them. To this point, we have used the term "politics" in its narrow sense, referring to those who seek and cast votes in the process of community decision making. But, of course, decisions are also made by other factions in other scenarios. These decisions also affect the distribution of power, money, and status—all hallmarks of politics as an activity. We turn to one of those now, in charting the parallel development of Springfield's economic leadership over the past several decades.

MONEY SPEAKS

In the years following World War II, the writing on the political wall was clearly in the hand of the city's white ethnic Catholics, but the writing on the local account books remained that of the Yankee business community. From the late 1940s well into the 1970s, relations were uneasy between the town's political and economic elites. While the former were left with the chores of day-to-day municipal management, the latter became increasingly anxious about the city's longer-term future. In fact, Springfield's business leaders formed a series of special councils, commissions, and committees to look over and beyond the shoulder of city hall. However, by this time many of the individuals involved in monitoring the city had moved to the suburbs. This added tension to a situation already strained by divisions of economic interest, status, ethnicity, and religion. While virtually all of these councils were publicly lauded for their "spirit of cooperation," the early history of such ventures was one of overlapping starts and stops, as high hopes were followed by sober reassessments.

The first of the city's postwar business councils was Future Springfield, Inc., formed in 1945 and described as follows by the city's mayor:

Future Springfield, Inc., is a group of citizens in many lines of work who feel that by studying our problems as they appear and by working together intelligently, the progress and development of our city can be promoted so that all of us may enjoy better homes, more security in our jobs, and more of the good things of life in the years to come. (*Springfield Union*, May 28, 1945, p. 1)

As one of the founding members also noted at the same time:

I believe that one of the reasons for Future Springfield, Inc., is to bring about a closer tie-up between the people who pay taxes on the money they make in

or off of Springfield, and those who spend the tax money after it is collected.
(ibid., p. 2)

But, if there was a potential here for considerable conflict, this was
considerably reduced by the group's composition. Its original seventeen
members well reflected the city's immediate postwar business and political elite. All were men, and almost all were Protestants with the exception
of a Jewish labor leader and the city's last elected Protestant mayor in
1938, Roger Putnam, who had returned from the war a converted Catholic. By this time, Putnam was a prominent local manufacturer who was no
more representative of Springfield's Catholics than he had been of its
Democrats. Even within Future Springfield, Inc., his stature was anoma-
lous, as this was more an organization of business vice presidents than
presidents. Lacking the city's true economic elite, the group was more a
source of counsel than a catalyst for change over its twenty-year existence.

Meanwhile, a different kind of group, the Citizens Action Commission
(CAC), was formed in 1958 during the term of the city's third Catholic
mayor, Thomas J. O'Connor, Jr. The commission began as an aspiring
grass-roots organization reaching beyond the economic elite to the city's
neighborhoods. Modeled more on a political party than a business corporation, it was a congeries of committees whose rosters included as many as
four hundred persons at the organization's peak, and it was born of the
same sort of enthusiasm and civic pride that led the city's off-street parking commissioner to proclaim a new facility as "the country's most beautiful parking garage" (*TIME for Springfield*, p. 6).

But CAC soon encountered difficulties. By 1961, there were more committees than tasks, and individual members complained about being
poorly mobilized and underworked. Then a feud developed between the
Daily News, supporting the incumbent Mayor O'Connor, and WWLP, a
television station owned by the family of former Mayor Putnam. In fact,
Putnam himself chaired the CAC even though he was at odds with the
CAC's executive director, who had been O'Connor's campaign manager.
As perceptions of political infighting increased, public enthusiasm and
corporate contributions waned, and the once full-time executive director
and his secretary were let go.

Under the next mayor, Charles Ryan, the CAC was pruned back to a
thirty-member executive committee and given new staff resources along
with new requests to study the feasibility of such possible city hall developments as a stenographic pool, a central mailing room, and a single automobile fleet. But by 1964, the organization was one of several such groups
in the city to have lost its momentum. In 1966, Roger Putnam himself
resigned and charged Mayor Ryan with "disinterest," "dragging his feet,"
and only maintaining the organization to meet federal requirements for
urban renewal and other funding.

Meanwhile, in 1961, several older business groups sought a common canopy to restore their languishing effectiveness and provide political economies of scale. The three principle organizations were Future Springfield, Inc., the Springfield Taxpayers Association (formed largely in response to city reevaluation in 1960), and the weak but enduring Chamber of Commerce. The newly formed Joint Civic Agencies (JCA) had its own paid staff, including an executive vice president recruited from outside the city at a salary not publicly disclosed and the subject of some controversy. The organization's functions were meted out to eight basic divisions, whose purviews ranged from trade development, government affairs, and civic development, to the concerns of women.

The JCA represented the public conscience and vision of the Springfield business community throughout the 1960s, a period of economic shriveling and downtown deterioration under the belied banner of urban renewal. JCA's large size and extensive scope became more liabilities than assets, and its record over the course of the decade was uneven. Finally, in 1970, the JCA was itself reorganized and reverted back to the Greater Springfield Chamber of Commerce. Future Springfield, Inc., was dissolved, and the Taxpayers Association regained its independent status without much hope of becoming a significant civic player.

And yet the 1960s did produce another organization that was later to develop into a very major player indeed. The Springfield Central Business District, Inc., was formed in 1964 as a smaller and more specific vehicle for the interests of the city's downtown business sector. In this first incarnation, the organization was relatively ineffective. In preaching growth and rebuilding, it was spitting into the winds of decline. After only a few years, the SCBD fell into a listless limbo, and it was not until the city's economic travails bottomed out some eight years later that the organization was revived and refashioned to become the single most powerful force in the city's more recent political and economic history.

It would be incorrect to depict downtown Springfield as a purely passive victim of economic deterioration even in the early 1970s. Two of the downtown area's most conspicuous buildings date from that period. Indeed, as the decade opened, the city's first major high-rise complex was nearing completion—a hotel mounted over a parking garage, both cheek-by-jowl with an indoor shopping mall—and the new civic center was under construction and proceeding towards its 1972 gala opening, featuring Bob Hope. And yet neither of these projects fulfilled their expectations. Although the civic center was locally celebrated as the "Showplace of New England," it proved too small to attract the major events anticipated. Here is how the new shopping mall was described only eight years later:

> It was supposed to be a magnet, attracting all sorts of people and businesses back Downtown. But its strongest pull was exerted right in its own shadows.

All the businesses and shoppers along Main Street were sucked in, leaving the street as a whole in worse shape than before. (*TIME for Springfield*, p. 5)

But if there was a single event compelling intervention, it was the 1976 closing of Forbes and Wallace, the city's largest and longest-continuing downtown department store, located on a prime corner just across the street (and an overhead walkway) from the new mall. This was an eloquent symbol of downtown economic decline that resonated throughout the community. Clearly, more comprehensive planning was required. With this cue, the Springfield Central Business District, Inc., was revived, and within a year it had assumed a streamlined role under a streamlined name, Springfield Central, Inc.

A Changing of the Guards

The Year 1977 was pivotal in recent Springfield history. It was no accident that it marked the beginning of an unprecedented surge of elite influence, for it involved a number of critical changes in the elite itself, including a new bishop, a new mayor, and a new newspaper publisher. Each represented a considerable break from the past, and hence each deserves a brief introduction of his own.

For the last several years of his tenure, Bishop Christopher Weldon had not been well and had lost much of his characteristic vigor and command. In fact, his successor had arrived on the scene earlier to serve as Weldon's auxiliary. Even before Joseph McGuire took over as bishop, it was clear that he was to mark a change. A Boston College graduate, McGuire was well integrated into Massachusetts political networks, and not long after his arrival in Springfield, he raised some local eyebrows and ire by delaying the start of a regular Sunday Mass to accommodate his late-arriving friend, Governor King. McGuire had served as secretary to Boston's aggressively activist Cardinal Cushing. However, he bore more resemblance to Cushing's own successor, Cardinal Humberto Medeiros, whom J. Anthony Lukas profiles in detail in his account of the Boston school busing crisis (Lukas 1986, pp. 372–404). Like Medeiros, McGuire succeeded a strong fount of authority and a self-styled "builder." Also like Medeiros, he was left to smooth some ruffled feathers both within and without the Church, while paying some overdue bills. Bishop McGuire remained genial through it all, and the contrast with his predecessor was remarked upon in a number of interviews:

> Weldon wasn't afraid to butt heads politically, though he preferred to work behind the scenes. McGuire comes across as a Boston pol working the crowd, but he's not a Cushing type. He talks a lot of what "the bishops say" rather than taking strong positions on his own. (interview)

McGuire is more people oriented. He doesn't step over the line or step on anyone's toes. Now, Weldon not only stepped over the line politically, but he would take money from the Mafia if it was for the churches and such. (interview)

McGuire's one of the greatest fellows I've ever run across. He has a completely different style than Weldon; he takes more time and consults more people before making a decision. Weldon tried to get the spirit of Vatican II, but it wasn't easy for him and many priests resisted. McGuire's not a pushover; he wouldn't allow something seriously wrong, but he overlooks more things and doesn't make a big deal over minor things. Weldon would pick up the phone. It would never hit the press, but it would be taken care of. And sometimes he'd send the chancellor or the vicar-general, who knew everyone from the Mafia to the saints. (interview)

Actually both McGuire and Weldon came out of the news releases, since both had been secretaries to cardinals, and similar cardinals at that. But McGuire is a centralist. He'll knock heads in his own house, but he won't make waves outside. While Weldon got out front on a few issues like civil rights in the 1960s, McGuire's not going to get caught by change, but he's not going to be the agent of change either. (interview)

It is possible, of course, that the difference between these two bishops—and the bishops who came before—simply reflects accidents of personality. But this not only runs counter to our own sociological bias, it denies the consensus of our ecclesiastical interviewees. One remarked specifically that, "O'Leary, Weldon, and McGuire were all bishops of their times." Another made the same point in contrasting Weldon and McGuire this way:

Weldon was a boxer; McGuire's more of a third baseman. But the difference between them reflects some real differences in the larger Church and its role. It's no longer a Church of uneducated immigrants needing protection or a fortress that needs defending. There are now a lot of middle-class Catholics who say basically, "We want to be Catholics in an Episcopalian way." Until we understand this, we're going to keep trying to raise money for a modern Church based on memories of an older Church. (Interview)

One important symptom of this change involved the increasing representation of Catholics in the city's corporate boardrooms. No longer was the odd Catholic bank president an exception to prove the Yankee rule; now the rule itself was becoming Catholic. But this was more the result of a decline in religious sensitivity than an aggressive increase. As religious filters were removed, the city's leadership began to reflect more accurately its basic demography, including the mobility of recent generations.

Indeed, by the mid-1980s two of the city's most powerful business leaders were each surprised to learn for the first time that the other was Catholic. But if the issue had never arisen between these two, it still comes up in other settings. Consider the following remark of a Springfield Catholic leader:

> I'm on the boards of several city businesses, and so are a number of Catholics. In fact, just the other day I heard a bank president—a Catholic himself—say, "Can't you find me a good Protestant layman? These Catholics are taking over banking." But really I don't know them as Catholics. They are far more educated and have a much more critical mind-set toward Catholicism. They don't seem to regard the old Catholic issues as seriously as in the past. (interview)

The increase in religious tolerance also extended to ethnicity, albeit more begrudgingly. A second major personnel change in 1977 involved the election of the city's first Italian mayor, Theodore E. Dimauro, who was to serve from 1978 to 1984. A Springfield native who returned to practice law after undergraduate studies at St. Michael's College in Vermont and legal studies at Boston College and New York University, Dimauro worked his way up the political ladder through earlier elections to the School Committee and the City Council. He was well positioned to run for mayor in the absence of an obvious Irish candidate, and he won handily, succeeding a popular member of the old guard and former city clerk, William Sullivan, who had served since 1973.

And yet Dimauro's own Catholicism was an important factor in one of his major achievements as mayor. For almost a decade, city officials had been aware of the need for a new high school, but disagreements over priority, site, and budget had led to repeated referenda defeats in the absence of support from such important community leaders as Bishop Weldon. Dimauro acted quickly to put together a new coalition of supporters, including a number of prominent clergy, the most important of whom was the new bishop. McGuire quickly acceded to the mayor's request for assistance. As one high-ranking member of the city hall team recalled:

> We did a study of the demographics of the high school opposition, and it was clear that the elderly and the Catholics were the most hostile: "Why build a school for blacks that my kids won't use?" But the new bishop turned it around. The Catholic voters who voted, voted for it; the ones who were opposed stayed home rather than vote against the bishop. Of course, the new site helped too. It drew off a lot of black and Hispanic students who people thought would cause problems in the parochial schools. (interview)

But, of course, Dimauro was more than a Catholic. As a downtown lawyer, he was well connected to the downtown business community. Indeed, Dimauro's willingness and ability to work with this community became a hallmark of his administration and was remarked upon by a member of his administration:

> Before we came in, there was a "business is badness" attitude. But we didn't have any resources. We had to form some partnerships, even if it meant giving up some power. Of course, you can't sell your soul to the business community. (interview)

This new eagerness to cooperate with business coincided with a major change in business leadership.

The third major change in the city's elite in 1977 involved a new publisher sent in by the nationwide newspaper chain that had owned the Springfield papers since 1960. A Jew from New York, David Starr was neither a disinterested chronicler nor a sidelines critic. He conceived of a city newspaper as part civic cheerleader and part corporate activist. Indeed his activism created uneasiness in his own newsroom, and by 1986 it had even earned him a "dart" of disapprobation from the prestigious *Columbia Journalism Review*:

> *Dart*: to David Starr, publisher of the *Morning Union, Evening [sic] News,* and *Sunday Republican* in Springfield, Massachusetts, for putting politics above professionalism and chairing a testimonial fundraising dinner for U.S. congressman Edward P. Boland, who represents the paper's district. Might not his role in the $100-a-plate event deter his reporters from writing critical stories about Boland, a reporter for the weekly Springfield *Valley Advocate* asked Starr. "I don't know what there would be to criticize about Mr. Boland," the publisher replied. (*Columbia Journalism Review*, January/February 1986, pp. 24–25)

Locally, however, Starr's posture received more applause. Several longtime political observers commented on his stance:

> Believe me, we were very lucky the day Starr came to town. He's a doer; he rolls up his sleeves and wants to be involved, whereas his predecessor was a knocker. If his successor turns out to be a knocker, the city will go limp again. We need the boosting for the psychology of the city. (interview)

> There's no question that Starr has suborned journalistic standards for the good of the community, and he's done a lot of good. With others, it's been just the opposite: anything to sell papers. (interview)

> Sure, he's a newspaperman, but he's a citizen first. . . . It's easy for a newspaper to kill a project; just cast enough doubt and the politicians won't touch it. But newspapers too often stand aloof; they become dead hands, naysayers, and malcontents—like his predecessor. But if you're a publisher, you can also

get things agreed to. He has power, he likes to talk about it, and he knows how to use it. (interview)

Still, the closer one gets to the actual political fray, the more divided the judgments become:

I remember once when a couple of city council candidates received unsolicited donations from the wrong people. They hadn't done anything to get them, but they'd look bad if it were revealed. I went to the head of the newspapers and presented the situation. I finally asked him, "Who runs this paper—the reporters or the owners?" It wasn't printed. (interview)

There was one time when Starr was meeting with a bunch of community leaders, and he kind of copped a plea saying, "I never interfere with my editors." Well, [a black activist woman] said, "Mr. Starr, you just insulted my intelligence," and she got up and walked right out of the meeting. As you might imagine, he remembered the incident and just about shut her out of Springfield politics from that day on by the way the paper covered her campaigns. (interview)

Predictably, such episodes produced sufficient resentment to provoke a few political candidates into running on partly antinewspaper platforms. But if few have tried, virtually none have succeeded, as was most recently discovered by Martin Reilly during an abortive campaign for reelection to the State Senate in 1988.

Meanwhile, Starr's zeal on behalf of the city's development and economic well-being found a natural outlet in Springfield Central, Inc., where he quickly assumed command. Some found it ironic that such an outsider should so rapidly become one of the two or three most influential citizens in a heavily Catholic city—a city for which kith and kin have long held the keys to influence. But there is long-standing scholarship on the power of outsiders (cf. Georg Simmel 1903); there is even a literature on the peculiar importance of newspapers within urban power configurations (Molotch 1976).

For whatever reason, the publisher soon became president of Springfield Central, joining its two cochairs: Charles Ryan, the Irish-Catholic former charter-chair, mayor, and congressional candidate, on the one hand, and James Martin, the Protestant head of Massachusetts Mutual Insurance Company, long among the city's largest and most important corporations, on the other.

This was a troika made in an ecumenical heaven. But in addition to combining a Jew, a Catholic, and a Protestant, it spanned several other important cleavages within the city's power ranks—politics versus business, old money versus new, Yankee versus ethnic. In fact, the mix was made even richer by close cooperation with the mayor and the appointment of another Italian Catholic (and former city assessor), Carlo Marchetti, as Springfield Central's executive director. The thirty-two additional members of its board of directors represented a critical mass of city influentials from various sectors, including corporation presidents and CEOs rather than seconds and thirds in command.

This was by no means an old economic elite pitted against a new political officialdom. It was soon to become a new and newly integrated political-economic constellation. And although its objective was limited ostensibly to rebuilding only the immediate downtown economy, its potential influence extended far beyond both the downtown area and purely economic issues. As one businessman noted, this was a major departure from the city's Chamber of Commerce:

> Springfield Central grew out of the Chamber of Commerce but then was taken over by people who excluded the traditional Chamber power structure, and that produced some hard feelings with the old-line business leaders, including the last of the old Yankees who had given the Chamber a WASP-ish attitude that was a heavy political negative. Besides, although most business leaders don't like friction and power struggles, the people in Springfield Central seemed to thrive on competitiveness. (interview)

Of course, the success of any agency is only partly dependent on its people; budgets also matter. Springfield Central planned to pursue federal, state, city, and corporate funding for its various downtown developments. However, as part of the process, it needed a fund of its own not only to cover staff and overhead but also to provide a "mortgage pool" for seed money and leverage in initiating projects. Here the troika was tellingly effective, especially its publisher-president. In fact, the fund-raising began with his call to the insurance head and cochair, asking directly for one hundred thousand dollars "to start the ball rolling." The money was quickly forthcoming, and with this and several other contributions in the bank, the publisher-president convened a meeting of Springfield's corporate heads to exact a proportional toll from each. Rather than ask for voluntary contributions of an amount to be determined by the donor, he had done his homework to determine how much each should contribute, and he distributed bills accordingly. As one person present described the meeting:

> They didn't all love Starr, but no one really had the guts to oppose him openly. But he kept talking about what's best for the public, and finally one guy challenged him and asked, "Just who is the public?" "The people." "And who are the people?" "The newspapers." "Yeah, well what will you do if I don't go along and give you what you want?" "Just wait and see." Well, the power of the press was pretty clear, and fifteen minutes later, the guy endorsed the plan. (interview)

The new Springfield skyline of the late 1980s, featuring (*left to right*) Massachusetts Mutual's BayBank tower, Monarch Capital's Bank of New England tower, the campanile of the municipal complex, the spire of First (Congregational) Church, and the former Hampden County Courthouse.

Over the next decade, turnover among Springfield Central's major players involved a new mayor and a new corporate cochair. The mayor was Richard Neal, an Irish-Catholic Springfield native, who had taught history in the local parochial high school prior to service as special aide to Mayor Sullivan from 1973 to 1977, followed by three terms on the City Council from 1977 to 1984, when he was ushered into the mayor's office. Dapper, well spoken, and a tireless presser of the flesh, Neal was a political natural who was seen early on as a likely successor to Edward Boland as U.S. congressman—a seat he finally won in 1988. In fact, there may be an instructive parallel in the succession to power of Mayor Neal and Bishop McGuire. Each followed a head-knocking power wielder who tended to keep his own counsel; each became known for his public relations savvy and handshaking flair. Perhaps Springfield's politics and Springfield's religion were both changing in the same direction.

Meanwhile, the first corporate cochair of Springfield Central, James Martin of Massachusetts Mutual, retired. He was succeeded by Gordon Oakes, the aggressive young head of Monarch Capital, the city's fastest-growing insurance and financial corporation whose downtown high-rise building of the 1980s was slightly higher than Massachusetts Mutual's Bay State West complex of the 1970s. Oakes did not live in the city proper, but as a birthright Catholic, his replacement of the Protestant Martin only underscored the new hegemony.

By this time, Springfield Central had become the preeminent force in reshaping not just the city's downtown skyline but its very sense of itself. While other business organizations also contributed, including the Chamber of Commerce and the Western Massachusetts Area Development Corporation, it was Springfield Central that dominated both the local headlines and a small group of some fifteen business leaders who formed the Task Force for Development that met most frequently with the mayor and stood by to donate corporate resources to civic projects.

Colloquial understandings of the Springfield "power structure" began to shift once downtown development gathered new momentum. Older structures were restored or replaced with new buildings, usually emblazoned with a corporate name or logo. Both pedestrian traffic and automobile traffic were reconfigured. And as the downtown area became increasingly adapted as a center for business and tourism, it made new homes for older city-activity groups such as the symphony orchestra, a resident theater company, and the Basketball Hall of Fame.

In fact, the very concept of "downtown" was redefined. As retail shopping moved out to the malls and the new high school was built several miles to the east, downtown became increasingly peripheral to the daily lives of Springfield citizens. Rather than "the city's first neighborhood"—as it is so often described—downtown became more of a western New

England regional center for banking, business, conventions, and tourism. Even the employees necessary to the revitalized downtown economy came increasingly from surrounding cities and towns. In fact, a number of business leaders have made a point of faulting the city's public schools for foundering on the shoals of drugs, delinquency, and illegitimacy and failing to produce the skilled and disciplined work force necessary for the new white-collar jobs required in a predominant service economy.

Trouble on the Nightwatch

Perhaps inevitably, Springfield Central's power was not always applauded, and even its proudest accomplishments had their detractors. In May 1986 the architectural critic of the *New York Times*, Paul Goldberger, was invited to inspect the downtown area and deliver his judgment to a meeting of the city's assembled elite in the old First Church on historic Court Square. To many who came expecting a laurel wreath, the verdict must have resembled poison ivy:

> I come away after a day in your city with both optimism and pessimism. You have a noble cityscape with a truly great stock of older buildings and as good a sense of what to do with them as any city in America. But you've been decimated in recent years by arrogant architects and city planners. . . . [The new downtown high rises are] the real Achilles' heel of Springfield . . . banal in the extreme, dull, stark, cold, and indifferent to the street. (*The Valley Advocate*, May 12, 1986, p. 20)

The response from the Springfield Central president was more than a little defensive: "Whatever we've done badly, we've planned it that way" (ibid., p. 21).

But even the planning itself came under fire. There were sporadic volleys aimed at the tax concessions that the city had granted to corporations putting up new downtown buildings. These included property tax exemptions ranging from fifteen to forty years under a recently passed Massachusetts law (121A) intended primarily to facilitate new housing starts and neighborhood redevelopment. Downtown developers were accused of gaining disproportionate shares of federal Community Development Block Grants (CDBG), which were also intended for broad neighborhood distribution to benefit low- and moderate-income residents who were to be involved in the decision-making process. In 1978–79, the U.S. Department of Housing and Urban Development raised questions about Springfield's allocations in communications with the mayor. The responses to both HUD and the public on these matters stressed the importance of downtown development in creating new jobs and new economic benefits for Springfield as a whole. The often repeated phrase involved the "rising tide that lifts all boats," but there was a persistent skepticism among some of the local sailors.

As the chapter's next section indicates, downtown development was not nearly so high among the public's priorities as among the elite's. But tensions involved more than priorities. Especially among the city's minority and populist leaders, there was a continuing suspicion of high-handedness among the high rollers. One black activist put it this way:

> I often call the city "Spring-gate"—you know, like Watergate. The politicians aren't any more corrupt here than anywhere else, but it's the corporate folks led by the newspaper that will really fight you down and dirty. They really have a hold on the city, though of course they go home to their houses in the suburbs at night. (interview)

And a recent unsuccessful mayoral candidate expressed his doubts more pointedly in a televised campaign debate:

> As long as corporations control city hall, the Block Grant money is going to go downtown. But I'll tell you one thing: If I'm elected mayor there won't be any consultants earning $317,000 out of community development money. (televised debate)

Even apart from the planning, the development itself had its share of snarls and snarling. The most critical involved a project to reconfigure the civic center, with added parking and a nearby high rise to include hotel, retail, and office space. An open competition in 1986 elicited four proposals for the site, two from within the city and two from outside, each with preliminary drawings and financing plans. All four were given front-page coverage in the morning newspaper as they were being considered by a selection committee appointed by Mayor Neal, with heavy representation from Springfield Central.

From a political standpoint, the odds-on favorite was the proposal from Monarch—the local insurance and venture-capital firm that had experienced meteoric growth and was just completing the city's largest (and highest) downtown project to date. Monarch Place was a $118-million office, hotel, and shopping complex on the site of the old Forbes and Wallace department store, which had closed in 1976. This appeared to give Monarch strong local standing, and its influence seemed considerably abetted because both its CEO, Gordon Oakes, and its legal counsel, Charles Ryan, were major figures within Springfield Central.

In fact, no one was more surprised than the Monarch CEO himself when the contract was awarded to an outside development firm from Boston, a firm with no Springfield track record or connections whatsoever.

There are competing explanations for the choice. According to those who were part of the selection process, it was based solely on the merits of the proposals, and there is no doubt that the Boston proposal was more fully elaborated while offering more developmental bang for the buck. There is also no doubt that the local proposal was somewhat vague. As one of its sponsors put it:

> Sure, it was just a sketch. After all this was a busy time for us. But we were certainly prepared to add details and to mold them to the city's own interests. If that's what they wanted, why didn't they ask? (interview)

Why indeed? Some knowledgeable observers of the city's political scene saw the results as a slap at the local corporation and its CEO, who were "getting too big too fast." One city political official noted:

> There's still some tension between the Catholic pols and the Protestant money men. It's not as much as it used to be, but the locals still resent the bankers and business types who live in Longmeadow, and they in turn tend to look down on the ethnic political establishment. (interview)

Actually, this explanation would seem inappropriate to the Monarch case, since its president is Catholic and lives not in Longmeadow but in a far less affluent community to the north. And yet the explanation applies at another and perhaps deeper level. Because of Oakes' corporate status, he is widely perceived as a Protestant suburbanite in the traditional mold.

But there are other possible explanations, too. Some of our respondents saw the decision as the mayor's attempt to manifest his political independence from the downtown economic elite prior to his imminent race for Congress. Still others saw the choice as representing a kind of civic maturation insofar as it was based solely on the merits of the proposals rather than local political ties and loyalties. However, if that was the case, there is still another irony involved. Within a year following the decision and the award of the contract, it had become clear that the Boston firm could not secure the necessary financing and was on the brink of defaulting. Even after reducing the size of the project, their ability to execute it was in considerable doubt. Thus, a decision defended on the most professional grounds had encountered quicksand and become a major civic fiasco. If there had been widespread dissensus over the initial choice, there was now equally widespread consensus over its results:

> The civic center was a mistake. People thought the city was farther along than it was. I mean the city didn't really *earn* Monarch Place; it was kind of artificial and more razz-a-ma-tazz than sound business, and its success chances even now are pretty marginal, though the people at Springfield Central didn't realize that. Anyway, of the four civic center proposals, three of them

had solid money behind them, and they took the fourth. The mayor rubber-stamped the decision, and it's been a disaster. (interview)

This interpretation by a knowledgeable insider suggests that the city itself may have gone too far too fast, as its political leaders suffered from an unwarranted confidence in its autonomous power and resources apart from its major corporations. If this was the lesson to be learned, it was conveyed in no uncertain terms by Monarch itself. As the city began to cast about for a substitute developer for the civic center project, Monarch was no longer available. Only days after the original competition ended, Monarch announced that it was withdrawing from further projects in Springfield's downtown area, including a much-anticipated riverfront project. Instead it purchased a large property in nearby Holyoke and began to invest heavily there. As another of the city's corporate leaders described the situation:

> There's no question about it: we're losing a major player. Gordy's picking up his marbles and moving to Holyoke. He's made no bones about it. He was really steamed about the civic center contract, and he can be difficult anyway. Gordy is a very bright guy, but his idea of negotiating is to set a position and stay there. He can be a nice guy, but he can also be the most unreasonable son of a bitch I've ever had to deal with. (interview)

Springfield and its political-economic elite both lost considerably from this episode. The push on behalf of downtown development and a heightened city skyline was at least temporarily brought to its knees. The decline in available private money was matched by a decline in both federal and state funds. Not only was the civic center project put aside, but several others shared the same fate, including major plans for further developing the city's riverfront, a new theater and office high rise, and an effort to reclaim an old hotel for new condominiums. So much, then, for a lengthy description of Springfield's political development up through the mid-1980s largely in its own terms. It is now time to check the perceptions of the citizenry.

The People Respond

As mentioned at the outset, this is a multimethod study that combines historical materials with personal interviews and a small questionnaire study. Having already drawn on the first two, this section introduces the third. In the spring of 1986—at the peak of Springfield's redevelopment effort—we conducted a mailed questionnaire survey of both a small sample of the Springfield voting-age population and several strategic elite groups, including clergy of all faiths, public school teachers and principals, and the city's second-echelon political and economic leadership—those with whom we did not conduct interviews. The questionnaire itself is included in Appendix B. Here, we want to report briefly on perceptions of the city overall and its power configuration.

Certainly, the 256 members of our general sample tended to be positive in their overall sense of the city. As part of a larger set of items, we asked them to give their reactions to three broad statements concerning Springfield as a community; for each, they could select one of six responses running from strongly agree to strongly disagree. Fully 78 percent agreed to one extent or another that "All things considered, Springfield is an ideal community in which to live," and 16 percent answered "strongly agree." At the same time, 71 percent disagreed to some extent with the statement "With so many groups in Springfield, the city is not a real community," and 18 percent disagreed strongly. Finally, 62 percent expressed some degree of agreement that "In Springfield, people from different backgrounds basically get along as equals," although only 4 percent did so strongly.

All three of these items tap a general phenomenon that might be termed civic idealism. This is a key aspect of what Robert Bellah (1967) referred to at the national level as "civil religion." The emphasis on the ideal society with a sense of community and equality is all part of America's reverential sense of itself. Bellah's concept makes more of a common denominational religious heritage than our items and the Springfield reality allow, and we have elsewhere (Williams and Demerath 1991) noted several ways in which the apparent conflict between America's civil religion, on the one hand, and its separated church and state, on the other, has been resolved. Still, a civil religion is part of the broader panoply of cultural solidarity that Emile Durkheim (1912) once described as critical to any enduring society or community and that need not have conventional religious trappings. Clearly Springfield has emerged from its divisive social and religious history with a sense of the whole. In balance, its citizens see it as not only viable but desirable within the perspective of what might be best described as the city's "civic" religion.

In addition, we asked our respondents to assess city governance and politics more specifically. In many ways, the halls of Congress are less urgent than city hall to most Springfielders, and we asked our respondents three questions to gauge their reactions to city politics and governance. Here it is also worth comparing the responses of the general sample with those of the political-economic elite. First, city government gets high marks for efficacy in that only 32 percent of the general sample and 19 percent of the elite agreed to any extent that "the problems of this city seem beyond the control of the city government." Of course, one could also note that almost one third of the general sample found city hall wanting in this respect. However, more than half of these respondents (18 percent of the whole) were in the most tentative category of agreement, and only 4 percent of the general sample—and none of the elite—agreed strongly with the sentiment.

Local government also rated favorably in terms of integrity. When asked if "Springfield's city government is basically honest and free of corruption," some 36 percent of the general sample disagreed, but only 7 percent disagreed strongly. The elite provided a more ringing endorsement with only 15 percent disagreeing, 3 percent strongly. However, the political elite cast more aspersions than the economic elite (25 percent versus 8 percent disagreeing that the government is honest; 6 percent versus none disagreeing strongly). This could mean that the politicos are closer to the action, hence in a better position to judge, while the economic leaders are inclined more to sideline boosterism. On the other hand, it could also mean that the political elite includes a higher proportion with specific axes to grind as a result of past political campaigns and enduring antagonisms.

Lest responses to the two questions thus far suggest a whitewash, one additional item salvages credibility. Consider the proposition: "Almost every major decision made in city government reflects the influence of a small group of people behind the scenes." Here, 76 percent of the general sample agreed, 15 percent strongly. Nor was the elite far behind, with 67 percent agreeing and 14 percent agreeing strongly (again with a preponderance of strong suspicion among the political leaders as contrasted with their economic counterparts: 25 percent versus 6 percent). While this need not be in conflict with the two previous sentiments, it does imply possible reservations about the democratic character of local politics.

Taken together, these last three measures provide at least a qualified affirmation of city government. But how do these three relate to the previous three? One can combine both groups into aggregate measures, calling the earlier set an Index of Civic Idealism, and this one an Index of Political Confidence. Not surprisingly, the two indices run together ($r = .58$ for the general sample). Put another way, approximately one third (.58 squared) of the variation in one is statistically accountable by the other.

Clearly the prevailing judgment is that there is more to city politics than meets the eye or clears the vote. However, responses to the previous questions suggest that neither the electorate-at-large nor the elite felt this pattern had produced major problems of incompetence or corruption. Politics may be a tainted business, but Springfielders do not seem to feel that it has fatally flawed their city.

Here too, however, interpretations may vary. On the one hand, this could be seen as a measure of legitimacy and an expression of confidence that those in political control basically have the public good in mind. On the other hand, the pattern could also reflect feelings of resignation and a lack of personal efficacy on the part of the citizenry. Recent studies of alienation suggest that it is more apt to lead to fatalistic withdrawal than activist revolt (cf. Wright 1976). Perhaps this is part of a general political fatigue in American life that involves a loss of both innocence and idealism. After several decades of investigative reporting and antiestablishment filmmaking, it requires either an enormous act of faith or an incredulous level of naïveté to believe that what one sees is what one gets at any level of American politics. What may have been scandalous in the movies of Frank Capra has become commonplace on the evening news.

Finally, let us return to religion with the one item that most alarmed respondents during questionnaire pretests: "Catholics are likely to have more influence around City Hall than non-Catholics." It is testimony to the issue's sensitivity that a number of respondents expressed uneasiness about answering, agreeing with one pretester who said she "wouldn't touch that question with a ten-foot pole." However, most persevered, and the results are arrayed in Table 3.1, where some 46 percent of the general sample agreed to some extent (though only 7 percent strongly). Note, however, that when the sample is separated by religion and ethnicity, the results are widely divergent and inversely related to what most insiders perceive as the reality. Within every category of the general sample or the elites, Catholics expressed the most disagreement with the premise of

TABLE 3.1

Percentages Agreeing (to Any Extent) that Catholics Have More Influence than Non-Catholics around City Hall

Group	% Agreeing
General Sample	46
Catholics	35
Liberal Protestants	48
Irish	32
Italians	55
French	34
Blacks	63
WASPS	71
Jews	88
Roman Catholic Clergy	27
Protestant-Jewish Clergy	82
Political-Economic Elite	59
Economic Elite	54
Political Elite	65
Catholic Political-Economic Elite	47
Protestant and Jewish Political-Economic Elite	88

disproportionate Catholic influence. This denial was particularly striking among the Irish Catholics and the Catholic clergy, although Catholic members of the political-economic elite were actually more likely to agree with the statement. Of course, the response of blacks, Protestants, WASPS, and Jews is predictable in a city that has undergone the kinds of changes we have described thus far. The real point here, however, is not to posit a truth but to note a continuing bone of contention and source of perceptual variance in Springfield, one that applies at the level of both "what is" and "what ought to be." The issue will recur.

In the meantime, there are other potential sources of influence in city politics, and less provocative ways of assessing them. Political theorists since Thomas Hobbes in the seventeenth century have recognized that "the reputation for power is power," and no account of community politics would be complete without considering such public perceptions. Hence, at another point in our questionnaire, we asked respondents to rate the influence of various community groups on two hypothetical issues that might face Springfield: a proposed property tax increase and a proposal for the addition of an X-rated channel to the cable television offerings. Respondents did not have to rank-order the groups in their influence, only rate them on a five-point scale. But few respondents chose to lump all the groups under the same rating, and the influence "ladders" developed from the answers are remarkably consistent across subsamples.

Table 3.2 shows the ratings ladder generated by the general population sample. Clearly, the elements we have identified as spearheading the

TABLE 3.2

Ratings of Community Influence on Hypothetical Property Tax Increase
(General Population Sample, $N = 256$)

Group	By Combined % Answering Great or Moderate Influence		By Mean		By Median	
City Council	1	(90)	1	(4.53)	1	(4.74)
Mayor	2	(87)	2	(4.47)	2	(4.72)
Downtown Business	3	(80)	3	(4.22)	3	(4.49)
Springfield Newspapers	4	(70)	4	(4.00)	4	(4.24)
General Public Opinion	5	(51)	5	(3.34)	5	(3.54)
Neighborhood Councils	6	(43)	6	(3.19)	6	(3.24)
Roman Catholic Clergy	7	(38)	7	(3.07)	7	(3.12)
Jewish Leaders	9	(31)	8	(3.00)	8	(2.98)
School Committee	8	(32)	9	(2.99)	9	(2.90)
Protestant Ministers	10	(22)	10	(2.62)	10	(2.50)

downtown revitalization—businesses, city hall, and the newspapers—
were viewed as the dominant players on the city's economic court. The
high ratings assigned to the City Council and the mayor generally accord
with city governance procedures in such matters; the strong showing of
"downtown business" and "Springfield newspapers" no doubt owed much
to the publicity surrounding the economic activities of Springfield Central. There follows a large gap in influence ratings before reaching the rest
of the ladder. While one must be careful not to overinterpret these ratings, it is worth noting that both Catholic clergy and Jewish community
leaders were accorded greater economic power than the Protestant ministers bringing up the rear. How the mighty have fallen over both the long
run of three and a half centuries and the short run of some fifty years since
the 1930s.

Compare these results to the same ratings ladder generated by the combined political-economic elites in Table 3.3. While the ratings here are
not as consistent across all three measures, they demonstrate even more
dramatically the perception that a political-business coalition influences
city economic policy. The same four groups are in the uppermost tier,
their scores closely bunched. There is the large gap between position four
and the rest of the field, even more dramatic for this subsample. And the
influence of the business community is rated even more highly.

But what about influence over another hypothetical case, the addition
of a pornographic cable television channel? Here we move from the city's
economy to its public morality. Table 3.4 presents the percentages of both

TABLE 3.3

Ratings of Community Influence on Hypothetical Property Tax Increase
(Political-Economic Elite Sample, $N = 69$)

Group	By Combined % Answering Great or Moderate Influence		By Mean		By Median	
Mayor	1	(99)	1	(4.78)	1	(4.88)
Downtown Business	2	(92)	2	(4.64)	3	(4.80)
City Council	4	(91)	3	(4.63)	2	(4.84)
Springfield Newspapers	3	(91)	4	(4.54)	4	(4.72)
General Public Opinion	5	(64)	5	(3.78)	5	(3.95)
Roman Catholic Clergy	6	(58)	6	(3.52)	6	(3.68)
School Committee	7	(46)	9	(3.12)	7	(3.31)
Neighborhood Councils	8	(43)	7	(3.30)	8	(3.25)
Jewish Leaders	9	(41)	8	(3.20)	8	(3.25)
Protestant Ministers	10	(27)	10	(2.85)	10	(2.85)

the general sample and the political-economic elite answering "great or moderate influence" for each influence source. The overall structure of power is somewhat similar to that for a property tax increase, and basically consistent for the general sample and the elite. However, there are several significant differences worth noting. Predictably enough, the estimated influence of religion is greater for the moral issue than the economic, as seen in the altered positions of both Protestant and Catholic clergy. Indeed, among the elite respondents, the Catholic clergy were rated the single most influential group concerning a matter such as pornography—and these are presumably the people who should know. Conversely, the influence of the downtown business community plummeted with respect to the moral question—from very close to the top to virtually the bottom. This provides a kind of common-sense validation for these findings. Although organizations such as Springfield Central and the Chamber of Commerce have recently shown signs of venturing into such moral issues as drugs and teenage pregnancy, they may have an uphill battle in the pursuit of credibility and influence.

In fact, downtown business leaders have had difficulty enough in persuading the general citizenry of the importance of the downtown area itself. We asked our respondents to indicate what priority the city should give to some eight different activities, including "downtown business development, city care for the homeless, reducing crime, responding to the needs of the poor and disadvantaged, improved maintenance of city streets and parks, development of [a black business] area, improving the public schools, and responding to the needs of minorities such as Blacks and Hispanics." In terms of the proportions indicating each was "ex-

TABLE 3.4

Ratings of Community Influence on a Hypothetical Pornographic Cable Channel

	% Answering Great or Moderate Influence	
Group	General Sample (N = 256)	Political-Economic Elite (N = 69)
Mayor	86	85
City Council	85	85
Springfield Newspapers	81	90
Roman Catholic Clergy	80	94
General Public Opinion	74	73
Protestant Ministers	72	76
School Committee	67	69
Neighborhood Councils	66	54
Jewish Leaders	65	71
Downtown Business	57	67

tremely important," downtown development ranked sixth out of the eight
with a rating of 26 percent in the general sample. However, it is worth
noting that it ranked fourth for the political elite (31 percent) and third for
the economic elite, with 50 percent of these respondents judging it extremely important. Clearly downtown development had greater urgency
among the elites than among the population at large, especially the increasing proportion of the latter that functions elsewhere in the city. Here
is yet another indication that Springfield's politics are not always soothed
by the warm waters of consensus, and that when elite and mass perspectives differ, it is the former that prevail. This, however, implies more
overt conflict than typically occurs. Successful elites often prevent such
matters from ever becoming matters of public debate, much less decision.
To a great extent, this was true of Springfield's downtown development.

All of the ratings so far apply to political sources involved with political
decisions. But at another point in the questionnaire, we asked about nine
more broadly constituted groups and their overall influence in the community. Again, the respondents were asked to rate rather than rank, and
here they had four levels of influence to choose among: a great deal, moderate, a little, and no influence. The groups are arrayed in Table 3.5 according to the percentages of the general sample that placed them in either of the first two categories. In light of the city's recent history, it is
hardly surprising that Catholics should score so high on this reputational
measure, or that the Irish should outdistance the Italians. However, it is
noteworthy that Jews rank higher than Protestants. Despite its considerably smaller number of people, the Jewish community is well represented
among the city's educated upper echelon, including several prominent
businessmen, a mayor who served from 1968 to 1972 and is now a local

TABLE 3.5

Ratings of Community Influence for Various Groups by General Sample (N = 256)

Group	% Answering Great or Moderate Influence
Irish Catholic	92
Italian Catholic	79
Jews	72
Protestants	60
Organized Crime	56
Blacks	49
Suburban Residents	48
Hispanics	33
Born-Again Christians	16

federal judge, and, of course, the publisher (as well as the editor) of the city's principal newspapers.

In fact, "Protestants" only barely exceed the score for "Organized Crime," and if one looks solely at the percentages estimating "a *great* deal of influence," organized crime has a higher profile than Protestants: 27 percent versus 11 percent. We shall be examining the power of various religious groups, including the Protestants, throughout the remainder of the book. But it is worth pausing briefly to flesh out the role of organized crime in the city's power configuration.

It is difficult to probe the shadow world of any American city with confidence. Rumors are rife, and there is a tendency to blame the city's problems on the city's villains, while engaging in the inside dopester's game of turning insidious innuendo against one's opponents and the high and mighty generally. In some ways the survey results we have just examined may be more trustworthy than the interview accounts ahead. But these accounts are also valuable, especially if we are concerned less with a totally objective depiction of the city and more with the city's sense of itself—its civic culture. For example, one involved observer of the city scene described it in these terms:

> The three really dominant forces in town are the Catholic Church, Mass Mutual, and the Mafia. But the Mafia keeps the really nasty stuff out of Springfield because they live here. Some of them give a fair amount of money to the Catholic Church for good works and a kind of moral dispensation. You can see them with the clergy down at Ciro's restaurant on the south side, and I heard that five priests did Big Nose Sam's funeral [the funeral of the reputed "head of the local Mafia"], and the mayor was there too. (interview)

Although virtually no one argues that city government is wholly without corruption, no specific ties to organized crime have been established, and the prevailing image is one of a backstage influence removed from the lights but never far from the action. As one respondent suggested:

> Springfield politics seem blemish-free only because no one's been caught. How could there not be corruption in a city government this size? The current mayor seems clean, but there have been others involved in some pretty shady dealings; and don't kid yourself, the Mafia is never too far away from city hall either. (interview)

But an ex-mayor drew this somewhat surprising parallel between how both organized crime and religion relate to local politics:

> Organized crime is like the clergy; they're there if you want their help, but otherwise they don't really get involved, and they don't control any political seats. (interview)

And another political figure described "the Mafia's" political impact in these terms:

> Does organized crime have more influence than the liberal Protestants? Oh, absolutely. I remember a mayor once kidding, "There are more of them than there are League of Women Voters, so I'm with them." They give a fair amount of money to political campaigns and, of course, to the church and to help the poorest section of the Italian community; one priest was a major character witness at a Mafia leader's criminal hearing. It sure doesn't pay to attack the Mafia, because then you'd just alienate a lot of Italians who aren't involved. Besides, they're not dealing with prostitution or drugs. They control the beer and local gambling, and their only real agenda is: "Leave us alone." (interview)

Meanwhile, the remaining groups in Table 3.5 also offer surprises. The slightly greater estimated influence of blacks vis-à-vis Hispanics no doubt reflects their greater numbers and longer local history, although some observers feel that this too may be changing, as we shall see in Chapter Six. The relatively low standing of suburban residents as a collectivity is belied by the power of many specific individuals within it, and this may be a case where the exceptions disprove the rule. Finally, the low ratings of born-again Christians may reflect Catholic unfamiliarity with the term as much as the community reality. As we shall see in Chapter Seven, there are some issues—especially concerning abortion and sexuality—where "born-again" evangelical Protestants have been very influential indeed.

FRAMING POWER IN SPRINGFIELD

If this were being written twenty years ago, it might have been cast in terms of the debate over "power elites" versus "pluralism" as the key to urban politics. Fortunately, that debate has been largely put to rest, and this is not the time to rouse it. Predictably enough, they were both right (cf. the excellent summaries by Friedland and Palmer 1984 and Waste 1986). Yes, there is a power elite in Springfield, but it is also subject to important limitations and qualifications.

First, the elite is by no means invariant. As this chapter and its predecessor have shown, Springfield's leadership has undergone several major changes, including first a separation and then a reuniting of a political-economic coalition, based largely on changing religious and ethnic grounds. The shift between a dominantly Yankee-Protestant power core and a heavily Irish-Catholic nerve center has been perhaps the single most important transformation to occur in Springfield over the past half-century.

Second, the elite is not simply an instrument of the economic infrastructure. Springfield has seen periods in which the political and economic leadership has been badly split and in quite different hands. For almost forty years, the local economy remained in the hands of the Yankees, while city hall came under the control of Irish Catholics. Clearly, considerations of religion and ethnicity have proved critical to the exercise of civic power. On the one hand, divisons between them can lead to lack of coordination and open conflict; on the other hand, commonality among them can produce a degree of bonding that transcends other differences, as was the case with Springfield Central at the peak of its power. The importance of religion and ethnicity offer yet another rebuttal to the vulgar elitist perspective that money is all.

Even within the camp of the moneyed material interests, there are important differences. Neither in Springfield nor in recent scholarship is the "business class" uniformly interested in or equally committed to the civic power struggle. For example, manufacturing firms that market their products outside the city have less stake in local development and economic growth than do those that depend upon investments in city projects, such as banks, insurance and venture-capital corporations, or real estate firms. Sometimes this leads to conflicts over priorities. However, it is also common for less interested businesses to defer to the development agenda, preferring to "sit one out" rather than contest and confuse matters. This has been the usual pattern with Springfield's manufacturing industries, none of which has either supplied or opposed major political leadership in the community. But in addition to those firms directly dependent on development, there are still other businesses whose interests are indirectly allied with the civic growth. Both a city's media and its legal community are cases in point, and Springfield provides classic evidence for each. No institution was more vitally involved in the city's recent surge than its newspapers, and as with virtually every other city, its law firms have been the chief seedbed of its political candidates.

Another variable that divides the business sector concerns the extent to which a firm or corporation is locally rooted or regionally affiliated. A large corporation that is not locally controlled and dependent is likely to have less political involvement than many smaller firms that have cast their lot with the city. Moreover, the officers and managers of regional firms are often auslanders with neither the interest nor the connections to become politically effective. Thus, while Springfield has offices of many of New England's largest banks, the local officers are rarely among the political-economic elite. They operate on orders from Boston or Hartford rather than by local initiative. Springfield's well-being is important to their organizations, but their own marginality and short-term tenure—their "capacity to exit"—insulates them from local conditions while truncating their local influence. According to one source in the Chamber of Commerce orbit:

> From a political standpoint, Springfield's business community has begun to get weaker, not stronger. Sure it has more corporations, but this includes fewer corporate headquarters. And although there is more money filtering through the city, there are fewer local people controlling it. Maybe the city as a whole is becoming just one big "branch bank." (interview)

And another traced the consequences this way:

> There's a real feeling of inferiority among the Springfield elite because they're not in Boston or New York. There's a drive to change that, but it's an uphill battle because the city's banks and major businesses are becoming more regional than local, and that tells you where the big time is. Besides, this means that their relation to community affairs gets more remote. And it gets harder and harder for local organizations and activities to get funds and support. (interview)

This leads to yet another important factor in the exercise of community power; namely, the size and nature of the context. In 1972, Michael Frisch titled his account of nineteenth-century Springfield *Town into City*. The title was technically apt since Springfield was formally incorporated as a city under the Massachusetts Municipal Code in 1852. But a legal change is one thing and a sociological change another. If, in sociological terms, a "city" is marked by impersonal and bureaucratic forces engaged in long-range struggles on behalf of a large and heterogeneous population on a multisplintered and differentiated turf, Springfield doesn't always qualify. Indeed, a common refrain among our respondents is that even a century after its incorporation, Springfield retains many characteristic of the more warmly personalized and face-to-face interactions of the town. Several political figures made a point of the matter while remarking on the importance of neighborhood, class and ethnic ties:

> City hall is gradually becoming more professional in its appointments. There are fewer family friends and political hacks being brought in and more promotions of deputies who deserve the chance on grounds of proven competence. But city politics is something else again. Springfield is too small to get away from tribal, "he's-my-buddy" politics. There's still a lot of old working-class ties, even among people who are now pretty middle-class. If you have the right working-class, ethnic, and neighborhood ties and you're on board with the downtown interests, you can disagree on an issue and still get elected. Except abortion, of course. (interview)

It's just a big town, and you really feel it in politics. I remember backing one candidate not because I liked him but because his father got one of my kids off on a disturbing-the-peace rap one time. Some things you just can't forget around here. (interview)

After Boston, Springfield feels more like a small town. It's easy to get around and meet people. My ethnic background made it easier to fit in, and I wouldn't have been accepted so easily without it. Actually after I got my first job, the first question I was asked was, "Who did you know to get it?" And even though I first got into politics as a newcomer, after a while it seemed pretty important to people to think of me as a native. They'll occasionally come up to me and say, "I knew your mother so well" or "My son grew up with you and speaks well of you." (interview)

This politician is luckier than others who have some difficulty "fitting in." Indeed, one city official was plagued at election time by a style and appearance that led many to misperceive him as a Protestant. His political competitors knew that he felt anxious about winning when he ran what they called his "Notre Dame ad," a brief television spot in which he discussed his loyalty to this very Catholic alma mater. It served the purpose well.

But there are other ways in which Springfield resembles a town. Just as its political process depends upon close personal links forged in the fires of neighborhood, class, ethnicity, and religion, its business community is marked by much of the same. When we asked the president of one of the city's major corporations to assess the civic commitments of various other business firms, he responded by naming not the firms but their CEOs, generally by first names and often in the diminutive. For him, like many others, Springfield's corporate world is more a collection of individuals than of organizations. The community is small enough that people within similar orbits know each other personally; it is provincial enough that they have often grown up and gone to school together. Without a rich array of private clubs and private schools, there is relatively little internal divisiveness—especially now that both "The Club" and "The Colony Club" accept Catholics, while the parochial schools serve many Protestants as a kind of disciplined urban academy.

All of this can produce a capacity for coordination that larger cities often lack. As one person involved in a civic improvement project noted:

Springfield is a good manageable size. You can make contact with people to get things done. It wasn't that way in Cleveland, where I worked on a development council. There, we had no contact with city hall, and it seemed we were always being introduced to strangers. (interview)

There is also a premium placed on cohesion. In order to protect the personal relationships that undergird the political-economic elite, there is a persistent effort to avoid conflict and minimize tension.

But all of this has its drawbacks too. The strain toward consensus leads to an idealization of the city by romanticizing its past and exaggerating its prospects. In fact, because Springfield falls somewhere between a town and a city, it tends to foster the former image in the face of the latter reality. What appears to be a warm and supportive town on the surface can become a disputatious city of deeply divided institutional forces underneath. Personal relationships can be poised precariously on the crest of a breaking organizational surf. And perhaps more than is usual in politics and elite management, there is a tendency to manipulate the presentation of a civic self to accord with townlike expectations. When these expectations are not met, the consequences can be all the more onerous for being so disappointingly at odds with the facts. Springfielders talk a great deal about their neighborhoods, their homes, and their families, but these intimate references are often belied by impersonal realities.

While the city's cross-cutting interpersonal ties facilitate leadership and support for sociopolitical initiatives in the short run, the city's compact size means there are fewer shoulders to share the load in the long run. The membership lists of charitable and civic organizations reveal the same names over and over; the boards of directors of the city's ten largest volunteer groups share fewer than one hundred different people. Business groups also have largely overlapping memberships—again as much a commentary on city size as on oligarchical exclusiveness. And when the city's political leadership canvasses the economic elite for financial support for special projects (see, for example, later chapters on the homeless and the school health clinic), the same people are consistently in the forefront of the giving.

This undoubtedly confers political benefits on particular businesses, but according to several of our respondents from downtown businesses, it may also be wearing out the economic leadership. Any economic contraction is likely to result in a withdrawal of civic-political involvement by many businesses and business leaders who are simply tired, depleted, or beginning to lose in public favor. In two different interviews, separated by over a year, two different respondents remarked that public actors in a small city like Springfield have a certain "shelf life." This has already begun to constrain what the current cohort of city leaders can accomplish.

To a large extent, deciding whether Springfield is a town or a city involves answering an insoluble riddle. As was mentioned above, it is both, and partly because the same may be said of every urban center. To quote the oxymoronic title of Herbert Gans' important work (1962), there are "urban villagers" everywhere. In Max Weber's sense (1905), both "town" and "city" are ideal types, and both have been subject to ideological and mythological embellishments. Just as many have pined wistfully for the lost intimacies of the town, so have many decried the harsh impersonality and bureaucratic intransigence of the city. But in reality, it is the interaction between the attributes of town and city that lies at the heart of most municipalities. Certainly that interaction is critical to the dynamics of power in Springfield.

Meanwhile, there are two other factors bearing on the exercise of civic power that need only be mentioned here because they will be elaborated in the chapters to follow. According to the classic formulation, the study of politics is the study of "who gets what, where, and how." So far we have concentrated on the first of these issues—the "who"—to the neglect of the latter three. By "what" we refer to important differences in the issues themselves, since even the most obdurate interpreter of urban elites now concedes that in most settings, elites vary in their interests and their capabilities according to the issues involved. This also relates to the question of "where." Thus, it matters where an issue fits on a city's agenda, and only a few will directly involve religious matters and religious constituencies.

Finally, perhaps the most neglected issue concerning community power involves the question of "how?" Recently, scholars have begun to realize that there are a wide variety of techniques for mounting power. Most studies in the past have focused on conventional political mechanisms involving electoral politics and coercive networking—what we shall call "structural power." However, our analysis of religion's influence has alerted us to a broader form of power wielding that we shall treat under the rubric of "cultural power" in Chapter Five. Illustrated by religion but by no means confined to it, this involves the use of moral appeals and cultural symbols to shape the political agenda and the political discourse. It is an important component of the relations between religion and politics, and it is invoked frequently by representatives of both spheres.

SUMMARY

This chapter concludes the introduction to Springfield and provides a richer context for the more specific analyses of religion and politics to follow. We have introduced the major players and the major forces at work within the city. We have supplied a historical grounding and provided a sense of the major changes that have occurred and are still under way.

By the mid-1980s, Springfield had all the characteristics of a second religious establishment, this one Catholic rather than Protestant. The political system had been under Catholic control for some thirty years, and over the last decade, the local economy followed suit. But what does it mean to speak of a religious establishment in late-twentieth-century urban America? How does this civic case relate to the concerns of the Constitution's Bill of Rights passed some two hundred years earlier: "Congress shall make no law respecting an establishment of religion, or prohibiting the free exercise thereof"?

In many ways, Springfield provides an ideal test for this dimension of the state of the Union. Precisely because the city's social, political, and institutional deck is so stacked in favor of a Catholic hegemony, one must wonder what form this has taken and what limits it has experienced. In the next chapter, we begin the examination with an overview of church and state in this local context.

Chapter Four

CORNER CHURCH AND CITY-STATE

IN EVERY AMERICAN CITY, the winter holiday season has become not only longer but louder as a result of its clashing sacred and secular symbols. The center of Springfield's holiday display is its Court Square. This city-owned block of grass, walkways, and monuments is bordered on the south by the red-brick facade of the city's oldest commercial block and on the east by the prestressed-concrete civic center. The park's other two sides represent corner church and city state explicitly. Anchored on the west by Old First (Congregational) Church with its characteristic white clapboard exterior and needlelike steeple, the square is bordered on the north by the city's municipal complex with a tall campanile, flanked by the twin, classically columned buildings of City Hall and Symphony Hall.

The symbolic interweaving of church and state is enough to make a strict antiestablishmentarian squirm. A traditional Christmas crèche with life-size figures arrayed around the swaddled infant stands on First Church property just across a driveway from the public square. The church flies a large American flag the year around, though we have yet to hear any protest about state symbols on church property. Both municipal buildings are adorned with large green wreaths conspicuously mounted on their upper facades. And assuming pride of place within Court Square is nothing less than a fifteen-foot Jewish menorah with its nine (electric) candles in honor of Hanukkah.

It was not always thus. Prior to the 1981 lower-court decision holding unconstitutional a municipal Christmas display in Pawtucket, Rhode Island, Springfield's city-owned crèche was mounted on the square itself. But with one eye on the courts and the other on the local religious and political scene, the mayor leased the crèche to First Church for one dollar with the understanding that it would be displayed in the church's side yard when out of storage space provided by the local newspapers. According to one city official, there was an initial question as to who would do the work of transporting and setting up the display: "Finally, one of the mayor's aides gave some city employees the afternoon off and a case of beer, and they very quietly drafted a truck and did the job" (interview).

The menorah came a year later when it was donated by a group of Hasidic Jews at the nearby state university. As the same city official put it: "We allowed them to put it up on public property; after all, we didn't own it, and we didn't use any city funds or workers to do it" (interview). Of

Court Square in 1974 (pre-Pawtucket court decision), featuring the city's Christ-mas crèche.

course, the menorah represents another in a litany of ironies—one that was especially appreciated by some of the city's Catholic political leaders who delighted in using it to defuse a potential community controversy. By replacing one religious symbol with another, city officials filled an impor-tant symbolic space and could not be accused of running from clouds on the legal horizon. It has become customary for the mayor to participate personally in lighting the menorah every year.

Court Square in 1983 (post-Pawtucket court decision), featuring a fifteen-foot menorah; the crèche has been moved to the bordering property of First Church.

In recent years, the square has added a Christmas tree and a Frosty the Snowman as concessions to the Supreme Court's reversal of the lower-court Pawtucket decision (*Lynch* v. *Donnelly,* 1984), allowing a mixture of religious symbols as part of the secular celebration of the season. However, the menorah remains the dominant religious emblem. Although a decision of the Second U.S. Circuit Court of Appeals in June 1991 up-

held the unconstitutionality of a similar menorah in Burlington, Vermont,
Springfield's case has never been litigated. Neither Catholics nor Protestants protest publicly, perhaps for fear of appearing anti-Semitic. In fact,
the only significant objections have come from the city's Jewish Federation and several Reform Jews who have written the local papers
and appeared on local talk shows to decry the breach of church-state
separation and point out the misleading parallel between the major Christian holy day and the less significant Jewish observance. As one rabbi
noted:

> Oh, there are a few protests every year from liberal Jews, but each time the
> mayor just says, "Go settle your own problems." Deep down, the Jewish
> community is pleased with it. They want to rub the Christians' noses in it as
> a response to the crèche. (interview)

All of this reflects the character of Springfield's recent church-state relations. As much as national headlines and federal court decisions might
suggest a pitched battle elsewhere in the nation's trenches, the tension is
managed here with relatively little confrontation. This is not to deny the
stress between the faiths of religion, on the one hand, and government, on
the other. But the strain is often more symbolic than substantive, and it is
rarely allowed to break into the kind of open conflict that would mar the
city's public equanimity.

But what do Springfield's church-state relations involve more specifically? This is the first of four chapters in search of the localized meanings of the First Amendment. Here we begin with an overview of two
sorts. First, we shall use our questionnaire data to examine how Springfielders themselves conceive of the issues in their private political attitudes and opinions. Second, we shall examine a series of actual church-
state imbroglios and entanglements in the city's recent history.

CHURCH AND STATE IN THE POPULAR EYE

From a constitutionalist's standpoint, there is an important difference between an established religious community and an establishment religion.
The first may represent the slipshod judgment of the social scientist, but
the second requires the precision of a jurist. Of course, it is the latter at
issue in the First Amendment's one pregnant phrase concerning religion:
"Congress shall make no law respecting an establishment of religion, or
prohibiting the free exercise thereof." This is the legal essence behind
America's civil religious shibboleth concerning the "separation of church
and state." Here, we want to examine Springfield's own response to the
law and its various overtones.

For the most part, Springfielders have kept this element of the constitutional faith—at least in the broadest sense. Early in our questionnaire, we

asked our respondents to indicate shades of agreement or disagreement with a series of propositions, including "The separation of church and state is a good idea." Some 84 percent agreed, though it is worth noting that, of these, only 37 percent *strongly* agreed," and some 29 percent either agreed only "somewhat" or actually disagreed to some extent.

Of course, these sentiments varied among subgroups. Overall, non-Catholics were more likely to agree strongly than Catholics (47 percent to 29 percent), as were those with college education compared to those without (39 percent to 34 percent). As the latter might predict, strong agreement was more common among our elite samples than among the general population; 50 percent of the political elite strongly agreed, along with 49 percent of the economic leaders. While only 36 percent of the clergy were in strong agreement—a figure almost identical to the general sample—this masks an important distinction. Whereas 49 percent of the combined Protestant and Jewish clergy strongly agreed, the figure dropped to 14 percent among Catholic priests and sisters. This reflects a major difference in theology. Whereas church-state separation is a staple of both mainstream Protestant and Jewish traditions in this country, the European roots of Catholicism have long stressed the sharing of power and responsibility with the state, and it is not surprising that American Catholic laity and clergy should reflect this heritage. Note, however, that it is reflected more in a sense of reservation concerning American separation rather than actual disagreement. No Catholic clergy reported "strong" disagreement with the sentiment, and only 28 percent "disagreed" or "disagreed somewhat."

But theology is not the only source of hesitancy here. Church-state separation may be clear enough as a cultural cliché, but it has been considerably muddied in the application. Even informed observers of the passing judicial scene are sometimes bewildered and frustrated by its lack of consistency in the church-state area. The problem may be compounded among those with only passing knowledge of its accumulated decisions and indecisions. To examine our respondents' knowledge at a more specific level, we asked them to consider a range of issues about which the courts have spoken in recent years, and to indicate their personal views as to whether the practice should be "legal" or "illegal" (and within these options, whether "definitely" or "probably"), or "not sure." Table 4.1 presents results for only those issues on which the courts have been generally unambiguous; for each, it notes the position of the courts and then the percentage of the general sample who "disagreed" with the prevailing judicial precedent (both definitely and probably), or who opted out as "not sure."

This is hardly an exhaustive inventory of recent church-state cases. However, the list is generally representative and provides at least a provisional measure of the potential gap between the judiciary and the citi-

TABLE 4.1

Disagreement with Prevailing Court Judgment on Church-State Issues
(General Sample, $N = 256$)

Issue	% Disagreeing	% Not Sure
Organized prayer in the public schools (illegal)	49.0	22.0
Students refusing to salute flag or recite pledge of allegiance for religious reasons (legal)	47.0	16.0
Parents educating children at home for religious reasons (legal)	43.0	26.0
Religious groups not paying taxes on their church properties (legal)	43.0	21.0
Atheists teaching in the public shhools (legal)	37.0	16.0
Teaching the Bible's version of creation in public school science classes (illegal)	35.0	29.0
Hospitals or clinics performing abortions (legal)	33.0	11.0
Allowing critically ill patient to refuse medical treatment for religious reasons (legal)	30.0	16.0
Exempting persons from wartime military service because of deep personal convictions (legal)	28.0	24.0
Allowing a book against religion and churches to be available in the public library (legal)	26.0	14.0
State certification of religious (or parochial) school teachers (legal)	9.0	18.0
Mean Percentage Scores:	34.5	19.8

zenry. Only state certification of religious-school teachers appears to evoke an accurate consensus, indicating that the city's Catholic parochial schools have made their peace with the Massachusetts Board of Education. Ironically, this is the one issue that was recently adjudicated in the Springfield area, when a suburban evangelical Christian school lost a court case on the issue after our questionnaires were administered (*Springfield Union-News*, January 5, 1990). As for the remaining ten practices, disagreement with the courts ranged from one fourth to almost one half, and the overall mean was 34.5 percent of our general sample. Perhaps even more revealing was the proportion "not sure." Here the mean was nearly one fifth or 19.8 percent. In fact, for seven of the table's eleven issues, a majority of the sample were in either disagreement or uncertainty.

As always, there was variation within the sample. In order to examine it more efficiently, we constructed a simple aggregate Index of Agreement with Court Decisions. This involved summing scores for all eleven items in Table 4.1, awarding a 2 for a correct answer, a 1 for not sure, and a 0 for an incorrect response. The result is a somewhat awkward 22-point scale that can be broken into more meaningful categories, including those in "high disagreement" with scores of 12 or greater. Not surprisingly, theological differences again appeared pertinent, as 44 percent of the Catholics fell in this category, as compared to only 26 percent of the non-Catholics. But education was also a factor. More than half of those with no college education were in high disagreement (55 percent) versus only 22 percent of those with college exposure. Disagreement was much less common among our several elites. The incidence of "high disagreement" ranged from 12 percent among the economic leaders, and 19 percent among both the political leaders and the combined Protestant-Jewish clergy, to 24 percent among the Catholic priests and sisters. At the other end of the scale, fully 34 percent of the Protestant-Jewish clergy were in very low disagreement.

Once again, it is important not to overinterpret these patterns. They are consistent with other surveys of American attitudes concerning the Bill of Rights (e.g., Selvin and Hagstrom 1960; McClosky and Brill 1983). Certainly the results for the general sample should not be construed as an indictment of Springfield for either civil disobedience or ignorance. As noted above, the problem may rest more with the courts and the issues than with the citizenry. The courts have never been paragons of consistency in the church-state area, perhaps because the issues are ideologically contorted and complex. Even a dull lawyer could imagine extenuating circumstances that might change the legality or illegality of the practices noted in the table, and it is little wonder that nonlawyers should have difficulty toeing a constitutional line that has long since been blurred in the dust of politics and litigation.

Quite apart from the degree of agreement between Springfielders and the courts, it is worth examining citizen attitudes on these issues for their own sake. Here we can follow the customary distinction between the two components of the First Amendment's religion clause. The first concerns the "establishment" of religion within the state as a result of the government's religious policies or actions; the second involves the "free exercise" of religion or the extent to which religious (or nonreligious) groups or practices are exempt from governmental control or constraint. At first glance, the two would appear to be simply mirror images of each other; after all, to the extent that there is an establishment, there is no free exercise, and how else would free exercise be curbed, if not by some sort of established religious regime? Indeed, one can imagine a number of court cases being adjudicated on either grounds. And yet the choice of grounds is by no means idle from a lawyer's standpoint. The two have spawned quite different traditions and precedents within the law. The question here is whether the citizens also view them as distinct.

In order to facilitate analysis, we constructed aggregate indexes of support for both the free exercise and nonestablishment of religion, combining four issues for each (see Appendix C for details). All four of the "free exercise" issues are drawn from Table 4.1, including wartime military exemptions, educating children at home, the refusal of medical treatment, and refusing to salute the flag. While two of the "nonestablishment" issues overlap with Table 4.1—prayer in the schools and the teaching of creationism—two others are new; namely, beginning City Council meetings with prayer and having a Christmas nativity scene on city property. The latter two have been important issues in the courts of late. However, because recent court decisions concerning them have been somewhat ambiguous, we did not include them in the test results of Table 4.1, though we can include them in the current index where there are no "right" answers.

If the "religion clause" is perceived as a single, unitary constitutional principle, then support for its two subdimensions should be highly correlated. In fact, the correlation among the Springfield sample is only .10, and this indicates that only 1 percent of the responses to one index can be explained or predicted by responses to the other. Apparently the citizenry found these two traditions as distinct as does the judiciary.

Another measure of their difference comes from their respective response patterns. Each index has values ranging from 0 to 8, and we have subdivided each into four support categories of low (0, 1), moderately low (2, 3), moderately high (4, 5) and high (6, 7 and 8). The sample percentages falling into each of these categories in order for free exercise is 13 percent, 25 percent, 28 percent, and 34 percent, respectively; compare these with the following for nonestablishment: 33 percent, 31 percent, 20 percent, and 17 percent. Clearly there is far greater support for the free exercise of religion than for avoiding the symbols and situations that smack of a religious establishment. Indeed, if one combines the two highest categories of support in each case, they total 62 percent for free exercise but only 37 percent for nonestablishment.

Perhaps this is partly because the free exercise issues tend to be matters of private conscience and private rights with idiosyncratic exceptions to the general rule. After all, the country is hardly overrun with conscientious objectors to the draft, children being educated at home, patients refusing medical treatment, or students refusing to take the patriotic pledge. While these are all nonconforming practices, they reflect more passive aberrance than the sort of aggressive nonconformity that threatens the whole.

This difference seems precisely at issue in two other cases broached in the questionnaire. First, only 25 percent of the general sample expressed any disagreement at all with the abstract proposition "A minority religious group should be able to practice its rituals and beliefs even if it offends the religion of the majority"; of these, only 4 percent strongly disagreed. On the other hand, when asked their reaction to "City authorities should strictly control the efforts of religious cults to recruit and convert young people," fully 58 percent agreed to some extent, with 24 percent in strong agreement. Here the issue is posed less as tolerance and more as protection, in this case protecting "our" youth from "their" religious predation, including such ritual practices as possible drug use. While the sample was generously constitutional in the first instance, it was much more willing to suspend free exercise in the latter.

But why is the nonestablishment position so much less popular overall than that of free exercise? Again the majority-minority distinction seems important. As long as the majority includes "me," what is wrong with reflecting its positions in public policies and displays? But another distinction is also important; namely, between symbols and substance. As long as the practice at issue is confined to the symbolic, it is perceived as innocuous; once it begins to involve actual political or educational substance, reservations increase.

In fact, these two distinctions are apparent in the two extreme cases within the Nonestablishment Index. Only 9 percent of the general sample expressed any disagreement at all over displaying a Christmas crèche on city property during the holidays—most likely because this was perceived as a purely symbolic expression of a majority tenet. On the other hand, 36 percent felt that teaching creationism within the schools should be illegal, and another 29 percent were unsure about this practice, which carries substantive bite in addition to its symbolic bark. Much the same logic appeared to govern responses to two questions concerning the political sphere more specifically. Whereas only 31 percent felt that a prayer before City Council meetings should be illegal, fully 68 percent had such doubts about "clergy using their pulpits to support particular political candidates." Ironically, while the latter is more substantive and hence more potentially divisive, it is a fairly common practice that has never been directly adjudicated by the courts—the primary reason we did not include it in the Nonestablishment Index. Another item omitted from the index confirms the point more directly; 68 percent basically agreed to one extent or another that "religious groups should keep separate from what goes on in city politics and city hall."

Since church-state litigation began to burgeon after World War II, many more cases have involved establishment than free exercise, and two critical establishment areas have involved prayer and religion in the public schools and aid to parochial schools. Our questionnaire included separate batteries for each. For example, we asked our respondents whether they supported or opposed (to varying degrees) seven hypothetical religious practices in a public junior high school (see questionnaire in Appendix B). Whereas a high of 89 percent offered some degree of support for "a moment of silence at the beginning of each day," a low of 50 percent lent support to "prayers led by local clergy from different faiths." Concerning parochial school aid, a high of 74 percent supported "Access to public school facilities where needed (e.g., labs, gyms, classrooms, etc.)" compared to a low of 46 percent supporting "Enough support so that parents do not have to pay extra for children to attend a religious school."

As one might predict, both batteries reveal a difference between Catholics and non-Catholics. While the average percentage in support of various forms of religion in the public schools was 69 percent for the overall sample, the mean was 72 percent for Catholics as compared with 62 percent for non-Catholics. And while the sample's mean support for different forms of aid to parochial schools was 62 percent, the average was "fully" 75 percent for Catholics but "only" 45 percent for non-Catholics. Not surprisingly, the religious factor was considerably larger where the vested interests of parochial school education were concerned. But even here, the average level of support was almost 50 percent among that segment of the population least likely to benefit from such aid. This shows substantial support for a form of religious establishment that does not include oneself. This may be partly a result of living in a community where the Catholic majority has begun to influence the attitudes of the non-Catholic minority.

In light of all of the foregoing, citizen attitudes toward the Supreme Court may be predictable. We asked for responses to the proposition that "U.S. Supreme Court decisions are more and more out of touch with the views of the people." Alas, this is a textbook example of how *not* to phrase a question, since disagreement could conceivably mean that the courts were already so out of touch in the past that no "more" disjunction was possible. And yet the dominant response here was one of agreement, with fully 65 percent in assent. Insofar as religion provides the governing framework for response, the problem lies less with free exercise than with nonestablishment. Only 27 percent agreed at all that "U.S. Government policies have greatly limited the freedom of religion in our country today." In fact, most of the difficult and celebrated religious court cases of recent years have concerned establishment matters, and these appear to form the primary rift between the courts and the government, on the one hand, and the citizenry, on the other.

The very existence of such a rift in attitudes concerning "what ought to be" makes one wonder all the more about possible gaps concerning "what is." It is not just that Springfielders have attitudes concerning church-state issues that are at odds with the courts; Springfield also has a new religious establishment that would stand to benefit considerably from a new church-state coalition. If the Congregationalists in their heyday used the city-state to cement their preeminence, should we expect any less of the Catholics who have assumed dominance in recent years? With this question in mind, it is time for a first consideration of how local church and state actually interact, as opposed to how the courts, on the one hand, and public opinion, on the other, say they should.

FROM WASHINGTON TO SPRINGFIELD

One of the historical paradoxes of America's church-state relations is that the acknowledged separation of the two spheres was itself a product of the country's unacknowledged Protestant establishment. Indeed, it was not until this founding establishment began to atrophy in the mid-twentieth century that the jostling between church and state became a significantly contentious issue on the judicial docket. With the increasing diversity among Protestants and the mounting growth of other faiths—most especially Catholicism—America's vaunted religious pluralism shifted from a cliché to a reality. This involved a new contest for religious influence within a new context for political action. The expansion of public power into the hitherto private spheres of education, health, and welfare upped the stakes of state control. And while the underlying causes of church-state litigiousness were more social than legal, there were important changes in the courts as well. These included a widening base of judicial appointments more responsive to social change, and the enhanced social standing of grievants more likely to file suit (Demerath and Williams 1984). Suddenly religious comingling emerged from the smoke of suppressed resentment to the fires of open competition. In the phrase of Jurgen Habermas (1975), the result was a "legitimation crisis," or a new confusion over old political understandings.

Here again Springfield is a microcosm, and it is not surprising that its own church-state history follows a similar course. We have already noted the city's early status as a Congregationalist stronghold. This included abundant violations of current church-state practice, which often choked in the swallowing but were rarely protested formally. As the late-eighteenth-century conflict among Protestant denominations was overshadowed by a nineteenth-century cleavage between Protestant and Catholic, Springfield's governance continued to reflect its dominant religious majority. During the first decades of the twentieth century, the pattern began to shift. Protestants continued to control both politics and the economy, but Catholics were rising to the challenge and becoming a city constituency to be reckoned with. By 1938, the diocesan newspaper noted the amount of money that the growing parochial school system was sparing the public educational budget, and commented:

In view of the tax relief afforded the general public annually, by this huge
Catholic contribution to the common welfare, is it not egregious bad taste—
to say nothing of elementary justice—for the bigots to set up a howl about
"State Support of Private (they mean Catholic) Schools," every time an effort
is made to treat Catholic children as the little citizens which they are? (*Catholic Mirror*, November 1938)

The echoing chords of the civic chorus were gradually becoming more
harmonious. This was especially true of the public schools, which began a
self-conscious pedagogy of pluralism known as the Springfield Plan, designed to teach tolerance across religious as well as racial and ethnic lines.
In 1940, the school system trumpeted the virtues of its holiday "festival of
lights" celebrating both Christmas and Hanukkah (cf. Chatto and Halligan
1945). Catholics as well as Jews were finding city hall to be increasingly
professionalized and increasingly neutral—at least between religions if
not over religion itself.

As we have already described in Chapters Two and Three, the fifteen
years following World War II were a time of political transition. But as the
Irish Catholics took over the city's political reins, the Yankee Protestants
remained in control of both the local economy and the most prominent
layer of the civic culture. This was a period of buoyant church membership and attendance—a momentary high before the decline of the sixties.
It was also a period in which churches crusaded on behalf of public morality. Clergy did battle with city officials over the granting of liquor licenses
to businesses within the proscribed five hundred feet of churches. They
inveighed against the unsavory character of bars and X-rated movies.
They opposed a state lottery. And in one specific burst of interfaith consensus, clergy struck an ecumenical coalition in support of discussing politics in the pulpit when moral standards were at stake (*Springfield Union*,
November 4, 1958).

The decade of the 1950s marked the end of Protestantism's last major
offensive on behalf of virtue. Early in the 1960s, the churches were
thrown back on the defensive by a state beginning to enact more constraints. In fact, it is useful to examine the next thirty years of Springfield's
church-state history under the twin rubrics of "state over church" and
"church over state." As Thomas Robbins (1987) has shown with a similar
distinction, there are strains in both directions, but each reveals different
patterns of initiatives and response. This is preferable to following the
Constitution's own distinction between "establishment" and "free exercise" cases for several reasons. First, the classic free exercise cases concern federal obligations such as conscientious objection to military service, and there are relatively few pure instances locally. Second, there is
a sense in which this is a distinction without a difference. The two are

really opposite sides of the same jurisprudential coin, since it is generally an establishment of the many that denies the free exercise of the few, and one abuse generally entails at least the potential for the other. Third, we want to avoid becoming entangled in narrow constitutionalism. Without skirting the specific legal issues of church and state, we want to go further in pursuit of the broader question of who is influencing whom. To what degree does government at any level influence religion, the churches, or one church in particular—and in what way and on what issues? To what extent does religion, the churches, or one church in particular influence government—again, in what way on what issues?

STATE OVER CHURCH

When the First Amendment was initially drafted and adopted some two hundred years ago, the basic problem was to protect a young and precarious federal government not only from the established clutches of the states but also from the establishment impulses of the various religious denominations that were strong in different regions. Since then, of course, the fragile flower of national government has been transformed, in the eyes of many, into so much kudzu. From this perspective, the central church-state problematic has been reversed. Instead of protecting the state from the churches, it is now the churches and religion at large that must be shielded from the state. Perceived government incursions upon religion can occur at both national and local levels. Within Springfield's recent history, the former is illustrated by U.S. Supreme Court decisions concerning religion and the public schools, and the latter involves a series of less celebrated instances of the influence of city hall and the city bureaucracy on civic religious groups.

Religion in the Public Classroom

As early as the late 1940s, it was clear that much of the judicial jockeying over religion was to involve education. The first major postwar Supreme Court decision concerning religion approved New Jersey's use of public busing to parochial schools despite a pointed clarification and warning of the dangers of violating the First Amendment's religious clause (*Everson* v. *Board of Education*, 1947). The Court's next two decisions set a pattern of seeming inconsistency that was to plague its rulings in the religious area for years to come. In *McCollum* v. *Board of Education* (1948), the Court ruled against released time for religious education in Illinois; in *Zorach* v. *Clauson* (1952), it allowed released time in New York, ostensibly because there the religious education was to occur off school premises and with no coercion of children to participate.

In 1962 the "Warren Court" acted decisively in shifting "separation" from a platitude to a principle. The basic issues concerned Bible-reading and prayer in the public schools. In *Engel* v. *Vitale* (1962), the Court held that government-written prayers at the beginning of the school day in New York were unconstitutional. In *Abington Township School District* v. *Schempp* (1963), the Court extended its proscription to compulsory use of the Lord's Prayer and to Bible reading as found in Texas. Actually both praying and the reading of Bible selections were standard practices in the Springfield public schools at that time—schools whose religious tone was still largely Protestant despite a rapidly increasing number of Catholic teachers drawn from nearby Elms College. As one of our interviewees recalls:

> Prayer and Bible reading in the schools ended while I was teaching there. In fact, I remember they had Protestant Bibles, and I used to sneak in my own Catholic Bible. (interview)

But it would be erroneous to infer that religious observances in the schools ended abruptly and absolutely on the heels of the Court's decisions. Kenneth Dolbeare and Phillip Hammond (1971) reported a considerable gap in compliance in their study of responses to the "prayer decisions" in a midwestern state. They cite four principle reasons for it:

> First, we saw that all state and local power holders . . . had what seemed to them good reasons for not taking the actions and suffering the probable costs necessary to carry out the Court's mandates. . . . Second, we saw that this inertia was rationalized in at least two major ways: by "misunderstanding" the requirements of the Court rulings so as to permit teacher discretion, and by resisting knowledge about the extent and character of prayers and other religious observances in the schools. . . . Third, we saw that local elites were not so much against the Court or the decisions as they were wary of conflict in their communities. . . . Fourth, we saw that there were no institutional channels through which local citizens could effectively activate the rulings. (p. 148)

Certainly the issue provoked debate and response within Massachusetts. By order of its School Committee, the North Brookfield schools observed opening day in September 1963 by reciting both the Lord's Prayer and the One Hundredth Psalm. An assertion of independence on the part of a small community seeking to "retain their 137-year-old right against the 'dictates of those nine men in Washington,' " the practice was quickly ended by the State Supreme Judicial Court at the request of the Massachusetts attorney general (cf. Christopher R. Clarke 1964).

During the same year, a mood of less incendiary insurrection surfaced in Springfield. The city's dominantly Catholic School Committee voted

5–2 to replace the Lord's Prayer and Bible readings with a moment of "reverent silence" at the beginning of the school day. This followed a ruling by the state's attorney general that such a practice would be constitutional. It is worth noting that the two negative votes were themselves split. One opponent continued to insist on prayer itself; she was a long-time power in school politics as an Irish-Catholic Democrat, and only two years earlier had persuaded the committee to ban Jean-Paul Sartre's *No Exit* from the high school reading list "because he didn't believe in God" (interview). The second dissenter argued that religion "is best founded and taught in the home" and wondered whether it was "worth challenging" the courts on this matter (*Springfield Union*, August 6, 1963). She was one of the last Republicans elected to city office before the change to nonpartisan politics—a young Smith College graduate who had defeated a rising Italian pol in 1959:

> It was pretty strange. He was endorsed by several officers of the League of Women Voters, but she benefited more from the support of "Big Nose Sam" (the local Mafia boss), who turned out his boys in her behalf following a rift with his fellow Italian. (interview)

As in other communities across the country, there was considerable sentiment on behalf of a constitutional amendment that would permit school prayers. For instance, in May 1964, several dozen high school students picketed major intersections and shopping centers while seeking signatures on a petition to restore prayer and Bible reading to the schools because, "Separation of church and state does not in any way mean separation of God from state" (*Springfield Daily News*, May 4, 1964). But there was also considerable objection. The objections of the Springfield office of the Civil Liberties Union were predictable enough in finding the First Amendment's religion clauses the "heart and soul of American democracy" and supporting its "essential inalienability and inviolability" (*Springfield Union*, May 26, 1964). Similar arguments from the mainline Protestant clergy were also to be expected. But the opposition of a number of prominent Catholic clergy raised more eyebrows. In fact, the editor of the diocesan newspaper argued in a signed editorial that such an amendment would expose a new generation to the same "Protestant ethic" that had originally led Catholics to establish their own parochial school system (ibid.). Clearly church-state relations are affected by church-church tensions, both current and recalled.

The School Department appointed a three-person committee to develop alternatives for setting a "moral tone" at the beginning of the school day. The recommendations included singing patriotic songs, reciting the Pledge of Allegiance, meditating on "something that made you happy," and reading inspirational quotations, poems, or short stories. They were circulated despite the reactions of the chairman of the local Civil Liberties Union, who found them "stupid," potentially undemocratic, and consistent with the School Committee's general effort to emulate "parochial education" (*Springfield Union*, May 26, 1964).

Silence has been the policy of the Springfield public schools ever since the early 1960s—both moments of silence within classrooms (whether reverential or not and usually at the teachers' discretion) and silence, or as little said about the issue as possible, from the superintendent's office. But the issue continued to surface locally as well as nationally, and other communities were less compliant—some even defiant. In 1969 in the nearby village of Leyden, the School Committee voted explicitly to resume teacher-led prayers and Bible reading. The case attracted the attention of both the press and the courts. In fact, the Massachusetts Supreme Judicial Court enjoined the school from any religious observance until the case could be decided by the U.S. Supreme Court. When the latter declined to hear the case, the injunction stood until it was subsequently settled by state action, which we shall consider momentarily.

The pressure for a constitutional amendment continued to ebb and flow. In 1971, it was well noted that Springfield's congressman, Edward Boland, had voted against a constitutional amendment that would authorize "voluntary prayer" in public buildings and the schools. The measure fell only twenty-eight votes short of the two-thirds majority needed for passage, and Boland's negative vote as a Democrat was contrasted locally with the positive vote of western Massachusetts' only other congressman, the Republican Silvio Conte. Although well known as a Catholic, Boland justified his position in the classic separationist terms identified with such Protestant "founding framers" as Madison and Jefferson (*Springfield Daily News*, November 9, 1971).

Massachusetts remained troubled by the civil religious void at the opening of the school day. In 1976 the state legislature passed a law allowing, but not requiring, a moment of silent meditation before classes began. But the issue continued to rankle. A year later in an episode that was widely, if not freshly, aired in the 1988 presidential race, Gov. Michael Dukakis vetoed a State Senate bill requiring teachers to begin the day with the Pledge of Allegiance. His veto followed a preliminary judgment of the Supreme Judicial Court that the measure was likely unconstitutional. Even so, the veto was overriden in the House by a lopsided vote accompanied by the refrains of "God Bless America" sung by two hundred standing legislators (*Springfield Union*, June 18, 1977). However, in the intervening ninety days before the bill was to become effective, it was indeed struck down.

School prayers surfaced again in Springfield and in the rest of Massachusetts in 1979. As if to finally make an honest village of Leyden some eleven years after its own action, the Massachusetts state legislature tried once again. This time it voted to replace its 1976 optional moment of meditation with a requirement that school begin with an opportunity for voluntary school prayer led not by teachers but by volunteering students. By the time the law was to be implemented in February 1980, the responses of town and city school districts had varied from early compliance to outright resistance on the grounds of likely unconstitutionality. Springfield opted for a middle course of nondefiant noncompliance. Although school and city officials were privately skeptical about the law, any public response was deferred pending advice from the city's law department. The advice itself was purposefully delayed until the issue was obviated by an eleventh-hour ruling of the Massachusetts Supreme Judicial Court, which voided the law on constitutional grounds. Thus was dodged another bullet of potential church-state controversy. With an almost audible sigh of relief, public school professionals in Springfield and the state as a whole reverted to the 1976 provision for moments of silence. The provision remains in effect today.

Public Attitudes toward Religion in the Schools.   As always, the relationship between the law, public opinion, and actual behavior resembles a nonequilateral triangle viewed through a kaleidoscope. Our questionnaire included a battery of items concerning religion in the schools: "Thinking of a public junior high school, how do you feel about the following [seven] kinds of activities?"—with six response categories for each, ranging from "strongly support" through "support" and "moderately support" through the same three categories for "oppose." Recall too that, given the importance of the schools in recent church-state activity, we created a small sample of some fifty-five public school teachers and principals and asked them to answer an additional page of questions, both because we valued their opinions and because we wanted to use them as observers of the school scene. Table 4.2 compares the responses of this group with our general sample in response to the question described above.

Several patterns are striking. Earlier in the chapter, we noted that Springfielders have a considerable tolerance for symbolic manifestations of established religion. The bottom four items in Table 4.2 suggest that the public schools are something of an exception, perhaps because of the headlines accorded court decisions. Even the single most favored form of observance among both the teachers and the general sample can be interpreted in secular terms. Thus, a "moment of silence" at the beginning of the school day not only reflects state law but fits within the generally accepted parameters of constitutional propriety. Although a 1983 New Jersey statute calling for the practice was voided by a federal district court

TABLE 4.2

Support for Various Religious Activities in the Public Schools among Teachers and the General Sample:

| | % Strongly Supporting and Supporting | |
Religious Activity	Teachers (N = 55)	General Sample (N = 256)
Moment of Silence	73	75
Moment of Silent Prayer	61	62
Religious Music for Holidays	54	57
Class Instruction about Religion	38	46
Coaches Leading Prayers before Games	29	40
Prayers Led by Different Local Clergy	26	28
Teachers Leading Prayers	20	44

judge, this had less to do with the practice itself than with the obvious religious intent behind the legislation. It is true that "moments of silent *prayer*" have been struck down by the Supreme Court (most recently in the Alabama case of *Wallace* v. *Jaffree*, 1985), but there is sufficient ambiguity between silence and silent prayer to account for its support in Table 4.2 on grounds of confusion rather than willful disobedience. As for "Religious music as part of the school's holiday assembly" and "Classroom instruction about [as opposed to indoctrination in] various religious faiths," both are acceptable practices according to prevailing judicial opinion. Their more controversial standing within the sample may be because they lack the legislative imprimatur accorded moments of silence in Massachusetts.

A second pattern in Table 4.2 involves the close overall similarity between the judgments of the teachers and the sample. Majorities of both favor not only moments of silence but silent prayer and religious music as part of holiday celebrations—in that order and with very similar percentages. After all, these tend to be broadly symbolic religious expressions without divisions of denominational substance. However, a third result concerns those items on which teachers and the general sample disagreed: by and large, the general sample was more supportive of teacher-led religion than were the teachers themselves. This was true of coaches leading prayers before athletic contests, classroom religious instruction, and, most especially, teachers leading prayers at the start of the school day. Of course, the last was specifically proscribed by the widely publicized Supreme Court rulings of the early 1960s, though it remains the stereotypic image of "religion in the schools" and a specific goal of the religious right. In fact, fully 67 percent of the teachers expressed some degree of opposition to leading prayers, and fully 42 percent "strongly opposed" the practice. Here the degree of personal religiosity made virtually no consistent difference among the teachers, although there was a slight tendency for non-Catholics to be more opposed than Catholics.

If these were the opinions, what were the behaviors? The subject is understandably sensitive in a city with a history of religious tension. But the school system insiders whom we interviewed were generally consistent in their responses. A number commented that a certain "tone was set" in a city whose mayor frequently began School Committee meetings with a moment of silent prayer and the Pledge of Allegiance. All of our respondents agreed that the "separation" was not perfect. As one official noted, "We have several faculty who are actually clergy; they have to be watched or they'll slip some religion in" (interview). At the same time, there was also consensus that the superintendent's office ran a "pretty tight ship" and was wary of violating the law in the face of a number of outside watchdogs, ranging from parents' groups to the state board of education, which provided a lion's share of the budget. As one state monitor put it:

> Most of the schools don't even have the moment of silence that the law allows. Things are just too hectic and unmanageable at that time of day. By and large, the schools are pretty good about keeping religion out. However, I wouldn't say there is *no* prayer in the schools, and we make it a point not to visit classrooms after December 18 when most of them put up their Christmas stuff. (interview)

Predictably, the holiday season is a particular headache from the standpoint of both constitutionalists and non-Christians. According to one member of the School Committee: "There is no administrative policy with respect to the Christmas season. Schools have a kind of local option to do whatever they want in their own buildings" (interview). A local rabbi commented on the results:

> Sure there are some problems in the public schools around Christmastime. We do object to crèches and pageants, but we don't care much about Christmas trees or wreaths. Part of the problem is that people sometimes want to be sensitive, but they don't know enough to know how to be. On the other hand, I don't really agree with one of my fellow rabbis, who says: "We're assaulted at Christmas." (interview)

Of course, Jews are understandably vigilant concerning Christian observances in the public arena. In recent years, however, many have moved to the suburbs and into Hebrew schools. This has made a difference, according to one school administrator who summarized the religious situation this way:

We get very minimal mail objecting to religion in the schools—whether too much or not enough. The issue has died down a lot, since we have fewer Jews. But not long ago I did have a Jehovah's Witness family who were ready to go to court, claiming their kid had a right to preach in school. I had them in, and we talked about it. I said he can do it in a corner of the cafeteria where other children can walk away, but not in a classroom. They seemed satisfied. (interview)

In fact, the community as a whole seems satisfied. Apart from isolated cases such as that of the Jehovah's Witness family or "one women who has a little group that is concerned about secular humanism in the schools and occasionally gets vocal about it" (interview), our respondents echoed the judgment that "there's no organized pressure to reestablish religion in the system" (interview).

However, the issue of religion may persist as a residue, if not a conspiracy. Here several additional questionnaire items are pertinent. First, we asked our sample of public school staff about religious practices in their classes and other classrooms in their schools. Table 4.3 provides the results in terms of the percentages saying "never" or "none" for six different activities. This confirms our interviewees' judgments that religion was not rampant in the city's public schools, although there was enough slippage to vex the constitutionalist stickler, and the results may reflect a teacher corps that was sufficiently knowledgeable to know what to deny. It is true that teachers are somewhat more likely to cite religious activities in classrooms other than their own. But even there, the overall pattern reflects little systematic violation of constitutional rulings. The two activities that are cited as majority occurrences in both columns are legally permissable—religious holiday festivities and moments of silence. The same is true of the third-ranking practice—teaching about religion—though this apparently is a less common occurrence. As for the last three activities—silent prayer, religious training, and spoken prayer—their rarity appears to reflect their formal proscription.

TABLE 4.3

Incidence of Religious Activities in Teachers' Own and Others' Classrooms
(Teacher Sample, $N = 55$)

Religious Activity	% Saying Never in Own Classroom	% Saying No Other Teachers Practice
Religious Festivities	31	13
Moment of Silence	46	43
Teaching about Religion	82	72
Moment of Silent Prayer	96	83
Religious Training	100	94
Spoken Prayer	100	96

As a side note, we asked the teachers about the characteristic response of their students to such moments of silence as do occur. The most commonly cited response was "respectful contemplation," as 59 percent cited this for a majority of their students. Only 11 percent cited "prayerful meditation" as the majority reaction, with 7 percent noting that most students manifested "bored resignation," and 4 percent indicating a norm of "noisy indifference." Overall, then, the dominant mood seemed to be one of tolerance rather than piety.

Finally, we asked those parents in our general sample who had had children in the public schools to indicate whether they had experienced religion in any of the forms indicated in Table 4.4. Here, the results suggested a somewhat broader set of constitutional violations. Almost half (46 percent) answered that their children had experienced "spoken prayer," while more than one third cited "silent prayer." On the other hand, 10 percent or less claimed that their children were exposed to the Bible's version of creation, participated in religious groups on the school grounds during nonschool hours, or "felt uncomfortable about some school program or activity for religious reasons." Of course, these data are hardly paragons of rigor, in part because parents are not always reliable informants concerning their children. Still, the table suggests that, while religion was more of a presence in the public schools than recent court decisions or enduring separationist convictions might allow, it was more of an epiphenomenon than a bone of contention.

TABLE 4.4
Children's Religious Experiences in the Public Schools, as Cited by Parents
(Parent Subsample, $N = 64$)

| | % Parents Saying | | |
Experience	Yes	Don't Think So	Don't Know
Spoken Prayer	46	40	14
Silent Prayer	35	56	10
Teaching Biblical Creation	10	62	28
Religious Groups after School	7	77	16
Religious Discomfort	9	79	12

City Hall and Secular Agency

For the most part, religion in the schools reflects federal policy rather than local resolve, although this is not to deny the importance of state and local implementation. We turn now, however, to a different facet of "state over church" and the extent to which the city-state has exerted its own power over Springfield's religion and religious groups. Few will be surprised to discover that this is a relatively brief section. The more critical question concerning city hall is the extent to which it reflects the religious preeminence of Springfield's Catholics, and thereby provides secular reinforcement for a sacred institution. We shall turn to that issue shortly, and it will occupy us in one way or another for the remainder of the book. Meanwhile, any city has a secular agenda shaped by its political officials and enacted by its bureaucrats. Issues such as taxation, licensing, zoning and building codes, and the provision of city services may entail frequent conflict with the local religious community. It is even conceivable that city hall may become a secular despot striking out at religion in all of its manifestations, especially where it conflicts with the fiscal and regulative interests of the municipality at large.

There is some evidence of this scenario in Springfield—but not much. For example, the odd city councillor has questioned the range of tax exemptions offered for, say, church-owned real estate development at the expense of the city's middle-class tax payers (e.g., *Springfield Union*, May 18, 1972). On the other hand, the odd church organization has donated money to the city "in lieu of" taxes (e.g., *Springfield Daily News*, July 21, 1977). Not surprisingly, both are rare exceptions to the rule. In fact, the rules themselves are best described in this account of the municipal tax system by a city hall denizen who has followed it closely:

> Some 30 percent of property in the city is tax exempt, and this was worth about $1.4 billion in 1987. Of this, churches account for about one fourth, although this is just a rough estimate because, when the city reevaluated in 1983, it really didn't bother with the churches since that would have been pretty academic.
>
> Occasionally, the city gets on the churches; for example, if they buy property and exceed the two-year grace period in putting it to religious use. We once taxed the bishop for the Gate of Heaven cemetery. But they appealed to the Appellate Tax Board and won—the only time I know of that the city and the diocese ever went to court. It's true that the bishop only paid something like $25 in taxes for 1987. On the other hand, he does own a lot that he leases to a private parking operator who he sends the tax bill to. The assessors got a tip on this from a private parking lot owner and had to follow it up.
>
> In general, the city doesn't chase the churches, and there's a fine line over what constitutes "religious use." But then I guess there's also some question about what constitutes legitimate city expenses. About ten years ago, we had some flak when we first separated sewerage user fees from the general property tax and asked exempt organizations to pay them. Some saw this as an attack on the charitables, but it really wasn't intended that way at all. (interview)

Of course, references here to "the bishop" are not to his private financial portfolio but are a common way of personalizing the local Catholic diocese.

Tax assessments aside, there are other manifestations of the city's secular power. One involved the issue of homelessness, which we shall treat in more detail in Chapter Five. In 1984, a local Protestant church sought to establish a shelter for the homeless in its basement just as city hall was anxious to set up its own consolidated facility. City hall prevailed as, according to one staff member, "The health people came in and raised all sorts of problems" (interview). But a colleague from another congregation put it more sharply: "When they tried to open a shelter, the city threatened to close down the church, and the church leaders blinked" (interview).

Although this case involved a highly visible and much respected Protestant church, it is perhaps predictable that the more frequent victims of adverse city rulings have been the more marginal and less affluent religious sects. For example, in 1963 the Seventh-day Adventists were refused a permit for "tag day" fund-raising on the city streets by a board of public welfare that was chaired by a prominent member of a still-influential Congregational church. In 1977, a local black Baptist church complained that the Springfield Redevelopment Authority reneged on its commitment in allowing the Greek Orthodox church to expand upon land contiguous to both; the Baptists filed suit but lost. In 1985, a Pentecostal church was closed down for violations of the city's building code and held Easter services outside the structure as a "clamor unto God" (*Springfield Daily News*, April 6, 1985). And also in the mid-1980s, a large Assembly of God congregation was forced to move to the suburbs by what it considered the calculated unreasonableness of the city bureaucrats. As one of its officers described the development:

> Sometimes when we'd fail to get permits and things from city hall, I knew that if we were Catholics, we'd get them. In fact, the city really forced us out of downtown. They set up all sorts of roadblocks to our expansion, and we were just splitting our seams. We needed more parking, but they wouldn't let us take down two houses for a lot because that would take them off the tax rolls. There just seemed to be all these technical and legal ramifications to everything. But I don't think we'd have to face them if we were Catholics. (interview)

Although we saw in Chapter Three that many Springfielders suspect Catholics of disproportionate influence around city hall, specific charges were surprisingly rare. Actually there are good reasons to suppose that religious groups serving less advantaged adherents would be forced to occupy the kind of quarters that might be questionable from a building code standpoint. Whether or not city officials were unduly harsh on a few such groups, most had no grievances to report. This is in contrast to the small New Life Baptist Academy in suburban East Longmeadow, which refused to have its nonreligious curriculum approved by the local

public school board in 1981 and took eight years in pursuing its position to
the U.S. Supreme Court in vain. A typical Springfield response comes
from the administrator of a similarly small and non-Catholic religious
school:

> We try to cooperate with the state as best we can and avoid conflict. Actually,
> we have a very good relationship. It seems like there's less state controls in
> Massachusetts, maybe because of the long history of prep schools and paro-
> chial schools. The state is mostly concerned with health and physical educa-
> tion requirements, and that's very amicable. We have more contact with the
> local School Department over things like busing and also curriculum and
> facilities. They don't really cause us any problems. But actually our college-
> preparatory curriculum may be better than theirs. (interview)

This is consistent with the experience of a former public school administrator, who described his perspective on the relationship in these terms:

> I guess you'd say we had a kind of "benign neglect" policy with the so-called
> Christian schools. We never really had to confront them on curriculum or
> teaching competency. Sure we saw some things differently, but we never
> made an issue of it. As for the Hebrew schools, we're technically responsible
> for their programs too, but we never really monitored them. Oh, yes, there
> was the Malcolm X School too in the late sixties and early seventies. But that
> finally went out of existence. They just closed their doors one day; I don't
> know why. (interview)

Certainly more established Protestant and Jewish groups had few com-
plaints. One minister described his relations with the city and city police
this way:

> The attitude at city hall is kind of an old-fashioned paternalistic deference.
> They don't raise any questions on things like tax exemptions for church prop-
> erty. They know if it ever became an issue, the Protestants could have some
> influence because the community is very sensitive to questions of discrimina-
> tion or favoritism. And as for the police, they're okay. As one of them told me
> when I asked for some help on parking, "No problem, Rev. We don't hassle
> churches." (interview)

Still another minister with a public history of sensitivity concerning
civil rights and civil liberties offered a similar account and an especially
intriguing explanation:

> In a city where one church is dominant, maybe it provides an umbrella for all
> churches to be treated in the same way. I mean the city power structure is
> very anxious not to offend the Catholic Church, and this extends to every
> church. Here churches get away with murder compared to where I used to

be where we were terrorized by city inspectors, the health department, zoning changes, and that sort of thing. Here you just get a wink on your taxes for commercial rentals, and you can get away with a TV antenna dish for a long time despite the zoning violation, although it's true the Jewish Community Center finally had to take theirs down. Some people say that if we were Catholic, the city plows would get here earlier. But basically I don't have any problems with the city or its services. When I asked my attorney about it, he just smiled. (interview)

This respondent's "umbrella" theory has a counter-intuitive charm. Many students of American religion have argued that religion as a whole gains more from the competitive pluralism of church-state separation than from the complacent establishment of a single denomination. However, the competition for adherents is one thing and the protection from secular power quite another. Today, there is no question that secular authority has more muscle than most of the sacred organizations on the civic beach, and the latter may well draw comfort from the knowledge that one among them is strong enough to withstand an assault. Thus, while Springfield illustrates the impact of federal secular authority in religion's retreat within its public schools, it evidences relatively little impact of local secular power in its various religious rounds. However, there are still several issues that remain problematic. Just how secular is the city-state, and how neutral is it in the competition between religious groups and their moral judgments? To what extent does the Catholic Church find it more in its interest to side with city hall than to align itself with religion at large? It is to these issues that we turn next.

CHURCH OVER STATE

At the outset of the book, one of our fundamental questions concerned the results of a power reversal in Springfield over the past century. Catholics have moved from the bottom of the social ladder to very near the top; at the same time, many mainstream Yankee Protestants have moved off the ladder altogether in their stretch to the suburbs. To what extent, then, have today's Catholics begun to emulate yesterday's Protestants in dominating city power and politics? Of course, the larger issue concerns religion more broadly within the municipal arena. Although Catholics represent the principal case and the leading wedge, there are other religious groups also contending for secular influence and civic favors. Still, we shall begin by highlighting the Catholic case with specific reference to another school issue; namely, aid to parochial schools. We shall then turn to a wider range of matters in considering religion's overall standing within the recent political sphere.

Public Aid to Parochial Schools

Like the parochial school systems in every American city, Springfield's has evolved considerably from its nineteenth-century beginnings. New England's parochial schools have traditionally served a smaller proportion of its Catholic population than in, say, Chicago (cf. D. P. Ryan 1983; Sullivan and O'Toole 1985), partly because of the initial reputation of the Yankee public schools, and partly because of the increasing Catholic control of the same public schools. Indeed, by 1988 Springfield's Public School Department was presided over by a superintendent and a ten-person administrative "cabinet"; of these eleven, nine were Catholics, eight were Irish Catholics, and seven were male Irish Catholics, including the superintendent himself.

Springfield's parochial schools have been an important part of the cityscape for almost one hundred and fifty years. Originally the lair of lower-class immigrants, the schools have reflected the upward mobility of their charges. Once a way of serving the faithful, they became mechanisms for protecting the faith in the crucible of religious competition and growing secularity. At one time an exclusively Catholic religious franchise, they are no longer justified by faith alone. Until recently, the schools were tuition-free because they were able to count on teaching as a labor of sisterly love. However, a faculty that was once almost exclusively "religious" but that is now 79 percent secular requires more worldly recompense. Hence, the city's parochial schools began charging tuition in the mid-1970s, and the amounts have increased steadily since. As of 1989–90, annual fees in the diocesan primary schools ranged from $600 for parish students to over $1300 for students from outside the parish. In the case of the Cathedral High School, the comparable costs were $1200 and $1830.

And yet Springfield's parochial schools have remained more Catholic than those of many other cities. Despite changes in all of the above directions, their enrollments are 95 percent Catholic, and they have remained both smaller and more religiously focused than their counterparts elsewhere. In fact, their percentage of total school enrollments has dropped since the advent of tuition charges in the 1970s. Between 1984 and 1989 alone, the total percentage of parochial school students declined from 17 percent to 14 percent of the total, and while the parochial system had a slightly higher proportion of the high school population, this too fell over the same period from 24 percent to 22 percent (source: Research Department, Springfield Public Schools). These figures were considerably less than the parochial school enrollments of more than 30 percent of the total in nearby Holyoke and the recent 44 percent in Boston.

The city's parochial schools have also not become the agencies of minority mobility as they have in other cities, where they function as private academies for the aspiring disadvantaged and the arriving lower middle class of diverse denominations. With a minority enrollment of less than 5 percent black, Hispanic, or Asian, Springfield's parochial schools are considerably different from the local public schools. The public schools have had a far different history. Since Springfield adopted its racial-balance plan in 1974, the public schools have seen their percentage of white students fall from 62 to 38 percent, while the proportion of minority students has increased from 38 to 61 percent, including some 28 percent blacks and 31 percent with Spanish surnames (source: Research Department, Springfield Public Schools).

Much of this change has involved a shifting of white enrollment into nearby suburban schools. But there is no question that there has also been at least a small "white flight" into the city's few small "Christian" academies as well as its much larger parochial system where enrollment numbers may have changed less than enrollment motives. One staff member commented on the changing tone of the parochial schools this way:

> The reasons for sending children to parochial schools have changed. It used to be religion, then just discipline. Now parents seem to want a different atmosphere which is genuinely more conducive to learning. Ours are basically white-middle-class schools with "middle-of-the way" students, in terms of their abilities. We have more control over our schools, and there are fewer outside controlling agencies than the public schools have. We even have more control over our problems. . . . But we also try to maintain a strong Catholic identity; it's a big priority along with our academic quality. We teach Catholic doctrine in the religious curriculum, but even our religion teachers have to be certified to teach religion. Of course, we don't teach religion in a calculus class, and daily Mass is now optional. But there are some required school Masses on certain dates, and the religion class is required in the high school. (interview)

Reactions to the parochial schools predictably differ outside their orbit. One recent candidate for the local School Committee described the city's Cathedral High School as "a working man's prep school with a mythology of excellence based on its low percentage of minorities" (interview). And a veteran observer of the Springfield schools noted that, "There is a tendency now for them to have the children of the upper middle class who can afford it and [of] the working class who get waivers. The middle class has started to leave, and they have to take more non-Catholics to survive" (interview). If Cathedral gets fewer high achievers than the newly consolidated public Central High School, it also has many fewer low achievers since it has no obligation to retain students who are problematic or disruptive. Indeed, there are many who cite its willingness to invoke the quick exit as a major factor in its strong reputation.

With this as preamble, we turn to the question of public aid. The complexity of the issue is reflected in the inconsistency of U.S. Supreme Court decisions since the Court first authorized public busing to parochial schools in the landmark *Everson* decision of 1947. Among its more recent decisions, the Court decided 5–4 to uphold a complex system of tax deduction to private (and parochial) school parents in Minnesota (*Mueller* v. *Allen*, 1984) but by an equally close margin ruled that special-needs instruction by public school staff under U.S. Title I could not be given in the parochial schools of Michigan (*Grand Rapids* v. *Ball*, 1985) and New York (*Aguilar* v. *Felton*, 1985).

Rather than consult jurists on such matters, we asked our several Springfield samples. Specifically, we asked about the six possible forms of public assistance listed in Table 4.5. For each item and for each sample

TABLE 4.5
Support for Various Forms of Public Aid to Parochial Schools

Forms of Aid	General Sample		Elite Samples			
	% Catholic	% Non-Catholic	% Public School Teachers	% Political-Economic Elite	% Catholic Clergy	% Protestant-Jewish Clergy
Access to needed public school facilities	85	59	51	76	95	63
Nonreligious textbooks	77	52	42	69	97	44
Special public school teachers in parochial schools	76	52	44	64	87	50
Tax credits for parochial school parents	75	33	41	62	95	51
Busing to parochial schools	74	49	51	59	97	49
Enough support so no fees	61	21	29	38	92	17
Mean percentage support:	75	45	43	61	94	46
(Sample n's):	(144)	(107)	(55)	(69)	(60)	(35)

segment, we have summed up all three categories of "support" ranging from strong to moderate. In light of the religious specificity of the issue, we have divided both the general sample and the clergy sample into Catholics and non-Catholics.

Turning to the results, consider first the bottom row and the mean levels of support for aid of all sorts. Not surprisingly the Catholic clergy (priests and religious) have by far the highest percentage of average support, followed by the Catholics in the general sample. On the other hand, and despite a composition that is 55 percent Catholic, the public school teachers have the lowest percentages of support, though their percentages are not significantly different from the non-Catholics in the general sample and the combined Protestant and Jewish clergy. But there is also variation among the forms of aid. It is worth noting that the one type unequivocally endorsed by the courts—school busing—did *not* leap to the top of the chart. Although most of the items are closely bunched, a slight edge in support goes to providing "public school experts to teach special subjects in parochial schools." At the other end of the spectrum, there is least approval of a blanket provision for "enough support so that parents do not have to pay extra for children to attend a religious school." Taken as a whole, however, there is more support for parochial school aid among Springfielders than one would likely find in a sample of jurists. Thus, one can calculate a "mean of means" to yield an average level of overall support of 61 percent—a majority average across all items and for all subsamples. While this masks considerable variation among both samples and items, fails to reflect gradations of support from strong to only moderate, and is actually overweighted with non-Catholic responses, it is another indication of support for an established religion, even one that is entangled in the public purse strings.

Bloom versus the School Department.   Aid to parochial schools is one church-state issue on which Springfield has its own judicial history. In 1977 the School Department's budget for textbooks and library costs included $200,000—some 32 percent of the total—for the purchase of textbooks to be loaned to students in parochial and private schools. This marked a sharp increase over the preceding year, when thirty-six books were distributed to students at the (Catholic) Cathedral High School, and another nineteen were given to enrollees at a nonreligious private school. However, even the earlier transactions had been enough to prompt the local Civil Liberties Union to launch a church-state challenge. The suit was filed, on behalf of thirteen city taxpayers, in Hampden County Superior Court, where it was known as *Eleanora F. Bloom et al.* v. *William C. Sullivan et al. as members of the School Committee.*

It is almost axiomatic that conflicts within the courts reflect wider conflicts within the host community. But if that is the rule, this was an

exception. In fact, "Bloom" involved cooperation between city and civil
liberties officials in a larger assault upon the state. In 1973, the Massachusetts state legislature had passed a law requiring public schools to loan
books to private and parochial school students on the request of their parents. The Springfield School Committee requested a ruling on the statute's constitutionality from the city's law department. It is perhaps not
incidental that the ruling came from the city's associate city solicitor who
happened to be Jewish, since the city's Jewish community has always
been especially sensitive to incursions of civil liberties and church-state
separation. In any event, when the ruling indicated that the law was indeed unconstitutional, the School Committee was placed between the law
of the state and the legal advice of the city's own counsel. Acting Solo-
monically, it decided to comply with the law while inviting a test suit
against it.

The suit took two years to find its way to the Massachusetts State Supreme Judicial Court. Finally in July 1978, "Bloom" won as the state statute was declared unconstitutional, and the city was let off its hook. As all
of this suggests, there was little controversy over the matter in Springfield
at the time, and it is little recollected today. Indeed, when we asked one
of the plaintiffs about the case some ten years later, he had forgotten that
he had been involved at all. Meanwhile, this proved to be the local Civil
Liberties Union's last church-state litigation. Shortly after the Bloom decision, the CLU gave some consideration to attacking a pattern of public
reimbursement for parochial school transportation rather than having parochial school students use the public school buses. However, the chapter
chairman at the time recognized that this was a different sort of issue both
legally and politically, and he declined to pursue it, "not having a death
wish, and not being suicidal" (*Springfield Daily News*, July 24, 1978). Interestingly enough, another member of the CLU at the time now mistak-
enly recalls the Bloom case as "unsuccessful and another nail in the coffin
of the local chapter, half of whom didn't care that much anyway" (interview). Springfield no longer has its own Civil Liberties Union local, and
the nearest branch is twenty miles upriver in Northampton. It is instructive that the Bloom case should be remembered as a blow received rather
than delivered.

Church and State-wide Referenda. If the 1978 Bloom decision was a
clarifying relief to many, there were others to whom it was a challenge,
inciting response. The powerful president of the Massachusetts State Senate, William Bulger, tried not once but twice to pass a state referendum
that would reverse the state's own long-standing constitutional amendment prohibiting the use of public monies for the "founding, maintaining,
or aiding" of any private school. Bulger argued that the original amend-

ment passed in 1855 was a poorly disguised and gratuitous slap at immigrants. While the amendment was itself amended in 1917 with the support of a number of Catholic legislators, he and others felt that it remained excessive in the light of U.S. constitutional developments and could be eliminated altogether. The point was not to automatically begin aid to private (and parochial) schools, but to allow the state to follow any national developments in this direction (Bulger Seminar, University of Massachusetts, Boston, October 9, 1986).

The issue was first submitted to state referendum in 1982 by an overwhelming vote of the predominantly Catholic joint House and Senate (144–44). Although supported by each of the state's four Catholic dioceses and opposed by the Massachusetts Teachers Association, the Civil Liberties Union, and the League of Women Voters, the campaign was relatively low-profile—perhaps by its proponents' design. The referendum lost statewide by substantial margin (62–38 percent); it lost by a smaller margin (55–45 percent) in Springfield. Meanwhile, the state senate leaders were unbowed. Four years later, they persuaded their legislative colleagues to approve another attempt, but by a much closer vote (107–87) following the pressurized reconsideration of an earlier defeat. Two things were to be different about the 1986 referendum. First, the campaign on its behalf was to move from low to high gear. Second, it was to be joined on the ballot by a second referendum item that would allow the legislature to restrict state assistance for abortions.

There is no doubt that the 1986 campaign was more intensely contested by essentially the same cast of supporting and opposing forces. Boston's Cardinal Law sought to energize the state's Catholics, and opponents responded in kind. In Springfield, both referenda were opposed by the *Morning Union,* and while most local Catholic politicians offered at least soft support in keeping with the Church's position, the issues made many uncomfortable. The bishop's own response was variously characterized by knowledgeable interviewees. Some agreed that they "had never seen him so politically active"; but others shrugged and felt that "while his heart didn't seem to be in it, he at least went through the motions."

We attended several Sunday morning Masses as the campaign approached election day, including one with the bishop himself presiding at St. Michael's Cathedral. Even here, however, his political campaigning was limited to a brief mention in the weekly bulletin, describing each referendum item and asking the parishioners to "Please give [them] careful consideration" (cf. Chapter Seven).

The bishop enlisted several Catholic lay leaders to host a series of neighborhood coffees concerning the referenda. But these too were pitched in a low key. One of the leaders recalled convening and chairing a Saturday-night gathering in a local parish hall:

It wasn't exactly a rousing success. In fact, there were only two people there—me and the hired film projectionist. Of course, the timing didn't help. It happened to conflict with the sixth game of the Red Sox–Mets World Series. (interview)

In fact, each referendum lost both statewide and in Springfield itself. Question 1 concerning a cutoff in abortion funding tallied 39 percent "yes," 54 percent "no," and 7 percent blanks statewide compared to 39, 44, and 17 percent, respectively, in Springfield. Question 2 concerning aid to private schools lost by 28, 65, and 7 percent statewide and by 36, 50, and 14 percent in the city. Springfield was somewhat more conservative than the state overall—and perhaps considerably more in doubt, as suggested by its substantially higher proportion of blank votes. When compared to the immediately surrounding communities, however, Springfield fell between its liberal suburbs, who rejected both questions handily, and its traditional working-class neighbors, who actually supported them.

The Springfield vote on school aid seems surprising in light of the majority sentiment for aid to parochial schools revealed in our questionnaire survey above. And yet there are several plausible explanations. Certainly it was not helped by being coupled with the even more controversial abortion item (Question #1) on the same ballot. Also, it may have backfired as an aid to the "ticket" for reasons to be explored in Chapter Seven. Second, the school aid question may have lost votes by its repeated phrase "private schools" rather than the more straightforward "parochial schools." In a state whose private schools include such privileged centers of higher education as Harvard University, MIT, and Amherst College, not to mention secondary schools such as Andover and Deerfield, some may have construed the referendum as a boon for the elite rather than the oppressed.

A final overriding negative factor may have been the statewide Catholic effort on behalf of the two questions. The vote may reveal the diminishing utility of an aggressive offense as the best defense for New England's Catholics. Of course, many Catholics did support the referenda, but a surprising number did not, and even a diocesan chancery staff member remarked later: "We were not all that disappointed" (interview). To the extent that conflicts of church and state involve contests between favored and beleaguered religious groups, the fading sense of Catholic marginality may be a critical clue to the future that we shall be considering in more detail.

Informal and Ad Hoc Aid and Cooperation. If the success of the Bloom suit and the failure of Question 2 served to ward off formal public aid to parochial schools in Springfield, there remains the possibility of informal and ad hoc assistance. In fact, not all public school aid has gone to Catholics, or for that matter to religious schools. In the early 1960s, space in several public schools was leased to local churches for confraternity classes, and in three cases—two Catholic and one Protestant—for religious services while church buildings were under construction. Although a local CLU petition of protest to the Superior Court was rejected, the practice gradually receded (e.g., *Springfield Union*, November 15, 1962). More recently, the U.S. Congress has made a point of the matter with its 1984 "equal access" law in which public schools were required to allow access to facilities either by all religious groups requesting it, or by none. A former public school administrator recalled the previous practice and reflected on the likelihood of a change:

> Sure, we used to let churches have religious classes in our schools when they were strapped, and we always tried to accommodate churches that burned down—at least we did until there was some question raised and then it went away. But overall we have a pretty good record, and I don't think the new equal-access law will have much effect. There seems to be a good equilibrium, and we try not to upset it. (interview)

Meanwhile, there is ample anecdotal evidence of small-scale assistance to parochial schools that is generally covert, uncontested, and not the stuff of a major constitutional contretemps. Here, for example, is how a parochial school administrator reflected on the relationship:

> We used to work pretty separately from the public schools. Now the relationship is excellent. They have a great attitude toward providing services, involving us in things like the Bicentennial and the "clean city" campaigns. They are also very cooperative with the busing. Chapter One [government group] uses our facility for meetings, and, of course, we get federal Block Grant money through the city—it's now seven dollars per student, which comes from the superintendent's office, and which we can spend on anything as long as it's nonreligious. (interview)

A somewhat murkier view comes from a parochial school parent who is sensitive to the law and finds amusement in the ironies surrounding it:

> I'm on the board of a local parochial school, and guess where we get our paper? You got it: the public school system. Even with books, all you have to do is have them stamp "obsolete" on them, and they can give them to us—and that's legal. Well, it may not actually be legal, but it's okay in Springfield, ha! . . . Sure we get materials from the public schools and occasional access to their facilities; but it's always on a case-by-case basis, and I don't think we'd get it if it weren't for one of our board members who is a city official. After all, it's just one city official asking a favor of another, isn't it? (interview)

Meanwhile, a state educational administrator placed such assistance in a different and more diffused light:

> I don't think there's much illegal aid to parochial schools. They know if they give them money, they get us in return. On the other hand, there is a fair amount of cooperation and exchange. For example, Cathedral High School would take nonambulatory students tuition-free because no public school could accommodate them. At the same time, because the parochial system doesn't have middle schools, a lot of kids switch over to the public schools for three years before returning to Cathedral. They try to make sure the two curriculums are lined up with each other, and there is a lot of communication and record-switching. (interview)

Certainly there are other instances of cooperation and assistance between the two school systems. Consider, for example, the recent judicial decision that the instruction provided to disadvantaged and special-needs parochial students by public school teachers could not occur in the parochial facilities. Communities across the nation have varied in their responses—some requiring parochial students to go to the public schools, others setting up public school trailers near the parochial schools, still others encouraging a full-time return to the public schools by the parochial needy, and virtually all witnessing a decline in the number of students participating in the special-needs programs. Springfield also experienced a decline, but this was despite the device of holding the instruction in space leased from one of the Catholic churches. As one administrator recalled:

> We had some problems at first with the Hope Center. The city was cooperative, but the state held to the letter of the law. But it's okay now. The city agrees that there's no real alternative. (interview)

Once again, however, a bemused parochial school parent applied an ironic touch:

> Well, the kids and the Title I specialists don't exactly meet on neutral ground despite the court decision. After all the Hope Center is in the basement of Our Lady of Hope Church, which the bishop rents to the city for a dollar a year. Of course, they keep church and state separate—ha! "Hey, Father, turn up the heat!" (interview)

But tensions persist in the midst of such church-state cooperation. The culture of both school systems includes a wariness of each other. One former public school administrator, Daniel J. Bresnahan, provided a historical backdrop to this uneasiness in his 1971 doctoral dissertation on the post–World War II demise of the Springfield Plan. This educational effort to promote interracial and interreligious harmony rankled a number of important Catholics in its tendency to relativize competing religious claims. Bresnahan (1971) cites Catholic opposition as a prime factor in the plan's ultimate atrophy and quotes a 1947 editorial from *The Catholic Mirror* as a case in point:

> Since the departure of Superintendent Granrud, we hear less and less about the Springfield Plan, and we cannot say that we are sorry. For what the "plan" may have done to bring about civic and social friendliness among national and religious groups, we can only be appreciative. For what it tended to do in making Christian Revelation just another "ism," we had grave forbodings, which we have not yet found reason to relinquish. (p. 179)

Over the more than forty years since 1947, the specifically religious sources of suspicion have declined. Many Catholics have followed their bishop into a more "commmunitarian" mode, and, as noted in Chapter Three, Catholic support was crucial in pushing through the bond issue for the city's new public high school in 1977. Still, an uneasiness remains among public school administrators. Although it is not uncommon for a majority of the city's School Committee to be parents of parochial school children—an issue on which our general sample was closely divided— there are many public school staff members, including Catholics, who tend to use the term "parochial" as a pejorative. A recent source of conflict involved allegations of raiding by public schools in their teacher-hiring practices:

> Priests used to call and charge the public schools with stealing their teachers by offering them more money, and the rumor was that the superintendent made a deal with the bishop to back off. It's not true, but the public schools are sensitive about stripping the parochial schools. We hire 'em. Why not? They deserve the salaries. But we don't actively recruit them. Besides, there's a big credential gap, and there aren't that many who qualify. (interview)

Meanwhile, there are also rumors among the public school staff about the Catholic schools. These include unsubstantiated claims that the parochials spend their federal Title I funds on all students, not just the disadvantaged, and that in a few parishes some parents are allowed to make tax-deductible charitable contributions to the Church in lieu of nondeductible tuition. In addition, there is resentment among the public school staff for the way in which the Catholic schools are able to select and reject their students:

> There's no question that Cathedral High School really keeps the lid on over there. They recently expelled seventeen kids for pot, and they were going to deny diplomas to four seniors until a public school official went to the bishop

and got the decision reversed. It's kind of like Mercy Hospital; they don't take the tough cases, but only those that are no trouble. (interview)

The parallel between the parochial schools and the Catholic Mercy Hospital is apt and worth a postscript here. The comment above is mirrored by the following comment from a staff member at the city's large nondenominational hospital:

> Mercy is good at skimming the light stuff, and there's a lot of competition at that level. They subtly shut the door on Medicaid, and we get more dumps from Mercy than anywhere else since they won't take the detox cases, for example. I mean they have good nursing, good food, and they're a very pleasant place to stay. But if something's really wrong, people come to Baystate. (interview)

That is certainly the prevailing community opinion. The two hospitals are often contrasted in terms of technology versus humanity. Baystate is seen as cold, corporate, and technically competent; Mercy's own logo features the implicitly comparative slogan: "We care." But Mercy has sought to extend its care on a nondenominational basis; it sees itself as an increasingly competitive hospital on both medical and economic grounds—not just a religious alternative. It is widely thought to have abandoned its obstetrics and gynecological services in 1970 partly to avoid controversies associated with abortion and contraception. Recently, it entered into a purchasing agreement with several secular hospitals to provide economies of scale, and it has been aggressive in pursuing state authorization for more complicated and technically demanding procedures. Still, it remains a religious institution, and this is reflected in some of its tactics in the statewide politics of health care. One of its staff described a recent problem this way:

> In this state, the large teaching hospitals dominate, and we have problems as a small community hospital. For example, recently Mass General in Boston put a prominent state senator on its board to co-opt him and get his support against the "Underfunded Hospital" bill. We'll counter by going after his parish priest and do it that way. (interview)

Municipal politics is apparently somewhat different. As one Baystate staff member noted, "The city is very careful not to discriminate in providing services to Mercy and Baystate. They're very responsive" (interview).

And yet there is one religiously related grievance concerning the Springfield medical scene from the early 1970s that continues to rankle as a rumor. At the time, the University of Massachusetts was planning to start a medical school and teaching hospital; the critical question concerned whether the location should be in the already-teeming medical center of Boston, at the university's flagship campus in Amherst only twenty miles north of Springfield, or possibly in Springfield itself. One of the new university trustees at the time was Springfield's own Bishop Weldon. When the final decision was reached to locate the facility midway between Springfield and Boston in Worcester, Weldon's role in the closed-door deliberations became the subject of considerable second-guessing. One local Catholic businessman asked with a sardonic sneer: "Our own bishop, and what did he do for us?" (interview). Still others conjectured that the bishop actively opposed location in Springfield in order to ward off competition with Mercy Hospital, in which he had made substantial investments. However, according to one participant in the decision-making process, Springfield was never a politically viable option. From the standpoint of western Massachusetts, the only feasible course was to oppose the Boston phalanx and at least place the hospital somewhere closer west:

> Chris Weldon was crucial, especially after one of the Boston group tried to nail down the vote of another trustee, who was living in an unapproved marriage not far from Springfield, by having Cushing himself come out and bless it. Weldon knew that Springfield was out of the question, but he really hung tough against Boston and at least helped force the Worcester compromise. (interview)

Clearly, the church was implicated in state decisionmaking, if not in the way subsequent rumors have suggested.

Religion in City Politics and City Hall

Asking politicians to disdain religion is like asking them to slap babies. But perhaps more than in most cities, Springfield's politics fairly quiver with religious overtones. Politicians rarely miss opportunities to attend religious functions—even those not of their own faith. This is partly because of the moral legitimacy afforded, but also because other contexts in which to press the electoral flesh have dwindled in an age of home entertainment and the decline of once critical "mediating institutions" such as political parties, labor unions, and neighborhood associations. It is not uncommon for Catholic candidates like Mayor Neal to launch their campaigns with a Mass. And the recently established "Mayor's Prayer Breakfast" has required an annual command appearance by virtually all politicians.

The prayer breakfast also testifies to the tensions behind the religious facade. Surprisingly enough, the event was first suggested by Protestant Evangelicals to a Catholic mayor disinclined to inspect a religious gift horse too closely. However, the evangelical control of the occasion became more obvious year by year, and soon the breakfast became more a source of squirming discomfort than ecumenical solidarity. The language was highly Christocentric, and liberal Protestants and Catholics alike shared the offenses taken by Jews. Indeed, one Jewish respondent was somewhat bemused at the reaction of some of his Christian colleagues:

> The prayer breakfast is the thing to do for some of the downtown insiders, and a lot of the clergy go because they have to. But the rabbis go more to act as watchdogs. I'm there to tell the mayor, "I'm watching you every step." Actually the only real teeth-grinding comes from the Liberal Protestant ministers, and everyone sort of accepts that. Those guys are so darned mechanical. (interview)

Several letters to the editor of the local newspaper have made a public issue of the event's religious content. But it is likely to remain a conservative Protestant occasion with heavy attendance by Catholic politicians who can ill afford to spurn it regardless of content.

Political opponents are sensitive to the way religion is displayed and deployed, and they are reluctant to allow one another to corner the symbolic market. It has been a long while since religious differences between candidates have been made an explicit issue, although several interviewees doubted that a Protestant could be elected mayor, and there was some feeling that the 1986 referenda concerning aid to abortion and to private schools may have been biased on religious grounds:

> When we had those questions on abortion and state aid to parochial schools on the ballot, some of us thought it wasn't right to have polling places in the churches. We even complained to the city election commission, but all we got was a shrugged shoulder. (interview)

In fact, having polling places in churches is a long-standing practice in the city, though officials draw a distinction between church assembly halls, which they use, and church sanctuaries, which they do not. According to one staff member, "The black churches are especially useful. We give them fifty dollars or so, enough to cover the heat and to keep their telephones free" (interview).

But religion plays more than a routine role in the city's political culture. It is also an ace in the hole in times of crisis. As we have already noted, in 1977 a mayor desperate for community approval of a badly needed new high school turned to the city's new Catholic bishop for public support, and it made the difference. As we shall see in Chapter Six, the city has a history of religious interventions in the midst of racial crises, including an ecumenical cadre of black and white clergy that led a key civil rights march in 1974 while the city was on a hair trigger. More recently, a closely contested state legislative race was won by a trailing African-American candidate who mobilized the black churches with only hours remaining at the polling booth. Chapters Five and Seven also illustrate religion's potency in both creating and smoothing crises. In the former, a liberal religious coalition fans the political fires over the issue of homelessness; in the latter, conservative religious voices shout down both city hall and the School Committee on issues of abortion, contraception, and sex education. As an indication that political officials are often compliant victims, let us turn to an early instance in which abortion intruded in city hall.

City Hall and the Tel-Med Tapes. One question we asked routinely of our interviewees was whether they could recall any instances of church-state conflict in Springfield. The most common response was a considerable pause, a bit of head scratching, and then a hazy recollection of the "Tel-Med tapes." In 1978, the city entered into an agreement with Blue Cross–Blue Shield to provide some one hundred and eighty brief telephone messages offering medical counsel on a variety of health subjects. The service was city sponsored, one-fourth city financed, and located in the city's municipal hospital.

The mayor had enthusiastically endorsed the service on the eve of its inception. But less than two weeks later, he ordered that six tapes dealing with abortion and birth control be withdrawn from the program and held by city officials, pending reconsideration of their "appropriateness for children." While the mayor denied that his position was religiously motivated, it was widely known that this Italian Catholic and his wife had been cofounders of Birthright, one of the city's early pro-life organizations, and it was later revealed that he had asked several members of the local pro-life movement to listen to the tapes and advise him concerning their disposition.

Community responses varied. On the one hand, the *Springfield Morning Union* charged censorship and mounted a major editorial campaign for the tapes' reinstatement. At the same time, the Civil Liberties Union petitioned successfully for a county superior court injunction to restore the tapes to Blue Cross–Blue Shield and its service. On the other hand, a group of sixteen physicians and nurses opposed to abortion produced their own tape and demanded that it be added to the service as a way of exposing callers to their moral perspective. While this was opposed by the newspaper, the CLU, and Blue Cross–Blue Shield, it was supported by the still-new Catholic bishop. A member of the mayor's staff recalled the imbroglio this way:

> We didn't worry too much about the tapes on contraception, but we did worry a lot about the abortion tapes, and the mayor told someone to pull them before the thing opened. Well, someone goofed, and it wasn't done, so we had to pull them after it opened. God, the city exploded. The CLU called him a book burner; the Council of Churches and the Jewish community both came out against him. But the bishop supported him, and it played out okay. (interview)

In fact, the bishop's public involvement was limited to the following brief comments, which reveal a good deal about how his style of church and community leadership was to differ from his predecessor:

I have felt that leadership in the civic and professional community has exercised moral responsibility in this matter. I respect the sensitive and articulate defense of positions during this controversy. . . . It is one of my duties as a bishop to defend the right of every person to present his or her side of an issue and to protest when freedom to speak out is threatened. (*Springfield Morning Union*, December 28, 1978)

This is a far cry from the moral imperatives that have thundered so authoritatively from the old guard of the Catholic ecclesia. In reaching beyond the diocese's immediate constituency to the community as a whole, it is one part ecumenism and another part good public relations.

Neither the church nor the community had the stomach for a protracted dispute. One of the CLU plaintiffs was surprised at how little reaction he encountered:

When I agreed to get involved in the case in response to a quick phone call, I thought there'd be at least twenty of us, but I then found out I was damn near alone. The morning paper applauded me for my courage, but it was hardly that. But actually there really wasn't any hassle. I never got any phone calls, threats, or reprisals. (interview)

In fact, the issue dissipated almost as quickly as it arose. In less than three weeks, the mayor arranged to dissociate the city from the service and have it switched back entirely to Blue Cross–Blue Shield. Since the city's financial support had been largely in terms of space and telephone, it was easily brought to a quiet end. Indeed, both the city administration and its opponents later claimed a victory. The political crisis was settled even though constitutional issues were left dangling. The pattern is by no means unusual.

Actually the Tel-Med episode illustrates only one of two types of religious influence in city hall. Here religion was activated internally according to the conscience and judgment of the political officials themselves. But the more provocative scenario involves city officials succumbing to church pressure from outside. Certainly there are suspected cases in point. For example, one knowledgeable respondent, albeit with a political ax to grind, alleged that, "The bishop didn't want low-income housing across from Mercy Hospital, so it just plain didn't happen" (interview). In another instance, a canny political observer who is himself a Catholic recalled when, "the mayor's office had X-rated movies thrown off cable TV in negotiating a new contract. The Church had a voice there; you can bet on it" (interview). Still one more case was also recalled by a longtime Catholic observer of the political scene:

Ward redistricting can get a little dicey. For example, when Our Lady of Hope Church was put in Ward 1 rather than Ward 2—you know, Spanish rather than Irish—there was pressure applied to put it back, and it was. In fact, some people in the Church were hysterical. Then in another case, some Irish Ward 6 committee members were moved to Ward 3 where the constituency was Italian and Spanish. The Election Commission was once again "prevailed upon by a higher wisdom," as they say. (interview)

But it is not the Catholics alone who seek to wield influence. A largely Protestant coalition of local black churches and suburban white churches opposed a reputedly immoral video arcade in the major predominantly black business area, and it was finally closed despite the support of the one black City Council member on largely economic grounds.

One issue that has periodically surfaced to both unite and divide Springfield's religious community is the licensing of church-hosted bingo—or "beano" games, as they are called locally. First officially legalized in Massachusetts in 1933, they were prohibited a decade later, only to be revived for nonprofit institutions in 1971. Despite the continued opposition of the largely Protestant Council of Churches of Greater Springfield, which formed originally in the 1930s to successfully oppose a local dog-racing track, bingo has become a major staple of the city's "religion incorporated," and one that knows no denominational boundaries. With hugely successful games in Catholic parishes, Orthodox Jewish synagogues, and a few Protestant churches, Springfield is the largest bingo-playing city in New England, with an annual religious take approaching $1.5 million. Although there have been occasional calls for closer city supervision and even delicensing, it is hardly surprising that no city administration has mounted the cause. Money is not be trifled with, whether in church or state. It is no more likely that the city will end the churches' bingo than that Massachusetts' churches would prevent the development of a state lottery, block the establishment of off-track betting in nearby Chicopee, or fend off the repeal of the commonwealth's blue law once the yen for new state income and Sunday shopping gathered legislative momentum in the late 1970s.

The next three chapters present three extended case studies in which city hall has been a palpable target of religious influence. But in some way, they are important exceptions to the general rule that effective religious influence is relatively rare in Springfield. Here is the attempt of one political official to put the matter in perspective:

Sure the Church sometimes asks for favors, but they're not always granted. On the one hand, the Church was successful in getting a building excluded from a historical preservation zone, so this beautiful building could be torn down. The Church and one of the largest Jewish temples in town also scuttled an effort to petition the state for a city bingo game. On the other hand, when the old Putnam mansion was no longer needed by the Ursuline nuns, the Church wanted to sell it and tried to get it zoned commercial rather than residential to get a higher price. I even got some calls from lay Catholics about the plight of the nuns. But the city planning department turned it down in a straight bureaucratic decision. Like most city departments, they acted fairly apolitical—in fact, amazingly so. (interview)

It is true that there is a widespread belief that Catholics have dispropor-tionate influence around city hall. And many Springfielders might well agree with one political insider who said:

Don't kid yourself. The mayor and the bishop don't have to look each others' phone numbers up in the book. Besides, they sit side by side at some dinner or another at least once a week and have plenty of chances to talk then. (interview)

However, our interviews with one mayor after another indicated that, while they kept in touch with the chancery, the bishops never once called them to apply heat:

The bishop was always there, and if I wanted I could call him. But he never got involved in any issue I had to deal with, and he never called me. (inter-view)

I never spoke to the bishop about politics—or even called him. My predeces-sor might have asked his permission to do something, but I just go ahead without asking. (interview)

As mayor, I kept in touch with the hierarchy. Nothing was said, but I did have a certain sense of obligation. Of course, it was good to be seen with the bishop, but I also did it with Protestant, Jewish, and black clergy. (interview)

Independent observers of different stripes give ample reason to accept this testimony on good faith, if not literally. According to a former Catho-lic political official with long years as both spectator and participant:

Catholic politicians were out there on their own, and the bishops and the Church were in a different compartment, so to speak. It was hard for a bishop to interfere in politics—even for Weldon. But they really didn't have to. People knew what their positions were, and they were pretty well accepted. (interview)

Or consider the following from a priest well versed in diocesan affairs of the vote and the flag:

The mayor's not in the bishop's pocket, but still the bishop's the bishop, and he does call him pretty regularly to keep him informed. But the pols aren't really interested in the Church as such. They just see it as a base, so they go to services and do the parades. (interview)

And according to a recent city councillor:

> There's a fair amount of deference to the bishop in the City Council, but in all the years I was on it, there was no direct or overt intervention by the Church, whether from the bishop or the clergy. (interview)

Finally, a journalist who spent time on the city hall beat offered this summary assessment:

> Look, I saw the mayor every day, and I never even heard the bishop's name. Generally, politicians don't need the Church. They won't offend it, but aside from abortion, everything else is negotiable, and the bishop is basically marginal to the daily political life and the decisions that get made. They pay him symbolic homage mainly, though he does have real control over some of the older Catholics on a strictly generational basis, and the politicians know it. (interview)

SUMMARY

In providing an overview of church-state relations in Springfield, we have moved from the attitudes and judgments of its citizenry through a series of points of potential conflict and entanglement in the city's actual rounds. Given Springfield's history, one might expect an inordinate sensitivity to such matters as they have been reflected in the nation's evolving constitutional law. And yet our questionnaires reveal a considerable gap between current church-state law and the citizens' own knowledge and attitudes. While there is great respect for the "separation of church and state" as a general principle, there is considerable deviation from the courts in preferences concerning actual practice. This is less true of the protection of "free exercise" than the prohibition of an "establishment"—especially where the issues concern symbolic display rather than political nitty-gritty. But in both instances, there are substantial pockets of disregard, more because of perceived irrelevance than willful disobedience.

Turning from opinions of "what ought to be" to the ongoing historical reality of "what is," Springfield's actual church-state relations range midway between a strict constitutionalist interpretation of the courts and the more indulgent opinions of its public. The city has witnessed probable violations of virtually every major U.S. Supreme Court church-state decision of the last thirty years. But these do not constitute consistent patterns of law avoidance, much less civic rebellion; indeed, there are several instances in which the city itself has taken care to test for and avoid the unconstitutional.

Clearly Springfield is no den of constitutional iniquity. As the realms of politics and religion have grown more distant and autonomous, the rela-

tions between them have generally become more symbolic than substantive. The city administration is by no means a secular tyrant; but nor is it
obsequiously deferential to either "the Church" or the churches. Religion
asks but does not always receive. And while there is no question that
Springfield is a Catholic city, the Catholic Church of today is not the same
civic force as its Protestant predecessor of yesteryear.

But if this is an accurate description of the city at peace, it does not
always apply to the city in conflict. Moreover, the relationship between
what surfaces and what remains hidden can be problematic. It is one thing
to note episodes that make the news and quite another to uncover patterns that escape it. The paucity of public church-state conflicts in a community may indicate either that there is too little contact to be made an
issue, *or* that the comingling of church and state is too ensconced to be
disputed. As we saw earlier in this chapter, the ways of violating constitutional and court requirements of separation are many and varied. They
may involve entanglements suggesting government endorsement or support of religion; they may also involve infringement on the free exercise of
religion—or nonreligion. While there is much to be said for keeping one's
eye on the commonplace rather than the anomalies, it is also true that
anomalies frequently expose the underlying social and cultural issues.

The three confrontational episodes to follow were the three major public issues in which religion was implicated during our research. Each allows us to probe beneath abstract generalizations into more specific details. The overall objective is a richer sense of local church-state relations
in all of their deceptive nuances. We also seek a firmer grasp of religion
and power, as they extend beyond the constitutional and the institutional
into the realm of culture. Religion in Springfield may be in decline, but it
is hardly in demise. Any attempt to understand civic power and politics
without it is sadly myopic. Issues of homelessness, black-neighborhood
development, and sexuality have all evoked major religious responses.
Religious protagonists have had their say, if not always their way. In the
process, they reveal a dimension of urban power that is frequently
neglected.

Chapter Five

HOMELESSNESS IN THE CITY OF HOMES

FOR MORE THAN A CENTURY, Springfield has relished its nickname as the "city of homes." A phrase born of late nineteenth-century affluence, it has been an important ingredient in the city's civic pride. In 1892, the local founding publisher of *Good Housekeeping* magazine, Clark W. Bryan, produced a poetic panegyric to this dimension of Springfield life. The first and last of its seven stanzas read as follows:

> Nestled peacefully down, by Connecticut's waters
> Full mirrored each day from the stream,
> A City of Homes, as fair as the fairest,
> Reflects from the river's bright gleam.
> Creeping up from a valley, a beautiful valley,
> In New England's fruitful domains,
> Creeping up from the crest of sunny-set hillsides,
> And out o'er the neighboring plains.
>
> . . . .
>
> A wide world of beauty lies ever around us,
> And beckons with well-displayed charms,
> That win new recruits for the army of duty,
> Who go from our hearts and our arms.
> Some go, others come—some go out to tarry,
> But loyal each pilgrim, who roams,
> To the world whence they go, to our valley and hillsides,
> To our beautiful City of Homes.
>
> (*Progressive Springfield*, 1892, vol. 1, no. 1)

Another example of the civic optimism that marked that period of Springfield's history is the Springfield Creed, written, posted, and circulated among city business leaders in 1925. Here are its first, third, and last of five dogmatics:

> I believe in Springfield, a city that preserves the best traditions of its patriotic founders; a city of high ideals that provides amid attractive surroundings the fullest opportunity for its people to enjoy the fruits of their labors. I respect its honored past, believe in its present endeavors, have faith in its destiny. Its advantageous location, its diversified industries, its substantial citizenship are its treasure and security.
>
> . . . .

I believe in Springfield as a city that ministers to the comfort, convenience
and welfare of its citizens; that possesses unsurpassed educational facilities,
active churches, extensive parks and playgrounds, efficient civic organizations, solid financial institutions, commodious hotels, and progressive stores.

. . . .

I believe in Springfield, this fair city of the Connecticut valley, because its
achievemetns [sic] have been such as to justify my confidence in its future
growth and development.

                        (*Springfield Union*, December 29, 1925, p. 6)

While neither the poem nor the creed are on the tip of the city's tongue
today, their sentiments are still represented in local mythology, both in
the community's public opinion and in the imagery used by public officials. Of course, there is a fine line between pride and piousness, and
there is often a mocking gap between ideals and reality. On the other
hand, the abrasive dialectic between "what ought to be" and "what is"
constitutes fundamental fuel for the motors of change. Ideals divorced
from reality can seem banal, pompous, or even hypocritical. But reality
without ideals can be a grinding force indeed.

In some ways it is unfair to juxtapose Springfield's recent problems of
homelessness with its long-standing reputation for homes. And yet the
irony underscores the point that civic politics operate within a civic culture. As this chapter will show, Springfield's efforts to come to terms with
a mounting homeless population have not been confined to city hall alone,
much as the mayor might have preferred it so. Instead, the problem has
elicited responses from a range of city organizations, many of them specifically religious. Few issues in the city's recent experience so highlight
the tensions between conventional politics and the cultural forces on the
political margins. The day-to-day governmental routine may rest increasingly with professional specialists, but an acknowledged crisis may quickly
expand the political "power field" and its roster of players.

In what follows we begin with an orientation to the problem of homelessness in Springfield and the organizations that have confronted it. We
then describe the struggle to establish an effective emergency shelter for
the homeless, noting the various conflicts between political officials, social
work professionals, and religious activists. Following this ethnographic
narrative, we shall examine some of its various implications and overtones
in the light of church-state precedents as well as prior research on both
religious organizations and community power. This latter, more analytic
portion of the chapter will also inform the two chapters that follow. These
are also case studies of religious influence, but with respect to the very
different issues of black-neighborhood development, on the one hand,
and the swirling vortex of sexuality, on the other.

Introducing the Issue and the Combatants

Homelessness, as a public issue, is relatively new to Springfield. Like virtually any city, Springfield has had a long experience with a relatively stable homeless population parceled out to a variety of facilities, all of which are either run by, or were founded by, religious groups. But only in the last decade has the homeless population come to exceed this capacity and require intervention through emergency overflow shelters. With the growing specter of persons foraging for food and cover on winter nights, community unease has given way to a growing sense of crisis.

As in any crisis, fact and rumor have intermingled. Estimates of the city's homeless have ranged from 200 to 3,500, although such numbers are often based more in ideology than methodology. Thus, an estimate of 1,500–3,500 appeared in the newspapers several times in late 1984 (e.g., *Morning Union*, October 17, 24, 1984). In June 1985, a city consultant calculated that there were between 366 and 521 homeless people on any given night. The newspaper used an estimate of 500 homeless in a December 4, 1985, story, but one of our interviewees was convinced that the publisher was determined to keep the estimates as low as possible. Meanwhile, shelter operators reported that use of their facilities increased as much as 30 percent between 1984 and 1985 (*Morning Union*, April 15, 1985), and a study of the 1983–84 winter indicated shelters reported that they had turned away some 1,250 persons, although this count would obviously have included some persons more than once (*Morning Union*, November 24, 1984). In late November 1986, an advocacy group attempted a census of the homeless population, the first in Springfield's history (*Morning Union*, November 13, 1986). The social worker coordinating the count reported estimates ranging from 200 to 2,500, the latter total including the "marginally housed" and others at risk. A clergyman active with the homeless told us that the number actually homeless is "in the hundreds, not the thousands," but other activists continued to use the figure of 2,500, including those "at risk" (*Morning Union*, December 3, 1986).

It seems that unreliable estimates of homelessness is yet another national problem of which Springfield has a local version. This illustrates again how political battles are fought over the "definition of the problem." In fact, both national and local politics have been involved in such definitions. Cities across the country "discovered" this malignancy in their midst partly in response to the media attention devoted to homelessness as a national disgrace and challenge.

But homelessness in Springfield is by no means chimeric. It is a product of altered circumstances as well as altered consciousness. One critical

change involved a statewide Massachusetts program for deinstitutional-
izing the chronically mentally ill. By late 1987, the Massachusetts Coalition for the Homeless estimated that 28 percent of the homeless adults in
emergency shelters throughout the state were mentally ill, while another
20 percent reflected some combination of mental illness and alcohol or
drug abuse (*Boston Globe*, November 29, 1987).

Another major source of the problem is rooted in the local economy.
The city's accelerating shift from a manufacturing to a service-oriented
economy has reduced the number of low-skilled jobs that pay sufficient
wages to enable people to afford adequate housing on the local market.
Meanwhile, the city's emphasis on revitalization of the downtown area has
contributed to homelessness at three levels. First, in the eyes of many,
the development has usurped priority over more pressing human issues
and discouraged debate concerning them. One Protestant pastor described the change this way:

> The push for economic renewal has pushed social and religious issues to the
> sidelines. They don't want to rock the boat because they want to keep
> everyone in it. (interview)

A second effect of development was more direct. It led to the demoli-
tion or the conversion to condominiums of a number of the single-room-
occupancy hotels (SROs) that traditionally served as the bottom of the
housing scale. As the city's overall housing vacancy rate dropped under 3
percent, people were forced onto the streets. Third, as the downtown area
was preened as a showplace, the rising numbers of the visibly homeless
became a major problem. According to one advocate for the homeless:

> The city is in a bind. It staked its reputation on downtown development, and
> the street people are an embarrassment. But at the same time they've gotten
> rid of most of the SROs, and the low-income housing is disappearing too.
> Where are these people going to go? (interview)

A member of Springfield Central made the point more personally:

> The city is pretty small, and the issues are all related. Hell, I meet myself
> coming around the corner. The homeless are a particular problem. Sure, I
> want to be humane and help people who don't have a place. But I also want
> the downtown to be clean and good-looking. Do I have to take care of them
> in my entranceway? (interview)

Clearly, some form of coordinated response was necessary if the downtown's human environment was to keep pace with its economic changes.

But homelessness was also salient for the city at large—at least by the
time we conducted our questionnaire survey in the spring of 1986, some
two years after the issue had come to a boil and been set to simmer on the

local political stove. It is impossible to know precisely whether the responses we received were causes or consequences of recent civic developments—and if the latter, whether the primary influences were national or local, since, by then, homelessness had become a staple on the network news. For whatever reason, Springfielders had come to regard homelessness as a relatively significant city priority.

Table 5.1 makes the point with numbers. The questionnaire asked respondents to evaluate eight priorities for city government. Possible answers for each ranged from "extremely important" to "important," "desirable," and finally, "not a priority." Since respondents had only to rate rather than rank-order the eight areas, any number of "extremely important" answers could be given, and any response of "not a priority" was clearly negative. Table 5.1 provides the percentages of the general sample that rated each of the eight areas as "extremely important." Of the eight issues in our "priorities" battery, care for the homeless rated fourth in terms of the percentage marking it "extremely important" (49.8 percent); in fact, it had the lowest percentage marking it "not a priority" (2 percent). Rated third, just above it, was the item "responding to the [needs of the] poor and disadvantaged," with 50.4 percent rating it "extremely important" and 2 percent rating it "not a priority." Both the items concerning the "poor and disadvantaged" generally, and the "homeless" specifically, rated higher on the priorities list than "downtown business development."

The responses of our elite samples to homelessness are also illuminating. The political-economic elite sample gave city care for the homeless only the fifth-highest priority, with 31 percent considering it "extremely important." However, the sample of religious clergy considered city care for the homeless the second-most-pressing priority, tied with "responding

TABLE 5.1
General Sample Priorities for Eight Areas of City Government
(N = 256)

Priorities:	% Indicating Extremely Important
Reducing Crime	75.3
Improving Public Schools	56.2
Responding to the Poor and Disadvantaged	50.4
City Care for the Homeless	49.8
Improved Maintenance of Streets and Parks	31.1
Downtown Business Development	25.8
Responding to the Needs of Minorities such as Blacks and Hispanics	21.3
Development of Winchester (Mason) Square Area	20.7

to the [needs of the] poor and disadvantaged" and behind only the need for "reducing crime." Although providing for the homeless was a higher priority for Catholic priests and sisters than for the combined Protestant and Jewish clergy (the percentages in the "extremely important" category were 68 percent and 41 percent, respectively), the issue was plainly salient for religious professionals.

This is hardly surprising since the religious community has been a prime mover in responding to the homeless. Of course, religiously motivated persons have long seen care for the homeless as a matter of social justice and ministry to the needy. Long before homelessness became politically contentious, religious groups had experience in operating food services and shelters of last resort. Once the city's responsibility for homelessness became a public issue, it was predictable that religiously based activists would become involved, both in pressuring public officials and in shaping the public opinion.

As we shall see, a cadre of local religious advocates were successful in generating attention for their positions and demands. At a time when city hall had neither the resolve nor the resources to become involved in the issue, the religious constituency made it too politically risky to duck it altogether. Nor could politicians attack the religious proponents as mere radicals or marginals, since they included Roman Catholic sisters as well as Protestant clergy. The issue's rise to public consciousness, its continued salience, and at least its temporary denouement all owe much to the moral and material leverage of the city's religious community and its representatives. In fact, before turning to an account of the political struggle itself, it is worth pausing to meet several of the groups most responsible for pushing it forward.

Council of Churches of Greater Springfield and Its Downtown Ministries. Forty years ago, Springfield might well have been called the "city of churches" as well as the city of homes. Indeed the two tended to go together within the domesticated, middle-class Protestant ethos that was so dominant through the 1950s. As we saw in Chapter Two, the city's mainline Protestant establishment enjoyed a rich legacy by whatever measure—members, finances, architecture, or civic influence. Nor was this restricted to the Congregationalists and their four proud bastions within the city. Episcopalians, Methodists, Lutherans, and Baptists were all major religious presences. By the 1960s this had begun to change—first gradually, and then with a rush. Springfield's mainline Protestant community was overtaken by the same trends that have been discerned nationally (cf. Wuthnow 1988; Roof and McKinney 1987). As Catholicism and evangelical Protestantism expanded, the old liberal Protestant denominations shrank from the civic center—many retreating to the suburban periphery.

A major theme of this volume concerns the decline of mainstream Protestantism against the backdrop of a surging Catholicism. It is therefore ironic that it was a mainstream Protestant organization that was responsible for initiating much of the community's activism on behalf of the homeless. Specifically, this was the Downtown Ministry project of the Council of Churches of Greater Springfield (CCGS).

By the early 1980s, the CCGS was a receding echo of Protestantism's longtime dominance of the city's cultural and political establishment. Located on the city's margins physically as well as socially, the CCGS was housed in shabby gentility in a once-elegant home near Springfield's border with its most affluent suburb. Still, the council provides its congregations with a kind of safety in numbers and an opportunity to act collectively rather than in isolation. The CCGS also provides a layer of political insulation in staking out controversial positions. As one staff member put it:

> Our main supporters are the heavily endowed churches. They can afford it. Besides, they like having the CCGS for referrals—both people, like the homeless, and issues, like, say, the death penalty. (interview)

And yet the controversies have tended to be more abstract than locally loaded. Indeed, the CCGS has earned a kind of community image in this regard. According to the pastor of a black church that was not a CCGS member, "Those folks all suffer from the same disease. They're stereotyped white Christian liberals—sort of pigeonholed" (interview). And in the words of a white Catholic City Council member, "You know those limousine liberals from the suburbs. They're too interested in the political process and not enough in its human impact" (interview).

Stereotypes aside, the CCGS has been involved in several programs that have been more immediate in both their impact and their conflict. It has provided economies of scale in taking on such service projects as a citywide winter fuel assistance program, although this began as a response to a request from a Catholic mayor, and although its largest recent donations have come not from member churches but from the local Farmworkers' Council. In the early 1980s, the CCGS also launched the Downtown Ministry to provide funding, counsel, and political empowerment to the disadvantaged, including prison inmates, drug abusers, and the homeless.

The young minister employed as director of the Downtown Ministry developed a confrontational style that became a double-edged sword. On the one hand, his challenge to the city establishment gave new impetus to other groups and movements entering the battle; on the other hand, he alienated many city hall officials and many civic-minded business people, including those involved in Springfield Central. This finally led to his undoing. As one Protestant clergyman characterized the project:

The Downtown Ministry used to give the CCGS some real color and a stamp of identity, but the two are now almost completely defused and submerged. The DM antagonized so many people that it finally lost its effectiveness. The CCGS won't reestablish that kind of presence again. (interview)

Ultimately, the director left Springfield, and the Downtown Ministry project became a shadow of its activist incarnation. However, this was not before the sword was passed to two other groups concerned with the homeless. Both Open Pantry and Service Providers, Inc. (SPI), were essentially offshoots of the CCGS's Downtown Ministry through small start-up grants. Both deserve brief introductions of their own.

Open Pantry.   This is the best-known provider of homeless services in Springfield. In addition to a shelter for the homeless, Open Pantry runs a soup kitchen ("Loaves and Fishes") and a day program ("Open Door"). The facility has experienced chronic problems in securing quarters, having had to move six times in less than six years. Three of the moves involved vacating buildings in the path of city redevelopment projects. Nor has location been its only source of tension with city hall. As we shall see, its director's public dispute with the mayor over the city's provisions for the homeless was perhaps the single most significant political event concerning the issue.

A major reason why that dispute loomed large was that the director in question was a Catholic sister. A member of the locally prominent Sisters of Providence, she was a native of nearby Holyoke where, like many of her coreligionists, she grew up "thinking everyone was Catholic." As a result of her career on behalf of the disadvantaged in Springfield, one political official referred to her as "our own Mother Theresa; she has enormous credibility all over town" (interview). However, this respect was not always negotiable as political currency. The ambivalence of the city's political-economic establishment was unintentionally revealed in the *Morning Union* of April 10, 1985. The editorial column included a paragraph of praise for the sister-director's selection as the Woman of the Year by the Women's Division of the Greater Springfield Chamber of Commerce; on the back side of the same page was a brief story describing the eviction of the Open Pantry's Loaves and Fishes soup kitchen from a downtown neighborhood targeted for redevelopment. In fact, the city had offered to help with the move, though one city councillor complained:

I wish the soup kitchen people would quit running to the press. . . . We're working on several alternatives and are very concerned about Loaves and Fishes. (interview)

This tension was chronic throughout the struggle on behalf of the homeless.

Largely because of the sister-director's public presence and the participation of others from her order, Open Pantry was widely perceived as a Catholic organization. However, as previously noted, it began as a program of the Downtown Ministry project of the predominantly Protestant Council of Churches. Although the Catholic Stewardship Fund did give the CCGS some $35,000 to assist in the launching, the Open Pantry's first location was in a Congregational church; its board of directors includes Protestants as well as Catholics, and over the years its politics have been decidedly "catholic," including alliances with virtually every other major city agency involved with homelessness.

Service Providers, Inc.   SPI was formed in 1983 by the activist director of the Downtown Ministry, and the bulk of its initial funding was a grant of $20,000 from the Home Ministries Board of the United Church of Christ. Originally staffed by both social work professionals and religious activists, SPI was torn by competing missions from its inception. On the one hand, it had a basic commitment to running homeless shelters with all of their logistical demands. On the other hand, it also took up the cudgels of community activism on behalf of the homeless, and many of its founding members saw its role as more political advocacy than custodial caretaking from the start.

Division over these priorities split both the board of directors and the staff, while producing considerable organizational uncertainty and tension. As one member described it, "We're really more of an ad-hocracy, but at least we're flexible and fast on our feet" (interview). With the clergy a minority on the board and with a staff composed almost entirely of secular activists, SPI came to be dominated by its advocacy. Not as well known as Open Pantry by the public at large, it earned a growing reputation as the most radical group in the political struggle for the homeless. As we shall see, SPI had its own struggles with the mayor, to whom it gradually became anathema after several purposefully embarrassing incidents.

But if SPI's relations with city hall were strained, its ties to the statehouse in Boston were far closer and potentially more lucrative. SPI received some state money early, with a promise of more if it could find a suitable building for a permanent shelter for the homeless. It had several important allies in the state's Department of Public Welfare (DPW). In fact, the DPW was only willing to release some $200,000 of state money for the homeless to Springfield on the condition that SPI be involved. Thus, the city was forced to reckon with SPI even though the group had alienated many political leaders as the most confrontational group on the homeless scene. At several junctures, the city tried to freeze SPI out of its plans to unify service delivery to the homeless.

Pioneer Valley United Way.   Although the local United Way has a history of concern and involvement in the area, it is similar to other UW chapters across the country in its disinclination to rock the boat in search of reforming change. One of its most visible officials—the full-time labor representative to the UW—was an incumbent City Council member who called the homeless one of "his" issues and was called upon to cochair a city task force on the matter. Although the United Way was not a major financial contributor to care and facilities for the homeless, it did underwrite the salary of a city staff member in the area.

The United Way was also responsible for distributing the money Hampden County received from the Federal Emergency Management Agency (FEMA). Significantly, the city's Housing Allowance Program, an SPI spin-off, received some FEMA money during the winter of 1984–85 while SPI was cooperating with the city, but it received no funds in the winters of 1985–86 or 1986–87, after SPI's confrontations with city hall.

Of all of the voluntary organizations involved with the homeless, the UW has been most firmly allied with the mayor. But it has also been involved with the Council of Churches. For example, several UW board members served on the allocation board that distributed money raised by the Council of Churches' annual Walk for Food and Shelter fund-raiser. Following SPI's dispute with city officials, the UW sympathizers on the allocation board attempted to redirect money away from SPI and toward another newly created umbrella organization, one with closer ties to city hall. Predictably enough, the move led to conflict within the Council of Churches itself. One pastor of a major CCGS contributor, and himself a SPI board member, threatened to withhold his church's contribution to the Council of Churches if the new allocation process killed SPI. This stopped the reallocation from the annual walk, but another walk was then organized to benefit the new and more establishment-oriented umbrella organization. Significantly, the CCGS's executive director sat on the board of this newly formed group.

These, then, were the major protagonists involved with homelessness in Springfield—and the churning currents beneath this channel of civic altruism. Clearly there were a number of organizations vying for influence; homelessness generated a confusing infrastructure of overlapping and conflicting alliances, including several not yet mentioned. Actually the homeless issue comprises a number of more specific controversies, but instead of chronicling them all, we shall focus on only one; namely, the pursuit of a citywide winter emergency overflow shelter. The events here involve all of the organizations above and bring into sharper relief the possibilities and limitations of exerting religious power in civic politics.

Side Steps toward a Permanent Emergency Shelter

In December 1983, Service Providers, Inc., opened a shelter on Prospect Street for homeless families. That brought the total number of beds available for the city's homeless to some one hundred and fifty. This still fell short of caring for all the city's estimated homeless population at that time, and because it included beds committed to families for up to three weeks or so, there remained an acute shortage of overnight facilities available on an emergency basis. Thus began a protracted political struggle during which religious groups and social service agencies alike pressured the city to acknowledge the problem and provide an overflow shelter in response.

The crisis was first catalyzed by a religious reaction. In February 1984, the dean of the Episcopal cathedral announced a plan to open an emergency shelter in the basement of Christ Church Cathedral. The Council of Churches' Downtown Ministry agreed to help by donating the $10,000 it had received from the state Department of Public Welfare (*Morning Union*, February 14, 1984). But the Episcopal shelter did not sit well with city hall, presumably because it would attract the homeless to the "quadrangle"—one of the downtown's most prestigious areas that the cathedral shared with the municipal library and museum complex—and perhaps more important, because it threatened to lift control of services for the homeless out of the hands of city political officials.

The city administration reacted in two ways. First, as we described in Chapter Four, health department officials responded to the church's application for a "lodging house special permit" by inspecting the basement of the cathedral, finding it unsuitable for such a shelter, and threatening to padlock the church if a shelter were opened. But in addition to a stick, there was also a carrot. The mayor asked the Episcopal rector to cochair a newly created "Mayor's Task Force on Homelessness." As an intimate of the rector put it: "He knew he was being coopted—those were the rules going in—but he wanted to get something done" (interview). His cochair was the city councillor and United Way employee who considered homelessness "his" issue. The task force was charged with studying the problem and presenting recommendations for city action.

By October 1984, the task force had made some progress. It applied for, and received, a multipart $100,000 grant from the state (this was before SPI had secured the informal state franchise in Springfield). The grant included money to expand the Open Pantry's Loaves and Fishes soup kitchen and move it *out* of the immediate downtown business area; it also funded the opening of a day program for the homeless, to be staffed by volunteers from a United Methodist church. Finally, $31,000 of the grant was allocated to begin an emergency overflow shelter, as soon as the task force could locate an appropriate site and administering agency.

The symbolic overtones of the site the task force selected were readily apparent; it was the old isolation ward of the city's municipal hospital. However, the city spent a reported $28,000 in renovating it for the task. Meanwhile, the Salvation Army and Service Providers, Inc., contracted jointly to operate the facility, and SPI agreed to apply to the state Department of Public Welfare for an additional $30,000 to keep the shelter open throughout the winter. To many, it seemed the problem of the homeless had been more or less "handled" (e.g., *Morning Union*, October 3, 9, 12, 15, 17, and 24, 1984).

On November 27, 1984, the mayor called a press conference to announce the shelter's opening, even though the actual opening was to be delayed. The announced problem involved difficulties in obtaining necessary insurance for the staffing agency, though there were suspicions that city officials were "dragging their heels." These suspicions erupted at the press conference itself when the sister-director of Open Pantry interrupted the proceedings to press the mayor repeatedly for a specific date when the shelter would open. For every reason he offered for the delay, she and her colleagues provided rapid rebuttal. Thus, when the insurance issue came up, the sister-director offered to staff it at once with the Sisters of Providence, one of whom testified that she had checked with their own insurance company and learned that it would provide an immediate rider until SPI was ready. Moreover, the sister-director had brought along ten homeless persons to dramatize the problem. Word of the shelter's opening had reached the streets, and homeless people were swamping the Loaves and Fishes soup kitchen in search of assistance. Ten people even paid an unannounced visit to the mayor's office, a move that some city hall insiders thought was choreographed by the sisters, one of whom remarked later, "Maybe now they [city officials] know there is a need."

The actions of the Sisters of Providence stemmed from several years of frustration in trying to prod city action. Although developments had occurred, the pace was slow, and the municipal hospital location was away from the downtown center, where the needy were concentrated without transportation. Throughout the two-week delay between the shelter's scheduled and actual opening, the staff of the Loaves and Fishes soup kitchen was faced with finding shelter for some twenty people each night. Many were lodged in local motels, with both the Roman Catholic chancery and the Episcopal Christ Church Cathedral picking up the bills (*Morning Union*, November 28 and 29, 1984). Ears were somewhat tinned to the mayor's defense that *he* was the driving force behind getting the shelter started at all, that it was the first municipal shelter in Hampden County, and that it would operate throughout the 1984–85 winter.

On the other hand, one can also understand the frustration behind a mayoral aide's response that they knew there was a need and were moving as quickly as they could (*Morning Union*, November 28, 1984). The press conference exchange was featured both in newspapers (e.g., *Morning Union*, November 28 and 29, 1984) and on television. Instead of appearing as a responsible administrator concerned with the welfare of all the city's residents, the mayor was caught off guard and made to look as if he were delaying the opening without good reason and then taking credit for services not actually provided. Most important, he was challenged by a religious figure who left him no way to win in a contest of public images. The mayor could neither counterattack nor dismiss the criticism; he was publicly embarrassed and privately angry, feeling both betrayed and hurt. One observer commented that, while the actual substance of the sister's remarks was rather mild:

> Even if Mitch Snyder [a nationally known advocate for the homeless] had been fasting on City Hall's steps, I don't think that would have had as much impact on him as a rebuke from a nun. (interview)

Actually, a number of our informants noted the disproportionate impact of Springfield's Catholic sisters on any issue they addressed. Most of the city's older politicians were educated in parochial schools by sisters, whose image is so entwined with Church authority that adult alumni continue to flinch in anticipation of a "sisterly" reproach and assent reflexively to a sister's request. As one particularly prominent political leader noted: "You'd think you can only say 'Yes, sister,' so many times, but the instinct never leaves you" (interview).

A member of the Catholic clergy gave a more organizational analysis of the religious authority and political influence of the sisters:

> When the sisters left the convents for community residences, it really changed the power equation. The diocese did it out of financial necessity, but now the nuns have a new independent authority, and they even challenge the bishop on a variety of matters. (interview)

A non-Catholic newspaper reporter put the situation more generically and more succinctly: "In this town, you don't mess with nuns" (interview).

Ultimately the city's municipal-hospital shelter did begin operations. But if its opening posed a crisis, so did its closing. The mayor was committed to keeping it open with SPI personnel until April 1, 1985. When that time came, however, SPI objected. There was still money in the budget, time on SPI's contract, and many cold nights in a Massachusetts spring;

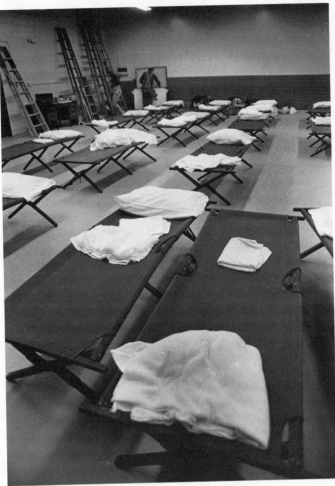

Workmen completing the wiring for the city's shelter for the homeless at 125 Armory Street—December 1, 1985.

there were also no provisions for the following winter. As a result, social
service advocates mounted a demonstration to protest the closing—a
demonstration staged at City Hall while the mayor was hosting a conference of the New England Mayors' Association. Although SPI's board of
directors had voted against the protest, it was led by several SPI staff
members, and the mayor held SPI responsible.

    Just as in the case of the Sisters of Providence's disruption of his press
conference the previous fall, the mayor was again embarrassed publicly
and politically. He was made to look stingy and callous even though he
had honored the city's commitment through March. Twice burned and

twice made to look foolish, he was determined that there would be no third occasion. According to sources familiar with city hall, the mayor now resolved to deny both Open Pantry and SPI any control over the city's next initiative for the homeless. And yet there was one major problem: SPI still had allies in the state Department of Public Welfare who encouraged it to apply for funds to run both a permanent facility and an emergency shelter. Accordingly, the city administration, represented by the city councillor from the United Way and the Commissioner of Human Services, cut a deal with the SPI board. The city would not oppose SPI's proposal for a permanent shelter, but the city itself would apply for, and then run, the emergency shelter. The project was assigned to the Springfield Redevelopment Authority (SRA), which convened a policy board called the Coalition for the Homeless. Although the Council of Churches agreed to manage the shelter (*Morning Union*, December 3, 1985), the city took almost complete control through the SRA.

On December 1, 1985, the city opened its emergency shelter in an old city-owned building up the hill on Armory Street, well away from the downtown center. Even apart from location, the building was inadequate. In fact, a year earlier Open Pantry had turned the building down during its desperate search for an alternative soup-kitchen site. More serious problems arose because of the lack of trained personnel to operate the facility. Several scandals also emerged, involving drug sales, prostitution, and violence. These not only occurred within the shelter but occasionally involved the shelter's staff, several of whom were disciplined, with two dismissed.

In light of the winter's bleak experience, the city allowed the state grant to expire in May 1986. However, to avoid the closing problems of the previous year, the mayor ordered the shelter to remain open at least through June at the city's expense. Looking forward to the year ahead, the administration began to seek a way to relinquish the actual running of the shelter, while retaining overall control of the facility.

Meanwhile, SPI faced continued frustrations in attempting to open its own permanent shelter, as city officials repeatedly denied zoning variances and rejected sites chosen (*Morning Union*, November 19, 1986; December 6, 1986). Once again, however, SPI was offered a deal. If SPI would give the city control over the state grant for the permanent shelter, then the city would facilitate its opening and staff it with SPI's professionals. SPI's board of directors generally favored the arrangement; they realized that the city could delay them indefinitely. However, the SPI staff rebelled. They felt betrayed by the city and were unwilling to trade away control of their money. They interpreted the proposal as yet another attempt to coopt their advocacy role and lure them into an establishment-oriented coalition.

At this point, the city's various social service providers solidified their opposition to city hall by coalescing into a federation called the Fund for the Hungry and Homeless (FHH). This federation included SPI, the Housing Allowance Program (HAP; a group of social service professionals with subcontracts to administer the family shelter that SPI founded in 1983), and several smaller advocacy groups, the best known of which was ARISE. Because FHH mirrored SPI's change-oriented critical thrust, it was virtually cut off from city hall and major business interests. However, it was an acknowledged political force because of its access to state money, its virtual monopoly on professional social workers, and even its somewhat ambivalent backing by the Council of Churches.

Realizing that this cadre of activists could not be pacified, city political leaders responded with a coalition of their own and gave it a similar symbolic claim, calling it the Friends of the Homeless (FH). Although the public initiative for the coalition came from the president and executive director of the Community Council of Springfield—a private, nonprofit clearinghouse for Springfield social services—there was little doubt that it had the blessings of both the mayor and the executive director of Springfield Central.

The first objective of the FH was a systematic canvass of downtown businesses to raise $250,000 locally for a permanent shelter, thus obviating the need for the state funds whose access was controlled by SPI. The drive was conducted in conjunction with the Community Council and the Chamber of Commerce by a policy board with representatives from most of the organizations mentioned above, including the executive director of the Council of Churches. Given FH's ties to city hall and city hall's linkages to Springfield Central, it is not surprising that the money was quickly forthcoming, especially when the plan was to build the facility on the periphery of the downtown area rather than at its core. Certainly there was no delay in obtaining the necessary building permits (*Union-News*, August 25, 1987), and ground was broken for the new shelter in November 1987.

While awaiting completion of the structure, the city continued to bear the cost of the Armory Street shelter. However, the mayor remained at odds with Service Providers, Inc., and their already sour relations curdled once again when a SPI boardmember (and activist Protestant clergyman) appeared on the local television news to criticize the mayor's "delaying tactics" as an effort to subvert SPI's own permanent shelter (*Morning Union*, January 10, 1987). But the mayor was not alone in his estrangement from the minister; many political leaders saw him and his confederates as grandstanders. According to a journalist who monitored events closely:

There is a staged aspect to some of the clergy's actions. Their posturing produces some resentment from people, and that Rev. ——has one of the worst and biggest egos I've encountered on the city scene. (interview)

Of course, within limits, "staging" and "posturing" are natural and indispensable components of the political theater that surrounds most public policy. Political actors who ignore them are likely to find themselves quickly back in the political wings. One seasoned political official understood the battle between the minister and the mayor—and between SPI and city hall—and commented on it in straightforward political terms:

A lot of the clergy involved in the homeless issue were there for selfish reasons. In fact, we had to kick the shit out of the clergy to get anything done, although there were a few of them who tried to kick the shit out of us. (interview)

But even within SPI itself, this same minister had incurred the suspicion of some staff activists over deals he promoted with officials of the Springfield Redevelopment Authority and the Community Council. In some ways, the minister was a victim of his marginality as a Protestant among Catholics, a pastor among social workers, and the voice of an upper-middle-class congregation on a lower-class issue. However, on the latter point, it is worth noting the words of one of his church colleagues:

Basically, he's got a lot of Republicans out there, so the parishioners don't mind their pastor causing problems for Democrat politicians. (interview)

Meanwhile, Springfield's new unified and permanent shelter was close to completion. But it was one thing to build the shelter and quite another to staff it. Again, SPI was a powerful resource, and the new coalition sought its cooperation. Although some members of SPI's board of directors, including the minister himself, urged compliance, the bulk of both the board and the staff balked. They saw the Friends of the Homeless as another device to co-opt their opposition, to gain access to SPI's money, and to produce a consensual solution that would neither embarrass the mayor nor tap the city's budget. Further, SPI staff members objected to the particular social worker hired to supervise services for the Friends of the Homeless; she was now paid by the United Way but had previously been on the city payroll as director of its emergency shelter. SPI personnel were not alone in their recalcitrance, as other members of the Fund for the Hungry and Homeless also refused to fall into step and join the gathering ranks.

And yet one key organization did enlist in the new establishment coalition and agreed to assume operating responsibilities for the new shelter;

namely, Open Pantry, under the leadership of its sister-director. This was a major coup, both substantively and symbolically, for the city's political elite. Although more than one civic leader referred to the sister-director as an obstructionist, she continued to command respect across the entire political spectrum. As a Catholic religious, she alone conferred an indispensable legitimacy on the enterprise, one not even matched by the entire Council of Churches acting on behalf of the city's mainstream Protestantism.

It had been two years since the sister-director had embarrassed the mayor at his press conference, but time was not the only healing agent; the bishop played an important and characteristic role in reconciling the two protagonists. After waiting almost a full year for the bruises to subside, the bishop invited both to lunch. Despite the mayor's grim reluctance to attend, there was a general ventilation of feelings, and the bishop gently advised the sister on the virtues of political tact and timing. After yet another year, both the mayor and the sister-director were prepared to work together.

At this point, then, the sides were drawn between two broad phalanxes of concern and action on behalf of the homeless. *First*, the Fund for the Hungry and Homeless (FHH) continued to further the interest of Service Providers, Inc., in pursuing long-range responses to homelessness. It retained some money, a corps of social service professionals, and important credibility with the Massachusetts Department of Public Welfare. However, it had no building and little chance of securing a city license for a facility. Although several of its constituent organizations were founded by religious-based activists or with church money, the coalition had become almost completely secular. *Second*, the Friends of the Homeless was a coalescence of the city's established political and business leaders and several additional groups with a primary interest in short-term, emergency interventions. While it had little access to state money, it had conducted a successful local fund drive to provide generous funding for a new "unified" shelter to house various programs for the homeless. It had no ready source of social work professionals, but it did include experienced religious staff and volunteers associated with organizations such as the Council of Churches and the more important Open Pantry. These religious personnel also brought with them a symbolic imprimatur that helped to offset the establishment onus of the political and business elite behind the operation.

From the standpoint of city hall, the absence of SPI and FHH from its new coalition meant that a loose cannon was still on deck. In fact, two activists allied with FHH ran aggressive if unsuccessful campaigns for City Council in 1987, centering their platforms around a criticism of the city's housing policies. However, given the disparity in fiscal, political, and symbolic resources between the two coalitions, the more establishment-based Friends of the Homeless was the likely winner in any war of attrition. Once SPI spurned membership here, it faced a future as a peripheral watchdog and advocacy group. The city's short-term care for its homeless population will improve, but the more enduring problems of low-cost housing will remain. In fact, they may well worsen as Springfield's last remaining SRO hotel was virtually destroyed by fire just as plans were afoot to upgrade it and convert it into profitable condominiums.

HOMELESSNESS AS A TEST OF CHURCH AND STATE

It may be difficult for many to read the foregoing without hearing echoes of Thomas Jefferson's injunction to maintain a "wall of separation" between church and state in this country. But if Jefferson, Madison, and others envisioned a society in which there should be an absolute wall between religion and government, then Springfield's treatment of the homeless would appear to mark a flagrant exception. On the one hand, city authorities have curtailed and constrained the capacity of several religious groups from rendering important services, thus inhibiting "religious freedom." On the other hand, the city and the state have also cooperated with religious groups in dispensing services. Assistance in the form of grants and building facilities might be regarded as favoring religion generally or some religious groups at the expense of others; as such it may conjure up the image of a government-supported "religious establishment."

In fact, Springfield is much more the rule than the exception in these practices. There are both national legal and local political reasons why the practices have not been contested on church-state grounds. State agencies have long had the right to encroach upon religious free exercise on behalf of the public interest and public safety (cf. *Sherbert* v. *Verner*, 1963). The state now has even more license as a result of the "Scalia opinion" in the Supreme Court's recent decision against the use of peyote in Native American rites in Oregon (*Employment Division* v. *Smith*, 1990). Whether for weal or for woe, impingements on religious freedom are now less constrained than are possible religious establishments involving church-state cooperation. In fact, the federal government has a long history of aid to religious missions and religious agencies. As Bruce Nichols (1988) recently pointed out, perhaps the two most obdurate separationists among the founders—Jefferson and Madison—both approved such arrangements when they were presidents, and Jefferson approved aiding Catholic missions to American Indians only a year after writing the letter that enjoined the "wall."

Despite these ample precedents, such issues have left an ambiguous wake in moving through the courts. Nichols discerns no less than four

positions in the pertinent Supreme Court decisions and opinions, which
he summarizes this way:

> The first approach, the "no-aid" theory, strongly emphasizes the concept of
> a wall of separation between church and state. While this view has not been
> discarded, subsequent decisions have moved in different directions, particu-
> larly concerning cooperation in state-sponsored welfare services. Here a sec-
> ond approach, the "evenhandedness" theory, attempted to allow cooperation
> between church and state as long as no particular religion was favored. A
> strict concept of a wall of separation has been replaced with efforts to deter-
> mine a "floor" and a "ceiling" of acceptable church/state interaction. The third
> approach of the Court has been the idea of the "benevolent neutrality" of
> government toward religion. This represented a government stance that nei-
> ther advanced nor inhibited religion, and left room for "play in the joints"
> between the two religion clauses. Finally, the most recent of the Court's
> approaches is summarized in what is known as the Lemon test, after the 1971
> case *Lemon v. Kurtzman*. Incorporating elements of previous standards, the
> test is a three-part examination of the establishment questions in any given
> case. (Nichols 1988, p. 220)

Basically, the "Lemon" test asks whether any given arrangement has a
dominantly "secular purpose," a "primary secular effect," and avoids "entanglements" between government and religion. The three tests are invoked seriatim, and if the answer to even one is negative, the arrangement is judged unconstitutional. Actually, more recent cases (e.g., *Lynch
v. Donnelly*, 1984, concerning the Pawtucket crèche) have alluded to a
possible fourth test involving the actual "endorsement" of religion. But
none of these tests is crystalline, and it is easy to imagine some of the
uncertainties posed. It is also easy to imagine how Springfield's services to
the homeless would pass the muster. Although the city has supported
several religious agencies, in all cases both the "purpose" and the "primary effects" have appeared to be secular. And, far from seeking "entanglements," the mayor has moved in the opposite direction.

Even if these arrangements had violated one or more of the *Lemon*
tests, it is not at all clear that they would have been declared illegal. It is
ironic that, despite the centrality of the nation's courts and Constitution,
the legal process itself is often initiated by persons perceived as misan-
thropic marginals who are prepared to invest heavily in pursuing a point
of principle, or perhaps a grudge. Few such persons exist in the midst of
Springfield's city pride and civic piety; those that do tend to lack the resources to pursue such a matter through the courts.

One source of protection may have been the ecumenical cooperation
that characterized the homeless groups and covered their religious flanks.
Catholics and Protestants sat jointly on several boards and worked to-

gether as volunteers in several organizations. The sister-director's several programs operated at different times out of two different Congregational churches; her Open Pantry received emergency housing funds from both the Catholic chancery and the Episcopal cathedral. Indeed, the most significant religious division was not between Catholics and Protestants as such, but between those Catholics and Protestants who favored direct action and political confrontation with city hall and those who did not. The latter group included not only many Catholics and members of the liberal Protestant orbit of the Council of Churches but also several evangelical Protestant churches that continued to run their own shelters with little controversy or outside assistance. The most active clergy and laity have been from larger congregations with the financial resources to provide some of the services needed and the political security to confront city officials over city policies. The two most activist organizations, SPI and Open Pantry, were started with grants from churches. Churches have also provided building space and service volunteers, sometimes to groups working under other auspices, both secular as well as religious.

If local responses to homelessness involved neither constitutional dilemmas nor religious conflicts, they did pose a series of major political problems. From city hall's perspective, the religious response to homelessness was a mixed blessing with an attendant quandary. As always, there was much to be said for letting private organizations provide services that would otherwise tax city coffers. But if turning the problem over to the religious community meant saving money, it also meant losing control. Further, because religious resources alone were inadequate for dealing with the problem fully, one could predict a steady series of requests—then demands—for city help. Because fiscal liability without political power was unappealing, the city decided to assume command and relegate both the religious community and the professional service providers to secondary status. With the help of the downtown business community, it was prepared to assume the costs of dealing with the homeless if it could also dictate the policy.

Even so, there were complications. By and large, the religious activists refused to bow out or bow down. Seizing the moral high ground, they continued to make homelessness a front-page issue and maintained public pressure on the city to respond. Unlike the secular activists, who were largely social service professionals and could be accused of both political and economic self-interest, the religious clergy and laity had unimpeachable motives. The opposition could portray them as impractical or naive, but it could not attack their motives. However, not all religious groups responded—or were responded to—in the same way. The largely mainline Protestant Council of Churches and the Catholic Church provide two differing cases.

Earlier, we noted the irony that many of the storm clouds surrounding the issue of homelessness in Springfield during the early 1980s were seeded by the declining liberal Protestants through the Downtown Ministry project of the Council of Churches. But when the rains came, the Protestants themselves got wet. In many ways, the Downtown Ministry and its offspring, Service Providers, Inc., represented local liberal Protestantism's last sortie into political activism. As the decade wore on, the list of alienated and antagonized members of the city's elite grew. By the time the elite founded its own umbrella organization, the Council of Churches moved under it quickly.

By this juncture, only a few mainline Protestant pastors had retained their prophetic roles. In the phrase of Glock, Ringer, and Babbie (1967), most had opted more "to comfort [than] to challenge." As noted earlier, some justified their political retreat in terms of the separation of church and state, an interpretation that is more convenient than constitutional. Meanwhile, the executive directorship of the Council of Churches itself had passed into and through more ameliorative hands. By the late 1980s, the council had undergone a major shift from provocateur to mediator, and it justified joining the Friends of the Homeless in order to adjudicate the group's continuing dispute with the SPI-dominated Fund for the Hungry and Homeless. As one staff member described the change:

> The churches are deliberately moving out of confrontational politics and into insider politics. They want to move in with the power types and work from the inside. We want to keep a lower profile so we can have more influence. All the same, Christianity locally is just a bunch of tired people. (interview)

Once again the specter of cooptation emerges. Perhaps predictably, the Council's mediation had little success, stemming more from weakness than from strength. Meanwhile, it continued to hold fund-raisers and to contribute emergency money to activities such as the Open Door day program. But city hall's decision to move forcefully on the issue—and the downtown business community's ability to raise $250,000 for a unified shelter—pushed the CCGS to the periphery. Like organizations such as SPI, HAP, and even Open Pantry, CCGS faced the choice of either joining the team or being relegated to the bleachers. It is a commentary on its somewhat loose and fragile federation that it had members who experienced both outcomes.

Not surprisingly, the situation was different for Catholics despite the ecumenism that described early responses to the problem. In dealing with any social issue in Springfield, protagonists and antagonists alike see themselves working in the looming shadow of "the Church." There is no denying Catholicism's moral and ecclesiastical presence. At the same time, it may wield as much influence through conditioned and stereotypic anticipations as through direct intercession. Often the other shoe that is yet to drop, it is frequently a shoe that need not drop at all.

From the Church's standpoint, this may be providential. As the Springfield diocese has grown over the years, it has become more variegated and less authoritatively monolithic. Even with regard to homelessness, there was diversity within the ranks. Clergy or religious who became involved had the implicit backing of the Church as a spiritual and institutional presence, but explicit support was more elusive. No parish took on homelessness as a special mission, and the priests of the diocese generally took a back seat to a small cadre of religious sisters as active participants.

This included the bishop himself, who was characteristically circumspect concerning homelessness. He avoided public involvement in controversial episodes, and he showed no signs of pursuing a prophetic role as moral entrepreneur or political troubleshooter. This is not to say that he was aloof or irrelevant; he was a member of the Mayor's Task Force on the Homeless, and while he attended relatively few sessions, another task force member indicated that he rationed his participation carefully and was virtually always present for major decisions. Then too, the bishop's periodic public statements on the deserving disadvantaged helped to shore up the community's overall sense of commitment while providing an encoded message of support to those Church members specifically involved, including lay politicians and the religious. The bishop stood behind—if well behind—the sister-director of Open Pantry in her embattled efforts on behalf of the homeless; and as we have seen, he played an important role in reconciling the sister with the mayor following their public contretemps.

Certainly, the Open Pantry's somewhat erroneous public image as a "Catholic" organization generated credit for "the Church." Indeed, one Protestant activist commented on the phenomenon with sardonic resignation:

> Sure, we get our noses out of joint when we provide the dollars and the bishop gets the credit. For example, in one shelter, we pay the staff, and the bishop put up a building that was vacant anyway. Our costs are higher, but he's the only one who makes the news. (interview)

The Catholic image of Open Pantry also afforded it considerable political protection. Although the Open Pantry has had six different locations in Springfield and was clearly maneuvered out of the central downtown business area, the city went out of its way several times to ensure that the Pantry would survive despite the moves. While the sister-director was a frequent thorn in the side of the political-economic establishment, she too was protected by her religious status. That she finally won the battle, if not the war, was symbolized by the city's new permanent shelter and the choice of her own Open Pantry to operate it. To be sure, this entailed joining the more establishment-oriented Friends of the Homeless coalition, but her politics were even more local than most. She consistently welcomed resources from all comers, just as she never hesitated to bite the hand that was failing to feed her charges.

Overall, then, city-provided care for the homeless illustrates both the capabilities and the limitations of religion's influence. Much of the result turns on the kinds of resources religious groups command as social movements. We shall treat this topic in more detail at the end of Chapter Six, to follow. However, it is worth noting here that several religious organizations had the money, the motivated volunteers, and the space to provide services that the city had eschewed. They were also able to use these resources to initiate and support a challenge to current sociopolitical arrangements. But here one additional resource was critical; namely, religion's moral legitimacy in calling for a response to injustice or human need. Because religious figures laid claim to public attention while transcending public criticism, they focused considerable pressure on the city government. Ultimately, both the religious leaders and the professional service providers were too marginal to the city's political economy to dictate the terms for resolving the issues, and they were forced to choose between going along or being left behind. However, the very fact that the city felt compelled to produce a solution at all is a tribute to the organizational and cultural resources of religious groups and activists.

Of course, all of the foregoing involves only one episode in one city, even though we shall find common themes in the two chapters to follow involving black-neighborhood development and controversies concerning sexuality. But these all concern broader questions of religion and power, and now that we have provided a glimpse of how they interact, we want to pause for a somewhat broader review of how others have depicted them. Put more pointedly, how does the scholarly literature help us to understand Springfield, and more important, where does Springfield provoke additions to that literature?

RELIGIOUS INFLUENCE AND CULTURAL POWER IN THE SCHOLARLY FRAY

By and large, previous work on religion and community circumvents questions of power, whereas prior research on community power waves a dismissive hand at religion. There are really two literatures here, and because they so rarely intersect, this suggests the same for the two spheres in question; namely, religion and power. And yet the suggestion is misleading. As the struggle over homelessness has just illustrated, religion can play an important political role in a city such as Springfield.

While religion is not politically dominant, it is not as politically impotent [7]
as earlier scholarship might indicate. In fact, the lessons to be learned
from that scholarship may reveal more about its own underlying assumptions than about the basic phenomena at issue.

Part of the problem lies with the reigning motifs in research on religion.
Over the past quarter-century, studies of religion have been preoccupied
with patterns of individual religiosity within conventional churches and
unconventional sects, often using surveys and demographic data. Corre-
lates such as age, gender, education, and socioeconomic status have important implications for potential religious power, or the lack of it, but
only seldom have they been drawn out and examined directly. More a
social psychology than sociology of religion, the chief unit of analysis has
been the individual adherent, and the operative social context has been
the denomination rather than the community or city at large. While there
have been several studies that have argued the case for religion's continuing influence in urban and community contexts, often their macro-
concerns have been subverted by their micro-methods. Both Gerhard
Lenski's classic *The Religious Factor* (1961) and the more recent restudy
of "Middletown" (*All Faithful People*) by Caplow, Bahr, and Chadwick *good point*
(1983) extrapolate from social surveys to social power without examining
the intervening social processes.

In fact, the role of religion in the community has tended to fall between
a concern with the individual and the parish, on the one hand, and a some-
what different order of concern with the larger culture, on the other.
There is a noble, even exalted, tradition that describes the importance of
American religion as a national cultural force and integrative mechanism.
This ranges from the classic observations of Alexis de Tocqueville (1848),
through the insights on "civil religion" of his contemporary heir Robert
Bellah (1967), to the various analyses of Varenne (1977), Wilson (1979),
Dunn (1984), and Reichley (1985). Bellah's more recent works, including
Habits of the Heart (Bellah et al. 1985), tend more to lament religion's
failure to fulfill its potential than to celebrate its centrality, a theme shared
with other cultural critics such as Daniel Bell (1976).

There is a long series of studies of religion in urban and community
contexts that has stressed religion's cultural salience in this context. These
include Liston Pope's work (1942) on Gastonia, North Carolina, and its
subsequent restudy by Earle, Knudsen, and Shriver (1976); Underwood's
book (1957) on Holyoke, Massachusetts; Vidich and Bensman's work
(1968) on "Springdale," New York; Baltzell's work (1979) on historic Boston versus Philadelphia; Caplow, Bahr, and Chadwick's restudy (1983) of
"Middletown" by Lynd and Lynd (1929, 1937); and Roozen, McKinney,
and Carroll's analysis (1984) of religious congregations in Hartford, Connecticut. But overall this literature pays remarkably little attention to reli-

gious power in the setting of the community; indeed, with the notable exception of Liston Pope's classic (1942), powerlessness is implicit throughout.

Once again, this may say more about where one has looked than what is to be found. Investigations of religion's role in a community or urban setting tend to begin and end with the congregation as the presumably critical unit. But as the religious landscape is increasingly differentiated, congregations have tended to turn inward so as to provide insulated support and solace for their members. As Robert Wuthnow (1988) has pointed out, other religious agencies have emerged to confront the community and its problems. He describes these special-purpose groups this way:

> Their causes range from nuclear arms to liturgical renewal, from gender equality to cult surveillance, from healing ministries to evangelism. They address issues both specific to the churches and of more general concern to the broader society. Yet they are clearly rooted in the religious realm. They take their legitimating slogans from religious creeds. And they draw their organizational resources, leadership, and personnel largely from churches and ecclesiastical agencies. . . . At the same time that the significance of denominationalism appears in many ways to be declining, then, these kinds of special purpose groups seem to be gaining importance in American religion. Students of American religion have generally paid little attention to these kinds of organizations, relative to the extraordinary interest that has been devoted to churches and denominations. But . . . the growth of special purpose groups constitutes a significant form of social restructuring in American religion. (pp. 100–101)

Wuthnow emphasizes the groups' role in animating and energizing more conventional religious forms, but he is also keenly aware of their wider political implications, including their pertinence for church and state:

> Despite a formal wall of separation between church and state . . . a growing mass of religious organizations has come into being with the state very much a part of their secular objectives. Like the secular world, where a growing number of nonprofit organizations have been founded to deal with governmental issues, the world of the sacred appears to have responded to the expanded character of the American state, either directly, or in ways as indirect as the titles by which special purpose groups choose to be known. (ibid., pp. 117–118)

Surely this squares with the Springfield case. Religion is indeed a source of community power and persuasion, but the direct activism comes from such special-purpose groups as the Downtown Ministry and Open Pantry rather than such conventional congregational or ecclesiastical structures as the Episcopal Church, whose own effort in the area was quickly faced down by the city. Attention to these newer religious forms has considerable potential as a corrective to prior scholarship on religion.

On the other hand, the literature on power and community has problems of its own. The nature of community power has been a concern of the social sciences since the 1920s, although its derived cliché, "community power structure," stems from the 1950s. Certainly the central problem has endured: Which individuals and groups are best able to shape civic arrangements in accord with their own best interests and/or the interests of those they serve? The long skein of provocative research includes studies by Hunter (1953), Mills (1956), Dahl (1961), Polsby (1963), Banfield and Wilson (1963), Rose (1967), Ladd (1972), Domhoff (1978, 1980), Whitt (1982), Clark and Ferguson (1983), and Waste (1986). Despite the divisions among these scholars, they appear united in an unspoken consensus that religion itself is not worth more than an occasional footnote to the power saga. No doubt this is partly due to their own secularity and to the conception of a weak and marginalized religious system that they shared with most of their fellow social scientists. But it is also an artifact of a deeper problem within the analysis of power: a bias in favor of strong structural components that give little credence to cultural agencies of any sort.

Scholarship on community power has been overwhelmingly "structural" in two senses. First, academic studies have focused on the stability and efficacy of political power over time—the patterned interactions and events that are the essence of "social structures." Second and more germane to our interests here, the sources of stable power have been found in so-called "structural" arrangements; that is, the institutionalized patterns of participation and persuasion in electoral politics, the interlocking interests, funds, and board members of the corporate community, and the various networks and coalitions that link political and economic leaders to each other. Such is the stuff of power structures, power elites, and power struggles—to cite but a few of the phrases that have echoed through this literature. The result has been a useful perspective fomenting a rich tradition of research and a lively series of debates, which have turned principally around the degree to which power is concentrated in the hands of a small and stable "elite" versus a series of shifting and "pluralistic" coalitions.

Unfortunately, power has been so identified with this analytic focus that alternative formulations have been stifled. The absorption with overt behavior, deliberate decisionmaking, public expressions of conflict, interest-group politics, and formal organizations has produced an overly narrow extension of Max Weber's classic conception of power (cf. Clegg 1975). Power is found only where it can be demonstrated that A was able to achieve his or her will against the intentional and manifest resistance of

B (or, in Dahl's terms, when "A . . . can get B to do something that B would not otherwise do"; 1957, p. 202). An assessment of power thus defined requires, first, an expression of intentions by *A*; second, an evaluation of what *B* would have done otherwise; and third, an observable outcome, whether a decision was made or an action taken.

But all is not static. As Stephen Lukes (1974) has pointed out, this "one-dimensional" viewpoint has spawned a supplementary perspective of broader scope. As typified by Bachrach and Baratz (1962), a "two-dimensional" conception attempts to account for *nondecisions* made in the face of perceived power as well as overt decisionmaking. In addition to actual issues, this requires identifying *potential* issues, which non–decisionmaking keeps from realization. Hence, nondecisions become decisions in their own right to be explained in terms of observable and articulated interests.

This marks an advance to be sure, but as much as the one- and two-dimensional images differ over the issues to be considered, they share an emphasis on observable conflict and the behavior that it produces. These premises ground most common conceptions of power and underlie some of the key debates within the power structure literature. They may also help to explain why that tradition has been relatively fallow of late, following a major surge of interest in the 1950s and 1960s. William Gamson (1968) noted that, for all their disagreements, both the pluralists (e.g., Dahl 1961; Polsby 1963; Rose 1967) and the elitists (e.g., Hunter 1953; Mills 1956) relied on similar conceptions of power and criteria for assessing it; namely, the ability of an actor or actors to achieve desired outcomes against resistance, as measured in policy decisions. Indeed, William Domhoff (1986) has dismissed the entire debate over the "faces of power" as a dispute among pluralists with at best a diluted sense of elitism. On the other hand, even the pluralists offered far from a grass-roots model; they did not deny the existence of elites, only their number and constancy.

Partly for these reasons, Aiken and Mott (1970, pp. 193–200) helped lay the traditional elitist-pluralist debate to rest by noting that the specifics of their respective research methods (e.g., positional, reputational, or participatory) were the most powerful predictors of their results. And in a recent critique of theories of the state, Alford and Friedland (1985) demonstrated that the concepts of "state" and "power" in pluralist, managerial (elitist), or class (Marxian) theory depend upon the underlying worldviews and theoretical "home domains" of the paradigms. They noted that each of the major research traditions uses "power" in a different manner: pluralists use power as "influence"; the managerial approach uses power as "domination"; and the class perspective regards power as "hegemony" (1985, p. 30).

The one- and two-dimensional views of power have thus relied upon criteria for assessing power that are formalist, behaviorist, and public; they have reinforced an individualist, rather than a systemic, model of politics. More important, the model *assumes* several things that should be problematic. Chief among these is the creation of the public agenda itself. The community power tradition generally ignores how issues become public, what forms they take when they do become public, and what terms of discourse frame the debate. Too often analysis is grounded in an overly simple and formal conception of social "structure." The symbolism, legitimation, and meaning-creation that are crucial to the construction of a political "order" are slighted for the "objective," structural evidence of overt decision making.

There is one research tradition that does focus on political culture. Led by Almond and Verba's work on "the civic culture" (1965, 1980; cf. also Devine 1972), this explores a nonstructural side to political order. However, it emphasizes individual rather than institutional ideas, beliefs, and values, and it stresses the degree to which persons develop an efficacious sense of "political self." This genre does not explore broader cultural "strategies of action" (Swidler 1986) that define what *is* the political, what "styles" of political behavior are legitimate, and what political outcomes are desirable. In defining culture as an aggregate of individual survey responses, it gives short shrift to the social creation of culture. The culturally constrained interaction among community forces and organizations receives scant attention, and the issue of power itself is largely ignored.

But how is power best dealt with and conceptualized? Earlier we noted Stephen Lukes' one- and two-dimensional perspectives and their limitations. As it happens, Lukes has offered a *third* dimension that is more promising. Here, he has included (a) control over the political agenda as well as decisionmaking; (b) issues and potential issues; and (c) observable (overt or covert) and latent conflict (1974, p. 25). In jettisoning the behaviorist criteria of intentionality, articulated resistance, and observable outcomes, this expanded conception emphasizes how social forces and institutional practices may keep potential issues *out* of public politics, and it allows culture and cultural agencies to play a role in shaping and defining issues if and when they become public. Lukes himself has highlighted such cultural concepts as political socialization and "false consciousness" in establishing political demands and separating "subjective" from "real" interests. This relates clearly to the domain of "critical theory" and its emphasis on the perpetuation of dominance through culture and ideology. But Wrong (1980) has noted that it is not always easy to distinguish between compliance due to "norm internalization," and thus generalized social control, and compliance due to power, with its ultimate implications of coercion. There is no question that the wielders of power often use cultural weapons in the process. But this is only one part of our larger concern with "cultural power."

Cultural Power Introduced

For us, cultural power is the capacity to use cultural resources to affect political outcomes. These resources include symbols, ideologies, moral authority, and cultural meanings. They can be used to legitimate or delegitimate both arguments and actors, to keep some issues public and others out of the public eye altogether, and to frame the discussion of those issues that become public. Finally, cultural resources can be used by those who seek power, those who seek to influence power, or those who seek to maintain and wield power with all of its prerogatives.

At one level, the phrase "cultural power" seems oxymoronic. The two terms conjure up discordant genres of social analysis—one soft, the other hard; one persuasive, the other coercive; one accretive, the other more abrupt. Of course, this very juxtaposition underscores the notion's utility. The combination gives the concept a breadth that spans different schools of analysis and different methods for both exerting and studying power. At the same time, such breadth requires delimitation, lest the part be confused with the whole.

Of course, cultural power is not the only power wielded by cultural institutions or agencies; nor is it restricted to them. Moreover, institutions often thought of as cultural—for example, organized religion, newspapers and other media, and many voluntary organizations—also have structural bases of power. They own property; they have members who can be mobilized; they have contacts with networks of influential community actors; and they often operate subsidiary institutions such as schools and hospitals. But as important as these structural resources may be, they are rarely sufficient to tip the balance in a contest with more conventional political forces. If cultural agencies are to exert significant influence, they must generally invoke their cultural resources. Their access to symbols, ideologies, and the moral high ground can provide a political purchase that reaches far beyond their structural instrumentality. This efficacy is *not* simply due to influence over the beliefs and values of individuals acting in the political arena (as the "norms and values" studies of the "civic culture" idiom would have it); rather, their cultural repertoire has a unique legitimacy—both nationally and locally—that gives it an impact of its own. While such influence is occasionally translated into conventional political terms as a card to be played in the next election or a key to other structural resources, the influence can also have a more direct impact on political institutions and decisionmakers by immediately mobilizing community sentiments and forces regarding a particular issue. Whether used directly or indirectly, cultural power can have effects far beyond what a conventional political metric would anticipate.

In fact, *all* institutions and organizations have *both* structural and cul- ✓ tural resources at their potential disposal. Certainly this is true of the major political forces contending in the urban ring, whether in the mayor's office, the downtown business community, labor unions, political organizations, or, indeed, religious groups. Because of this, it is tempting to reduce organized religion to simply another interest group and one whose pursuit of power is commonly episodic, even diffident. Most religious groups have only a limited political agenda restricted to a few specific issues. But when religious groups do become exercised and enter the fray, they offer a kind of critical test of cultural power precisely because their structural resources tend to be so limited and poorly focused. — *true is a* *variable .*

Springfield is by no means the only context in which religious groups have used their cultural power to appreciable effect; nor are we the only observers to chronicle the process. Certainly our survey is not alone among attitude studies showing that many citizens accord religion considerable deference and a proper place in secular politics; the sentiment even has some currency among those who are not themselves overtly religious in either belief or behavior. The British sociologist James Beckford speaks of religion as having a "moral power" that can mobilize large numbers of lay persons in pursuit of a political agenda that provides "specific and categorical notions of right and wrong in all spheres of everyday life" (1983, p. 24). Meredith McGuire discusses religion's contribution to the legitimation of power, and notes that "religious language" is a key element, since ritual and metaphor can "bridge between meanings in the spiritual realm and those in social, political and economic realms" (1983, p. 6). Of course, it is true that religious groups often use this cultural legitimacy in support of the community's status quo (cf. Pope 1942). But this same process can also be used to legitimate a *challenge* to the established order and its representatives. Here, too, it can be very persuasive indeed.

American cultural history is clotted with instances of cultural power, including the cultural power of religious groups on issues ranging from temperance, abolition, and prohibition to the civil rights and antiwar movements. While the overall influence of specifically religious and cultural institutions may be declining in an increasingly secularized and differentiated political economy, special-purpose religious movements have exerted important bursts of political influence even as the conventional churches have moved to the margins of the power structure.

In fact, we use the term "movements" advisedly. Much of the limited literature on religion and power focuses on mainstream religious institutions whose higher-status parishioners offer more individualized access to political influence. But as Wuthnow (1988) has pointed out, many of the most politically effective religious groups are far less congealed and conventional, and their memberships are both more fluid and less establishment-oriented. Whether associated with the Moral Majority on the right flank or with the tradition addressing economic rights, civil liberties, and pacifism on the left, these are more accurately depicted as "social movements" than either churches or, for that matter, sects. As noted earlier, we shall have more to say about such movements toward the end of the next chapter.

SUMMARY

This chapter began with a political ethnography concerning the issue of homelessness in Springfield. It charted the roles of both insiders and outsiders in the development of a political-economic infrastructure that would confront the needs of the homeless and reduce the tensions that make the problem a community issue. As a case study in church-state relations, it indicated that religious groups can be an effective voice in civic policy decisionmaking—even where they do not violate constitutional boundaries. Put another way, religion exerts more power than the literature on community power would suggest, even though it poses fewer constitutional violations than First Amendment watchdogs might anticipate.

All of this provides a challenge to the existing literature on both religion and power. Social research on religion has generally eschewed the power problem while giving primacy to religion's more social-psychological aspects in the context of its more conventional institutional forms. Conversely, research on power reflects a marginalized conception of religion as at best a weak protagonist in the arena of secular decisionmaking. This is partly so because there is a limited perspective on power itself and a tendency to restrict attention to its "structural" as opposed to its "cultural" facets. In developing a conception of cultural power that includes but is not limited to religious groups, we want to broaden the conception of both religion and the community power struggle.

The main evidence for religion's cultural power in this case is the "asterness" of the one exec. dir., hardly a solid evidentiary base.

Chapter Six

A COVENANT IN THE CRUCIBLE OF RACE

IT WAS A RESIDENT of a small hill town not far from Springfield—the poet Archibald MacLeish—who once remarked that "there are two classes of people: those who divide people into classes and those who do not." Sociologists and Springfielders both fall into the former category. As much as the city's residents might idealize its civic institutions, only a minority portray the community in completely egalitarian terms. Indeed, when asked their reactions to the statement, "In Springfield, people from different backgrounds basically get along as equals," only 26 percent of the general sample either "agreed" or "strongly agreed." While there was more overall agreement, albeit lukewarm, than outright disagreement, it seems clear that perceptions of community stratification are themselves divided.

We pursued the matter in our interviews, asking respondents to identify the most important sources of division in the community. Class was mentioned prominently, and in the socioeconomic rather than the MacLeishian sense. According to one former mayor: "Class is more important than religion or race. Look at the tension between the Irish who've made it versus the working-class Irish" (interview). And according to a liberal Protestant pastor: "The biggest cleavage is economic, and the major issue for the future is the disappearing middle class. Soon it's just going to be the haves versus the have-nots" (interview).

Like most cities, Springfield has taken major hits from suburbanization, and many of its remaining residents share the sense of manning a listing ship. Two decades ago, the suburbs were seen as Protestant havens, residential refuges of a business class that could no longer control a city politics dominated by Catholic Democrats. But the suburbs now have significant Catholic and Jewish populations and are marked more by economic class and race than by either religion or ethnicity. One former mayor, recalled an agreement he had reached with one of the city's largest employers that, henceforth, its newly hired executives would live in the city: "But, of course, they didn't." Still another former mayor noted that suburbanization was considerably boosted when the city dropped its requirement that city employees had to be city residents.

Despite its residents' flights to the suburbs, Springfield has fared better than some other New England cities. And while our general sample ran the full gamut of income, educational attainment, and occupational prestige, respondents clustered in the middle when asked to assess their own social class. Some 55 percent thought of themselves as "middle class," while another 41 percent considered themselves "working class"; only 2 percent each identified with the upper and lower classes—again evidence that the city's press toward consensus runs counter to its actual diversity, although our survey sample underrepresented the bottom end of the socioeconomic scale (as compared to census figures) and therefore provided an artificially low estimate of the lower class.

There is no question that economic distinctions cut deeply into the community. Both census data and our survey responses show considerable overlap between the cleavages reflected in household income, educational attainment, and occupational status. Changing the unit of analysis from individuals to neighborhoods sharpens the portrait. Table 6.1 offers strong testimony to the way in which class segregates the community. Median family incomes range from a 1988 high of $21,361 in East Forest Park to a low of $5995 in the North End; these same two neighborhoods frame the range of percentage of families below poverty level at 3.6 percent and 57.4 percent respectively. Similar spreads are apparent with respect to unemployment and to the percentages graduating at least from high school. Clearly these several dimensions of class are interrelated; for example, the best predictor of median family income by neighborhood is the percentage of high school graduates in the neighborhood.

As important as these socioeconomic distinctions are in a city such as Springfield, their wounds may be either salved or infected in relation to other sources of division, including the invidiousness of ethnicity, race, and religion. Table 6.1 provides more than a hint of this in its data on the percentages of whites, blacks, and Hispanics in each neighborhood. The percentages of whites range from a high of 97.9 percent in East Forest Park to a low of 10 percent in Old Hill. Correspondingly, the percentages of blacks range from 83.6 percent in Bay to 0.8 percent in East Springfield, while the percentages of Hispanics range from only 0.5 percent in East Forest Park to fully 67 percent in the North End.

Of course, it is no surprise that race is a major source of segregation in any American city, and we shall turn to it shortly as a major focus of this chapter. However, ethnic differences among whites alone have been sources of almost castelike isolation and insulation in Springfield. A local journalist covering the political scene said: "The first question I always ask is 'Who's Irish?' " (interview). And there are many, including significant numbers of our interviewees, who see ethnicity as even more divisive than class.

ETHNORACISM IN THE SPRINGFIELD EXPERIENCE

Earlier chapters have provided abundant evidence that ethnic conflict is one of Springfield's primary historical motifs, especially that resulting from the changing relations between the old Yankees and the new Irish.

TABLE 6.1
Springfield's Neighborhoods Described in Socioeconomic Terms

Neighborhood	Median Family Income	% White	% Black	% Hispanic	% Family Poverty	% High School Graduates	% Unemployed
East Forest Park	$21,361	97.9	1.4	0.5	3.6	78.8	3.3
Sixteen Acres	20,143	87.5	10.5	1.3	6.2	78.2	4.5
East Springfield	19,136	97.8	0.8	1.0	7.7	64.5	6.7
Forest Park	18,185	96.2	1.2	2.0	10.3	70.6	5.8
Hungry Hill (Liberty Hgts)	17,640	89.2	2.8	7.7	11.0	60.2	6.9
Pine Point	16,934	74.8	22.0	2.8	10.8	64.6	5.5
Indian Orchard	16,498	90.8	5.7	3.2	15.3	51.2	8.5
Boston Road	15,484	89.8	7.6	2.0	5.9	57.4	7.2
Upper Hill (WS)*	15,115	40.0	57.5	2.0	17.8	59.6	9.4
McKnight (WS)*	12,959	23.6	66.8	8.7	26.2	60.1	13.5
Bay (WS)*	11,266	10.0	83.6	6.2	30.6	52.2	9.7
Old Hill (WS)*	10,662	11.6	74.1	13.8	27.5	44.6	11.0
South End	10,000	68.7	10.4	20.6	28.2	45.1	8.4
Downtown (Metro Center)	9,794	73.8	15.1	10.2	28.7	59.8	8.4
Six Corners	9,298	49.0	31.0	19.6	41.7	56.9	12.2
Brightwood	6,838	20.9	16.2	62.7	54.1	29.8	20.2
North End (Memorial Square)	5,995	29.1	3.6	67.0	57.4	32.0	19.6

Source: Data compiled by the Union-News, April 1988, from Springfield Planning Department documents and 1980 United States Census.

*(WS) = Neighborhoods composing the Winchester (Mason) Square area.

But the Irish were merely the first among unequals, and rivalries persist as the conflict among immigrant groups has given way to an uneasy coexistence among ethnic communities. One priest recalled an old Irish saying: "Never trust the French"—a major reason why Springfield's French residents have never had significant political representation despite their longtime status as the city's second-largest ethnic group, with almost 18 percent of the population. And as we noted in Chapter Two, a local historian recorded the same sentiments phrased slightly differently, but just as directly: "Do you want to know why the French are Republicans? Because the Irish are Democrats" (Burns 1976a, p. 28).

However, similar Irish enmity has been far less successful in stemming the political mobilization of the third-largest group, the Italians. According to one Italian politician, even their shared Catholicism provided all too little bonding:

> Just like the Irish Catholics were always identified more as Irish than as Catholic, I was always more Italian than Catholic. It was tough. There was a lot of discrimination. You were always seen as a Mafia suspect. But I was proud of my heritage and learned to fight hard for it. Listen, if I were Irish, I'd be king. I got the style they like. In fact, I remember one of them saying, "Too bad he's not Irish because he hates the same people we do." (interview)

As this suggests, suspicion has sometimes given way to grudging respect. Another Italian politician actually relished his reputation around the still predominantly Irish city hall as the "top wop." And since the 1970s, there have been important instances of ethnic cooperation and coalitions. The county sheriff has replaced his Irish grandmother as a major political kingmaker, and rather than conduct politics solely in the shadowy lair of Irish Hungry Hill, he now gives an annual picnic for political figures from all backgrounds. As one observer put it: "Attendance is mandatory. This isn't an old-time ethnic fete. It's more like a Noah's ark, where everybody buries their differences to get on board" (interview).

The ark metaphor may be especially apt in Springfield for African Americans and Hispanics, since one can imagine two—but only two—of each at the very end of the procession. Even this may be an overrepresentation. A Hispanic respondent recalled considering a candidacy for School Committee and exploring the possibility with a member of the city's elite, who responded: "There's already one minority candidate. Why would you want two?" (interview). In Springfield's version of urban "ethnoracial" relations (Eisinger 1980), there is a tendency to hold both Hispanics and African Americans at arm's length in the same "minority" category. Their representation in city politics has been disproportionately minimal. Despite their accounting for more than one quarter of the city's population, there has never been more than one "minority" member of the City Council or School Committee at any given time, and there is yet to be a Hispanic city councillor.

Part of the problem is that the two groups do not form a politically cohesive minority faction despite their common stereotyping by the majority. Although such a coalition has been a vision of a few leaders from both communities, it has been neither compelling nor consensual. One local black social worker noted that "There really isn't a civil rights movement here anymore. There really hasn't been a unified minority block ever since the Puerto Rican community began to speak up on its own" (interview). According to a long-prominent black civic leader: "There's not too much tension between the black and Hispanic communities. But then there's no romance either" (interview). And as a white liberal activist put it: "If the blacks and Hispanics united, they could really control things, but *they* keep 'em divided" (interview; italics added).

Of course *"they"* refers to the elite mentioned above by the prospective Hispanic School Committee candidate—the predominantly white Irish Catholics whose current position at the top of the city's political ladder redresses their previous grievances at the bottom of the social ladder. It is not that "they" have ignored blacks and Hispanics, but rather that majority politicians have often sought to mobilize minorities only for their own political purposes. As only one example, the current and multiterm state representative from Springfield's North End is a Greek American whose concern for the dominantly Hispanic community is assiduous. Several older observers have noted the similarity between the way white Catholic politicians court the black and Hispanic vote now and the way white Protestant political officials began wooing Catholic supporters in the 1920s. A Hispanic neighborhood leader described a change that occurred following a period of high tension in the mid-1970s:

> Before the riot in 1978, we were headed toward a real ghetto. But that scared city hall, and they began to take the North End seriously. The police and fire departments began to step up their recruiting efforts. Politicians started coming around. You could almost hear the mayor counting the votes. (interview)

But for all of the Hispanic alienation from the city's political system, Irish politicians have been far more successful with Hispanics than have Irish ecclesiastical leaders. Springfield has a history of gradually including ethnic political blocs, as any politician will pay heed to potential votes. The Roman Catholic Church, with its historical division into ethnic parishes dominated by an Irish ecclesiastical hierarchy, has been slower to adjust. A number of clergy joined in lamenting the Church's inadequate response, one that has sent many Hispanics into the embrace of Pentecostalists who conduct more aggressive ministries:

It's a problem for the Church to deal with the Hispanics. We've sent dozens of priests to learn Spanish, but it's one thing to learn the language and another thing to know the customs and the culture. One Hispanic kid became a priest, but he felt so isolated in the Church that he finally asked the bishop to let him go and work in Puerto Rico, and he's still there. (interview)

In fact, this priest was passed over twice for a parish of his own, both times in favor of Irish clergy. As of the mid-1980s, there were only two priests in the dioceses who spoke Spanish, and neither of them were regarded as "Spanish-speaking" in view of their French and Irish surnames. Hispanic Catholics were increasingly frustrated:

> The Church has had a hard time. We Hispanics tend to be young, poor, and devout, but you can't just take care of our souls anymore. Of course, whatever the Church gives to us creates problems with Irish, Italian, and middle-class members. In the midseventies, the diocese created Blessed Sacrament to get the Hispanics out of Sacred Heart, and then they transferred *all* the Spanish-surnamed to Blessed Sacrament. This really outraged many families. (interview)

While the Hispanic sense of being shunted aside is understandable, others have argued that what the community needed most was a distinctively Hispanic parish akin to those of long standing among the Irish, the Italians, and the French.

In many ways, the story of Springfield's Hispanic community has only recently begun. By contrast, the city's black community has deeper and more variegated roots. It spans both a small middle class and a large underclass that suffers from the lacerations of both racial and economic disadvantagement. It includes some families virtually indigenous to New England, others who arrived in the nineteenth century, and many who migrated to Springfield following World War II. According to one recently arrived black pastor:

> There's no difference between New England's indigenous blacks and whites. They hold their "Yankeeism" in common, and both tend to have an insider's viewpoint. (interview)

Actually, two of the city's largest black churches—St. John's Congregational and Third Baptist—both antedate the Civil War; the former has a considerable legacy of political activism, while the latter has been more traditionally otherworldly.

Race has an equally long legacy as a civic issue. On the one hand, there are the noble cases of the Underground Railway and John Brown's brief residence in Springfield in the 1850s; the integrationist Springfield Plan that was meant to reduce ethnoracial and religious tensions in the public schools of the 1940s; and school desegregation through busing in the early 1970s, arguably Massachusetts' single most successful such program. On the other hand, Springfield shares with virtually every other American city a historical record smudged with civil rights grievances and protests. These have been along both racial and religious lines, often intertwining the two. Both Catholic immigrants and southern black migrants had difficulty finding acceptance, and even employment, in the community. When the Ku Klux Klan held rallies on Springfield's outskirts in the 1920s, its themes were as much anti-Catholic as anti-black (cf. Jackson 1967). And every minority group has found it difficult to scale the walls of city government, at least initially.

Race and religion have remained intertwined. Although the definition of Springfield's "elite" has changed over the years, discrimination has not disappeared; nor has community consciousness of group identity and status. One respondent recalled the 1960s when the nearby Catholic women's school, Elms College, turned down a scholarship program for blacks on the grounds that its dormitories had "no single rooms"; Cardinal Cushing reached out from Boston to intervene indignantly. And even though Springfield's school desegregation went peacefully, a number of knowledgeable respondents reported a continuing "white flight" into the suburbs, into the new "Christian" schools, and into the older parochial schools. The syndrome was publicly deplored and rejected at the time of the busing plan by then Bishop Weldon, and it continues to be disavowed by even those administrators who would appear to gain from it. In the words of one former School Committee member, " 'White flight' is something everybody knows about but nobody talks about" (interview). Such flight was an important, if publicly unacknowledged, reason for pressing forward toward the building of the city's new Central High School. The group-relations situation was summed up awkwardly by a recent mayor when he remarked somewhat defensively: "Sure there's subtle discrimination against blacks, Hispanics, and Jews, but it's on ethnic, not religious, grounds" (interview).

There is no question that many white religious leaders have been involved in integrationist efforts, occasionally mounting ecumenical demonstrations of their support for the cause and for keeping the peace while pursuing it. On the first day of the city's school busing program in 1974, the Catholic bishop joined two locally prominent Protestant pastors—one black and one white—to march arm in arm down State Street in an attempt at moral suasion. But there is also no question that many have been frustrated by the difficulty of converting lofty symbols into something more concrete and enduring. According to one white Protestant minister: "I heard blatantly racist talk in the School Committee in the 1970s for the first time since I left the South a long time ago" (interview). And following

Winchester Square, with its boarded-up "shoppers' plaza" and the shell of the once-proud Indian Motocycle plant in the background—1986.

the celebration of Springfield's 350th anniversary in 1986, a well-known local Protestant wrote a letter objecting to the note of Irish and white ethnic triumphalism that penetrated the festivities:

> It is Blacks against whom American [churches] have grievously sinned, and if there is anyone who remains shut out of Springfield today, it is the Blacks. (private letter)

It is one thing to be "shut out" literally like the Quakers and the Baptists in the seventeenth and eighteenth centuries; it may be worse to be allowed in and then shut out in other ways like the Catholics in the nineteenth century and more recent migrants. For the most part, these tensions remain a buried subtext in the city's public rhetoric. While latent ethnoracial consciousness has often led to an "us" versus "them" mentality and has served as a major filter of city power, politicians have learned to treat the issue delicately, if at all. Candidates on winning ethnic tickets, whether Irish or Italian, are aware that this ethnic consciousness is an advantage even when it goes unmentioned. Many indulge the political luxury of offering rhetorical bromides on inclusion, knowing full well that it is in part the covert politics of exclusion that will elect them. Candidates whose ethnicity is stacked against them are often advised to seek an opportunity to "serve the whole community" instead of dividing it. Probing ethnoracial differences publicly from the perspective of either winners or losers is the stuff of both bad manners and bad politics, no matter how real the effects.

Finally, in addition to locating this chapter's case-study issue culturally, it is also worth locating it geographically. If the prevailing direction of national black migration has been south to north, it has been the reverse within Springfield. The city's North End has been the traditional point of ethnic entry, having been home at some point to the Irish, Jews, French, blacks, and currently Hispanics. In time, groups have fanned out into other parts of the community. Following the urban renewal of the 1960s and the arrival of increasing numbers of Hispanics, the primary black residential center moved south and east to an area known for years as Winchester Square. It is here that this chapter's central drama is concentrated—a confrontation between the city's elite and a small group of black clergy covenanted to pursue economic development for a neighborhood left moribund in the city's downtown revitalization.

A Ghetto on a Hill

Winchester Square lies sprawled across a rise overlooking the downtown center and its changing skyline. However marginal the square may be in social and economic terms, it lies at the city's geographic center. The area is home to the federal armory historical park, Springfield Technical Community College, American International College, and the now-defunct Indian Motocycle plant. It is bisected by State Street, the city's major east-west traffic artery and longtime route to Boston. But most traffic speeds through the square without stopping, because there is so little to stop for. Only a few businesses remain open among the boarded storefronts. The once-proud Hope Congregational Church has given way to the Shiloh Seventh-day Adventists; the building that formerly housed Holy Family Parish school is now an Evangelical Christian "academy."

As this suggests, the area has not always been downtrodden or dominantly black, although its defining plot was sold to the city in 1868 by a black businessman, Primus Mason. At the time, it formed the eastern edge of the city, and was known locally as "Hayti," with Mason himself often referred to as the "King of Hayti." However, the park within it was named for the white Charles Winchester, then Springfield's mayor. The term Winchester Square has since been generalized beyond the park and its immediate vicinity to embrace at least parts of five formally recognized neighborhoods that abut State street and the square itself: Bay, McKnight, Old Hill, Upper Hill, and Six Corners, as noted in Table 6.1. But now that the area has become a referent for the "black" section of the city, its boundaries are more emotional than ecological.

And yet it was only recently that the area's population returned full circle to its black roots. Forty years ago, the square was primarily an Irish-

Italian lower-middle-class area, with several pockets of black middle-class residents. A 1955 master's thesis described the main ethnic tensions in the area as being between Irish and Italians (Clough 1955, p. 60), but by then momentum was already building in a rapid ethnoracial and economic transition. Between 1930 and 1950 the poorest of the five neighborhood areas—portions of Old Hill and Upper Hill along the main State Street corridor—had a 1 percent decrease in total population but a 112 percent increase in black residents (Clough, 1955). And while a *Morning Union* article for April 4, 1959, entitled "Winchester Square Now an Active Shopping Center," described the square's bustling retail activity, this too was to change quickly. Just ten years later a prominent article in the same paper featured a city councillor deploring the rapid deterioration of the square and warning that it threatened to become an "economic wasteland" (*Morning Union*, October 17, 1969)—a phrase recently used by a more recent generation of black activists.

Between 1965 and 1980, approximately 2,000 families moved out of the five-neighborhood area surrounding the square. As we described in Chapter Two, the effect was as profound on the area's churches as on its business community, especially on Hope Congregational Church, which went from being the state's largest congregation in the early 1960s to disbandment in 1976.

There were other similar cases. For example, in 1973 the once-thriving and predominantly white First Presbyterian Church called its first black pastor; by 1980 it had become almost exclusively black and was renamed the Martin Luther King, Jr., Community Church. Nor did the historically strong Catholic parish, Holy Family, escape transition. In 1977, it was forced to close its parochial school after a declining parish population left it with a small pool of students, many of whom were unable to afford the newly instituted tuition. And yet Holy Family persisted as a reconfigured black parish, as did the area's Episcopal church. In fact, it is significant that the churches that did survive the transition were those with "episcopal" polities; that is, controlled by a central authority such as a bishop rather than by a locally autonomous laity. Both the Catholic and the Episcopal dioceses maintained commitments to the Winchester Square area that were in some measure independent of the local members and their declining resources (cf. Holstead 1982).

The politics of the square's redevelopment have been characterized more by promising hopes than by actual economic change. A series of bright starts have led to bleak disappointments and angry recriminations. For example, in 1982 the mayor appointed a commission to market the abandoned Indian Motocycle plant that looms over the main intersection of the square; Springfield's only black city councillor was made the commission's chair. Within a year, the councillor charged that city officials were "insincere" in their revitalization efforts. He noted that while the city's Community Development Commission never wavered in its support for downtown ventures, it used myriad problems as excuses to evade responsibility for the square (*Morning Union*, February 17, 1983).

As another instance, in 1983 a group of area residents formed the Winchester Square Concerned Citizens Group (WSCCG). Twenty-five families put up $2000 per family to underwrite development-grant applications and to act as a supporting organization for the Upper State Street Community Development Corporation (USSCDC), a nonprofit organization led by the area's state representative and focused on a series of projects around the square. The WSCCG was the main force behind the 1984 renovation of Midtown Plaza, a small shopping center in the heart of Winchester Square that has struggled fitfully and with high turnover ever since. But the WSCCG was also critical of the city government's lack of support, again singling out the Community Development Commission (*Morning Union*, June 30, 1983; *Valley Advocate*, July 13, 1983). Thus, for several decades there was a growing sentiment among black community leaders that the city had neglected their neighborhoods both politically and economically. In particular, many saw a striking contrast between city hall's enthusiastic backing of downtown development projects and its hollow gestures on behalf of the square.

CIVIC PRIORITIES AND PUBLIC OPINION

A key question in the study of political power is the extent to which decisions by political officials reflect opinions of the electorate. In terms of the relatively low priority given to Winchester Square and its economic redevelopment, there is ample evidence that the city's mainstream politicians were swimming with the current rather than against it. As part of our questionnaire survey, we asked our respondents to evaluate some eight priorities for city government, with answers ranging from "extremely important" to "important," "desirable," and, finally, "not a priority." Table 5.1 in the previous chapter summarized the results in terms of the percentages responding "extremely important" for each area.

Rather than reproduce the table here, it suffices to note that the development of Winchester Square scored lowest of the eight issues listed (20.7 percent), even though the survey was conducted at a time when the issue was very much in the local headlines. In addition to receiving the fewest "extremely important" responses as indicated, it also received the most mentions as "not a priority" (13 percent). Given the stigma of the politics of race in Springfield's political culture, it is not surprising that "aiding Blacks and Hispanics" should also be near the bottom of the priorities ranking (21.3 percent). Indeed, one measure of race's negative salience is the contrast between these two items and the more general "responding to the needs of the poor and disadvantaged," which ranked near the top of the priorities in third place, with 50.4 percent rating it extremely important. Clearly, adding the specter of race changes the issue from one that enjoys general community support to one with which many city residents want little involvement.

Economic development of Winchester Square is often juxtaposed politically with downtown business development. As we have already described, Winchester Square activists have consistently contrasted the city's cooperative attitude toward projects in the Metro Center with its political and bureaucratic foot-dragging concerning the square. While that may well be the case, Springfield's citizenry appear not to see the two issues aligned in this way. Downtown revitalization did not emerge as a high priority for city-government involvement for our sample; it was ranked sixth out of the eight priorities, with only 25.8 percent judging it extremely important.

Turning from the general sample to our more specific elite samples, Winchester Square continued to rank low. For example, the political-economic elite sample rated Winchester Square development next to last of the eight issues, essentially tied with "responding to the needs of Blacks and Hispanics." However, an interesting difference emerged when we separated those respondents included in the sample for their *political* connections from those respondents included for their *economic* standing. While 28 percent of the political leaders rated Winchester Square's development as "extremely important," this was true of only 11 percent of the economic elite; the political elite subsample rated Winchester Square development as the fifth-highest priority, while the economic elite rated it last. On the other hand, while 50 percent of the economic leaders rated downtown development as extremely important, this was true of only 31 percent of the political group. It is also interesting to note that this division between subsample ratings was larger for these two issues (Winchester Square and downtown development) than for any other pair. Clearly, Winchester Square was seen as a more important issue to those who were primarily concerned with the city's politics than it was to business leaders. This may have been a recognition that the square had emerged as primarily a political problem requiring political attention rather than an economic opportunity or necessity.

There was also variation among the religious leaders in our sample. Looking at the percentage answering "extremely important," Winchester Square development ranked next to last among the eight possibilities. But there was a difference between Catholic and non-Catholic clergy. Only 25 percent of the Catholic priests and sisters accorded Winchester Square development the highest priority rating, whereas 47 percent of the Protestant and Jewish clergy did so. It is true that 12 percent of the Protestant-

Jewish clergy group were black, but this is not in itself sufficient to account for the difference. Overall, the Protestant-Jewish subsample considered Winchester Square development the second-most-important priority, while Catholic clergy rated it last, and the only clergy to rate Winchester Square as "not a priority" were Catholic.

Public opinion can be both the cause and the consequence of political action. On the one hand, it can be a source of instigation or at least a reservoir of preexisting sentiment that politicians draw upon to bolster their positions and provide leverage for deal making. On the other hand, public opinion can also be the result of manipulation by politicians and political events. The foregoing pattern suggests that Winchester Square development had little preexisting citywide support to draw upon, and most politicians were neither eager nor effective in lending their leadership to the cause. As the situation developed, the concern expressed by the city's political elite seemed primarily reactive. Without the serious support of the community's business establishment, it was more of a gesture than a commitment.

The survey provides more support for this interpretation through a comparison of attitudes toward Winchester Square development with our earlier indexes of general civic idealism and specific political confidence in city hall. As we noted in Chapter Three, idealism of both sorts runs high within Springfield; the community is considered a good place to live, and its government is believed to be relatively honest and competent. In fact, there was a slight tendency for those who scored higher on either index to give *lower* priority to Winchester Square development. Thus, 14 percent of those scoring high on civic idealism judged Winchester Square development as "extremely important," but this was almost doubled by the 27 percent among those scoring low on the civic idealism index. Whereas only 13 percent of those scoring high on political confidence rated the square "extremely important," this rose to 22 percent among those scoring low on this second index.

Clearly, assisting Winchester Square was not high on the civic agenda by the mid-1980s, either as a political priority or as a general public concern. For some it was an unwelcome reminder of the downside of city life, a breach in the consensual faith in the community itself. For others, it was dismissable as a mere "neighborhood problem." While pledges to care for "the neighborhoods" are part of every city political campaign, programs targeting specific neighborhoods for special treatment can seem like an inappropriate intrusion into downtown civic politics. As one political observer noted: "City hall can lay off a lot of things to the neighborhoods, when you don't have a ward-based political system to fight back" (interview). And as our survey data imply, questions of neighborhood and race intermingled. A local journalist and practiced observer of the back-ward scene noted:

I've heard some people say that if you build up Winchester Square, where will the ghetto move to next? Some are worried that it'll be [the dominantly Irish] Hungry Hill. (interview)

But perhaps the most common framing of Winchester's Square's difficulties was as a "black problem." Blaming the blacks for the area's deterioration is consistent with Springfield's historical hostility to those lowest on the ethnoeconomic ladder (cf. Chapter Two) and is also part of the common urban syndrome of "blaming the victim" (Ryan 1971). Indeed, the very concept of blame may be a contributing factor in its own right. Time spent finding the "culprits" responsible for the square's deterioration was time not spent working on solutions. It was also a way for those politically responsible to get off the hook.

Thus, while volleys of prejudice have echoed through the area, and the general search for villains has reemerged periodically, an unintended and unacknowledged "institutional racism" may account for more of the square's intransigent economic difficulties. The city's changing political system, macro changes in the structure of the regional economy, and the history of local migratory patterns have each played significant roles. Yet even this fails to fully explain the complexities of the issue, since it portrays Springfield's black community in simplistic monolithic terms. The situation was more complicated, in the words of one black observer:

Winchester Square is not just a power struggle between downtown and the neighborhoods, or between whites and blacks. It's also a power struggle within the black community itself. (interview)

We shall see abundant evidence of all these sources of enmity and suspicion in the pages ahead—along with yet another important factor, religion. Meanwhile, it is clear that many Springfielders see Winchester Square as a "bad part of town," whose difficulties are doubly dismissable as problems of both neighborhood and race. To many of Springfield's white population, the arguments calling for city attention to the square's economic problems sounded like "another black demand for special consideration" (interview) in an area where both public and private investments had proved risky ventures with low payoffs. It was against this backdrop that religion and politics conspired to dramatize the strengths and weaknesses of each.

THE COVENANT AND THE SQUARE

Up through 1983, the political actions and recriminations concerning Winchester Square received scant attention in the press or on the hustings. But this was to change quickly as a new group of players joined the cast. Suddenly, debate about the square's economic fortunes was to blossom into a full-blown political issue, becoming enmeshed in local electoral races, city budget and administrative processes, and even the internal politics of the black community. This in itself was remarkable, for it occurred despite the low-profile preferences of a formidable coalition of the city administration, the dominant downtown businesses, and the newspapers. The explanation for this sudden prominence lay with a small group of predominantly black clergy, who began meeting in early 1984 and called themselves "the Covenant."

The clergy forming the Covenant all had congregations in the Winchester Square area, and they shared a deep frustration over the city's lack of response to the area's plight. Their objective was to use the concerted voice of the black religious leadership to draw attention to the structural problems underlying the neighborhood's economic distress, and to redirect some of the city administration's support from downtown development to the square:

> When we first met, we didn't want religion to be a doormat any longer, and we knew that if we protested solo, we'd be dismissed as self-righteous or as kooks. We also knew we had to be ecumenical, even though there were sure to be divisions; for example, between those who were theologically educated and those who weren't. (interview)

The group began with eleven members, but not all of Springfield's black churches were represented. In fact, the Covenant included few of the older, established black clergy, or those with Evangelical or Pentecostal congregations. A canvass of the Pastor's Council and the Ministerial Alliance—both organizations of black clergy—yielded only one new member. These two groups helped plan and sponsor such events as the Inter-Faith Thanksgiving Service, and they tended to avoid controversial issues. One pastor called them "watchdog agencies," but noted that they spent most of their time watching each other.

Variations in church polity also appeared important in determining involvement with the group. With the exception of one Congregationalist pastor, the most active members of the Covenant were from more episcopally organized denominations such as the Methodists, the Lutherans, and the Episcopalians themselves; that is, parishes operating under a higher ecclesiastical authority that often provides support for controversial programs and insulation from the constraining backlash of either laity or secular authorities. The pattern is by no means unique to Springfield; it was also a major characteristic of the white churches involved in the Southern civil rights movement (cf. Campbell and Pettigrew 1959; Wood and Zald 1966; Hadden 1969; McNamara 1969).

However, in 1985 a highly significant new member joined the Covenant from the prototypic episcopal polity. This was the newly appointed priest in charge of Holy Family Church, the only black priest in the Roman

Catholic diocese. A Springfield native, he had grown up in the Winchester Square neighborhood when it was predominately white. Beyond his personal assets as a bright and energetic advocate, his Catholicism provided the coalition with important new legitimacy. He carried the general authority and implicit approval of the most influential religious leader in the city, the bishop. City politicians could not interpret the priest's presence in the square as accidental, and the chancery made no public attempt to rein in his involvement with the Covenant. Local observers began to draw their own conclusions:

> Either Father has real connections in Rome, or the bishop actually wants him doing that. Otherwise, he would have been transferred over the hills to North Adams in a hurry. (interview)

Sources close to both the chancery and the parish reported that the relations between them remained positive throughout the strains that were to follow. According to one chancery official:

> Father is very able and gifted. We asked him to be in close contact with the black clergy up there. He's been a spokesman for the diocese, and a very effective one. We haven't had a call from anyone asking us to put pressure on him. (interview)

The reports from Holy Family were almost, but not quite, as affirmative:

> The bishop has never told Father to cool it, and whenever the mayor complains—and he has—the bishop tells him that this is Father's parish. On the other hand, he hasn't been very publicly supportive either. He only responds to the middle class, and his basic answer to Winchester Square is, "I put [Father] there." (interview)

Certainly, other members of the Covenant became quickly aware of the importance of a Catholic priest as teammate:

> We'd have been blown out of the water without him. He can get through to people we can't. He even demanded and got an apology from a city councillor who had insulted me. The guy turned wimpish on the spot, as if he'd been scolded by a parent. We who work in similar appointive systems know that priests aren't appointed indiscriminantly. He was part of a larger agenda. The bishop will be there when he's needed, but he won't fire a shot until it's a sure shot. Every time the papers are on the verge of tearing into the Covenant, there is some public ceremony when the Father, the bishop, and the mayor can be seen together. It helps, believe me. (interview)

Faith in the bishop's "sure shot" was to be sorely tested. The priest's participation was valuable, but it was no panacea. Most Covenant members were politically marginalized threefold as, first, clergy; second, predominantly black; and third, predominantly Protestant. It is true that a combination of race and religion can confer a moral martyrdom; in the words of one city councillor: "How the hell do you take on black ministers?" (interview). And yet martyrs are known more for losing than for winning, especially when they lack access to the direct levers of power. Certainly the Covenant members were outsiders, and they were made all the more so by an agenda characterized by structural challenges and incendiary rhetoric. One member of the Covenant summarized their argument this way:

> The city's refusal to develop up here amounts to economic racism pure and simple. We don't need more housing. We need small businesses, a skills center, seed money, block grants, and, most of all, a sense of priority from the city. We also need a good department store to pull back in some of the $20 million a year that the residents now spend elsewhere. And there are businesses that would come in, except that the downtown effort has shut them out. The Indian Motocycle building should have been taken down a long time ago. The whole community is held hostage to that hulk and to the few people that are trying to make money off of it. We also should have had the new high school located here as a cornerstone for the area. But the bottom line was getting "those raggedy kids" as far from downtown as possible, and the bishop made the mistake of supporting it. A lot of people now feel they're left with nothing up here, and some are really angry. (interview)

Some members of the business community agreed on some of the particulars. For example, one member of Springfield Central noted that the program to convert the Indian Motocycle building into condominiums was "the wrong project, at the wrong place, and at the wrong time. But . . . people in Boston got excited by it, and now they're caught in it" (interview).

Overall, however, the agenda challenged Springfield's basic political and economic arrangements and thus carried the potential stigma of radicalism. The Covenant realized its need for a theological rationale to justify its demands and legitimate its involvement in this seemingly secular arena. In order to transform economic issues into moral issues within the public consciousness, they drew on circulating drafts of what was to become the national Catholic bishops' 1987 pastoral letter on the economy. They also sought to forge a sociomoral linkage by pointing out that the square's crescendoing problems of drugs, teenage pregnancy, and crime could all be reduced through economic enhancement, with its jobs and family support. The Covenant's ideological work converted a theodicy into a sociodicy. While perhaps too rarefied for political slogans, newspaper headlines, and bumper stickers, this had at least an initial effect in

recruiting a number of ostensibly neutral onlookers within the community. It was also a major factor behind the official endorsement of the
board of directors of the Council of Churches of Greater Springfield, and
more important, the tacit approval of the Roman Catholic bishop.

There was some resistance to the political challenge by a segment of the
Covenant's parishioners. Development of Winchester Square was not the
highest city priority among our black survey respondents, although it did
rate second. Nonetheless, the Covenant clergy were operating within a
rich tradition. As a local black social worker commented, "In politics, the
churches are where it happens—at least among blacks" (interview). At one
City Council meeting, a Covenant member made the point explicitly by
invoking the hallowed image of the Rev. Martin Luther King, Jr., taking
his crusade into the streets as a political and economic struggle (*Morning
Union*, January 22, 1986). Of course, there is no more revered name in the
annals of American moral politics, and the Covenant sought the aura of
King's courage and charisma. But in addition to providing moral leadership, black clergy have had a long tradition as "ward heelers." Since alienating the Covenant risked alienating potential voters (both blacks and
white liberals), every city politician was obliged to maintain a posture of
public deference. Thus the civic leadership, which had devoted twenty
years to its own vision of Springfield's development, had a delicate task in
meeting this challenge. A duel was inevitable.

The gauntlet was thrown publicly on November 6, 1985. After more
than a year of shadow thrusting and parrying, the Covenant's media
broadside caught many in city politics off guard. It combined a critique of
the current economic and political status of the square with a call for a new
master plan of revitalization. It called the existing plan, lying dormant in
the city's planning department, "grossly flawed and deficient," and described the Upper State Street Community Development Corporation
(whose president was the black state representative from the Winchester
Square district) as unable "to engage in any competent and effective economic development planning or implementation" (*Morning Union*, November 7, 1985). Press conferences and press releases featured the kind
of heated charges that threatened to melt the constraints against an open
confrontation.

Privately, many of the city's elite gnashed their teeth and clenched
their fists, spoiling for a fight. One person within Springfield Central conveyed both the logic and the prejudice of many business leaders this way:

> Their arguments are all wrong; we'd blow them away in five minutes. There
> just isn't good planning for that district. The business community has taken
> a "Big Daddy" approach and written them checks, hoping they'll go away and
> without being involved hands-on. So they squander the money, as kids will.
> (interview)

But this was not the mayor's public tone or preference. Even then he was an unofficial candidate for the city's soon-to-be-vacated congressional seat, and he had amassed a campaign war chest of close to $200,000, raised through two mayoral campaigns that were essentially uncontested. The mayor's political style reflected Springfield's distaste for public controversy and its penchant for decorous consensus. His image depended upon his constant contact with the electorate, tirelessly attending ceremonies and meetings of every conceivable voluntary association, spanning the entire ethnic, racial, and religious gamut. As one rabbi remarked, only half in jest:

> He comes here constantly. In fact, he has a better attendance record than some of our members. You only have to call and tell him about a presentation and, boom, he's here. (interview)

The mayor was well known for his place in the Irish-Catholic Democratic succession, but he also had well-nurtured relationships in almost every other organized sector of the community. A politician who managed more through handshakes than brandished fists, the mayor preferred both his collars and his issues buttoned-down. At one point, when accused of breaking an agreement with the Covenant, he expressed "surprise" and claimed: "I spoke to a member of the Covenant last week who assured me that there would be no public comment on this" (*Morning Union*, December 10, 1985). In fact, public disagreement of any sort was risky. On the one hand, the mayor's political future would be greatly enhanced by the support of the city's minority groups; on the other hand, his future also depended upon the continued backing of the downtown elite, who would not look kindly on his "giving in" to the Covenant's pressure. Thus, while the Covenant's opening charges seemed to pick a fight, the mayor and his allies seemed to shy away from one, opting instead for coolly worded responses on the inappropriateness of carrying out this debate through the papers (e.g., *Morning Union*, December 5, 1985; December 10, 1985).

A first key element in the city's response to the Covenant was an emphasis on the putative civic consensus that so many politicians claimed as characteristic of Springfield. The objective was to keep the community's politics under control by stressing an assumed commonweal that would benefit everyone. According to this emphasis on a whole larger than the sum of its parts, city decision making was not a zero-sum proposition but a way of adding value to the totality. The effort was to deemphasize divisiveness of any sort, including rude reminders of historical injustices or gauche promotions of special-group interests. Working more by implication than accusation, the city administration hoped to persuade Springfielders that the black clergy of the Covenant were petty and self-interested grandstanders who insisted on dredging up the past rather than addressing the real problems of the present.

Ironically, a second major theme in the city's response to the Covenant involved one of the parts in the civic equation, namely, its neighborhoods. Residential patterns have long dominated Springfielders' sense of place, even if the city's self-described identity as the "city of homes" has gathered some dust. Longtime residents still think of themselves as coming from a particular neighborhood, and neighborhoods are identified in local terms by their ethnic composition. There are currently sixteen "recognized" neighborhoods, each with its own neighborhood council funded at least partly by the city itself. In 1985, the city's presentation in the national All-America City competition was centered on its neighborhoods (*Morning Union*, November 18, 1985). During the 350th anniversary year of 1986, the facade of City Hall was festooned by neighborhood banners. Virtually every election has been marked by expansive pledges to respond to neighborhood concerns and preserve the community's residential character.

Not surprisingly, however, Springfield's neighborhoods are highly disparate and defined less by location than by their ethnoracial and economic attributes. Recalling Table 6.1 presented earlier, only two of the sixteen recognized neighborhoods have less than two thirds of their residents from one ethnoracial group (white, black, Hispanic); seven have fully 80 percent of their residents from just one group. Thus, generalized pledges to "the neighborhoods" play on a cultural image of community that is often wide of reality. When resources are scarce, the game often becomes zero-sum despite its rhetoric. Where Winchester Square is concerned, an emphasis on neighborhoods has frequently pitted the one against the many.

The irony of having a neighborhood focus is underscored further by the city's recently relentless policy of developing the downtown area. Several successive city administrations actually used the neighborhood theme to justify the downtown emphasis. The current mayor frequently invoked a slight variation on the theme:

> It's not downtown versus the neighborhoods of Springfield; it's downtown *and* the neighborhoods. But most importantly, downtown is everybody's neighborhood. (Konig 1986, p. 47)

However, the new downtown area is no longer a retail or small business center geared to the city and its residents alone. As it has become a regional center of banking, insurance, finance, and convention business, city residents have tended to stay away and shop increasingly in the suburban malls.

Concomitantly, the neighborhood councils have seen a decrease in both their city funding and their civic influence. This was partly due to the Reagan administration's preference for block grants, which put city neighborhoods into competition with each other for federal funding. But critics have also noted city hall's declining commitment to the neighborhoods overall (e.g., Catabia 1979). Several city budgets contained cuts for the neighborhood councils, although the mayor restored some monies in response to protests (cf. *Morning Union*, October 30, 1984; June 5, 1986; and April 21, 1987).

Meanwhile, a third city hall response to political challengers like the Covenant was to present city decisionmaking as a matter of technical problem solving that emphasizes expertise rather than political or economic interests. In his classic work *Ideology and Utopia*, Karl Mannheim once suggested that "The fundamental tendency of all bureaucratic thought is to turn all problems of politics into problems of administration" (Mannheim 1936, p. 118). The mayor echoed the point in his frequent remark that "There's no Democrat or Republican way to collect the garbage." In fact, there was a good deal of political dispute over the delivery of city services. But the mayor sought to cast the legitimate alternatives solely in terms of existing political parties, while setting boundaries around perspectives that were "rational" as opposed to "irrational" (Clegg 1975, p. 23). The effect was to delegitimate conflict and controversy and depoliticize city administration generally. To define all politics as disreputable, save that involved in elections per se, also obscures the values, choices, and disparities that enter into public policies.

All of this is doubly disabling to minority communities. On the one hand, they tend to be excluded from access to the technical, administrative arena, such as it is; on the other hand, the ideology discounts the value of their one ticket into the game—namely, the politics of interests and morality. The Covenant members were well aware of both handicaps, but they resolved to play the game notwithstanding. Instead of acceding to the norms of reasonableness defined by the city's political elite, the Covenant accentuated its nonconformity and increased its provocation.

UPPING THE STAKES AND CHALLENGING THE RULES

If the tenor of Springfield's civic discourse was already strained, there was a risk of total rupture following the Covenant's public charges of racism and possible corruption in city hall. Whatever the substance behind the allegations, many in the community regarded the charges as a breach of civic faith, hence more alienating than persuasive. But the Covenant went beyond mere name-calling. It added insinuation to insult by demanding that the city authorize an audit of all monies spent for economic development in the five-block Winchester Square area for the period 1965–85. It also pushed for the appointment of a master plan task force so that the square would not be developed piecemeal by real estate speculators. All of this came at a time when the city's political leadership was already

reeling from a bitterly contested election campaign for the state representative seat representing the Winchester Square area. In fact, these three
specific issues—the election, the audit, and the task force—all illuminate
the Covenant's complex and changing relations with both the city's elite
and Winchester Square itself.

The Election

As described in Chapter Three, in the aftermath of the city's charter
change and its shift away from the old ward- and party-based system,
Springfield's politics have generally involved more selection than election, and campaigns have often involved more ceremony than genuine
competition. Decisions are typically managed behind the scenes, and the
results are rarely in doubt, much less subject to public rancor. However,
the 1986 election for state representative was a clear exception. It was
perhaps the single most vitriolic contest in two decades, largely because
its candidates and their campaigns crisscrossed traditional alignments and
awakened a series of dormant political issues that produced both high
emotion and high confusion. Of course, Winchester Square development
was an important issue—indeed, so important and so volatile that both
candidates tried to use it to their advantage. But the election was not
about specific issues per se; rather, it pivoted around broader images of
race, ethnicity, and religion. And it was the Covenant members who kept
the pot boiling by withholding support from their "natural" candidate, the
black incumbent, and extending it at least implicitly to his young, white,
Irish-Catholic challenger.

What was especially surprising about this particular contest was that it
should be a contest at all. The incumbent had held the post since 1978
with the consistent support of the reigning political elite. With a tall and
handsome physical presence, tailored for the campaign stump, he was one
of the city's very few politically successful blacks. As such, he was an ironic
source of legitimacy for white control; just as the city needed one, but only
one, minority member of the School Committee or the City Council, so it
was useful to have one minority "state rep." But he was useful in other
ways as well. As one white political official put it:

> If he lost, there would be even greater division between the city establish-
> ment and the black community, and he doubled the turnout in the black
> precincts. He gives each mayor a short list of names for city boards and com-
> missions, in return for which he guarantees no hassles from his faction. (inter-
> view)

A similar dynamic operated at the state level. As one of the few blacks
in the commonwealth's General Court (or state legislature) on Boston's
Beacon Hill, he had the clout of conspicuous tokenism. This assured him

of sufficient prominence to become a minor fixture within the House. And according to a city councillor who was grudging in his assessment:

He's the only "black rep" west of Framingham, and he can use his color to get things for Springfield; and that's not bad. He may not be the straightest shooter or the brightest light in town, but the business community doesn't care as long as it gets what it wants. (interview)

As this suggests, the representative's political standing was not as solid as his longevity would imply; but in this he was no different from any other black politician in the city. In the words of one white political veteran, "In Springfield, black politicians make it on white votes; that's why they're always running scared" (interview). A former black officeholder put the matter even more succinctly: "They elect our black representatives, not us" (interview).

Although the state representative was widely perceived as an important figure in the politics of Winchester Square, he was not commonly beloved by either whites or blacks. Indeed, other black community leaders were noticeably cool in their assessment of him. According to one conservative elder statesman: "Well, he does pretty good, for a politician" (interview). And a younger, more radical organizer noted the representative's ties to the white elite this way: "He's just a black Irishman, and he's so afraid of the newspaper publisher that he won't say his name out loud. He whispers it" (interview).

Covenant members had their own grievances against the representative. They saw his unwillingness to close ranks with them as a sign of both weakness and arrogance. As one noted, "He told us, in effect, 'You be Stokely Carmichael and I'll be Martin Luther King, Jr. You take on the moral questions, and I'll handle the politics' " (interview). But it was precisely his politics that made them skeptical. They accused him of selling out his district to downtown interests in return for their political support and an opportunity for financial gain for himself and a small circle of associates. They noted that he had been a consistent supporter of downtown development, including the move of the Basketball Hall of Fame from his home district to a new building on the downtown riverfront. His Upper State Street Development Corporation was the instrument for reconfiguring the abandoned Indian Motocycle building into housing units, a move that prompted opposition from many in the Winchester Square neighborhoods. Finally, there was ample evidence of the political assistance he received from downtown interests. In particular, the newspapers were a consistent source of praise and support (e.g., *Daily News*, March 3, 1986; September 3, 1986; *Morning Union*, December 9, 1986).

Meanwhile, the challenger in the 1986 election was an ambitious young city councillor whose family had been active in Springfield politics for several generations, though never at the very top level. Clearly this candidate sought to take advantage of the divisions that had developed within the district's electorate, especially within the black community. Although he was scarcely a political paragon from the standpoint of the Covenant, he viewed the emerging rift between the Covenant and the incumbent as an opportunity too promising to pass up.

Another wild card in the race was that the challenger's candidacy produced a rift of its own within the white political community. Because the representative was a team player with important symbolic value in a city whose minorities were greatly underrepresented politically, he had chits to cash. Many city politicians urged the challenger not to run, and when he spurned their counsel, many took to the sidelines rather than support either candidate openly. The mayor and several longtime city councillors took this tack. It was not true of the newspapers, however, which came out early on behalf of the loyal incumbent.

The challenger was not one to back off coolly in such circumstances. Instead, he used both press interviews and paid advertisements for dramatic attacks on the newspapers. In particular, he criticized their publisher for not only trying to talk him out of running but threatening him in other ways as well. In Springfield's city politics, running *against* the newspapers is rare and rarely sound. The race had become a test of community power all around.

The newspapers responded to the challenger's attacks in two ways. First, they soft-pedaled the charges, using language that implied they were false without denying them outright (*Morning Union*, September 11, 1986). Second, they regained the offensive with a hard-hitting investigation into financial statements given by the challenger to the state ethics commission (*Morning Union*, September 1, 1986). As one newspaper staffer put it proudly but privately, this "alienated him from his natural constituency" (interview). Certainly it blunted and counterbalanced the challenger's allegations of the incumbent's corruption.

The Covenant as a group did not publicly endorse either candidate, but its involvement in the issues and its obvious disaffection with the incumbent helped to further polarize the contest. According to one reporter closely attuned to the situation:

> A lot of people thought the Covenant was setting up [the incumbent] for a loss. . . . This was a real concern to both the black and the white establishments, each of which saw him as their man but for different reasons. (interview)

This is another way of describing how black politicians are pulled in two quite different directions by their black and their white constituents. Any minority hoping to play a public role in the city's political system must navigate the at-large process and finesse the competing demands of two more or less antipathetic constituencies. The problem was further compounded by splits within both the black and the white ranks.

Meanwhile, the white challenger, along with two allies on the City Council, sponsored the Covenant's call for an audit of the development money spent in Winchester Square (*Morning Union*, January 16, 1986), and he repeatedly positioned himself in accordance with Covenant positions. Thus, while the Covenant did not directly support the challenger, they were paired by association when he took up at least part of the group's cause. But if this was politically expedient, other parts of the challenger's platform were much less so. For example, he accused the black incumbent of running a campaign with racial overtones. On the one hand, some regarded this as a shrewd ploy in a city with considerable backlash sentiment against "reverse discrimination." On the other hand, this was another development that, along with the newspaper's investigations, alienated moderate and liberal white and black supporters. And it was another violation of the polite civic discourse that usually surrounds city politics.

Still, as the campaign headed into its final months, it was clear that the incumbent was in jeopardy. Once the threat to the only established black political voice in the area became palpable, it forced the reluctant support of many who were more committed to the cause than to the candidate. This included one Covenant member, who had enjoyed personal support from the representative in his own political efforts and was obviously cross-pressured. This member finally quit the Covenant, citing "schedule conflicts." But most members of the Covenant were unfazed and were determined to shake up the downtown political-business coalition even if it meant entering a de facto alliance with an opportunistic white candidate and turning their backs on a fellow black. There is no question that the Covenant's unrelenting obstreperousness was unpopular with most of the area's black middle class. Indeed, when a parishioner faulted one member of the Covenant for risking the representative's seat, the minister responded without a hint of appeasement: "Whether you elect a person from the White Citizen's Committee from Biloxi, Mississippi, or [the representative], the effect will be the same" (interview).

The election results confirmed the advantages of incumbency. The veteran black state representative held off his young white antagonist by a margin of 53 percent to 38 percent, surprising even those political handicappers who had predicted the win. And yet many observers noted that the race went to the wire, even on election day itself. According to one member of the Covenant, the incumbent's organization learned by midafternoon that he was in fact trailing, whereupon "they just combed the community and really shook it down; that did it" (interview). A white political official with long experience in election postmortems described a similar scenario, and noted that "the black churches played a big role in revving people up when the chips were down" (interview). However, the black conservative churches had carried a larger share of this mobilizing role, since the incumbent had generally failed to win the support of Covenant clergy leading the more liberal congregations.

Regardless of how close the contest was, there are a number of explanations for its outcome. Although blacks slightly outnumbered whites in the electoral district, white *voters* generally outnumber black voters. Nevertheless, the incumbent's name and organization, the black solidarity engendered by the white challenge, and the efforts of downtown interests, especially those of the newspapers, all proved formidable advantages. If it was an election pitting race against political structure, the latter carried the day. To the extent that the outcome hinged on race consciousness, it may well have backfired against the challenger and the Covenant because of the way each violated the city's political etiquette. And if all of these explanations seem too conventional, there is this from one of the city's longtime inside-dopesters:

> The real trump card [that the representative] had going for him was an Irish staffer from Holy Cross Church, whose mother was very well known in the district and really undermined [the challenger's] natural base of white support. (interview)

Perhaps. But it did not take long for the challenger to regain his local standing. After the election and its attendant upheaval, city politics reverted back to its homeostatic routine. The many city officials who "sat it out" were privately regretful of having missed an important opportunity to be associated with a black winner. The challenger himself admitted defeat and went out of his way to make peace offerings to the incumbent and the newspapers. Two of our interviewees described him as being "back on the team." This was confirmed a year later when he ran a highly successful campaign for reelection to the City Council in 1987.

As for the Covenant, neither result of the election would have signaled success in their longer-term agenda. Although the representative's victory further confirmed their marginality among blacks as well as whites, it did not diminish their resolve to pursue the larger issue of Winchester Square's development. If anything, the campaign had increased their visibility and focused more attention on their basic cause. They were to need every bit of this momentum in pushing forward with their demand for a twenty-year audit of monies directed toward Winchester Square.

The Audit

A common response to the Covenant's demands by those connected to downtown business and political interests was that the city had already invested a great deal of money in Winchester Square with virtually nothing to show for it. The response was sometimes muttered beneath the breath and sometimes euphemistically encoded as a public rebuttal. Certainly the financial record seemed to offer support. A figure of $90 million spent over the past sixteen years was reported more than once (e.g., *Morning Union*, April 8, 1986; June 6, 1986), although this figure was later revealed to include the $24 million spent on the new public high school at the edge of the district—a location many blacks had opposed—as well as other monies spent on nondevelopment projects such as sidewalks and housing rehabilitation.

City hall also argued, without noting the paradox, that most investments were not the results of political decisions made by the administration but of economic decisions made by private capital. However, city hall's opponents saw this as disingenuous in light of the cooperation between city government and business over downtown revitalization. Moreover, the local political culture was replete with stories concerning the way politics intruded into the expenditure of federal money. For example, one city staffer described the following episode with some bemusement:

> I remember when [an earlier mayor] brought a guy on board to help manufacture a target area for outside urban development funds for Hungry Hill, where they both were from. They had to finagle some per capita income figures and throw in an unattached North End neighborhood to bring the income level down below the trigger point. (interview)

Such stories were widely circulated, and it is hardly surprising that similar suspicions surfaced regarding Winchester Square. According to one Covenant pastor:

> There's a lot of feeling in the black community that things aren't right downtown. It's not that [the mayor] has personally benefited from development rake-offs, but there are people who have their hooks into him. A lot of people around here feel that if you dig deep enough, a couple of ex-mayors might be in real trouble. But how do you break into that white Irish group? I mean the mayor's so strong that I've heard his last campaign paid $5000 to a guy just so he would run against him and make the election look good. And without some sign of public white failure, the black community won't really get organized. (interview)

Realizing that its own allegations of political interference, administrative mismanagement, and personal corruption in Winchester Square investments carried little weight, the Covenant dared the city to risk an independent investigation. Specifically, the clergy proposed a twenty-year "performance management audit" to evaluate not only how much was spent but also whether it was spent appropriately. They persuaded three city councillors to endorse the audit, including the challenger for the state representative seat. With these sponsors, the City Council as a whole approved—at least in principle.

However, the struggle had just begun, and there developed a substantial gap between preliminary approval and final implementation. The City Council first considered the audit resolution in January 1986, but it was almost two years before an actual audit was released. To begin with, the council felt it could not responsibly order an audit until it had a cost estimate from the city auditor (*Morning Union*, January 22, 1986); the city auditor agreed to provide such a figure, but needed records from the city's Community Development Commission in order to do so (*Morning Union*, April 8, 1986); the community development commissioner claimed he was "doing nothing" in terms of providing those records because there were already audits available, and he was too busy to get back into the original contracts (*Morning Union*, April 26, 1986); the City Council considered this an "abuse of power" and sponsored a resolve ordering his cooperation (*Morning Union*, April 28, 1986)—and so on. The coup de grace of this bureaucratic and perhaps political delay came when it was discovered that a "typographical error" in the City Council's order caused the auditor to only consider the costs of a *ten*-year audit (1975–85) rather than the twenty-year one requested (*Morning Union*, April 23, 1986). Another month elapsed while the city auditor repeated the process of receiving bids from interested accounting firms.

Once the council received the estimate of $300,000, it rejected a twenty-year audit as too expensive (*Morning Union*, June 5, 1986). Even sympathetic city councillors gagged on the price, and the newspaper accompanied its account of the council's decision with an editorial taking the political high road of civic boosterism and forgive-and-forget consensus formation. Entitled "Let's Go Forward" (*Morning Union*, June 5, 1986), the editorial faulted audits for looking backward and supported the council's rejection of the twenty-year audit as too expensive "to go fishing." It urged instead that "all parties concerned must put past differences and rancor behind and work together." Asking the minority community to forget about past discrimination, the paper proposed that "officials, clergymen, developers and residents" unite behind a mayor's task force representing "the community and the city's business-industry interests" to produce a master plan "looking forward" and "in an orderly fashion." Of course, the editorial mirrored the mayor's position and strategy on the issue.

However, calls for an audit continued. Several months of haggling produced a compromise five-year audit with a cost not to exceed $50,000. From the City Council's point of view, this was a gesture of concern and cooperation over the square. But from the Covenant's perspective, the change was driven more by politics than by budget. A twenty-year audit would have included an examination of the Model Cities Program run in the mid-1970s when both the current mayor and the state representative for Springfield's North End were mayoral aides involved in administering the program. This was the period in which the Covenant and other interested bystanders most expected to uncover misappropriations. Rumors of potential "jail terms" for city officials notwithstanding, there was considerable feeling within the black community that the Model Cities Program had been intentionally inadequate for the square: they were "funding for failure," in the phrase of a Covenant pastor. There was also considerable suspicion that the current city administration was not eager to dredge up old memories or old account books.

Finally the five-year, $50,000 plan was negotiated, the resolution was passed (*Morning Union*, July 8, 1986), and the mayor indicated his approval. But by October the work had not yet begun, and the Covenant again voiced public criticism of the mayor. According to one member in the press, the delay was "orchestrated by the mayor," and "we feel that he owes the entire city an explanation" (*Morning Union*, October 2, 1986). "That's a joke . . . it's foolishness," was the mayor's quoted response. Nevertheless, snags and delays continued.

In November it was revealed that the audit would cover federal community development monies for the *entire* city, not just the Winchester Square area, and another round of finger-pointing ensued. The Covenant accused the City Council and the city auditor of duplicity. The City Council blamed the mistake on a subcommittee report, the city auditor asked why the Covenant members had not caught the error in their review, and the Covenant claimed not to have received a copy of the order (*Morning Union*, November 18, 1986; November 24, 1986). In December, the city auditor accepted a letter from the accounting firm outlining the revision of the audit in order to focus on the square (*Morning Union*, December 5, 1986), the City Council appointed a panel of its members to monitor the audit's progress (*Morning Union*, January 2, 1987), and the mayor signed off on the revised audit (*Morning Union*, February 19, 1987). By the spring of 1987 the accounting firm announced that not every Community Development Block Grant contract for the five-year period could be reviewed since that would exceed the $50,000 limit (*Morning Union*, May 8, 1987). And in early October the City Council's review panel announced that the audit would be released sometime in that month (*Union-News*, October 10, 1987). By that time, however, city elections were at hand, and the decision was made to wait and release the findings after election day, ostensibly because of the difficulty in finding a meeting date that would fit into the busy schedules of all interested parties.

The audit was finally released in early November and revealed no corruption or systematic malfeasance (*Union-News*, November 6, 1987). City

hall and the newspapers concurred that the report amounted to a validation of virtue. But other interpretations were possible. Among other
things, the report stated that "the City has neither consistently nor ade-
quately enforced . . . contract terms" and that "the City's ability to monitor effectively the overall financial results of project activities [was inhib-
ited]." In particular, the audit report found that "management controls are
weaker at the Springfield Redevelopment Authority than at other sub-
grantees reviewed." It found no fraud or abuse, but lax management was
systemic (*CDBG Program Review*, Peat, Marwick, Main and Co. Final
Report, November 5, 1987). Because these more negative findings received almost no coverage in the local press, the audit quickly faded as a
public issue.

Once again, the Covenant was the loser, having sacrificed yet another
portion of its dwindling political capital. While it was still accorded respect, there was a patronizing courtesy to it all. The private remarks of
a local banker captured the public sentiments of the enlightened establishment:

> I think the Covenant didn't understand the difference between a lack of wis-
> dom and an actual misappropriation. I'm sure there was a good deal of the
> former, but I don't think there was much actual graft. (interview)

The Task Force

Along with the call for an audit, the Covenant also pushed early on for a
master plan, so that the square would not be developed piecemeal by real
estate speculators and profiteers. If the audit was a look backward in
search of political culprits, a plan would be a look forward in search of
economic resources. The objective was systematic economic development
sufficient to produce the jobs and income necessary for neighborhood stability. But in the world of politics, plans are cheap, and plans to plan are
cheaper still.

The mayor had readily agreed with the Covenant's call for a master
scheme in early November 1985. However, a month later the Covenant
charged him with "breaking faith" and delaying the planning process
(*Morning Union*, December 10, 1985). The mayor responded at his sec-
ond-term inauguration in January 1986, when his speech included a paragraph outlining the creation of a task force to produce a new master plan
for the square (*Morning Union*, January 16, 1986). The Winchester
Square Task Force was to include twenty-six people, eleven of whom
would constitute an executive committee to write the report itself.

This had the effect of both doing something and doing very little. In
providing a sense of attention and action, it took the initiative away from
the mayor's critics. Already an adroitly rumored candidate for the not-yet-

vacated congressional seat, the mayor was eager to side with the Winchester Square community, at least symbolically. At the same time, sending a troublesome issue to committee could be akin to a political quarantine, and perhaps a burial. The mayor's past task forces (such as the one on homelessness) had combined high visibility with political moderation. One could reasonably infer that he had similar hopes for this one.

The issue quickly shifted from planning itself to the planners who were to compose the task force. Covenant members were asked preliminarily about their willingness to serve on the task force, if not on its critical executive committee. They quickly refused in order to preserve their independent eyes and voice. At a meeting of the Community Development Commission, seventy Winchester Square residents appeared and demanded that a majority of the task force be people from the neighborhood itself. In response, the community development commissioner said that he would recommend to the mayor that two-thirds of both the general and executive committees be from banking, business, and the city administration, while the other third would be from the Winchester Square area. When asked who some of these people would be, the commissioner replied: "Those have been confidential inquiries." The head of the local NAACP responded: "That's the problem. Everything has been too confidential" (*Morning Union*, January 23, 1986). Later in the same meeting, another black community activist articulated the frustration more fully:

> I'm just a little bit weary of people who live in Longmeadow and Wilbraham [two decidedly middle-class suburbs] who have businesses or are lawyers downtown . . . develop[ing] my neighborhood. [I'm interested in the] master plan not being orchestrated from the corner of [Liberty] and Main Streets. (*Morning Union*, January 23, 1986)

The offices of the Springfield Newspapers, Inc., are at the corner of Liberty and Main, and interviewees within the newspaper reported that the publisher was incensed by this comment. In the following weeks, he met with the activist and members of the Covenant, alternating attempts to cajole them into dropping their objections to the task force with threats to end his personal involvement and hence Springfield Central's support. A member of the Covenant described one such meeting at which, by all accounts, passions boiled over:

> Both he [the publisher] and the mayor came out to meet with us at Holy Family so he could clear his name. Well, things got a little hot. One of our clergy called him a weasel and said downtown development was a failure, and that Bay State West [the downtown shopping mall] was a vacuum cleaner sucking money from all over the city. [The publisher] jumped up and said, "I don't have to take this; I won't even sit on the executive committee of the

development task force." But one of our guys said, "Oh yes you will. In fact, my money's on you chairing it; you couldn't stand not having your name on it and controlling it." Then he said he'd had as much as oppression as anyone in the room, whereupon Reverend —— said, "Bullshit, Jew-boy." Well, needless to say the reverend heard from folks about that. He got strong letters of protest from seven members of his congregation, and [the black state representative] told him, "You don't have long to be in Springfield." (interview)

The remark apparently reflected both over-zealous retaliation for past grievances and the giddy put-downs of locker-room humor gone too far. It was one more incident in the Covenant's increasing isolation. And yet even in its aloofness, the Covenant continued to exert influence. Despite the efforts to undermine its impact, the group's opposition to the task force's composition remained obdurate and vocal. Finally, in February, the mayor agreed to pick a majority of the task force from the neighborhood area and met with the Covenant to receive five nominations for the eleven-person executive committee. The NAACP and the Urban League were also asked to submit lists of possible participants (*Morning Union*, February 4, 1986).

In April the Covenant once again publicly criticized the mayor—this time for intentionally stalling in appointing the actual task force. The mayor called the comments "patently unfair" and noted that he needed only one more response before completing the membership (*Morning Union*, April 2, 1986). The next day fifteen appointments to the task force's general committee were announced. Although a member of the Covenant was quoted as being disappointed that the crucial executive committee was still unnamed, the heads of the Urban League and the NAACP pronounced themselves "very much pleased" and said the names were "credible [and they] will do an excellent job" (*Morning Union*, April 3, 1986). The Urban League president added that "It serves no useful purpose to focus on the negative," a statement that marked his differences with the Covenant and underscored once again the latter's marginality within the black as well as the white community.

Almost six months elapsed before the eleven-person executive committee was announced, along with its cochairs, the newspaper publisher and the black director of the local Housing and Urban Development office (*Morning Union*, September 20, 1986). In late November the task force opened an office in Winchester Square to solicit public opinion; in late December the executive committee released a list of eight goals for the revitalization plan. And in April 1987 the executive committee released the master plan for developing the square, complete with the kind of full-page newspaper stories and architect's drawings that had always accompanied Springfield Central's downtown projects (*Morning Union*, April 16, 1987). In an ironic footnote to the role that race had played in the entire Winchester Square controversy, several readers wrote the paper noting that the artist's renderings of the future square did not include a single African-American face.

The first change proposed by the plan was to rename Winchester Square as "Mason Square," after Primus Mason, the nineteenth-century black businessman who had donated the central plot of land to the city and its white mayor, Charles Winchester. The formal renaming occurred in July 1987, and in August the newspapers announced that henceforth they would use the Mason Square designation for the entire area (*Union-News*, August 19, 1987). The change was far slower in general usage, and when we asked community activists from the square area about the switch, they shrugged their shoulders diffidently. During a subsequent interview with a member of the Covenant, he made no particular attempt to use the "Mason" designation.

A more important aspect of the master plan was the creation of the Mason Square Development Corporation—a nonprofit, public-private conduit for economic planning and implementation modeled explicitly after Springfield Central, Inc. The use of Springfield Central as an exemplar no doubt reassured many downtown business figures that the square was in the capable hands of those who knew where the city's *real* priorities lay. It also brought predictable editorial praise from the newspapers (*Morning Union* April 17, 1987), whose publisher was a leader in both ventures. However, many members of the Covenant remained dubious, and their skepticism seemed confirmed in September 1987 when a former U.S. Department of Housing and Urban Development administrator from Hartford, Connecticut, was hired as executive director of the new development corporation. From the Covenant's perspective, this marked the cooptation of development strategies for the square by the city's dominant business interests. The Covenant feared that new development in the square would be no more responsive to the needs of the black community than downtown development had been. Once again it appeared that the people of the square's neighborhoods would not be in control of their own economic destiny.

A FAILED SOCIAL MOVEMENT?

Any assessment of the Covenant requires some conceptual basis for comparison. Certainly not a church or a sect in its own right, it is more like one of Robert Wuthnow's "special purpose groups" (1988) and qualifies within the broader category of "social movements." Such movements occupy a position midway on the continuum between an informal collective enthusiasm and a formally structured organization. Broadly speaking, these groups share a single objective and are bound more by ideological conviction than by a code of rules and procedures. Often cohering around a charismatic leader, they tend to begin as small clusters of like-minded folk who pool their energies and resources voluntarily in the short run with little thought of what the longer haul may bring beyond the specific goal at hand.

Of course, there is a substantial literature concerning such movements. While its primary focus has been on nonreligious groups, it offers instructive clues to the power process and potential of cultural agents of all sorts, including the religious. In recent years, scholarship has moved from analyses of who joins movements and why, to the conditions necessary for movement success. Research has been dominated by a concern for the "resource mobilization" of social movements, to use the phrase of McCarthy and Zald (1977). As summarized by Jenkins (1983), this perspective tends to emphasize the importance of structural resources such as money and members.

Toward the end of the last chapter, we urged that more attention be given cultural, as distinct from structural, power in the world of community and society politics. Here we have a similar message in urging that more attention be given cultural, as distinct from structural, resources in the analysis of social movements. There is no question that successful social movements must pursue such structural resources as an adequate financial base and a continuing supply of committed and effective members; but there are also cultural resources that can neither be dismissed as idle nor taken for granted. These include ideological arguments, moral appeals, and symbolic vocabularies, which must be mobilized in the sense of being selected, filtered, agreed upon, articulated, and broadcast. Generally these cultural chords must resonate *before* other resources can be mounted. Finally, if for many social movements, the problem is one of finding the appropriate symbols and frameworks (cf. Snow et al., 1986), religious groups sometimes face the problem of scaling back the vast moral and theological armaments available. Just as a movement may be poorly served by too few cultural resources, so may it be subverted by too many. The latter can produce a form of cultural overkill, and the deployment of the wrong arguments in the wrong contexts.

Even prior to this chapter, we have seen that Springfield offers examples of movements using cultural means in pursuit of political ends. This was certainly a major theme of the struggle over homelessness in Chapter Five. Both Open Pantry and Service Providers, Inc., were social movements of a sort, as their respective leaders were self-consciously calculating in their use of moral symbols as major weapons. While city officials frequently tried to rebut in kind, they were ultimately left little choice but to follow the movements' lead while trying to maintain city hall control over developments as they occurred.

The Covenant's success is more difficult to measure. With the reelection of the incumbent state representative, the five-year audit's failure to turn up significant malfeasance, and the composition of the Mason Square Development Corporation and its master plan largely on downtown's own terms, the Covenant's basic ammunition was spent. By 1988 three of the original members had left the group, and two had left Springfield. The Covenant had become marginal to more recent political and economic developments in the square, and it no longer commanded headlines. When we asked a member of the task force executive committee what the Covenant's reaction to its plan would be, he shot back: "I neither know nor care" (interview).

Like the religious activists who challenged the city on behalf of the homeless, the Covenant qualifies as a "social movement" on several counts. Its political objective drew a small but generally steadfast membership that transcended the traditional distinctions that divide conventional religion—church versus sect, Catholic versus Protestant, black versus white. Further, it had a clear commitment to political tactics outside the institutionalized political framework, and a preference for ideological purity over group maintenance.

At the same time, there were several respects in which the Covenant fell short of a full-fledged movement. As social movements go, there is a sense in which this one was both antisocial and unmoving. Its short history appeared to rebut one of the major themes of the "resource mobilization" school; namely, that all social movements share basic organizational exigencies and be responsive to the need to develop a critical support base. In fact, neither money nor members—the two most commonly prized support resources—were Covenant priorities. The group restricted itself to local clergy, preferring media releases and closed-door negotiations to a strategy of mass mobilization, and given our survey results on the relatively meager grass-roots support of square development, the latter may have reflected more necessity than choice. Instead, two other resources seemed more critical to the Covenant: first, and more cultural, was the prophetic moral appeal directed at the community as a whole; second, and more structural, was the political leverage on and political support from both the black community and the city's predominantly white power network.

Normally these latter two resources must be complementary for successful movements. After all, broad public legitimacy is often a crucial component of the power needed to make specific political deals. But the Covenant case suggests that the two resources may conflict for challengers to power who are riding the crest of a self-generated political crisis. As one Covenant member said of another who defected during the state representative election, "[He] had a problem being prophetic and being political at the same time" (interview). The respondent was implying, consciously or not, that the Covenant's prime resource—its moral authority—had driven it to a position where the need for ideological purity kept it from being able to make the *realpolitik* deals that grease the wheels of community action. Whether the members themselves recognized it, the Covenant as a whole confronted the same dilemma, although their group response took the opposite path of prophetic radicalization.

Prior to 1984, the combination of conventional politics and conventional pulpit prophecy had done little to advance the cause. The Covenant was well aware that risks were required, and that a moral escalation was necessary to secure headlines and provoke response. Reasonableness was too easily dismissed; extremism at least promised a hearing. As William Gamson (1990) has pointed out, "feistiness works," and the history of social protest underscores the "success of the unruly." Given the polite deference that marked most of Springfield's politics, the Covenant's switch to a public confrontational stance was a type of "tactical innovation" that documenters of the civil rights movement have shown to be highly effective (e.g., McAdam 1983). By shifting to a call for justice that stressed a sense of Springfield as a moral community, the Covenant shifted the terms of political debate and forced the city administration into a reactive and defensive posture.

However, the Covenant's basic abandonment of a centrist strategy in favor of an end run was critically compromised by a switch from the high road to the low. Certainly there was an exhilaration to the combat, perhaps especially for men who had operated for so long under priestly constraints—although, as one summed up his character, "I'm an antagonist" (interview). Gradually, however, lofty ideals were displaced by shrill accusations, ends were tainted by the means, and, in the eyes of public Springfield, "moral politics" gave way to "pressure politics." The respective roles of saints and sinners became more difficult to discern, at least in terms of their public rhetoric. In one sense, the Covenant clergy had squandered their most precious resources: their racial martyrdom and their religious authority. An interviewee, who had witnessed the confrontation with the newspaper publisher described earlier, put it this way: "When I heard him say that, he was no longer a clergyman to me" (interview).

The comment catches the mood of many in Springfield, for whom the charges of racism and personal corruption seemed gratuitous attacks that lowered the clergy from their lofty moral platform into a conventionally "political" struggle. It is quite possible that many people were simply looking for a reason to discredit the Covenant and dismiss their charges. Even so, the Covenant gave them a reason, and its reduced moral authority and public legitimacy left it in a contest for which it was overmatched. Down and dirty was not their game, and the mere act of playing it cost them dearly.

Ironically, the Covenant's confrontational tactics even cut them off from much of the black community. Earlier we noted that Springfield's black population is divided between those whose families are well rooted in New England and those whose families migrated north, particularly after World War II. By 1955, Clough had noted the distinction between the city's "conservative" and "southern" blacks (1955, p. 60). The former were clustered in and around Springfield's largest black Baptist church (Third Baptist, founded in 1844) and were conspicuously cool to the Covenant. Even the prestigious St. John's Congregational Church (also founded in the 1840s), which ran a highly visible community action program, and whose pastor was an important cog in the Covenant, had a large membership faction that was less than completely supportive. Lukas (1986) describes an almost identical social distinction between northern and southern blacks within Boston's African-American community during its busing crises. The parallel is not just a function of a common concern for racial justice but is also a common scenario of social movements generally.

Virtually every member of the Covenant felt pressure from parishioners. Some of this stemmed from a sense that the Covenant seemed to abrogate fundamentals of Christian forgiveness while elevating this-worldly concerns above otherworldly priorities. But there was an economic concern as well. As described by several community activists, the city's small but important "black bourgeoisie" had an implicit understanding with city government and downtown interests, which occasionally became explicit. Many of these persons worked for the city or various social service agencies; others were professionals or small-business owners highly dependent on their civic standing. The interests of this black middle class were represented by Springfield's Urban League and NAACP, and they provided the core constituency for the black state representative. Many felt jeopardized by the Covenant, and they joined some downtown figures in labeling the clergy as radicals.

But the Covenant clergy remained undaunted, and most echoed the following sentiments of one of their colleagues:

There were a lot of problems from our parishioners. They saw us as a threat to their jobs with the city or with white employers, and a lot were indebted to [the state representative]. Basically they said, "Keep your butts out of the economy." And I lost a number of them, including one $25-a-week pledge who just up and left. But my gospel's not for sale, and neither are my ethics going to be ghettoized. (interview)

Several of the city's political leaders used this dissensus as a rationale for inaction. According to one former mayor, "I would tell them to get their act together, then come back to us with a proposal their whole community supports" (interview). Thus, the black community, once criticized for coalescing too much around its own interests and therefore being divisive within the city as a whole, was *now* being faulted for not being united enough to represent its interests.

Meanwhile, the conflict was increasingly controlled by a city elite that realized the Covenant's lack of conventional political resources. One member of the elite described the results this way:

More than anything else, the Covenant has been an irritant. It's been pretty well neutralized because it has no constituencies with power. They're not prepared or capable of doing anything positive. If they could solve the loitering, drinking, and pilfering problems, that would be helpful. These things scare potential businesses. (interview)

Of course, this raises the troublesome question of which comes first, an end to social problems or the beginning of economic recovery. And it assumes that the primary problem is behaviors by the community that scare away private business, rather than an institutionalized political economy that has neglected the square. But the business leader was not alone in noting the Covenant's lack of conventional political strength, and a number of observers agreed that the Covenant suffered by "pushing development all the time instead of concentrating on social issues such as black teenage pregnancy" (interview).

Clearly this reflects a stereotypic image of the proper role of the clergy—one that Covenant members were anxious to change. However, the image is also consistent with a wide perception that the Covenant clergy were content to hurl bombast from the sidelines rather than enter the fray more cooperatively:

The Covenant's inconsistencies have made it hard for their friends. They lack a strong ideological base and tend to reflect their different personalities. I'm convinced of their basic integrity, but I sometimes wish I knew what they were up to. One of the last straws for [the mayor and the publisher] was the Covenant's refusal to be a part of the basic task force. They were afraid of being coopted, and they stayed out to be a watchdog. But when they refused to "come inside" and roll up their sleeves and get to work, this both mystified and infuriated the city's leaders. (interview)

Cooptation is a very real threat to any budding movement. But it is the way that elites do business in Springfield. And in successfully avoiding that danger, the Covenant also cut itself off from potential allies within the city's inner political circle.

None of this is to say, however, that the Covenant failed completely or had no impact at all. Quite the contrary. Covenant members themselves saw the state representative election as an important phase in "consciousness raising," and none was so enamored of the Irish challenger as to regard his win as an untainted triumph. Further, they claimed a victory in the city's decision to perform an audit, although they acknowledged that its scope and results were disappointing. They counted the formation and composition of the task force as a substantial gain, even though the resulting master plan reflected the dominance of the city's political and economic elite. Finally, at least one Covenant member used the city's own defensive retaliations as a measure of success:

> We've had different types of responses. We wouldn't be bought off with an awards banquet. . . . And when one guy offered to get our parishioners who were looking for housing in on the ground floor of his development, one of my colleagues told him point blank: "That's the sleaziest offer I've ever been made." Meanwhile, we've had city building inspectors showing up unannounced repeatedly; we've had trouble getting traffic control at events; we've even been denied police protection when it was needed and requested. And we've been hassled trying to get in to to see our people at the York Street jail. In fact, when we tried to see the sheriff, he was always "not in." (interview)

Of course, city officials denied any retaliation, and the truth probably lies somewhere in between. At the same time, there is no question that city officials were alarmed and provoked. Further, the examples of attempted deal-making in the quotation above indicate that the city elite responded at least in part to the Covenant as if they were representatives of a galvanized political constituency. They assumed that the Covenant merely wanted a slightly bigger slice of the pie, continuing to be cut by conventional means. Seeing themselves as the avatars of moral authority, Covenant members refused that game, instead questioning the very organization of the city's political and economic decision making. It was clearly a strategy of headfirst confrontation, whether designed that way or not.

More important than the Covenant's limited specific successes was its broader victory in compelling a new examination of the problems of the African-American community. Mason (formerly Winchester) Square is a blighted area whose political economy threatens to produce a permanent black underclass. It stands as a dramatic contradiction to the city's optimistic self-image. Even business leaders who disagreed with the Covenant's analyses, tactics, and proposals gave the group grudging credit. As one put it, "At least their rhetoric was good in focusing attention on the area, building community concern, and pushing toward a master plan" (interview).

Finally, the experiences of the Covenant's challenge illustrate both the power and the limitations of moral authority as a political resource and of moral politics as a movement strategy. As we have noted, the Covenant's collective status as clergy allowed it to break into the public political arena in a manner denied other groups concerned with Mason Square. As clergy, their moral arguments for developing the square carried great weight, and at least initially these protected them from public backlash by members of the downtown business-political coalition. Despite the newspaper publisher's firm commitment to downtown, the media was an accessible platform for the Covenant. The word "clergy" fit neatly into the headlines, and the sight of men in ecclesiastical collars (even some of the Protestants wore them) gave television news images an instant moral credibility. An interesting confirmation of this came from the city elite itself, as the mayor and the incumbent state representative appeared in the media with still other black clergy. During the two years this issue was hottest, virtually every black clergyman in the city had his picture in the paper at least once.

The Covenant's resource, however, was more than just its members' social standing. The *content* of its challenge, with its distinctly moralistic dimensions, captured the terms of the public political debate. While the city often responded with technical, managerial, or economic arguments, questions regarding social justice and inclusion in the moral community also came back. Hence the city's responses stressed community and neighborhood, images that played into civic religious sentiments about Springfield as a "decent" community. Of course, this was fighting on the Covenant's own terms. This underscores the damage caused by the Covenant's loss of moral legitimacy through tactics of political desperation. The clergy simply lacked the wherewithal to fight city politicians on the politicians' more narrowly structural terms.

But even if the Covenant had kept its moral authority untarnished, there are inherent limits to strategies that rely on moral politics. The Covenant presented itself as the representative of a moral position rather than a political constituency per se. While this offered its members protection from charges of self-interest, it cost them when the time came to effect political closure. Ideologically committed to a "pure" solution, the Covenant found that negotiation was beyond the pale. While this obviated the risk of cooptation, it also froze the Covenant out of what one politician called "the practical process of seeking practical solutions" (interview).

Summary

Springfield is a small city, and its political system discourages diversity and challenges to the status quo. Elections often function more as validations than real contests. Just as minority populations are seriously underrepresented in city offices, so are divisive viewpoints underrepresented in city caucuses. Rather than serve as an independent arbiter and spotlight, the newspaper itself is allied with the elite through its publisher's role as civic leader. It was against these rather considerable odds that a small group of largely black and largely Protestant clergy was able to redirect a major portion of the city's political agenda for two years, as it exacted both financial and organizational commitments from the city's elite. The Covenant has now receded from the headlines, and neither city politics nor Mason Square's economy has undergone the kind of transformation its members originally envisioned. Still, a master plan is in place, and the struggle continues.

As each of the three issues examined here demonstrates, small move- *so what?* ments can make big noises even when arrayed against the overwhelming forces of a prevailing "power structure." This depends on their ability to marshall a different kind of force against the conventional armaments of political establishments. Moral appeals to higher authority can gain at least a temporary hearing in the midst of the conventional political and technical babble that engulfs public policymaking. While it is by no means easy to convert these appeals into conventional political strength, they at least offer that possibility should lightning find its way into their bottle.

Such was not the case with the Covenant—a group that overplayed its moral hand and found it difficult to maximize both prophecy and politics simultaneously. But in other chapters, we find examples of other movements that enjoyed somewhat more success. And just as religion played a major role here in alliance with race, so has it loomed large in conjunction with issues of homelessness and sexuality. While the city-state may be relatively unencumbered by the church as an institution, it remains vulnerable to the assault of religion as a cultural force, especially when allied with the salient moral issues of the day.

Again, the story is interesting but the interpretation seems forced.

Chapter Seven

SEXUALITY AND SECTARIANISM

FEW CITIES can be described as sprinting eagerly into the future. Most are anchored to the status quo by elites who have benefited from it, by a culture that reinforces it, and by a structure that finds inertia more congenial than change. Most cities tend to avoid the very issues that form the rocky trail ahead. Certainly this is true of Springfield—a city often cited for its traditionalism and one with a preference for even superficial consensus over overt conflict. But not even here can conflict be closeted permanently. Despite the city's resolve, there are occasional subjects that disrupt the civic sanctum and require a confrontation with change. Sexuality is one such issue—or rather that complex of issues embracing sex education, abortion, contraception, teenage pregnancy, and, most recently, AIDS.

Of course, these problems are hardly unique to Springfield. Here again the city is a microcosm of the nation, especially in its "pre-Webster" phase. Prior to the U.S. Supreme Court's 1989 decision in *Webster* v. *Reproductive Health Services*, the pro-life movement seemed ascendant in pursuing a reversal of the Supreme Court's 1973 *Roe* v. *Wade* judgment and all of its pro-choice implications. The *Webster* case changed the arena from the federal level to the individual states. It also occasioned an astonishing political reversal as the pro-choice faction took to the hustings and began to realize the advantage long described for it in opinion polls. In state after state the pro-life movement began to suffer defeat and disarray. And yet Springfield has been slow to catch the changing tide. This chapter helps to explain why, by focusing on events prior to 1989 and a mood that may seem anachronistic to some outsiders but remains painfully contemporary to the community itself.

Whether resisting or complying with changing patterns of sexuality, Springfield does not operate alone. Like any community, it functions within national parameters of culture, politics, the law, and the courts. The city could not have banned contraceptives or abortions even if this was the overwhelming preference of its citizens. And it was not. Springfield's reaction to both increasing illegitimacy and escalating AIDS was conditioned by programs and regulations at other levels. Even its activist special-purpose groups were affiliated with national organizations that helped to define both the problems and the solutions.

As one might predict in such a heavily Catholic city, abortion has been a recurring cause célèbre. Pro-life demonstrations in front of abortion clinics began as explosive provocations, but gradually became a part of the civic ritual. Attitudes toward abortion have been a continuing litmus test for Springfield's political candidates and public officials, especially as these tests are administered by pro-life activists. While politicians are certainly anxious to pass the test, they are not eager to expatiate on the issues. In fact, where any controversial matter of sexuality is concerned, public debate has been more muted than disputatious. Americans have always been uncomfortable discussing sexuality, and this is especially true of public figures caught in the swirl of value flux and moral ambiguity.

But as much as public Springfield might wish to avoid a confrontation in this sphere, two developments have forced the issue. On the one hand, escalating rates of teenage pregnancy and illegitimate children have soared to staggering heights. In 1986 Springfield had Massachusetts' second-highest rate of teenage pregnancy and out-of-wedlock births; almost 41 percent of *all* Springfield births in 1986 were to unmarried women, compared to a state average of 19 percent (Teen Pregnancy Task Force, *Community 2000* Report, June 1988). On the other hand, another development involves the city's rising number of AIDS cases, a tragedy not only unwelcome in its own right but one that vastly complicates the morality of sexual intervention. Indeed, both illegitimacy and AIDS suggested to many the urgent need to begin *for the first time* a program of sex education in the schools, possibly even one linked specifically to counseling on contraception, if not to contraceptives themselves. The combination of sex education and sex intervention is, of course, volatile. As we shall see, city officials responded gingerly and with understandable sensitivity to a small cadre of conservative religious activists who threatened their political standing.

Here, then, is one more community sector in which to observe the interaction between church and state. The twin issues of abortion and sex education offer another mirror for reflecting changes in Springfield's religion and its politics. Once again we shall see politicians more at odds than at ease with their constituents. We shall also see more evidence of both the culture of power and the power of culture as well as the sometimes paradoxical dynamics of social movements. We shall examine various changes in the religious community itself, including the rise of Evangelicalism and the continuing transformations within Catholicism. We shall end by addressing a frequent characteristic of political and cultural change; namely, a quietly quivering tension between its short-run and long-term patterns and between minorities and majorities in the joust for power.

ABORTION IN SPRINGFIELD: ACTORS, ATTITUDES, AND ACTIONS

Bay State [Hospital] used to do the cheapest abortions on the East Coast, and
we drew cases from all over New England and as far south as North Carolina.
Now we've standardized the costs and the procedures. We're still the only
place that does them in the second trimester, but we've cut back on these too
and cut back the time from twenty-four to nineteen weeks. Of course, we get
picketed, and we were even visited by some Fundamentalist clergy who
threatened a boycott. But while we see a few boycott cards surfacing, it really
hasn't affected our volume. (interview)

The hospital staff member who made this remark understood its irony.
A city regionally renowned for its opposition to abortion had become a
regional center for abortion procedures. Nor was the nonsectarian Bay
State Hospital the only facility in the city performing abortions. Indeed,
if in late-twentieth-century New England, the "scarlet letter" stands for
abortion rather than adultery, the very first entries in the Springfield yel-
low pages provide a range of references under "Abortion Alternatives,"
"Abortion Information," and "Abortion Services."

This now seems like business as usual, but it was not always so. Kenneth
Underwood's book, *Protestant and Catholic* (1957), described a period in
nearby Holyoke, within the same Catholic diocese, when tensions over
contraception reached a fever pitch:

For a brief period in the Fall of 1940, Holyoke, Massachusetts, . . . held the
rapt attention of many religious leaders in the United States. The members
of Roman Catholic and Protestant faiths were set in conflict by the attempt of
Roman Catholic clergy to keep Margaret Sanger, America's foremost birth-
control advocate, from speaking in the First Congregational Church of the
city. The conflict occurred in a community which some Roman Catholic leaders called "the most Catholic city in America," and in a region which some
Protestant ministers termed the "birth land" of American Protestantism (Underwood 1957, p. xiii). . . . To understand the importance to the Roman
Catholic Church of the meeting sponsoring Margaret Sanger, it is important
to bear in mind that [the city] is located in one of the two states in America
which has legally forbidden doctors to provide birth-control information to
married persons, even if considered by the doctor necessary for health reasons. In the Fall of 1940, the New England Mothers' Health Council, affiliated with the Birth Control Federation of America, was engaged in a vigorous
attempt to secure twenty thousand or more certified signatures of the state's
voters on an initiative petition to force the legislature to vote (a change) at its
next session. (ibid., p.3)

Although the speaking appearance was successful, the legislative petition was not. In fact, similar statewide referenda also failed in 1942 and
1948, and it was not until 1966 that Massachusetts became the nation's last
state to decriminalize the sale or distribution of contraceptives by over-
turning a law originally passed in 1879.

Underwood's analysis of the Sanger incident took the form of a historical ethnography of Holyoke's religious conflict within the contexts of class,
ethnicity, politics, and ecclesiastics. He depicted the Catholic diocesan
structure up through the 1950s as both strongly centralized and hierarchi-
cal in its authority pattern, and he noted that the tensions between Catholics and Protestants might have been far more pronounced were it not for
norms of civility concerning church versus church and church versus
state. Then as now, the latter can provide a public veneer for private
unpleasantness and an excuse for avoiding unpleasantness altogether:

> The slogans of "equal status for all religions" and of "absolute separation of
> church and state" represent a vast fabric of truth and fantasy about politics
> and religion. It is a fabric which hides from the religious leaders their actual
> involvement in political life; it also hides from the general public the narrow
> tactical considerations for checking the power of the other religious groups
> which have gone into church action. . . . (ibid., pp. 357–358)

Of course, a great deal has changed since the 1940s, although even as
late as the 1970s, opposition to contraception and the new specter of abortion were seen as basically "Catholic" issues (cf. Hanna 1979). While abortion continues to galvanize political activities by Catholic laity and clergy
across the country, the issue is by no means confined to them. With the
rise of the so-called New Christian Right in American politics, a number
of non-Catholics such as Jesse Helms, Jerry Falwell, and Orrin Hatch
have become key figures in the national abortion debate. And lest one
think there is a monolithic "Catholic" position, the 1984 controversies
generated by such pro-choice Catholics as Mario Cuomo and Geraldine
Ferraro are a sufficient prophylactic.

Springfield's version of the abortion/contraception debate demonstrates
similar diversity. Our survey results indicate that a majority of Springfield's population favored the continued legality of abortion, although the
sentiment was by no means unanimous. The question occurred within a
battery asking whether a series of practices should be legal or illegal. This
particular entry involved "hospitals or clinics performing abortions." The
item was intentionally general. Eschewing the contingencies that complicate the issue for policy purposes, we simply wished to obtain a sense of
the respondent's overall perspective. We used four possible response categories. Just over 55 percent answered that abortion should either "defi-

nitely" or "probably" be legal, compared to one third who answered "definitely" or "probably" illegal. Further, "definitely" legal responses outweighed "definitely" illegal responses by 34 percent to 25 percent.

Appendix C provides a technical analysis of the sources of such sentiments in the general sample. Without recapitulating the details here, it is worth noting that there is a predictably negative relationship (Pearson $r = -.425$) between favoring abortion legality and one's degree of personal religious involvement (as measured by an index combining church attendance, religious beliefs, and the number of one's closest friends who are religiously involved). Put more graphically, of those who scored high on personal devoutness, only 14 percent thought that abortion should definitely be legal as opposed to 45 percent who thought it should be illegal. On the other hand, of those who scored low on religiosity, the comparable figures were reversed: 53 percent versus 11 percent.

What is even more remarkable is the variety within religious communities. Unfortunately, our sample of Protestants was too small to yield a reliable measure of the difference between liberals and conservatives, and the problem was compounded by race, since most of our conservative Protestants were black Baptists. However, it is worth noting that Springfield's Catholics were more heterogeneous than its Protestants on the issue. Whereas 75 percent of the Protestants favored legal abortions compared to 19 percent opposing them, Catholics were more evenly split and far from the monolithic stereotype. Here, too, opinions were skewed toward legality, as 46 percent of the Catholics answered that abortion should definitely or probably be legal, while only 40 percent answered definitely or probably illegal, with the percentages in the extreme categories roughly equal: 25 percent answering definitely legal and 27 percent answering definitely illegal. Finally, some 14 percent of the Catholic respondents remained "not sure" on the issue, as compared to only 6 percent of the Protestants. Given the continued clarity of the official Catholic position, the large number of "not sure" responses is itself noteworthy. It seems unlikely that these persons were unaware of the Church's position. This may instead represent a stage of transition out of the institution's basic grasp, an aspect of the secularization that we describe in the next chapter.

A different indication that Springfield's Catholics are not ecclesiastical lemmings in following the hierarchy on abortion is the outcome of the November 1986 Massachusetts state referendum described in Chapter Four. Unlike earlier referenda that sought to liberalize contraceptive statutes, this one tried to reverse the liberal tide by allowing the Massachusetts legislature to place restrictions on the availability of publicly funded abortions. As described in Chapter Four, the measure failed both throughout the state (39 percent to 54 percent with 7 percent blanks) and in Springfield (39 percent to 44 percent with 17 percent blanks). Of course, there was predictable variation among Springfield's various wards, depending in part on their proportions of older, working-class Catholics. In addition, the voting patterns split in the communities surrounding Springfield on the same basis: the two poorer, more traditionally Catholic neighbors (Holyoke and Chicopee) voted to pass the measure, but Springfield's more affluent suburbs (Longmeadow, East Longmeadow, Wilbraham) voted to defeat it.

So much, then, for an overview of the abortion attitudes of the population at large. But, of course, a city's primary political actors are not always in concert with the citizenry as a whole. Policy outcomes often fail to articulate the voice of the majority and tend to represent instead the temporarily resolved struggles among elites and organized interest groups. Certainly our community survey would be an inaccurate gauge of the city's recent history on these issues. To obtain a better purchase on Springfield's sexual politics, it is necessary to look more closely at several strategic sources of influence in the policy-making—and policy-breaking—process. These include the Catholic clergy and the bishop himself, the pro-life and pro-choice elements of the city's grass-roots activism, the Springfield newspapers, and a political and economic elite straddling a razor's edge of change and conflict.

Catholic Clergy and the Bishop

Although the distinction between Catholics and non-Catholics made less difference in predicting lay attitudes toward abortion than we had expected, for clergy the distinction was pivotal. Springfield's Catholic clergy were far more opposed to abortion and its legalization than their non-Catholic colleagues. Whereas 35 percent of Protestant and Jewish clergy believed that abortion should definitely or probably be illegal, the percentage leaped to 77 percent among Catholic priests and sisters. This percentage gap of 42 percent for non-Catholic versus Catholic clergy was considerably greater than the comparable gap among the laity (21 percent).

This is somewhat surprising in view of previous studies. When one considers attitudes toward social issues other than abortion, it is not uncommon for clergy to lead rather than lag in taking more liberal or change-oriented positions. As Jeffrey Hadden (1969) showed in his survey of Protestant ministers in the 1960s, in most denominations pastors have been considerably more liberal than the laity on the political issues of the day, and this presaged a "gathering storm in the churches." Survey data since that time have continued to find such differences (e.g., Quinley 1974).

But there is an important distinction between issues that are secondary to the Church and those that lie at its theological core and are critical to its basic identity. Clergy may be more rather than less conservative on a central issue such as abortion because professionals have both a tendency and a responsibility to cleave close to the defining tenets of their host institutions. On the other hand, abortion may now be undergoing a transition from a primary to a secondary matter within Catholicism. After all, it is also possible to read our survey results from an apostate perspective, noting that only 65 percent of the priests and sisters felt that abortion should definitely be illegal, while, some 12 percent felt probably so, 10 percent felt that it should probably be legal, another 3 percent definitely so, and some 10 percent were simply not sure. From this vantage point, more than a third of the Catholic clergy in this highly Catholic city wavered on what has long been regarded as a fundamental Catholic dictate.

For most clergy as for most issues, however, the bishop set the tone. He spoke often, both in public and in private, about abortion and contraception. One after another of our interview respondents remarked on how important the abortion issue was to him. One, recalling the bishop's address to a city task force of social service professionals, when he departed from his prepared text to speak out directly against abortion and any city policy connected to it, said: "A lot of the people there resented it" (interview). Another interviewee—a Catholic city official—suggested somewhat bitterly that the bishop, like the Church generally, "has used the abortion issue somewhat cynically—you know, like an organizing tool, a way to mobilize the troops and get the 25- to 45-year-olds active again" (interview).

While it is impossible to divine such motives reliably, it is clear that the bishop's position on the matter was more complex than customarily regarded. Interviews with him revealed strong but measured antiabortion arguments. He took great care to point out that the Church's positions on abortion and contraception were part of a broader "respect for life," which included strictures against euthanasia, nuclear war, and capital punishment, as well as a concern for economic justice. The bishop's theological opposition to all threats against human life and dignity were described as a "seamless garment" and associated him with Cardinal Bernardin's "consistent ethic of life" (cf. M. Johnson 1990). This was explicit in his pastoral letter to the Springfield diocese just prior to the 1984 presidential election, when he noted that war and poverty were as important to Catholics as abortion (*Morning Union*, October 2, 1984).

Further, the bishop's relation to the community conveyed an appreciation of its religious pluralism and its political realism. He seemed to reflect the buoyant fatalism of one whose finger plugs a leaky dike while water pours over the top. He was consistently compassionate toward those facing such moral dilemmas as an unwanted pregnancy. His counsel and message were neither judgmental nor retributional. For example, while admitting concern over the abortions performed at the city's secular Bay State Hospital, he returned from visiting a nun who had undergone heart surgery there, asking, "Can we condemn an institution for one evil when other good things are also being done?" While the bishop was firm in not retreating on the immorality of abortion, he was also quoted to the effect that this was not the only item that concerned the Church and "You have to have a sense of timing" (interview).

Of course, the bishop's position was as much a function of his institutional role as his private convictions. As the local embodiment of the Catholic ecclesia, he was often assumed to represent its positions in pure and uncompromised form. While this may have failed to reflect his personal nuances, it assisted him in his role as an ideological beacon in the community. The vast majority of Springfielders could state confidently the bishop's blanket opposition to abortion and contraception—even those who had never heard or read him on the topic.

However, sexuality was one area about which he frequently called civic leaders to express his views. For example, he called the president of a local television station to applaud his "courage" in refusing to run ads for condoms, although the president responded that he did not know how much longer he could hold the line. Also, the chancery often hosted groups of area political officials as occasions for sharing perspectives. One legislator may have exaggerated in contending that "the only time we hear from him [the bishop] was over abortion" (interview). However, our interviewees were unanimous in citing abortion as the political issue about which the bishop was most active. In the words of one prominent civic leader:

> You don't talk about downtown development without talking to the bishop first. You don't pick the site of the new jail without consulting the bishop. He doesn't call us; we call him. Except on abortion. There he takes the initiative, and you can be sure he calls the mayor. (interview)

And yet this bishop was known more for a light touch than a heavy hand when push came to shove in the political ring. He appeared to sense that a hard line could alienate increasing numbers of middle-class Catholics. It would also foreclose new opportunities for moving the Church into the center of civic life from its historical position on the edge. As he was more inclined to heal old wounds than open new ones, his political posture was noticeably less contentious than his predecessors, or those bishops in larger cities who preside over a still embattled Catholicism as part of a more impersonal struggle of conflicting forces. As one chancery staff member put it:

Abortion is an important issue to the bishop, and he brings it into a lot of his messages. We do all we can within the confines of the law, but nothing outside the law. We lay it on the table all the time to let everyone know where we stand. But demonstrations aren't his style. And I've never known him to make a deal. He never would. He just says, this is how I see it; that's it. He has good relations with political people . . . but he's not involved in politics. He sees politics as the realm of the laity, and [believes] they have the right to form their own conscience and opinions. He doesn't want them to shirk their responsibilities. (interview)

Like many politicians, the bishop sometimes seemed more interested in stating his positions than in implementing them. Here is another respect in which the "frontstage" performances and "backstage" understandings of public policy may diverge. It is one thing to put a law or a theological directive on public record; it is quite another to enforce them closely—or even believe this is possible. Bishops are not alone in looking away from exceptions to their rules. Jurists, legislators, and police officers all know the advantages of the averted eye. The point is not hypocrisy, but rather that public political symbols have a meaning and significance of their own. The logic of this cultural sphere must be observed, even when it does not accord completely with recognized structural realities.

Earlier, we recalled the statewide 1986 referendum to inhibit state funding of abortions (Question 1), which was linked with an additional referendum to facilitate state aid to private and parochial schools (Question 2). As noted in Chapter Four, in neither case was the diocesan political effort conspicuous for its zeal. The bishop expressly forbade priests from issuing direct voting instructions from the pulpit or as part of the liturgy (*Daily Hampshire Gazette*, October 15, 1986). However, the written programs distributed at services in the diocesan cathedral in the weeks just prior to the election did contain brief messages regarding both referenda. Here, abortion received the greater rhetorical investment:

Concerning Question #1: Up to 8,500 abortions per year are paid for with our tax dollars. That is about one abortion every 15 minutes of every workday. Every Massachusetts taxpayer is forced to support this destruction of unborn human life. On November 4, a "Yes" vote on Question #1 would allow our state legislature to stop tax funded abortion. Please consider this when voting.

Concerning Question #2: On November 4, by voting "Yes" on Question #2 voters in Massachusetts will allow students in parochial schools and other non-public schools to be considered for assistance allowed by the United States Constitution but now unfairly forbidden by the Massachusetts State

Antiabortion demonstrators outside Baystate Medical Center—December 1989.

Convention. Please give this careful consideration. (*Diocesan Bulletin*, October 19, 1986)

Again, as noted earlier, both referenda lost, although the margin was narrower in Springfield than for the state as a whole. Later a chancery staff member commented that the bishop was "not all that disappointed" at the results on Question 2. While he may have been more chagrined over Question 1, even here he was plainly reconciled. Two interviewees, one an antiabortion activist and the other a Catholic religious, claimed that the bishop put more effort into Question 2 than into the abortion measure. This may indicate their disappointment with his commitment to their issue of choice, but it is also a comment on the bishop's low-key political style generally.

For the most part, then, the bishop has taken the high road of public proclamations and tolerant pluralism in Springfield politics. However, one important reason for this is that there were others who exhibited a more militant intolerance and used occasional guerilla tactics. Indeed, the real activism in Springfield's sexual politics has come not from efforts organized by the Church hierarchy, but from those instigated by the grass-roots groups, to which we turn next. Although the bishop did appoint a

Springfield parish priest as director of pro-life activities for the diocese, even he took a position to the rear of the lay activists when the battles raged.

Grass-Roots Activists

Strictly speaking, there were two grass-roots groups involved in the struggle over abortion. We shall continue to focus more on the pro-life movement because of its religious grounding and more immediate involvement in the political process. However, the local pro-choice advocates were also a continuing presence whose contrast with the pro-lifers extended beyond the basic dispute between them (cf. Zurcher and Kirkpatrick 1976; Luker 1984; Wood and Hughes 1984; Himmelstein 1986).

For the most part, the proponents of choice were women of high status who came from the suburbs more often than from the city proper, and who saw restraints on abortion as affronts to their feminist autonomy (cf. Scott and Schuman 1988 for a confirming national portrait). Linked more by a concern for women's rights than by any dedication to abortion itself, they formed more of a loose coalition than a tightly bound cell. Insofar as they had direct religious connections, these tended to be with liberal Protestant churches or the Jewish Federation. But their more pressing affiliations were with local chapters of the National Organization for Women and the League of Women Voters, and specifically pertinent organizations as the local Family Planning Council, Planned Parenthood, Massachusetts Choice, the Coalition for Reproductive Freedom, the Religious Coalition for Abortion Rights, and Catholics for Free Choice.

When compared to the pro-life exponents, the pro-choice advocates were far less strident or contentious in pursuing their cause. This was partly a function of class, both in the sense of style and because these women already had greater access to power and the media by virtue of the connections their status afforded. They may also have sensed that history and the courts were with them, thus requiring fewer desperate measures in response. For whatever reason, Springfield's pro-choice movement never became a compelling public antagonist. While its representatives wrote eloquent letters to local editors and offered well-crafted testimony as part of their witness before the School Committee and the City Council, they resembled lightning bugs more than gadflies in the political air.

Such decorousness was often conspicuously absent among the approximately fifty lay activists at the core of the city's antiabortion movement, which also included much stronger male participation than did their prochoice counterparts. The pro-life leaders, two evangelical Protestants and a Catholic, were the Springfield chapter heads of the National Federation for Decency (NFD) and Massachusetts Citizens For Life (CFL). Remarkably enough, here the often virulent hostility between Catholics and conservative Protestants gave way to a shared agenda against common opponents. Such ecumenical cooperation is especially rare within conservative Protestantism, where evangelicals and fundamentalists are often at sword's point (cf. Guth 1983a, 1983b). "Fellowshipping" with those who do not share an identical theology is an understandable anathema to those for whom theology is critical and seemingly small differences of worldly and otherworldly views may become magnified with emotion. One consequence of this uneasiness is that much of the overt political work is organized not by congregations but rather by "parachurch" organizations (Guth 1983b), through which conservative Protestants of different theological persuasions can cooperate on common sociomoral issues. Only recently have independent Baptist and evangelical churches begun to work together politically, and although The Evangelical Association of Ministers of Greater Springfield (TEAMS) issued a press release endorsing the 1986 abortion referendum, even this limited form of concerted action at the congregational level remains atypical. Moreover, there was virtually no cooperation between white evangelical Protestants and black Protestants. Race remained a formidable obstacle, despite common theological and ideological positions extending to a shared opposition to abortion.

Overall, there was greater ecumenism among pro-life laity than clergy. Despite the pro-life position most Catholic priests share with conservative Protestant clergy, many priests reported feeling more comfortable in their limited contact with liberal Protestant pastors. Priests claimed to be uneasy around "true believers" and appreciated the more tolerant ideology and life-style among the liberals. Both liberal Protestant and Catholic clergy were more likely to have had more extensive educational backgrounds than the evangelical pastors.

Clergy of all stripes reported difficulties with the antiabortion activists themselves. Several liberal Protestant pastors had occasion to admonish pro-choice laity about the problems of using repeated abortions as a substitute for contraception and more preferable birth control measures. But virtually all of our clergy respondents confessed problems with the obstinacy and obduracy of the pro-life movement. One Catholic priest spoke for many clergy in describing his reservations:

> I have problems myself with the pro-lifers in the CFL and the NFD. They don't want moral discussion; they just want to give dogmatic answers. They are a real problem because they only care about that one issue. (interview)

In fact, neither the Catholic hierarchy nor many of its priests and sisters had much contact with, let alone control over, these antiabortion groups. Even many conservative Protestant ministers were uncomfortable around them. While a number of these conservative clergy had been involved in antiabortion efforts, they were not the linchpins of the local movement, and lay persons who had gone from church to church soliciting support and resources reported a sense of caution, even suspicion, from ideologically sympathetic pastors:

> The established churches want to stay established; they don't want to get involved with any conflict. Even the fundamentalist churches don't want to get involved. They might lose members, and besides, they're afraid of working with nonfundamentalists. Even our own church membership was sometimes a handicap. People were afraid we were recruiting for members. (interview)

Much of this is due to organizational pressures on the pastors. Competition for Protestant church members is acute in a Catholic city like Springfield, and high membership is necessary to pay the bills, including the pastor's own salary. Clergy were concerned not only that their own antiabortion activists would be stigmatizing, but also that activists from other congregations would proselytize among their members. Hence, while several churches organized antiabortion activities, these were rarely central to the churches' programs, the clergy's priorities, or the movement itself. One conservative pastor described his own conservative approach to social action in these terms:

> The church itself is not involved in social action, but we encourage our members to get involved—and they do in all kinds of things, from pro-life and the teenage pregnancy test and counseling center to "Toys for Tots" and food and clothing drives. We encourage voting and public involvement, but the church tries to be discrete in its stands on issues. (interview)

In the main, then, Springfield's antiabortion activists were laypersons who went beyond their church communities in the depth of their commitment and the radicalism of their political tactics. In the words of one clergyman, "These people have the noise but not the numbers. They're often a kind of stalking horse for the chancery" (interview).

In contrast to the bishop's broad sense of pro-life, including opposition to capital punishment, poverty, and nuclear war, the grass-roots antiabortion activists were more single-mindedly concerned with sex. For them, abortion was intertwined with contraception, sex education, teenage pregnancy, and pornography—all with the unifying theme of sexual morality, pursued relentlessly. In a letter to the local newspaper, one activist deplored any plan that would sanction the distribution of contraceptives, and asked aggressively: "Are we a nation gone sex-raving mad?" (*Morning Union*, May 21, 1987). On the other hand, there was little direct concern with AIDS. Pro-life activists were worried that any AIDS education campaign would implicitly legitimate homosexuality and promiscuity, particularly if condoms were offered as a solution. When two interviewees were asked about AIDS, their remarks were indicative of the general feeling. First one responded: "We say 'We told you so.'" And another asked rhetorically: "If homosexuality is a private matter, why should AIDS be a public problem?" (interview).

As noted earlier, Springfield was host to local chapters of several pertinent national organizations, each of which tended to focus on a particular issue. These were the National Federation for Decency, which focused on pornography; the Massachusetts branch of Citizens For Life, on abortion and contraception; the Concerned Women of America, on sex education; and obviously the Women Exploited By Abortion, on abortion. In practice these organizations comprised largely the same people, who used the organizational titles interchangeably, pooled their mailing lists, exchanged information, and shared the same political strategies. For each of these social problems, the solution was identical: a return to "traditional values" and a "Christian" code of personal sexual morality. The activists saw themselves as fulfilling a religious mission, and although, as one said, "We aren't telling anyone they have to be Christian," they left no doubt that there was only one possible Christian position on these issues. When asked about liberal Protestant involvement with the pro-choice forces, one responded: "You're saying that they might be Christian; we're saying they can't be" (interview).

Without the resources or community prestige to provide access to decision-making elites, the pro-life activists—like the Covenant in the preceding chapter—relied on highly visible confrontations to generate interest and publicity in the local news media. For example, in March of 1987, three members of the CFL were arrested for chaining themselves to the furniture in a waiting room of a clinic where abortions were performed (*Morning Union*, March 3, 1987). On another occasion they put leaflets on cars parked at Sabbath services at the Conservative Jewish temple. The leaflets, complete with swastikas, likened abortion to Nazi genocide and criticized a local Jewish doctor by name (*Morning Union*, January 13, 1987). At still another point they picketed the First Congregational Church after the pastor issued a pro-choice pronouncement (*Morning Union*, October 20, 1984). In addition, they picketed local hotels whose cable-TV service allegedly included X-rated movies (*Union-News*, August 3, 1987). Still other frequent targets were the convenience stores that carried *Playboy* or *Penthouse* magazine; some store owners admitted to discontinuing the sales because of the demonstrations (e.g., *Morning Union*, April 11, 1986).

For many social movements like this one and that of the Covenant, maintaining the motivation and participation of a cadre of highly committed volunteers often takes precedence over reaching out for the secondary support of those with less pervfervid beliefs. Because this often requires a continued escalation of tone and tactics to shore up the faithful and remain true to the initial commitments, there is a common tendency toward radicalization rather than amelioration. In this sense, ideology and organization (culture and structure) often reinforce each other in a social movement, each becoming both cause and effect. Thus, ideological inflexibility makes wider recruitment difficult, resulting in an even more isolated organizational core, which only reinforces the sense of ideological distinctiveness, and so on as the two tendencies feed on each other in cycles.

Meanwhile, the pro-life group also used a confrontational style in seeking influence over electoral politics. Consider Springfield's 1987 city elections. Just before the September election primary, the local branch of Citizens For Life (CFL) released its political endorsements. All the incumbent city councillors, except one, were endorsed, as was the only incumbent member of the School Committee running for reelection. With the exception of one black School Committee candidate, all of the endorsed incumbents qualified for the general election. The city councillor who was not endorsed also survived the primary, although his position in the final primary standings slipped several ranks from his showing in 1985 and presaged trouble ahead.

In the November general election, the CFL again released a list of recommended candidates. In this case, however, it singled out one challenger for the City Council and specifically recommended that voters not vote for him due to his position favoring abortion. To inquiring supporters, this Catholic candidate denied that he had taken such a position, but his denials received little publicity. While it is questionable how much coverage the CFL leaflet received, and because the candidate also had controversial family ties that his expensive campaign may not have overcome, he did lose, placing tenth in a race for nine seats. Meanwhile, all eight running incumbents were reelected in the November election, along with one challenger from a well-known Irish-Catholic family who was the wife of a former city councillor and who had been endorsed by the CFL. The incumbent city councillor who had not been endorsed by the CFL leaflets was also reelected, but only by placing ninth and last, and his showing was thought to dampen his prospects for long-term advancement to a higher position, including the mayor's office.

While the episode is not an unequivocal demonstration of the right-to-life groups' electoral power, it is the kind of political scenario that gives the movement credibility among local political observers. Two different local politicians estimated to us that the hard-core right-to-life electorate consisted of about 300 votes. That constitutes some 2 percent of the average primary voter turnout and only 1 percent of the general electorate. What makes the votes formidable, however, is precisely their "hardness";

that is, their rock-ribbed responsiveness to the issue and their certainty of being cast. Given Springfield's at-large system, where each voter casts nine votes and the top nine vote-getters win, such a block can have dispro-portionate impact when other voters vary widely over both issues and candidates, and sometimes cancel each other out.

Moreover, although 300 voters may not spell the difference in a two-person mayoralty race, they can have a considerable impact in a City Council or School Committee election with a crowded field. It is not unu-sual for such a small difference to make or break those on the bottom cusp, and votes of this number frequently influence the relative ranks of those elected (an important political barometer in Springfield's political weather where a potential mayoral candidate must generally finish as the top city council vote-getter at least once to be taken seriously). For example, in the 1987 City Council election, 5,000 votes separated the number-one vote-getter from the number-nine finisher (the incumbent mentioned above); but only 1,000 votes separated numbers five through nine.

Meanwhile, another incident illustrates a different tactic and reveals several of the competing forces surrounding abortion as a local political issue. A half-hour before officially starting, every regular City Council meeting has a "Citizen Speak" time reserved for questions, comments, and general input from citizens; special "land-use" City Council meetings do not have such a period. But before the land-use meeting of July 27, 1987, a representative of Citizens For Life showed the graphic antiabor-tion film "The Eclipse of Reason." Neither the council nor the public knew this was to be on the agenda; the council president had merely invited councillors to come a half-hour earlier than normal, without explanation. The president himself was not in attendance when the film was shown, and it was a matter of subsequent debate whether he had merely author-ized the showing after being approached by the CFL representatives or had actually taken the initiative in inviting them (*Union-News*, July 28, 1987; August 10, 1987).

The screening generated more controversy than the film itself. Al-though no councillor took public issue with the message of the film, sev-eral objected because it provided only one side of the issue, and most argued on still more neutral and procedural grounds that, if the film was to be shown at all, a regularly scheduled Citizen Speak time would have been more suitable (*Union-News*, July 28, 1987; August 10, 1987; August 29, 1987). Newspaper editorials weighed in heavily with both objections (*Union-News*, August 13, 1987). The City Council president reacted by claiming he was only responding to a citizen's request, and he offered other sides of the issue equal time. Planned Parenthood representatives accepted the offer, and unlike the CFL presentation, had a spot on the agenda that was announced in advance and occurred during a Citizen

Speak time. Perhaps predictably, only three of the nine city councillors were present (*Union-News*, September 18, 1987). Thus, while a generalized sense of fairness and "equal time" (plus the newspapers' considerable influence) were able to get a hearing for the pro-choice position, the political repercussions of alienating the pro-life activists kept most of the city politicians from listening. Avoiding controversy is a full-time pursuit for many politicians, particularly when the controversy is tied to such deep-seated moral divisions.

As this episode suggests, representatives of the pro-life movement were not strangers to city government meetings, including those of both the City Council and the School Committee. City officials could almost be heard to sigh with weary resignation at their appearance. Sheer persistence was a major factor in the pro-life influence, as was its constant threat to embarrass the officials by drawing a sharp moral line and publicizing the name of anyone crossing it. And it bears repeating yet again that numbers were no measure of its effectiveness. Even though it was the same small group of activists over and over, they could be quickly mobilized, and within the confines of a city chamber they both outflanked and outshouted the officials present. These were not conditions to maximize reasoned debate. Instead they represented an aspect of city politics that could be chilling and shrill, one that could easily spill over into other issues. Consider, for example, the following remark by an antiabortion activist—one that may combine both truth and paranoia in a particularly volatile mix:

> Actually a lot of police favor abortion. They say, "If you abort one Puerto Rican or [black], that's one less problem." Lots of people in this town feel that way. Genocide against minorities is okay. (interview)

It is a political truism that an ideologically cohesive and aggressive minority can overcome a diffuse and passive majority. Precisely because of its minority status and its sense that the tide is running against it, the minority is apt to be more desperate and more zealous than its mainstream opponents. It is also less likely to observe the etiquette of conventional restraint; indeed, there is a kind of special if perverse power that accrues to the uncivil. By pushing their arguments to extremes, vocal minorities can often gain a moral advantage, particularly if those arguments prey upon the uneasiness of those whose values or opinions are in transition. In any matter of controversy, there are many majority members who are ideologically secure in the privacy of their homes but discomfited by public scrutiny. This is both cause and consequence of an anxiety that their position may be turned against them. Threatened with exposure and the difficulty of defending a position that is still new to them, many would rather duck than fight even a small activist minority.

Springfield's politicians were especially troubled by this dynamic. Beyond their personal commitments, they sought to avoid taking positions that their constituents found morally ambiguous. Hence, policy outcomes on such issues frequently depended less on exerting power than on avoiding embarrassment. In a community whose political culture depends on consensus as much as Springfield's, becoming associated with controversy carries the risk of becoming a target. When the extremes are as polarized as they are in the politics of sexuality, being in the middle of the pack is comforting.

Clearly, the antiabortion activists took advantage of this vulnerability and exerted a quite different form of political influence than, say, the Catholic hierarchy. In fact, some members of the Catholic religious community scoffed at their tactics. The point is conveyed in the comments of a Catholic sister, a staff member in a Catholic hospital within the diocese, one that obviated the abortion issue altogether by simply abolishing its entire obstetrics and gynecological services by 1970. The sister recalled several visits from lay antiabortion activists who asked her to join them in picketing the private hospital that did do abortions. She dismissed the possibility with a wave of her hand, "as if I had time for that kind of thing . . . that's not my role" (interview).

The Springfield Newspapers

Like many beleaguered social movements, the pro-life phalanx was inclined toward paranoia concerning the opposition, and not without reason. Their concern was not so much with their opposite numbers in the city's pro-choice movement; it was directed more pointedly toward the "pro-abortion conspiracy" of the city's power brokers led by the chief agent of moral decline, the Springfield newspapers.

The pro-life leaders were convinced that the newspapers were attempting to "convert the city to a pro-abortion position." They were primed with instances where their antiabortion activities or press releases were underplayed in favor of pro-choice stories:

> There were 119 people at the talk by Eleanor Smeal [the president of the pro-choice National Organization for Women] and nine stories in the paper, but there were 647 people at our pro-life Mother's Day rally and only one story. (interview)

Our pro-life respondents were also quick to note that the newspapers had recommended a pro-choice "no" vote on the aforementioned statewide referendum (*Morning Union*, October 20, 1986). Perhaps worried that he sounded too fanatical, one respondent twice commented that he "used to dismiss all conspiracy theories." However, since becoming active in this issue, he has realized "how powerful a conspiracy by the media and political leaders could be." In part, this reflects the relative powerlessness and isolation of the antiabortion activists themselves.

Once again, this is in marked contrast to the Catholic bishop, who reported having been "blessed" with excellent relations with a very attentive media. In fact, one local newspaper commented on the distinction between the two political styles. During the 1984 presidential campaign and shortly after New York governor Mario Cuomo's address at the University of Notre Dame, an editorial (*Morning Union*, October 3, 1984) noted approvingly the bishop of Springfield's pastoral letter urging Catholics to consider not only abortion but also issues of justice, peace, and poverty. The pastoral letter called for nuclear arms control as well as decried abortion, but it did not endorse any particular candidate: "We don't have a right to do that. . . . We're not seeking to impose our morality on anyone." The newspaper editorial commented:

> Indeed, rather than using the strident tones of some pro-life advocates, [the bishop] called those who believe in freedom of choice "people of sincerity and good will who do not perceive abortions as a moral evil and a violation of a basic human right." . . . We do not support the Church's viewpoint in the pro-life, pro-choice debate. But we respect that position and those who advocate it. . . . There has never been any doubt that morality plays a role in government. . . . But we find it disturbing when one party or one segment of society claims to be the protector and interpreter of that morality. (*Morning Union*, October 3, 1984)

This left little doubt as to the paper's position on the issue, and which style of politics it considered legitimate in the local context. Meanwhile, the question of acceptable political activism appeared in another editorial written shortly after the United States Supreme Court upheld the *Roe* v. *Wade* decision in June 1986. The editorial quoted Justice Blackmun's majority opinion that "states are not free . . . to intimidate women into continuing pregnancies." It then continued:

> The word "intimidate" was well chosen. Strident "pro-life" advocates have been trying to do that since *Roe* vs. *Wade* finally gave women absolute control over their bodies . . . picketing of abortion clinics, violent acts . . . single-issue political movements, threats to pro-choice candidates—all have been aimed at intimidating pregnant women and those who would protect their right to make their own choices. (*Sunday Republican*, June 15, 1986)

It is little wonder, then, that the grass-roots pro-life activists thought of the paper as their opponent. Not only did it oppose their policy demands, but it criticized their political techniques and confrontational style—a style that they were virtually forced to use in the absence of the insider's access to decision-making processes or of the kind of community high status that could convey influence without politicking. Indeed, this provides another example of why such activists must "moralize" issues. In the press, the dominant discourse concerning abortion and sexuality pivoted around individual rights and freedom of choice in family planning (*Union-News*, June 17, 1987), and included an appeal to the community's well-being underlying sex education in the public schools (*Union-News*, June 29, 1987). To break through these moral injunctions, the pro-life forces needed equally urgent appeals of their own. They transcended the classical liberal individualism and a laissez-faire approach to government with a no less classically conservative invocation of a collective morality set in a traditional religion.

But, of course, few movements calculate strategies in such explicit terms, and it is dangerous to reify them accordingly. Often strategies seem clearer to the observer with hindsight than to the participants themselves. Moreover, it is hard to know the importance of other potential factors that may have set a dynamic in motion. For example, to what extent was the conflict between the newspapers and the antiabortion advocates fueled by the fact that both the publisher and the editor of the newspapers were Jewish. The point is not to allege anti-Semitism but to suggest the potentially powerful effect of religious and class differences combined. Insofar as this did operate to exacerbate the tension between the newspapers and the pro-lifers, the latter were by no means alone in their animus.

-strikes me that a comparison between pro-lifers + covenant would be instructive -- seem very similar.

The Political and Economic Elite

As we mentioned in Chapter Four, the single most commonly recalled instance of church-state conflict in Springfield involved the Tel-Med case of the late 1970s. The incident concerned a city telephone-and-tape answering service that Blue-Cross–Blue Shield established to provide health information to anyone who called. Although the insurance company funded this Tel-Med system, the city was to provide the site and secretarial assistance. However, one problem concerned the tapes on abortion and contraception that were part of the package. The mayor at that time was a Catholic and a charter member of a city pro-life group, Springfield's Birthright; at the same time, he was no doubt concerned about pressure from other antiabortion activists (possibly including his wife and brother-in-law, also charter members of the group).

For whatever personal and political reasons (and the Church itself was only marginally involved), the mayor withheld the tapes on abortion and contraception before he allowed the system to begin. The local branch of the Massachusetts Civil Liberties Union obtained a restraining order against the mayor to return the tapes. After only a few days, the matter was resolved when Blue Cross–Blue Shield moved the operation to a privately owned hospital and dealt the city out entirely. The issue burned brightly but briefly in the local media, and the church-state constitutional issues were never pursued.

A city councillor at the time described the mayor's reactions and their consequences this way:

> [He] got pressured on the Tel-Med tapes by some of his more puritanical pro-life friends. He's pro-life too, but more moderate. Later, he said privately he'd made a mistake. Actually he took flak from both the left and the right on that one. (interview)

The episode offers a revealing look at the response of political officials to dissension generally and to the abortion issue in particular—the initial conservative instinct, the quick resolution of the imbroglio, and the cooperation of political and business leaders in dousing flames before they can spread. At least in areas of controversy, city elites play dual roles as both the leaders and the led. On the one hand, they are obviously in a position to influence others through their views and activities; on the other hand, they are ringed by those who would constrain their actions, and their public status may require compromising their private positions. Often caught between community factions, they must either take a middle course or gamble that they will be followed down a bolder path.

The dilemma was especially acute concerning Springfield's abortion issue by the late 1970s. Here the elite was caught between a newly developing and still insecure community majority and a small but politically militant minority. Elite members who operated in the political background had some room to maneuver, but politicians and city officials in the public limelight were squeezed more directly.

Our questionnaire sample of the political and economic elite consisted mostly of those in the second echelon—ward leaders, city commission and committee members, heads of small businesses, and officers of major corporations. Some 70 percent held the private view that abortions should be legal, with only 21 percent feeling that they should either definitely or probably be illegal, and another 10 percent not sure. Perhaps predictably, the political elite were somewhat more conservative than the economic. Thirty percent of the political officials felt that abortion should be illegal, as opposed to 14 percent of the economic executives. This may be partly because the political leaders were closer to the electoral pulse and partly because they included a higher proportion of Catholics—55 percent, as opposed to 44 percent among the economic elite. Even among Catholic members of the entire political-economic elite sample, a majority favored legality (52 percent, as compared to 36 percent preferring illegality), but it is worth noting that 88 percent of the non-Catholic elites favored legal abortions, whether or not they actually approved of the practice.

One might suppose that the degree of personal religiosity would be as strongly related to abortion attitudes among these elites as we saw among the general sample earlier in this chapter. In fact, the correlation among the elites was considerably weaker (−.25 as compared to −.43) Two factors help to account for this falling off. First, the elite contained proportionately fewer conservative (and black) Protestants, and they tended to join traditional Catholics in sharpening the relationship within the general sample. Second, the more educated elites were subject to a wider variety of influences on their abortion attitudes than religion alone. They were also more likely to compartmentalize their religious practices from their ethical judgments. Thus, 30 percent or almost one third of the highly religious elite members felt that abortions should definitely be legal, and this included a large number of Catholics. In fact, there was an overall pro-choice majority for even those Catholic elite members who were devout in their personal religious activity. Appendix C provides a more detailed statistical analysis of this and related patterns.

Despite a likely majority of city politicians who privately favored the continued availability of abortions, only one elected official—a Republican state legislator—was openly pro-choice. Many agreed implicitly with the comments of two long-time office-holders:

> There are just some things you can express privately that you can't say publicly. I wouldn't want to be seen as pro-choice. It would seem like a betrayal, a walking away from my roots, and a disloyalty to tradition. (interview)

> I don't really see any difference between the rhythm method and contraception, and I sure prefer contraception to abortion. Actually a lot of politicians are just politically pro-life. Besides, most pro-choice Catholics will still vote for pro-life candidates. I think I could get away with almost anything but being pro-choice. (interview)

All of this lies behind two further ironies in the city's politics. The first is that cultural change is not always manifest in clashing symbols; quietude itself may be a measure of changes under way. Thus, as important as abortion was to the city's public morality, private doubts had begun to emerge, creating ambiguity, uncertainty, and a growing sense of uneasiness among rank-and-file voters. This in turn often produced an awkward silence on the issue. For example, one pro-choice activist recalled:

> A couple of years ago, I was on a forum on abortion on the radio—you know, a talk show. It was well advertised to be about abortion, but the only calls we got were about school prayer and aid to parochial schools. Not a single one on abortion. (interview)

Similarly, a recent aspirant for the School Committee described the typical "candidates night" held around the city:

> The only religious component of the evening involved the pro-life issue. Mostly, it was treated not as divisive but as a platitude, with heads nodding. People are afraid of raising questions directly. . . . They're scared heads will roll. (interview)

The paradox was underscored by another of our politically engaged respondents, who commented that as large as abortion loomed in the city's moral culture, it "has never really been raised in city affairs, let alone been placed on any city agenda" (interview). At least this was true until the mid-1980s when, as we shall see momentarily, the School Committee became embroiled in an issue involving a school health clinic and a sex education course. But even this required the provocation of pro-life activists "outside the system." Precisely because abortion was so potentially volatile, no mainstream politician wanted to contend with it publicly. A longtime participant in city politics recalled a candidate for City Council in the late 1970s whose entire platform was antiabortion. Her candidacy never went anywhere in the polls; she did not even survive the primary. Of course, this is true of most issues that reflect politically charged divisions. Except in cases where extremist movements and political radicals force an issue from the flanks, most established politicians—especially incumbents but often challengers as well—prefer to wage campaigns over less explosive matters more amenable to an insider's control and euphemisms.

Even some pro-life politicians recoil from the pro-life activists. Two elected officials, the first consistently weaker at the polls than the second, described the CFL:

> They are the only extremist faction in the city's political spectrum. They have overwhelming influence, and time and again I've seen them intimidate the School Committee. In fact, even though I'm personally pro-life, I actually like the pro-choice people better. If you disagree with the pro-choice folks, they'll just argue with you and try to change your mind; if you disagree with the pro-lifers, they'll try to destroy you." (interview)

> I've never seen a group like the CFL. I didn't fill out their form this year, and when they called, I said, "You know my views; do what you want." I later heard they endorsed me to keep up their credibility because they knew I would win. But they keep badgering us, and they try to embarrass you. They're represented at every meeting that even touches on sex, although there are only eight to ten of them at the most. The pro-choicers sometimes turn out three times that many, but they don't speak. (interview)

> The pro-lifers control about 300 votes, roughly the same as the teachers. They can make a difference, but maybe not as much as people think. In fact,

one of them told me flat out: "I know our endorsement isn't going to affect your election." But if I were to come out publicly as pro-choice, it would have a deep impact—though it's hard to say how much. (interview)

As a rule, politicians go along to get along. But there are occasional exceptions to this mute complicity—exceptions that may prove prophetic in the long run but are merely instructive in the shorter term. Earlier we mentioned the pro-life activists' tactic of endorsing candidates on the basis of their abortion position and distributing fliers at strategic locations prior to the elections. One incumbent Catholic decided not to endorse the CFL despite his basic pro-life position. As a result, he was conspicuously absent from a CFL endorsement leaflet and hence the target of allegations that he actually favored abortions. Although he won in spite of the treatment, his indignation boiled over:

> The CFL fliered every car at every Mass at every church before both elections. Although the churches have a rule—no leafletting in the parking lots; it must be off church property—they obviously ignored it here. I finally decided I'd had enough of this kind of pressure—all the hypocritical statements required to fend off the back-stabbers and the rumor-spreaders. Right after the election I went to see the bishop and gave him a hard time. He was nice about it and kind of sympathetic, but he didn't do anything. I told him, if you treat me like an enemy every two years, I'll start to act that way. I'm basically a moderate, but I told him that the Church was so rigid in dictating political positions and not tolerating others that it was driving some middle-class Catholics out. I know a couple of families in my neighborhood—one Polish, one Irish—who have joined the Congregational Church. (interview)

Ironically, the bishop was not a prime agent behind the antiabortionists' tactics, just as he was not in a prime position to stop them. Still, the message expressed a political insider's frustration at the absence of institutional levers to restrain such outside groups.

In fact, this suggests a possible *second* irony in Springfield's future politics of abortion, one that turns on the difference between voting and public opinion. Given the discrepancy between a city population that was in the main pro-choice and political candidates who were almost unanimously pro-life on the public stump (regardless of their private views), a day of reckoning seemed imaginable when a candidate would be defeated for being *too* Catholic. A number of politicians were sensitive to the possibility, but they were even more alert to the difference between the "public" at large and the far smaller voting segment that forms the critical mass in local elections, as described earlier.

City candidates are especially vulnerable to traditional moral appeals because, in addition to the conservative activists themselves, there is another group of near-certain voters among the older, politically captive

CHAPTER 7

residents of apartment houses and nursing homes who are transported to the polls in the time-honored fashion of the political machine. Often conservative to begin with, these voters are particularly responsive to the social and cultural traditionalism inherent in the appeals of groups such as the CFL—and politicians know it full well:

> We've made it easy for elderly people to vote by arranging transportation for them and putting polling places in their housing projects. As a result, they have become a very influential bloc, and since they tend to have very narrow views of issues like taxes, education, and old-fashioned family values over things like sex and abortion, they can be a real obstacle to progress. (interview)

Thus, while the antiabortion movement itself lacked the numbers to elect one of its own, its natural alliance with other conservatives represented a formidable obstacle to the election of a pro-choice opponent—or any other politician caught in the cross fire and deemed suspicious. Actually there is often little difference among candidates on major city issues, as local pols generally run on the basis of experience, family ties, and shared shibboleths. Hence, controversy on any one issue can be determinative, especially a moral matter that cuts deeply and heals slowly. This is yet another reason why most successful city politicians appeared to honor the Japanese aphorism: "The nail that sticks out gets hammered down."

By the late 1980s, change was clearly under way in Springfield's views of abortion, and abortion was a major source of community tension. As consensual certainty ebbed, private views shifted toward an uneasy limbo, and public exchanges grew sharper, especially when they were goaded from the margins by activists on both sides. But abortion was not the only question of sex and morality to occasion debate and dispute. Springfield's politics of sexuality found a second focus in the related issues of sex education and a school health clinic. The relation between sex and education proved predictably volatile, as we are about to see.

SEX EDUCATION AND THE HIGH SCHOOL HEALTH CLINIC

As in most communities, Springfield's schools have generally reflected the best and the worst of the civic culture. As noted in Chapter Three, the school system made national as well as local news in the 1940s for its effort to promote interracial understanding through a curriculum that became known across the country as the Springfield Plan. Soon after World War II, however, the program unraveled, due in considerable part to resistance from a newly mobile and politically powerful Catholic community, which saw interracial priorities competing with interreligious advances.

Of course, the growing influence of the Catholic community has had a major impact on the Springfield public schools. As Catholics were becoming the major force within Springfield's Democratic party and city government, they were also becoming increasingly prominent within the public school system. After all, city politics impinge directly on School Committee elections and appointments. As we noted in Chapter Two, there is now some speculation that Springfield's first Catholic public school superintendent was selected by accident in 1950, since both his name (William Saunders) and his education (Yale University) led people to assume he was Protestant. No similar accidents have been held responsible for the fact that every subsequent superintendent has also been Catholic.

As more and more Catholics pursued higher education, many Catholic women turned to education itself as a career. Our Lady of the Elms College in nearby Chicopee soon became a prominent source of teachers in the post-baby-boom expansion of the city's public schools. One former administrator described the development:

> Early on I guess you could say that we did recruit teachers from the Elms for political reasons. But then they turned out damn good teachers, and after awhile we didn't even want to know a teacher's religion. There was no pressure to hire Catholics while I was there, although people down at city hall and in the political machine did call us to take care of students or teachers who were constituents. (interview)

Today, the school system does not record the religious background of its faculty. However, 56 percent of our own small sample of teachers and administrators were Catholic—a far larger proportion than any other religious denomination.

Given such religious interpenetration, it is no surprise that the public schools should increasingly reflect Catholic values and sensibilities. But there has been an important reversal in the social-class base of the public versus the parochial schools. On the one hand, today's public schools now embrace the vast majority of underclass and disadvantaged youth who were once the staple of parochial school enrollment. On the other hand, the parochial schools themselves have a far more middle-class constituency as a reflection of the mobility of Springfield's white ethnic Catholics generally.

The parochial schools have changed in other ways as well. As we noted in Chapter Four, their faculties are now dominantly nonsectarian, owing largely to the sharp decline of female religious, or sisters, in the diocese. Ironically enough, parochial schools have also deemphasized some of the traditional moral constraints that still grip the public schools. A member of the city's Department of Public Health described the parochial high school's response to sex:

Actually Cathedral has a good sex-education program, which focuses on teen-age pregnancy and includes counseling. It's very quiet and involves both priests and parents. Ironic, isn't it? (interview)

And according to a representative of the Family Planning Council of Western Massachusetts:

Cathedral High School has the best sex-education program in the city, al-though it is formally part of their "religion" classes. They are not only willing to talk about abortion, but they even invited in one of our staff persons to make a presentation. (interview)

By contrast, the city's public schools only recently begun to move to-ward a sex-education program of their own—a move that was choked with controversy from the start. The problem was *not* one of widespread com-munity disapproval. Our questionnaire item concerned sex education in *junior* high schools so as to put the matter to a sterner test than among more mature high schoolers. Unfortunately the item was part of the con-stitutionality battery, and hence asked whether the respondent supported the legality of sex education in public schools rather than approved it more generally. But even allowing for a discrepancy between legality and broader approval, impressive majorities of our samples were positive about sex education in the public schools. Eighty-five percent of the gen-eral sample responded either that it should be legal, with 56 percent re-sponding "definitely," as opposed to "probably." At the other extreme, only 5 percent indicated either degree of disapproval. The elite samples provided even heftier support: 94 percent of the political-economic elite approved, as did 90 percent of Catholic priests and sisters, compared to "only" 71 percent of the Protestant/Jewish clergy, where a number of evangelical and black pastors expressed rare disapproval. Clearly sex edu-cation was not just a "Catholic" problem, and for most residents of Spring-field, it was not a problem at all.

In fact, the real issue was less about sex education itself than about the possibility that counseling on abortion and contraception should occur within it. One school committee member was sensitive to the point and noted that the local newspapers had portrayed the public schools inaccurately:

The newspapers have gotten pretty sensational with some flashy headlines, and they've hurt the schools with some overdone articles. For example, the article that said the School Committee prohibited teachers from even talking about condoms was just wrong. There's sex education in the schools, though it probably doesn't go far enough, and it sure doesn't push for contraception or abortions. (interview)

A high-level administrator within the office of the school superinten-dent conveyed the official position of the system, along with a keen aware-ness of at least part of the community's response:

> Contraception isn't even mentioned in sex-education classes, and AIDS is
> dealt with only in the context of standard diseases. Of course, some accuse us
> of having our heads in the sand. (interview)

The nub of the matter was whether sex education should be selective or systematic, and whether teaching the biology of procreation necessarily should include teaching techniques of prevention. While local pro-life ac-tivists could not lawfully prohibit abortions or the use of contraceptions in Springfield, they did attempt to ensure that the city would have no part in sponsoring them. And even though few of the antiabortion activists had children in the local public schools, education became one of their major battlegrounds.

The conflict began in 1981 when a coalition of educators and health professionals made the first of several efforts to institute a formal sex-education curriculum. It was to be a mandatory and comprehensive health course for seventh graders, conducted by teachers well trained in health education. However, its component on sex raised an immediate alarm signal to the sexual traditionalists. The program was no sooner introduced on the agenda of the city's School Committee when it was derailed by the militant opposition of a group known as the Citizens for Decency, which made its position abundantly clear: "We believe there can be no such thing as a 'good' school course on sex education" (*Morning Union*, June 11, 1981).

Following this episode, the mayor formed the Community Health Edu-cation Campaign for Children and Adolescents (CHECCA), a program sponsored by the city's Department of Public Health and administered by health professionals. It was to run media and workshop programs on health issues with special salience for teenagers. In the first two years, the program emphasized problems of drugs and child abuse. One involved participant described the choice of programs:

> When we set out to pick a major topic for our educational campaign, we knew
> to steer clear of birth control, abortion, or any issue involving sex. There was
> heavy Catholic pressure, but it wasn't just the Catholics. Some of the black
> Protestant clergy felt the same way, especially the older ones. (interview)

For the campaign's third year, however, the staff decided to ignore these obstacles and focus on teenage pregnancy. The mayor quickly ve-toed the choice without even considering how it might be packaged ac-ceptably. A member of the mayor's staff recalled his justification:

He just said, "No way," and he commented later that he had made their lives easier by keeping them away from controversy. (interview)

And yet controversy continued as both advocates and opponents of sex education persisted in their efforts. By early 1987 the School Department responded to the competing pressures by creating a large (thirty-seven-member) committee to develop a health curriculum. The committee was comprised of clergy, physicians, civic leaders, and parents, including the antiabortion activists at the head of the CFL. Skeptics alleged that this was a classic political strategy for avoiding the issue and pointed out that the mix of members virtually guaranteed protracted discussion and compromised actions. It did little to break the political stalemate; in fact, it did little at all.

Ultimately this committee gave way to another. The new Health Advisory Committee was equally large, included the Catholic bishop, and was described proudly by a School Department administrator:

Now we have a new community-based committee to look at the whole sexuality issue. It has thirty-five members who represent every faction in the city. We asked for volunteers, and we put some people on who we wanted there. There is one member from the National Federation for Decency who accused the health supervisor of giving out birth-control information and using his office as a front for an abortion clinic. She's on the committee too. (interview)

To be sure, there were also representatives of the liberal religious community. In fact, a Protestant minister made a futile proposal to include abortion in the curriculum.

Committee relationships were especially curdled when the new committee was handed the responsibility for developing a local curriculum for AIDS. When the mayor demanded that it seek outside input from "parents and religious leaders" (Union-News June 19, 1987), progress was slowed even more. The city's public-health commissioner—himself an Italian Catholic—estimated that the curriculum would be in place by October, although the mayor made no such promise. As the summer and the committee's fractious meetings wore on, the public-health commissioner urged the school system to adopt the state-provided AIDS curriculum, since local planning was taking too long and "none of the [local] politicians want to make a decision" (Union-News, July 15, 1987). The suggestion was not greeted warmly.

As one measure of the Health Advisory Committee's uneasiness, the newspaper reported that public school teachers were told that they could answer questions about AIDS only if students initiated the discussion (Union-News, June 19, 1987). Members of the School Committe denied the report, but they refused to respond to reporters' questions as to what the actual policy was. When a Health Advisory Committee member said there was no set policy, a School Committee member told a local reporter *that* was not true either, but again declined to delineate what instructions teachers had been given (interview). The situation was never cleared up, at least publicly.

Confusion and bad faith abounded both inside and outside the Health Advisory Committee. Perhaps predictably, the antiabortion activist members were highly suspicious of the entire process and were convinced that they were not provided with all the information that other committee members received. Members of both the Health Advisory Committee and the School Committee issued conflicting statements about what was and was not occurring—what the schools would and would not be able to do. A number of committee members, like the bishop, attended meetings selectively and strategically. Two Catholic priests attended more frequently until they were removed by the bishop after they had voted in favor of a controversial program. Their replacements abstained on crucial votes, following the pattern of the public-health commissioner himself.

Much of the tension was concentrated around the mayor. Publicly an adamantly pro-life Catholic like his predecessor, the mayor had made a point of speaking every year at the Citizens For Life's annual Mother's Day banquet. And yet our respondents differed as to whether his position was personal or political. One respondent remembered that the mayor was a "strong ideological liberal as a student, and he still is in private" (interview). Another commented snidely that he "has the courage of other people's convictions" (interview). For example, during the 1985 city election campaign, the mayor joined with the National Federation for Decency in declaring the week of October 27 to Novemer 3 as National Pornography Awareness Week in Springfield (*Morning Union*, October 27, 1985). On the other hand, pro-life activists also had suspicions: "The mayor says he's pro-life, but he's got his eyes on Washington, and you can never tell what he'll do to get there" (interview). Or, indeed, after he arrives. As one of our respondents noted of the mayor's mentor (and predecessor as U.S. congressman):

> Boland has voted pro-choice in Washington for years, but he's still seen as a good Catholic around here, and none of his opponents have ever made an issue of it. (interview)

Perhaps this was because Congressman Boland continued to be pro-life *locally*, attending the Citizens For Life dinners and meeting antiabortion marchers from his district when they demonstrated in Washington.

And yet cynicism concerning the mayor's pro-life position was in the minority. There is little doubt that most Springfielders saw him as a Catholic traditionalist who was close to the bishop, if not in his clerical pocket.

A confirming incident that was recounted identically in two different interviews is revealing. Both respondents were prominent business leaders,
one Catholic and the other Protestant. Both told of meeting with the
mayor over the need for adequate sex education, particularly with regards
to AIDS. Both reported that the mayor agreed in principle, but finally
slammed his hand on the table and said, "If you think I am going to allow
rubbers to be distributed in schools while I am mayor, you've got another
think coming" (interview). The mayor repeated that pledge publicly at the
Citizens For Life annual Mother's Day dinner, where he condemned public schools that promoted promiscuity, and vowed never to allow the distribution of condoms or abortion referrals in the Springfield school system
(*Morning Union*, May 15, 1987).

From Classroom to Clinic

Despite the Health Advisory Committee's inability to deal effectively
with either a sex-education or AIDS curriculum—or perhaps because of
that inability—the central political focus shifted to a new bone of contention: a possible health clinic at the city's new public high school. At the
same time, the political arena also shifted from the Health Advisory Committee to the more public School Committee, whose meetings, under the
chairmanship of the mayor, began with a silent prayer, although according
to one School Committee member:

> He [the mayor] has missed quite a few meetings this year as we've had
> more than the usual number of tough issues, which he tries to steer clear of.
> (interview)

Many factors influenced the clinic's turbulent and uncertain development, including a rivalry between the local medical society and the secular Bay State Hospital staff that developed the proposal. But, as we are
about to see, religious opposition was the most formidable obstacle.

The clinic issue began in early 1986 with an instigating inquiry from a
nationally prominent medical foundation. As part of its concern for city
health care and education across the country, the foundation had circulated "requests for proposals" (RFPs) to many cities that lacked school-
based health clinics and might be interested in establishing them. In
Springfield, the foundation found a local ally in the Bay State Hospital, and the two together made the request of the city's public-health
commissioner.

The mayor was quickly informed, and he just as quickly consulted
the Catholic bishop before discussing the proposal at a meeting with
the public-health commissioner, the director of the city's Community
Council, and several invited physicians. Here, the mayor reported his

conversation with the bishop and their shared concern about potential abortion referrals and contraceptive distribution. The concern was particularly pertinent since the foundation's grant specifications required that such services be available (though not necessarily on the same site or in the schools themselves). However, several physicians who had met with foundation officials suggested that the foundation might be persuaded to omit the requirement in light of the probable community opposition. It was on this basis that the mayor gave the group permission to develop a proposal, although he placed the public-health commissioner in charge and enjoined him to meet with the bishop before completing a draft.

According to one participant in the meeting between the bishop and the public-health commissioner, the tone was cordial, and the bishop responded characteristically. The participant reported:

> The bishop wanted an absolute policy of no contraceptive education, or distribution, and no abortion information. But he was very nice about it. He told the PHC [public-health commissioner]: "This is what I prefer; you're in a delicate position, and you must speak for the Jews and others. But Christ spoke for everyone, and I have no choice but to go by Church doctrine. I know you'll have a difficult time, but neither of us has any alternative." He was fair and understanding, and he didn't order the PHC. As it turns out, the policy statement finessed the issue, saying that nothing was to be approved that would jeopardize a healthy baby. (interview)

After this round of conferences, a group of Bay State Hospital medical professionals assumed responsibility for the initial draft of the proposal. This draft was to be presented to the Springfield School Committee for its approval before proceeding to the formal application. According to one of its members, the School Committee had always been considered a safe body, from the perspective of the Church:

> I think the bishop feels comfortable knowing that the School Committee is all Catholic and will take predominantly Catholic stands. I know the mayor has been meeting with him about the health clinic, but the bishop has never once called a School Committee member to give his opinion, and the mayor himself has only called once to say please vote his way. Actually, the bishop is sympathetic to the need for a clinic and sex education. After all, when you've got four to five thousand kids pregnant every year, it's pretty clear we've got to do something. (interview)

For this School Committee meeting, however, the public-health commissioner received a copy of the draft only four hours before the committee was to convene. He was alarmed that the proposal still contained provisions for contraception education, and that there was only a small role in the program for either the PHC or his Public Health Department. It was already clear that the draft would be unsatisfactory to the mayor and the School Committee.

Meanwhile, the pro-life leaders of the local NFD and CFL also obtained advance copies of the draft and appeared at the meeting in force. The School Committee chambers were packed with activists from both pro-life and pro-choice groups, but it was the former, including no Catholic priests but several evangelical Protestant clergy, who dominated the political stage. In a word, they were outraged. The draft did not expressly forbid abortion and contraceptive counseling; the fact that the sponsoring hospital was a private institution performing abortions raised suspicions; and they even charged the mayor of trying to "sneak something past" them.

At the mayor's suggestion, the School Committee immediately tabled the matter and required the drafting group to revise and resubmit the proposal along acceptable lines. However, the mayor was embarrassed by the confrontation, which was well covered by local television and the newspapers. He took several antiabortion activists aside and suggested a political quid pro quo: on the one hand, he warned them not to make another scene; on the other hand, he assured them that he would not allow any unacceptable proposal to pass—playing a kind of Horatio at the gates of civic morality.

Prior to the next School Committee meeting, the proposal was revised to put the Public Health Department more clearly in control and delete the offending passages. Once again, the CFL members had obtained advance copies of the operative documents; that is, the revised proposal and the foundation's guidelines. Both pro-life and pro-choice contingents were well represented at the meeting. The former made much of the foundation's stipulation that abortion and contraceptive counseling be provided, and they refused to accept assurances that the foundation would omit the condition. Further, their knowledgeable criticisms of another planned city health clinic—this one for adults rather than students—led some to believe that they had direct access to insiders in the Public Health Department itself.

Given the doubts raised concerning the foundation's response to a proposal that explicitly deleted abortion and contraception, and given further doubts about the foundation's willingness to become involved with a community so embroiled in conflict, the School Committee finally endorsed an alternative plan. While withholding final approval of a school-based clinic, it resolved to explore alternative funding sources that would allow the city to operate a clinic on its own terms. In effect, this meant seeking support from local sources—the same eleventh-hour strategy that allowed the city to avoid the conditions of state funding concerning the homeless.

Just as city hall finessed the homeless controversy by first establishing a task force, then seeking local monies for a shelter under its own control, here city officials first established a health committee and then sought local funds to deal with sexuality more conservatively.

The mayor appointed the public-health commissioner as chair of the funding committee with instructions to "make absolutely sure that the city controls this." Throughout the committee's course, the mayor checked frequently to be sure he was not surprised again. Meanwhile, the PHC made it clear that the school clinic would operate under the Public Health Department or not at all. After several meetings—all attended by pro-life activists—an acceptable draft was completed and funding was secured from a local bank foundation on the specific condition that no abortion counseling or contraceptive information would be available. Finally, the bishop himself endorsed the plan in the diocesan newspaper (*The Catholic Observer*, June 1987).

Thus, eighteen months after the originating idea of a school health clinic and after lengthy and sometimes raucous deliberation, a plan had emerged to claim the support of the city's principal forces of church and state. Both had found a way to divide the crow so as to avoid eating it whole. In fact, three basic changes had occurred since the first proposal: the removal of any provision for—and the explicit stipulation against—abortion or contraceptive services; complete control of the clinic in the hands of the public-health commissioner (a Catholic appointee with whom both the bishop and the mayor were comfortable); and a shift in funding from a national foundation to a local combination of public and private sources.

But uneasiness remained. Pro-choice advocates and a number of city physicians and health professionals were clearly frustrated by the apparent denouement. More surprisingly, the pro-life activists themselves remained suspicious. One of them noted:

> We killed the sex clinic three times, and each time the idea comes back well funded, and with our money through taxes. Meanwhile, there's still a lot of talk about liberal sex education in the schools as part of their "life-style education." But that's death-styles, not life-styles. (interview)

The CFL and NFD were far from persuaded of the city's good faith. As one of their leaflets, released not long before the September 1987 city primary election, explained:

> The most serious problems facing Springfield residents this year is [sic] the prospect of a school-based sex clinic in [a high school]. Don't let *anyone* tell you this is not a sex clinic. The leading exponents of the clinic are members of family planning groups who advocate distribution of prescription contra-

ception to teenagers without notifying their parents. . . . The largest abortuary in Western New England will help fund the clinic. (NFD-CFL leaflet, not dated)

Clearly, the pro-life group intended to monitor the clinic closely when—and if—it actually began. Indeed, one can imagine the uneasiness of clinic personnel and school officials whose jobs hung in the balance of student reports of services rendered. As one school administrator put it:

> Who can blame us for feeling nervous? Some have even suggested that we are being set up. After all, we can't control everything that goes on in a clinic, and it's not hard to imagine some foolish but well-meaning staff member telling a teenage girl after her second or third pregnancy how to get some contraceptive help. If that girl should mention the conversation to others and it gets back to the child of a pro-lifer, all hell will break loose and a lot of heads may roll. In fact, the pro-lifers aren't too happy about some of the school personnel to begin with. This could be just what they need to start a little head hunting. (interview)

School administrators were not alone in projecting such scenarios. One School Committee member concurred that "Realistically, the clinic probably will provide information about contraception and abortions" (interview). Under these conditions, it is understandable that progress toward the clinic and a curriculum ran consistently behind schedule. Indeed, even after endorsements by the major political actors of the community's establishment, the clinic was still some distance from opening.

Originally scheduled for September 1988, the clinic's opening was set back due to a controversy over the contents of an informational flier (*Union-News*, June 3, 1988; June 10, 1988). When the School Committee picked up the issue again, there was a further delay, which was partly due to technical matters concerning insurance coverage, but was primarily a dispute over whether students would need written parental permission to use the facility. Finally, written permission was made mandatory, and the clinic was scheduled to open on February 1, 1989 (*Union-News*, December 24, 1988).

FACTIONAL AND TEMPORAL DIALECTICS:
MORALISTIC MINORITIES AND SHORT-TERM POLITICS

All of the foregoing illustrates the power of conservative religion and traditional morality, even when they are represented by an embattled few against substantial odds. There is no question that Springfield's experiences with abortion, contraception, and sex education illustrate the short-run impact of one particular moralistic minority. However, it is important

to place the phenomenon within the broader perspectives of both politics
and religion. Both politicians and political analysts are apt to misperceive
vocal minorities and quiescent majorities; they are also vulnerable to the
hot seductions of the short run as opposed to the cool dominion of the
longer term. This is not surprising, since the relations between both pairs
are often interactive to the point of interdependence.

As we have already noted, minority movements depend upon being
accorded more headlines and political deference than their numbers
would indicate. Precisely because they are different, they are newsworthy. And precisely because they are moving against the tide, they often
adopt tactics of desperation that can make them especially compelling—at
least for a while. Threats, protests, boycotts, and personal intimidation
are all effective in a moment of crisis. As the squeaky wheels of politics,
organized minorities demand lubrication. When these demands take moralistic form, they frequently receive it. But noise and numbers can be
inversely related. Just as minority movements are often oppositional
responses to majority inertia, they can sometimes countermobilize a
majority opposition. Some of the very characteristics that win attention for
the minority have a tendency to alienate the mass and provoke its reaction. Minorities may well become self-defeating witnesses for their own
mission.

If minority-majority relations often constitute a "factional dialectic," the
relations between the short run and the long run frequently form a "temporal dialectic." Their complex relationship is another reason why appearances are so often misleading in the dynamics of politics and religion.
Short-run calculations and long-term considerations often lead in opposite
directions only to collide in the middle range. As each sets limits for the
other, they may feed off of each other in classic dialectical fashion.

If it is true that "all politics are local," it is no less true that "all politics
are short term." This is especially true of electoral politics. Because every
incumbent is keenly sensitive to the perpetually forthcoming election,
political decisions are generally controlled by those conditioned to fash-
ioning proximate solutions to ultimate questions. Many have made ca-
reers out of maximizing the short run rather than agonizing over the
longer haul. In fact, Peter Blau (1964) noted that many leaders are caught
up in a related "dialectic of legitimacy" as politicians promise pie-in-the-
sky fantasies to win office but are later thrown out of office for their failures
to confront pie-in-the-face reality.

But it is not just that short- and long-term frameworks are different;
they are often mutually compounded. Thus, short-term policymaking
often allows long-range problems to fester unattended. Following periods
of patchwork and neglect, these same long-range problems may burst to
the surface as short-run crises in their own right, whereupon the dynamic

begins again. It is perhaps worth noting that, if politics is a quintessentially short-run phenomenon and religion is based more on the longer
term—in some cases, the longest of all possible terms—this helps to account for much of the tension between them.

Of course, there are contingencies and exceptions to these factional and
temporal dialectics. For example, as much as incumbents and many challengers cleave to the short-term interests of the majority, the long-run
concerns of more moralistic minorities are the stuff of political upsets by
those who are outside the system and make a virtue of it—at least temporarily. Moreover, even for incumbents, it matters whether a minority
movement or a short-run imperative involves preventing or promoting
change, since it is generally easier to veto a new policy than to enact one.
Then too, some politicians have sufficient electoral security to resist short-
term pressures in one direction to pursue long-range programs in another. After all, incumbency may await the former, but posterity rewards
the latter. Significantly, however, for all of Springfield's electoral security, few politicians have taken the long term as their cause if it has meant
bucking a vociferous minority in the here and now.

At the broader community level, poll standing and vote talleys are not
the only factors involved. Nonelected elites often control the switches that
activate minority versus majority influence, and short- versus long-range
considerations. Insofar as an elite is able to insulate politicians from electoral vicissitudes, it can toughen their resolve rather than leave them
weak and vulnerable. Springfield's business leaders have bailed the city
administration out of several tight spots with their ability to generate
funds for social services. But under these circumstances, it matters
whether these elites are aligned with the majority or represent a minority
interest, including their own. Of course, where elites depart from the
majority, democracy itself may suffer. While this is not merely the stuff of
conspiratorial fiction, most nonelected business elites are seldom eager to
run the machinery of government, although they are often eager to make
end runs around it.

By and large, Springfield's business elite has reflected the city's quiet
majority throughout the politics of abortion and sexuality. That is, the
elite, too, have been troubled with doubts and changes. As we remarked
at the beginning of the chapter, Springfield was by no means a unified
sanctuary of sexual conservatism. Despite the influence of its pro-life
faction, its public opinion was in the main pro-choice, and the city was a
regional center for abortions. While sex and contraceptive education were
conspicuously absent in the schools, there were alternative programs administered by agencies such as the local Family Planning Council and the
city's large nonsectarian hospital. However, these did not stem the increasing rates of either teenage pregnancy or AIDS, both of which offered

eloquent testimony to the low quality of sex education available on the streets.

Clearly, city officials were paralyzed by a small activist faction that effectively blocked decisive action. However, other members of the civic elite have subsequently become involved, with the intention of pushing matters toward the changes needed. The core of this group clustered around Springfield Central and the city's Chamber of Commerce, circles in which it has always been hard to disentangle civic interest from self-interest. Although the primary focus continued to fall upon economic development—where a priority on black-neighborhood development was conspicuously absent—the group did reflect a broader view of the development process itself. Informally, many questioned aspects of civic life that had a negative impact on the city as an investment site and on the quality of its labor force. There was widespread disgruntlement concerning the educational effectiveness of the public schools; there was also increasing concern over teenage pregnancy. The latter was a major social and economic problem that was becoming ever more acute among Springfield's ethnoracial minorities. By the mid-1980s, some 40 percent of the city's children were either black or Hispanic, and 75 percent of all births in Springfield in 1984–85 were to minority women under the age of eighteen (Teen Pregnancy Task Force, *Community 2000* Report, June 1988).

Reacting to such problems and the city's hesitant response, one business leader put it this way:

> This city has a lot going for it. But, let's face it; it also has some pretty severe drawbacks which people don't want to recognize. There is a kind of head-in-the-sands mentality around here, and it is hard to get anyone to act. Look at the new high school. Sure, it's a great facility, but it is turning out more and more graduates who are almost illiterate. These are not the kinds of workers we need; in fact, we need better workers, not worse, as our businesses get more sophisticated. And the climbing illegitimacy rates are a scandal. Everyone knows it, but no one wants to do anything about it, especially if it means bucking the Church. Well, dammit, I'm Catholic too, but that doesn't mean that I don't think we need a good program to hand out contraceptives. The stakes are just too high all around for us to be hobbled by an outmoded theology. (interview)

And according to another elite member, also a Catholic:

> The Catholic Church and the local ethnic communities are the major forces in opposing the steps necessary to correct the issues of illegitimacy. They're really helping to increase the spread of the lower class and its illiteracy. (interview)

Of course, it is one thing to confide such sentiments in an anonymous interview with scholars from outside the city, and it is quite another to pursue them candidly among other leaders, or convert them into an agenda for public action. And yet the latter processes were slowly occurring. Such perceptions were neither isolated nor idiosyncratic, and they extended across the elite's diverse religious composition. Not only were they widely discussed off the record, but there was a growing disposition to place them on the record, specifically as part of a series of deliberations and reports sponsored by the Chamber of Commerce under the banner "Springfield: The Year 2000." As one of the project leaders indicated:

> For the first time in the city's history, the community leadership is beginning to come to grips with a whole series of problems. My guess is that the results are going to shake a lot of people up. After all, this isn't just a bunch of old Yankees or a group of local bankers. We've gathered together a broad coalition of leaders—including the bishop—and formed them into a series of committees to look at separate issues in depth. The overall mood is that it's about time we started looking honestly at our problems and facing up to what needs to be done in response. (interview)

One of his colleagues in the group elaborated on the position:

> A lot of the critical issues facing this city are political suicide for politicians. But business can be more aggressive in pushing for long-term solutions. Both business and religious leaders have a way of crossing political boundaries. And although religion is not really taking the lead role, business is doing more and more. . . . Unlike five years ago, there's real dialogue going on between Catholics and non-Catholics over issues like condoms and teenage pregnancy. People are trying not to push each other into corners or cross swords immediately. They want to deal with the issues in a "moral" way, so the atmosphere is more open here than it was in the past. (interview)

At this point, it is impossible to know whether this bold resolve will be matched by equally bold results. Large commissions are often subverted by internal differences; the bishop's participation may provide legitimacy, but only on his terms. Even strong recommendations may be greatly weakened during the politics of implementation, and the same traditionalist forces that have proved such effective constraints in the past are not likely to disappear in the near future. But despite the fetters placed on change in the short run, in the long run, change of some sort is inevitable.

Some hint of Springfield's longer run is available in the most recent developments concerning sex in the schools. After more than a year of fitful preparation, both sex education and the health clinic became tentatively operative during the 1988–89 school year. However, at the conclusion of that first year, both were again in jeopardy, ostensibly because of personnel layoffs required by a budget shortfall. According to one informed observer:

> In general, the School Department and even the School Committee have been quietly supportive, but they are also highly sensitive to political matters. Even one protesting parent can send shivers down their spines. (interview)

Finally, in January 1990, the School Committee approved a proposal from its new superintendent to use representatives from various community agencies to offer a course on AIDS to more than 5,000 students. This ended a period of more than two years in which the curriculum existed on paper but not in the classroom. According to one member of the Health Advisory Committee, teachers from outside agencies such as the Red Cross, the Family Planning Council, Dignilife, and the city's community centers were "needed to ensure that it is taught" (*Union-News*, January 26, 1990). It was the Community 2000 coalition that rallied the agencies and their volunteers to the cause.

The question that is unanswerable at this point is whether or when the crises of AIDS and unwanted children will produce a major change in the forces arrayed around these issues. There are two models for change of this sort, the leaking dike and the bursting dam. It is possible that further changes in both public opinion and public policy will be halting and gradual. It is perhaps more likely that, with continuing pressure from the elite, the traditional dam will give way in a more sudden break with the past. It is generally easier to effect a quick change in policy than in public opinion, but once policies shift, the remaining pockets of public opposition are apt to either adjust and follow or withdraw for another, perhaps even more desperate, minority action in protest.

SUMMARY

There is much received wisdom about the slow rate of change in New England's culture and politics, but clearly the winds are up. Responses to the abortion issue are swirling nationally, and change is precariously afoot even in Springfield. This redoubt of heavily Catholic traditionalism has experienced some of its most wrenching recent conflict over issues of sexuality. The conflict has occurred not just between religious groups, but within them. Indeed, it is possible that the storm over abortion and sex education will leave behind a far different Springfield. As a new cultural majority finds and asserts itself with the help of a newly purposeful elite, city politics may reflect a new openness of style as well as substance. But history provides little confidence for such optimism, and sociology even less.

This chapter has offered the last of three case studies of Springfield's church-state relations within the wider sweep of religion and culture, on the one hand, and politics and civic policy, on the other. Issues such as abortion and sex education are more volatile than either homelessness or minority-neighborhood development. But in all three instances, we have glimpsed the possibilities and limitations that apply to the influence of religious groups on civic affairs. Rather than attempt an overarching statement here, we feel it is best left to our next and last chapter. There we shall be "bridging the gaps" of several sorts—gaps between different types of political power, gaps between the spheres of religion and politics, gaps between distinct religious groups and communities, and most especially the gap between the twin processes of religious secularization and revitalization. Springfield is a city of bridges, both literally and metaphorically. But in the latter sense, this is true of all cities, regardless of topography.

- rel. influence most compelling in this chapter.

Chapter Eight

BRIDGING THE GAPS

ANY AUTHOR of a scholarly book is apt to be peeved by the casual question, "So what are your findings?" There is something trivializing in the implication that one's multilayered, multitextured, multichaptered work can be reduced to such terse summary. On the other hand, there is also something to the old New England tradition of boiling sap down to syrup. Books that defy quick summary may contain too much sap and too little syrup. The distillation process itself may concentrate the mind as it concentrates the solution.

Our own summary involves four conclusions at odds with what might have been predicted. First, despite Springfield's predominant Catholicism, there are fewer violations of the law and less bridging of church and state than many constitutional Cassandras might have expected, or than might have been predicted on the basis of community opinion. Second, this does not mean that religion has become a political cipher. Religionists of varying stripes—not exclusively Catholic—have exerted considerable political influence on selected issues, indeed more influence than many social scientists might have expected. Third, attempting to understand where religion does and does not exert civic influence leads to the realization that the contingencies and vicissitudes of power are themselves more complex than many political analysts have suggested. As one pointed example, most accounts have focused on the "structure" of power, but it is the "culture" of power—and the power of culture—that requires increasing attention. Fourth, and finally, religion's varying influence on civic matters is obviously related to larger changes in religion itself. Once again there are paradoxes to be confronted. A continuing religious influence in community disputes is not a rebuttal to long-term trends of secularization, as many students of religion might aver. Secularization and sacralization are more mutually dependent than mutually exclusive, and each tendency can only be understood with reference to the other.

So much for the reader in a rush. The remainder of this chapter will elaborate these findings. Having devoted most of the volume to relatively straightforward description, we now turn to more overarching perspectives. In what follows, we shall be bridging the gaps with spans akin to the conceptual codas in each of the last three chapters. The first two sections offer more summative accounts of, first, church and state, and then, religion and politics, in Springfield. The next two sections are more analytic

in exploring a range of political—and then religious—contingencies that
affect religion's influence in any community. Taken as a whole, this chapter offers a bridge in its own right between the particularities of
Springfield and aspects of American communities overall.

CHURCH AND STATE IN SPRINGFIELD

For more than two centuries in Massachusetts, any civic issue was by
definition a religious issue, and vice versa. It was not until 1833 that
church and state were formally separated in the commonwealth, as town
citizens chafed at the expense of maintaining the Congregational churches
in the manner to which they had become accustomed. Since then, the
relations between religion and government have become more problematic. In addition to the de jure separation between these spheres, recent
Massachusetts history has had the de facto effect of minimizing religion's
political impact. Nowadays most issues on the state's complex agenda are
perceived as having little or no religious significance. Any religious group
presumptuous enough to dictate state policy across the board can expect
overt resistance and covert snickers, although there are special issues
under special circumstances when religion plays a highly significant political role.

Much the same applies to the cities within the state, including Springfield. But here we must also confess to some surprise. We suggested
above that each of our four principal conclusions concerning the city vio-
lates the expectations of others. It is only fair to confess they did the same
to ours. Frankly, this is not the church-state conclusion we anticipated at
the study's outset.

As reviewed in Chapter One, there are persuasive arguments that
church and state should be far more entangled at the local level than either the Constitution or the courts have envisioned. Although Thomas
Jefferson's call for a "wall of separation" has echoed through almost two
centuries of the American experience, it has suffered the fate of echoes
generally. There has been a blurring of sound and substance as the nation
has changed in important ways. Thus, American religion has become increasingly heterogeneous in its dogmas, strictures, and constituencies.
This has produced new variations of religious "free exercise" that have
steadily challenged older parameters. As government has moved into
areas once considered private and even denominational—areas such as
education, health care, and welfare—it is little wonder that questions of a
religious (or irreligious) "establishment" should become steadily more
contentious. Moreover, this is an area of jurisprudence in which the
courts are especially plagued by the distinction between principle and

practice. It is one thing for the courts to rule, and quite another for the rulings to be implemented. The force of local practice and local preference is often too strong to be vanquished by even a magisterial decision from the U.S. Supreme Court itself.

For all of these reasons, we expected to find that a city so often characterized as "traditionally religious" had become a constitutional minefield. Over the last seventy years, Catholic dominance has extended from the census rolls to the voting booths, and finally to the corporate boardrooms. Surely this is the stuff of a religious establishment, and we anticipated ample evidence of a city hall in thrall to a chancery. We were prepared to find a civic infrastructure laced with ties to the Catholic diocese, and a wide variety of unofficial subventions of religious practice and unacknowledged tolerance of religious excess. We also expected to hear a small choir in discordant protest, one whose voices included members of both the displaced Protestant elite and the liberal separationists associated with organizations such as the American Civil Liberties Union. In short, we expected to find a community in conflict over religion and its legal improprieties.

As we have seen, each of these expectations has some basis in reality. If one scratches deeply enough, one can find instances of virtually every proscribed form of church-state collaboration in the city, ranging from prayer in public classrooms and unwarranted assistance to the parochial schools, to religious symbols on city property and discrimination among religions by city bureaucrats and agency heads. But to borrow a phrase from R. H. Tawney's (1926) neo-Weberian account of pre-Protestant capitalism, these practices are "represented in but not representative of" Springfield.

To argue the latter would require a triumph of stubbornness over serendipity. It is true that minority religionists are somewhat wary of majority Catholics. But there are few specific resentments expressed even privately, and the ACLU no longer has an office or a local branch in the city. Several Protestant leaders suggested tentatively that perhaps all religions benefit when one is dominant enough to compel respect and deference from city officials. In this sense, Springfield's Catholicism may be running interference for the city's other religious groups rather than simply outracing them in a competitive sprint to power and prominence.

Surely it would be inaccurate to portray the city as host to a confrontation of church *versus* state, as our separationist tradition is often described. In fact, several respondents suggested that some of Springfield's religious leaders have willfully misinterpreted church-state law as a cover for hiding from politics generally. There is a remarkable similarity between the two independent quotations below in which the charge is being leveled by Protestants against Protestants:

Many clergy just aren't strong enough to deal with government. In fact, they use the "wall of separation" argument as an excuse to back off and return to the "real work" of the Church; namely, evangelism and serving the needs of the congregation. This isn't true of the Catholics. But the Lutherans are especially inclined to use Luther's notion of the "two kingdoms" this way. Actually, regular politics are often cleaner than church politics. (interview)

Sometimes the younger clergy use the "separation of church and state" as a justification for retreating from politics. You hear it from Lutherans, Presbyterians, and some Episcopalians—not so much from Methodists or UCC types. Of course, the Evangelicals used to take this position too until Falwell brought them around. But they'll change too and become more like the mainline. (interview)

Whatever the reason or justification, there is no question that many Springfield churches have kept a lower political profile in the last two decades. The 1960s were a period of considerable tension in the city, especially over questions of race relations and Vietnam. Many churches and clergy were sucked into the political center, only to spin back to the city's sidelines as the era ended. While religion has continued to be represented in several key political disputes, this has involved more special-purpose groups than conventional church structures, although the latter have often provided important support and cover.

Meanwhile, political leaders have also stepped gingerly in their relations with religion. Although there are certainly instances of undue church-state collaboration, if not conspiracy, these are more isolated than routine. Springfield's officials have shown no inclination to flout the law. Many of the city's programs, including its public school system, are monitored by state authorities. It is perhaps ironic that the one instance of church-state litigation that directly affected the city as the losing defendant was a suit concerning the provision of public school texts to parochial school students—a suit actually initiated by city officials themselves who were concerned about the practice's legality.

There are two possible explanations for this general compliance with the law, one involving the law itself, and the other concerning a broader range of social, political, and cultural factors that have had law-abiding consequences for nonlegal reasons. We want to discuss the first of these explanations here; the second set of contingencies will occupy the remainder of the chapter.

As we saw in Chapter Four, Springfielders agreed overwhelmingly that "the separation of church and state is a good idea." However, many diverged over specifics. Short of the most astringent cults, there was more support for protecting religious free exercise than for preventing a religious establishment. But many seemed to distinguish between the cultural symbols and the political reality of such an establishment. Thus, a Christmas crèche on city property was generally regarded as unexceptionable, but soliciting votes from a religious pulpit was not. Overall, there was a widespread tendency to stray from the path of recent court decisions. On seven of the eleven issues that formed our church-state battery, a majority of the general sample were either unsure about what was legal or in disagreement with it. Indeed, it was perhaps prophetic that more than 60 percent agreed to some extent that "U.S. Supreme Court decisions are more and more out of touch with the views of the people."

As all of this implies, neither the Constitution generally nor church-state law in particular were major conversational topics around the city's coffeepots. We found virtually no disagreement with the terse judgment of a local rabbi that "The church-state issue is just not salient" (interview). However, agreement over the condition conceals a disagreement over its implications. Consider the following four remarks from a public school official, a social worker, a journalist, and a business leader, respectively:

> In this city, the links between religion and government are so insidious that it's hard to see the connections. (interview)

> I don't think "church and state" is an open topic, and the line is getting vague. In fact, it doesn't exist on certain issues. The church to this day hasn't come out of the closet. There's never been a public polling. (interview)

> There's a sort of benign agreement between church and state. Their relations are often informal and partly outside the law, but publicly it's all part of the same united front. (interview)

> There's not much attention given to religion in this city. But come to think of it, isn't that a sign of absolute power? (interview)

In each of these statements, quietude is accompanied by an ominous hum. All would agree that there is little public concern about the church-state paradigm as such, but all are uncomfortable with the most obvious conclusion that there is little to be concerned about. We know the syndrome. As researchers, we too were suspicious that the surface discourse failed to reflect a subsurface reality. It was only after several years of careful checking and cross-checking that we were no longer haunted by the possibility that we were failing to uncover a major church-state cabal tucked under the civic carpet.

Of course, Springfield has experienced religious tensions, and there is a lingering sensitivity over city politics that seem so disproportionately Catholic. In fact, respondents tended to interpret questions concerning church and state as questions concerning "*the* Church" and state; discussions that began constitutionally frequently ended institutionally with considerations of Catholicism in particular. But just as the Constitution does not deny religious influence, neither does it prohibit religious dominance. The critical questions concern means rather than ends. A "religious establishment" is unacceptable because governmental entanglements give religion in general or one religion in particular an unfair advantage over the competition. But a religion that wields political impact as an open function of its numbers, its persuasiveness, or its cultural heritage is acceptable so long as other religions and irreligions are free to practice and participate in the contest.

By and large, Springfield's religious contest is open, if openly dominated by the Catholics. The fact that eight of the last nine mayors have been Catholic is not ipso facto grounds of a religious establishment; nor, for that matter, is the frequent interaction between the mayors and the bishop. There is nothing inherently illegal about the strong tendency of mayors and city officials to hold prevailing "Catholic" views of such sensitive matters as abortion or sex education in the schools. Although there is the whiff of an establishment in the way committee agendas and city policies are set concerning such issues, even here the law remains basically undefiled. Politicians are elected to follow their own conscience as well as that of their constituents. While some nationally prominent Catholic officeholders (for example, Gov. Mario Cuomo of New York) have publicly set aside their private convictions for official purposes, this is no more a requirement of the Constitution than the Church. It might even be construed as an adroit political maneuver to have the best of two worlds—a publicized private conviction on one side of the abortion issue and a courageous public stance on the other.

In general, then, the role of religion in community decisionmaking is more a question of politics than of law. Although our initial purpose in Springfield was to provide a local test of the constitutional paradigm, it became increasingly clear that the more important issues were not so much church and state as religion and power. Thomas Jefferson notwithstanding, religion and power are often at arm's length, sometimes with arms entwined, and occasionally engaged in the moral equivalent of armed conflict. The factors that control these interactions—or the lack of them—are less legal than sociological.

A REPRISE OF RELIGION AND POLITICS IN SPRINGFIELD

Since this is a book whose title promises a report on the relations between religion and politics, it is hardly surprising that we have found some. But from other perspectives, this may seem surprising indeed. As we noted in Chapter Five, politics and religion have tended to occupy distinct scholarly traditions, and few studies have examined their convergence. Even in Springfield, the two tend to be regarded as separate spheres. Although a little bit of prodding will elicit a wink and a nudge to the effect that the "bishop and the mayor aren't exactly strangers" (interview), this is generally more of an afterthought than an inflamed sensitivity.

A number of our interviewees commented on the decline in overall religious influence. One veteran political observer put it this way:

> Religion was always the way the city was run, although there's much less conflict today than there was two generations ago. People realize that dogma is a source of conflict, so they play it down. Ritual too. . . . The Catholic Church has lost power and credibility. A lot of this is due to a better educated public—they're just more individualistic and critical in their thinking. This has particularly shown up with birth control, and this is an issue that has cost the Church a lot. But then I really don't think the Church has an agenda for city politics. Probably the Mormons have the only communities where the Church really has a handle on the government, and Springfield is no Salt Lake City. (interview)

Of such comments are comparative studies born. One wonders about a comparison between Catholic Springfield and perhaps Mormon Salt Lake City, Baptist Mobile, and Presbyterian Fort Wayne. It is possible that there is less religious influence in each city today than yesterday's stereotypes would suggest. But more important than the degree of influence is the kind of influence.

Our respondents agreed that Springfield's religious groups and their leadership were on the political decline. Here are three further comments about the prevailing community mood, the first from a local business leader, the second from a prominent figure in social-service delivery, and the third from a politically engaged black pastor:

> Religious representatives have been cooperative with the city's recent efforts at development, but they're not a driving force. They just don't provide any real input or initiative. (interview)

> If there is any religious tension in the city, it's very quiet. Social justice is an issue for some religious people, but it's not a religious issue per se. Only abortion is really a religious issue. (interview)

> Overall, I'd say that religion is pretty incidental and secondary. Ethnic politics is the big thing here. (interview)

These comments about religion in general reflect more specific judgments about particular religious communities. There was virtually no religious group whose members felt its political influence in the city was on the rise. All shared the sense of a growing distance and depowerment relative to civic decisionmaking. For example, one rabbi described Springfield's Jews in these terms:

> Jews could be important players in the city as supporters, backers, and that sort of thing. But instead, they mostly just back off. They're so pleased to be in the boat that they don't want to rock it. (interview)

A similar theme of retreat emerges from comments concerning the city's old-line Protestants. Although the two comments below come from a former Catholic mayor and a Protestant teacher, respectively, they share the same theme of depowerment, whether through suburbanization or a more general weakening:

> The biggest change in the liberal Protestant community is the move to Long-meadow. That's where a lot of the business community leaders live now. And believe me, it makes a big difference. (interview)

> There's still a Protestant elite around, but its voice is pretty feeble now. (interview)

Portraits of the largely Protestant Council of Churches of Greater Springfield (CCGS) reflect much the same theme. One Protestant minister described it this way:

> The CCGS defers a lot to the city, and we're even kind of obsequious to the Catholic diocese. They have a priest on our ecumenical committee, but there's no comparable Protestant pastor anywhere in their structure. And I remember the joint singles club where the Catholics didn't want divorced people, and we went along. The CCGS talks a lot about tolerance, but I think it's really just that people don't care. Like someone said, American religion is a mile long and inches deep. (interview)

A member of the city's Inter-Faith Council made perhaps the most succinct assessment of the old Protestant phalanx. He described it as having "lots of love but little action" (interview).

Nor do the Catholics escape such depiction. It is true that many Springfielders would agree with the statement of a prominent Protestant business leader that "Underneath everything that occurs in this community is the presence of the bishop in some form or another—never obtrusive, always appropriate" (interview). However, the choice of metaphor may be instructive in placing the bishop "underneath" rather than on top of the community. Contrary to the bishop's popular image in the city, virtually all political insiders were in accord with one of their Catholic peers, who said:

> I wouldn't put the bishop among the top movers and shakers in the city. He's more pastoral, and many Catholics don't want him to take a tough stand on

moral issues. He's not even a stand-up guy when it comes to just getting things done. If there is any controversy involved with a project either here or in the city's relationship with the folks in Boston, the ground beneath him gets a little like quicksand. (interview)

Another made the point more sharply in describing a shift from "the bishop as boss to the bishop as lobbyist" (interview). And a Catholic ex-mayor pointedly included the bishop in his more general formulation:

> Religious leaders are more like the rank and file in the political process than the heavy hitters. Not a single one of them would even rank in the top ten of people who can gets things done around here. (interview)

Some observers attributed this to the personal characteristics of the particular religious leaders now on the scene, including the bishop himself. Unlike the ecclesiastical scolds of earlier days, he is regarded fondly throughout the city. And yet few would describe him as charismatic. According to one Protestant leader who has had extensive relations with him:

> The bishop is really miscast. He may be a right guy in the wrong job. You really have to have something on him to get anything out of him. (interview)

But the problem goes beyond the interface of history and personality. As we have already seen, there is widespread recognition that even more critical than the bishop's lack of leadership may be his lack of followers. We will explore this theme in more detail in the chapter's last section concerning secularization.

The description so far generally accords with both the city's sense of itself and the prevailing social science literature. Citizens and scholars alike concur that, in the main, religion is losing rather than gaining as an urban political force. Even Catholic New England is a pale reflection of the more covenanted communities of the Yankee Protestant past. However, this is more of a gloss than a probe. When examined more closely, Springfield's religion is by no means irrelevant to its politics. For one thing, it provides an important symbolic adumbration. In a city in which mayoral candidates use a Catholic Mass to begin their campaigns in hopes of using it again to inaugurate their administrations, it is clear that the realms of cross and shield are at least semiotically related. What is less clear is the degree to which the relationship is politically binding. Even in the context of a lengthy interview, it is hard to plumb the depths of a politician's personal religious convictions or to infer private faith from public piety. Those who pray together in church do not always stay together in city hall, and religion is by no means a reliable predictor of city decisions.

To pursue these matters further, we explored three recent instances in which religion has played a critical role in Springfield's politics. Chapter Five chronicled the way in which an often divided group of religious activists held city officials' feet to the fire long enough to make homelessness at least a temporary priority on the civic agenda, eventuating in a new public shelter. Chapter Six described how a small band of highly contentious and largely black clergy sought to make black-neighborhood development a prime city objective. Here religion became entangled with race, and the results were mixed, though not yet fully determined. Finally, Chapter Seven concerned complexities and controversies of sexuality, especially abortion and sex education. Once again a small core of religious activists occupied center stage in an effort to hold city politicians to a pro-life position and to stem the move toward school-based health services and sex education, with all of their contraceptive overtones and implications. Here too the results are not yet all in. However, there is no gainsaying the effectiveness of this traditionalist coalition in forestalling city changes that would violate their values.

These three case studies represent headline-grabbing instances of religion as a potent political force. As such they contradict the general pattern of secularization in Springfield's politics. If religion is no longer a primary political institution, it can sometimes have primary political effects. Moreover, the circumstances of these particular issues help to inform a more nuanced view of religious and political interactions. In this spirit, we want to examine several important characteristics the case studies share.

First, none of these cases involved the city's overall political climate, moral bearings, or spiritual well-being. Religious representatives were not pontificating on the state of Springfield as a whole, casting an inclusive judgment. Rather, they took up specific issues, whether it was a city shelter for the homeless, staving off programs likely to increase abortion and contraception, or black economic development, although the latter issue was characterized by the most inclusive rhetoric. Each issue involved a kind of single-interest politics that has become increasingly common among political interest groups of all persuasions. And each embroiled its participants in a level of political action that was rare within ordinary religious rounds. Indeed, each entailed the sort of political infighting and highly charged confrontations that many religionists see as their mission to avoid.

In part, this is a matter of ends and means. Many politicians are less than fully committed to churchly ends because they are skeptical of churchly means. In their view, religious leaders are long on abstract moralizing but short on rolling up their sleeves to plunge into the muck of the political process, characterized as it is by compromises that are often less than morally ideal. On the other hand, insofar as religious activists

avoid practical politics due to reservations about the give and take of the
political brawl—or, for that matter, the separation of church and state—
religious reservations concerning political means restrict religious
influence over political ends. It is hard to know whether such moral or
constitutional compunctions are primarily obstacles or rationalizations. As
we shall see momentarily, there are other explanations for churchly reticence. At the same time, a number of clergy are sensitive on the point,
and some express chagrin on behalf of both themselves and their institutions. One former Springfield pastor characterized his stay in the city in
these terms:

> I saw my task in Springfield as getting my people involved in community
> issues. But I never got them involved as a corporate group, though some got
> involved as individuals. We didn't make a big splash, and I finally lost faith in
> "statements" (interview).

This may be as much an admission of reality as of failure. Both are common themes among today's clergy.

In light of the above, a second characteristic shared by the three case
studies becomes all the more understandable. None of the episodes involved conventional churches, synagogues, or other religious organizations as major protagonists; nor did they depend principally upon the intervention of what is known in Springfield as "*the* Church," that is, the
ecclesiastical hierarchy of local Catholicism, although virtually all of the
activists took comfort and legitimacy under its symbolic umbrella. Thus,
while Catholic religious and clergy of various faiths were involved in the
homeless issue, they were acting more on their own initiative than as
formal representatives of their basic communities. The same is true of the
dominantly black clergy who formed the "Covenant" concerning the economic development of Mason (formerly Winchester) Square. In fact, several of these clergy found themselves at odds with home congregations
that begrudged their radical tactics and belligerent behavior. Finally,
while it is true that the bishop issued periodic statements concerning
abortion, the basic thrust of Springfield's pro-life movement—especially
in its opposition to sex education in the schools—came from the ecumenical laity rather than the clergy.

This nonconventional face of religion both departs from and helps account for some of the erroneous stereotypes of religion's political impo-
tence. Insofar as conceptions of religion are limited to the conventional
church as a corporate community, it is understandable that religious
influence is so consistently underestimated. This is especially true of issues that call for politically innovative, controversial, or prophetic intervention. While established church structures serve as staunch bulwarks of
the mainstream and the status quo, they often leave more adventuresome

political action to smaller groups and individuals seizing initiatives on
their own—and sometimes sneering at their ecclesiastical betters in the
process.

There is a rich literature concerning the organizational factors that constrain prophetic actions within conventional churches, as we noted particularly in Chapter Six. Some of these factors are internal, such as ideological differences within the membership and between members and clergy,
or the distinction between patterns of authority that provide ecclesiastical
support to local pastors and those patterns that leave the pastors at the
mercy of their local congregations. Other factors are more external, such
as a church's relation to other religious institutions in the community and
its economic and political vulnerability to other community groups and
organizations. Earlier we noted that some non-Catholics feel that the
presence of a strong Catholic Church has made it easier for all religious
groups. This may be true of religion's overall place in the community routine, but it may be misleading where more controversial political involvement is concerned. In fact, one respondent described the religious scene
more in terms of division than unity:

> The competition among churches and clergy fragments the religious scene
> and keeps the pastors out of politics. I mean they're political in protecting
> their own interests but not as an active force. They just never seem to able to
> get together. (interview)

This suggests an important distinction between protecting one's interests in a competitive market and pursuing a more forceful agenda. The
latter is frequently left not to congregations but to more single-minded
"social movements." These ad hoc movements are generally smaller,
more flexible, and less enduring than the churches. They also share a
constant need to muster and maintain scarce resources. The most obvious
of these resources involve money and membership, but no less important
is a cultural message that confers legitimacy and compels respect. A resource of a different kind is cooperation with other groups and potential
allies.

In fact, this introduces a third common quality shared by the religious
representatives in our three case studies. It is perhaps surprising that
each of the three episodes of religious activism should involve a fundamental ecumenism. In each instance, the activists formed a coalition that
spilled over religious boundaries that had become entrenched in the
Springfield experience. The various coalitions on behalf of the homeless
involved changing religious compositions, but the cooperation between a
Catholic sister and the largely Protestant Council of Churches was critical
to the ultimate result. Turning to black-neighborhood development, the
Covenant included a Catholic parish priest as well as several Protestant
pastors, including a white Episcopalian representing an ecumenism of

race as well as creed. Both the pro-choice and pro-life movements within the city reflected religious diversity. The latter marked an especially productive collaboration of Catholics and evangelical Protestants.

Here, too, the reality is at odds with the stereotypes. Cooperation between Catholics and Protestants would seem a dim prospect in a city so historically divided along such lines. However, the chances are enhanced in view of the first two characteristics shared by these episodes: their single-interest focus and their dependence upon informal groups of clergy and laity as opposed to formal church structures. Moreover, these forms of cooperation may presage the sort of reshuffled religious alignments described on a national scale by Wuthnow (1988). A local Catholic priest and a Protestant pastor both struck this note in their independent comments on the future:

> At times I feel closer to Lutheran and Episcopal clergy than to my fellow Roman Catholic priests. There really is a major realignment going on, and finally it looks like we're going to get a real Inter-Faith Council—something a few of us have been working toward since 1968. (interview)

> Middle-class Catholics have more in common with mainline Protestants than mainline Protestants have with evangelical Protestants. And, come to think of it, a lot of Irish Catholics are now more similar to some of the Yankees than they are to Polish Catholics. At least this is true in terms of general culture and life style, which is often more important than religion per se. (interview)

Although the bulk of this volume is concerned with religion's impact on politics, this suggests the reverse. Politics may indeed make strange bedfellows; new interfaith political alliances may break down old interfaith hostilities. As traditional distinctions of theology and ritual wane in importance, there is a waxing of new sensitivities concerning ideology and politics. While these also divide as well as unite, they do so along quite different lines—lines that are more a product of educational, class, and ethnic differences than denomination alone. Some of these changes were already becoming clear to several of our respondents. In the words of one Protestant clergyman, "The big difference between Protestant and Catholic isn't a religious thing; it's an economic distinction" (interview). And a successful political official described a trend that is making issue-oriented movements more influential, as traditional institutions become less so:

> Traditional voting patterns are slowly becoming less important. Religious . . . influences are slowly giving way, as the media give more attention to the issues. (interview)

But as we have already noted, it is one thing to leap from the decline of traditional religious configurations to religion's disappearance from politics altogether. The former may well be under way, but the latter is easily overstated.

Finally, a fourth characteristic of our three case studies concerns their political methods. In each case, the religious activists used moral appeals to transcend the normal political fracas and take their case to the public. Realizing that they lacked the conventional resources to bring pressure to bear on city hall and city authorities, each found a way to provoke confrontations that placed their establishment opponents on the defensive. Each found the media important allies—if sometimes unwilling or unwitting— in seizing and maintaining the moral initiative. As small minority movements, each sought to capture majority support by invoking moral fundamentals.

Of course, moral appeals are not uncommon among politicians themselves, especially long-shot challengers to well-known incumbents and the system they represent. Sometimes these appeals are seen as cynical, and voters in Springfield as elsewhere have had occasion to gag on a surfeit of rhetoric tainted with disingenuousness. Partly for this reason, many of the city's cannier politicians are wary of such talk. Some moral rhetoric is indispensable as part of every politician's ongoing ceremonial rounds among neighborhoods, institutions, and particularly religious groups. However, many politicians seek to preserve flexibility by minimizing public commitments and making as many decisions as possible behind closed doors and on the basis of closely calculable circumstances, coalitions, and trade-offs. Moral overkill may create problems resulting from both too little and too much credibility. In the former instance, the politician suffers from insincerity; in the latter, he or she may become the victim of that special political curse, the unkept promise. Politicians learn early that if one is going to enter the moral debate, it is best to do so on one's own terms.

Each of the three cases threatened to get out of hand for Springfield city officials, because in each instance the moral terms were first dictated by religious activists who left the politicians on the defensive. With regard to homelessness, the mayor's failure to deliver a promised shelter on schedule led to an embarrassing press conference at which he was morally outflanked by homeless advocates, including an outspoken Catholic sister. A similar background of unfulfilled commitments finally led to the fulminating outburst of the Covenant over the economic development of the city's principal black neighborhood. Similarly, the battle over abortion and contraception had a long local history in which Catholic and evangelical Protestant pro-life advocates sought to hold a traditionalist line and bind the politicians to it. When city officials moved quietly to develop an externally funded sex-education program in the schools, this "betrayal" elicited a storm of moral indignation expressed quite publicly.

In each of these episodes, politicians spoke privately with gritted teeth of their irritation over the moralists at their heels. It was not, of course, that the politicians themselves were immoral, but rather that they felt themselves exposed to competing moral priorities with limited resources—political as well as economic. From the standpoint of most public officials, single-issue politics is a demagogue's dream but a policymaker's nightmare.

It is not surprising that the results concerning the three issues offered both successes and frustrations all around. Religious activists won the clearest victory concerning homelessness, perhaps because this was less a matter of moral persuasion than political resolve. There was virtually no public challenge of the merits of responding to homelessness, although there was considerable disagreement as to how, how much, and how quickly, not only between activists and political leaders but even among the activists themselves. But if there was a residue of suspicion and retribution even here, this was much more palpable in the two remaining issues.

With respect to both black neighborhood development and the issues surrounding sexuality, community sentiment was far more divided and the results combined short-term compromises with long-term uncertainty. Of course, racial demands will continue to surface as civic contentions. There will be periodic investments in black economic development, but these may never be sufficient to satisfy the demands of black activists. And given the deep problems of the black political economy—both internally and in relation to the city's priorities—they will likely produce more failures than successes. Meanwhile, disputes over abortion and contraception have also produced both gains and losses from the standpoint of politicians and religious activists alike. Arguably the most divisive cluster on the civic agenda, this is also the area least amenable to compromise. On the other hand, it may also be subject to the most sudden and radical change. There is already evidence that the city's (increasingly Catholic) elite may finally demand and facilitate a sharp break with a troubled and troubling sexual status quo.

CONTINGENCIES OF CONTEXT, ACCESS, AND ISSUES

Up to this point, we have concentrated on describing Springfield itself and religion's role in its ongoing politics; now we want to hazard more generalizable explanations, relegating Springfield to a source of illustration. Indeed, some readers may want to leave the remainder of the chapter to those more theoretically—or more masochistically—inclined. Actually, the task ahead would be easier if the description itself were simpler. But the reality conforms to neither a fully sacred nor an entirely secular model. On the one hand, organized religion is no longer the community's institutional colossus, and for many purposes it has become impotent, irrelevant, or both. On the other hand, there are certain contexts in which religious organizations have access to sufficient influence to affect particular issues. We have divided the explanation into two broad categories, one involving secular and political factors and the other involving aspects of religion itself. We have saved the latter for the next and last major section of the chapter. In dealing with the more secular explanations here, we want to focus on the three broad variables of differing community contexts, differing patterns of access to power, and differing issues at stake. Within each, we suggest several distinctions to illuminate the conditions and contingencies under which religious institutions can have political impact.

Variations in Community and Context

Any appreciation of religious influence on the civic scene requires some attention to variations in the civic context itself. While the word contextualization may be an offense to grammarians, it has become an important injunction to social scientists. Religion and politics interact within a community rather than a void, and it matters whether the community is large or small, simple or complex.

Town versus City.   If the relation between religious influence and community size were encoded within a multiple-choice question, surely the correct answer would be to align larger influence with smaller size. Caveats aside, religion exerts more power in towns than in cities. Indeed, one reason why political scientists attribute less community influence to religion than do sociologists is that the former have tended to focus more on large cities, while the latter have been more attentive to smaller settings.

Springfield's history appears to confirm the pattern. Over the grand sweep of some three hundred and fifty years, there is no doubt that religion has ebbed in influence as the population has surged. But of course, all other factors are hardly equal across that span. As we have noted in detail, both religion and power have been transformed over the years. And if one looks particularly at the past century and a half, it remains moot whether Springfield's changing size has in fact produced quite the shift from town into city that Michael Frisch (1972) describes in his insightful study of the period surrounding municipal incorporation in 1852.

To reprise our consideration of this matter at the conclusion of Chapter Three, there is no doubt that contemporary Springfield satisfies many city criteria, though Frisch himself despairs over the confusion here. It is certainly more citylike than nearby Holyoke, a more traditional mill town dichotomized between managers and workers, the hill and the flats, Yankees and ethnics—precisely the sort of community likely to engender and exacerbate the intense religious conflict it has in fact experienced. By contrast, Springfield is larger and far more variegated in its economic base and its cultural and class composition. But if one goes on to define cities in terms of New York, Los Angeles, Chicago, or even Boston, Springfield is an imperfect fit at best. In fact, one of the most consistent refrains from our interview respondents was that, as much as Springfield may be labeled a city, it often functions more like a town. The theme had a number of variations as exemplified in the following excerpts:

> This is more like a fishbowl than a big city. Everyone knows what you're doing and thinking. There's no real anonymity, and even though I'm supposed to be a professional, my job is incredibly personalized, and that really adds to the pressure. (interview with a school administrator)

> You know, this is really a small community, and sometimes leaders have a limited shelf life because people learn too much about them. (interview with a business executive)

> Springfield's just not what I would call an issue-oriented community. People don't like to face up to things, and the mayor's desire to avoid controversy kind of sets the tone. After all, this is a small town with a small town mentality. It's so incestuous with everybody knowing everything. (interview with a social-service administrator)

> We're really a big town, not a big city. There's a sense of familiarity, and geographically, things are just closer, and there's a closeness of the system to everybody. You have different boards but pretty much the same people, and the ties are more personal. I think it's easier and less complicated to change things as a result. I mean if you want something, you know who to see in city hall or Springfield Central. (interview with a political official)

All of these comments stress the degree to which one can know and be known among the local citizenry. City politics reflect more interaction among friends and families than impersonal organizations. There is a communal sense of civic pride, even *civic* religion. The line between public and private is frequently blurred, and candidates for office tend to be more successful running retrospective campaigns on their family pasts than prospective campaigns on their platforms for the future. Finally, to the extent that any community is more intimate than impersonal, this should enhance the import of every primary bond, including family, neighborhood, ethnicity, and, of course, religion.

But community size alone cannot account for variations in the distribution of power, political or otherwise. It may be a surface proxy for a less

obvious variable to which it is strongly—but by no means perfectly—related. This entails the degree of differentiation between major institutional sectors in the community. As a correlate of size, differentiation has
implications for religious influence at least as clear as those of size itself.

The Rise and Occasional Decline of Differentiation. From their very
inception, the social sciences have been an arena for bickering among a
series of master accounts of Western history. This has included such classic rivals as Karl Marx's class conflict, Max Weber's rationalization, and
the liberal emphasis on political development and democratization. A
more recent motif is particularly apt here; namely, the neo-evolutionary
perspective of "social differentiation" (cf. Bell 1976; Luhmann 1987). Dif-
ferentiationists argue that social units are pressed to evolve from tightly
bound to loosely coupled relations among their basic institutions. On the
one hand, earlier and smaller communities tend to enfold all of their institutions—familial, economic, political, educational, and religious—within
the same embrace; later, larger size and more complex interactions produce greater institutional separation and autonomy, as each sphere tends
to become more specialized in function as well as distinct in form from the
others. Once again, not all factors—or all institutions—are equal in this
process. While some, such as the economic, may remain potent and demand a increasing share of societal resources, others, such as religion,
may decline in general significance and experience increasing autonomy
from other institutions at the expense of a decreasing influence over them.

Here, too, Springfield's broad history is illustrative. There is no question that the city of today is far more differentiated than its seventeenth-
century original, whether that is regarded as a "covenant community" or
a "company town." As one moves through the eighteenth and nineteenth
centuries, it is no surprise to find different facets of the community becoming more separate as part of the differentiation process. It is also no
surprise to observe a decline in the basically religious character of the
community and the municipal influence of its churches. By the early
twentieth century, Protestantism in particular and religion in general
were already back on their heels and being pushed to the city's right flank;
Catholicism had yet to make its move.

But more recent developments are somewhat mixed. There are certainly patterns of differentiation in accord with the theory. Springfield has
shown steadily more cleavage among its various institutional sectors—
political, economic, educational, even religious. One indicator of differentiation is the extent to which each sphere has fewer horizontal ties to other
spheres at its level but is instead more vertically organized among the
local, state, regional, and federal levels within it. Put another way, a city
institution is increasingly differentiated when its policies are increasingly

controlled by larger state, regional, and national entities in the same sector. For example, Springfield's city hall officials spend more and more time filling out forms and fulfilling regulations sent down from Boston and Washington. The city's budget is now so fiscally dependent upon the state's treasury that a recent political candidate's statement of exasperation at a public rally was simultaneously understandable and ludicrous:

> I'm sick and tired of [the state] welching on their budget commitments to us, and if they keep doing it, I say we stop dealing with them altogether. (television transcription)

Local politicians everywhere may sympathize with the candidate's frustration without endorsing his strategy. After all, this is the same candidate who at the same rally denounced his opponent for providing campaign lunches to senior citizens and was "pleased to announce" that "the lunches will stop after this election." He went on to fault his opponent for never having served in the nation's military forces, perhaps the first time in the city's history that a woman had been so criticized. Perhaps not surprisingly, she won.

Meanwhile, the city's large public school system is also differentiated into a sphere of its own and is constrained by a myriad of state and federal laws. As mentioned earlier, the one actual bit of church-state litigation to originate in Springfield occurred in the late 1970s when the city made itself into a test case for a new Massachusetts law mandating the provision of public school textbooks to local parochial schools. As we described in Chapter Four, the city adopted the policy (allocating almost one third of its book budget for the purpose) but cooperated with a suit against it that ultimately won in the courts, taking down the law with it. Meanwhile, Springfield's leading economic institutions—notably insurance firms, banks, manufacturers, and larger retailers—also tend to play on regional and national fields where the rules are externally set and sustained. This reinforces their differentiation from other local interests; it has also led some observers to describe some of the local branch executives as "second-stringers sent to the provinces" (interview).

But lest differentiation theory become a master motif, there is some evidence of "dedifferentiation" as a countertrend. This is reflected in the city's single most important political decision of this century; namely, the 1960 charter change from a ward-based, two-party, bicameral city council system to an at-large, nonpartisan, strong mayoralty system. In insulating city officials from the wider political process, the change converted city hall from a pork barrel to a veritable agribusiness. It also effectively secured political dominance for Catholics—especially Irish Catholics—since, not coincidentally, it came just in time to preclude real political power for blacks and Hispanics through the kind of ward-based politics that had afforded white ethnic groups their first steps up the political ladder in the early twentieth century. After 1960, Springfield's choice of mayors depended more on the back-room negotiation process than on the actual elections themselves. It became clear that the old Democratic party had moved to the political center and was holding very well indeed. Where city elections were concerned, the Republican party became a very white elephant.

None of this would have occurred without the instigation and cooperation of the city's economic elite. In fact, charter change marked the beginning of a new political-economic alliance that provides another symptom of dedifferentiation. This alliance took on a new form and vitality in the mid-1970s with the birth of Springfield Central, Inc., as a means for the pooling of energies and money from the city's corporate leaders to work with city hall in reversing the long-term deterioration of the downtown business area. The results were impressive by almost any standard, the exception being the standard of some in the neighborhoods (especially the black neighborhoods) who saw federal monies routed away from their more pressing needs.

For the better part of a decade, the spirit of Springfield Central became a dominant force in shaping not only the local economy but also the city's sense of itself along a series of dimensions. Here, too, there is a strain toward consensus, though some might argue that it reflects less of a convergence toward the mean and more of a collapse into the middle. This was recently symbolized by the merger of the city's two remaining newspapers. Both had been purchased ten years previously by a national chain, which sent in its own publisher who ultimately decided on the merger, retaining the masthead and format of the Yankee *Morning Union* and the Sunday *Republican* rather than that of the old working-class and ethnically oriented *Daily News*. There is no question that the newspaper wields enormous influence in the city, because of both what it prints and what it decides not to print. In fact, its policy as a cheerleader for the city's downtown development and new political-economic elite has caused some to question its blurring of reportorial and adversarial functions.

What of religious influence in all of this? In some ways, it has been the victim of both differentiation and dedifferentiation simultaneously. The former process has moved institutional religion to the margins as a major civic force, but the latter has invited it back to lead the ceremonial parade of civic harmony and self-congratulations. Of course, these varied roles reflect the needs of religion's major constituencies in different historical circumstances. While it was once the preeminent vehicle of social control, religion is now more often a legitimating tool of groups who have "made it" in society and feel a strain in working within the community family. Here the bishop himself marches at the fore, no longer the community repre-

sentative for marginal immigrant groups (cf. Dolan 1983) but now the social conscience of a somewhat disparate middle class. Certainly many
mainstream Protestant and Jewish clergy are in step behind him; and
while there are faint whispers of cooptation from the more radical sidelines, there is no question that the city's established religious groups have
sought comfort in the images of consensus. And yet there are exceptions
to this pattern, and we have detailed three of them, noting in each case
that the activist core did not spring directly from conventional religious
organizations. It is precisely their status as exceptions that makes them
journalistically newsworthy and sociologically provocative.

Variations in Access to Power and Influence

As important as size and differentiation may be in accounting for institutional power, they are neither exhaustive nor predictive as contextual variables. Another critical factor involves patterns of access to civic power.
Posed most broadly, is such access open or closed? That is, does it allow
for widespread participation across institutional sectors, community
groups, and status strata? Or, on the other hand, is power restricted, with
its currency monopolized by a very few at the top of the community's
institutional structures? Nostalgic stereotypes of America's villages and
towns suggest that smaller and "simpler" communities would have more
open access than larger, more complex, "boss-controlled" cities. A careful
reading of the community studies literature (for example, Lynd and Lynd
1929; Pope 1942; Vidich and Bensman 1968) should put such Rockwellian
images to rest for the scholars, but they continue to be vibrant in public
politics.

Variations in access may be caused by a variety of factors, all of them
intimately tied to the nature and distribution of power. In a sense, any
discussion of access is also a discussion of the scope and completeness of
power. Cutting off access is a way of maintaining power, and political lore
is replete with stories of cabals and oligarchies that run their communities
from behind guarded doors. But restricted access is not merely a function
of political conspiracy; nor is the distinction between closed and open access merely a synonym for "elite versus pluralistic" power. Indeed, the
latter is only a debate about the relative size of the controlling elites.

Importantly, access may be limited for reasons other than the intentions of those on top. A closing of access may be an unintended and unacknowledged consequence of changing political form and scale. Thus, it may
reflect altered patterns of administration, such as bureaucratization and
staff professionalism. The organization of administration is an important
"face" of power—it is the "organization of bias" (to paraphrase Steven
Lukes 1974). But it is a dimension not commonly thought of as overtly

political. That such administrative processes obscure the restrictions they place on levers of civic power is part of their effectiveness. They often benefit from the kind of legitimacy granted to incumbents that is represented in this statement of confidence from an older city resident—one who had been involved with local politics himself:

> City government has been pretty good. You get good people in as mayor and you don't have to pay much attention. You just trust them 100 percent and know they'll do the right thing. (interview)

Just as Springfield has grown, and grown more differentiated, over its three and a half centuries, so has its power configuration changed. In terms of access to power, however, it is hard to discern a single unilinear course. In the town's earliest days, power was largely restricted to the founding Pynchon family. The eighteenth and nineteenth centuries marked a gradual opening of access, as city administration expanded and city politics became increasingly democratized. And yet, during this period, religion remained a tool of exclusion, intimately tied to ethnicity, class, and party. Once the tables were turned, and white ethnic Catholic Democrats wrested electoral politics from Yankee Republicans, access was once again limited—both through the formal mechanism of the charter change described above, and through the informal process of political patronage.

Clearly the opening and closing of access is also the story of the transition and consolidation of power. Access opens as the scope and completeness of power weakens, and then closes again with consolidation. Legitimation of power and conflict over its control follow such transitions and are inversely related to each other. Thus the mechanisms of power, whether structural features such as a political party system or a bureaucratized administration, or cultural features such as legitimacy and ideological symbols, are access points. They are levers of influence, used by a variety of politicians and groups to pry open some part of the control of civic life.

Springfield's current situation can be variously assessed. City Hall is a continuing Democratic citadel. This is not just a matter of the party's electoral dominance in a formally nonpartisan system; it is also a function of an increasingly insulated government bureaucracy with an incongruous mix of professionalism and patronage. Whether the Democratic hegemony is also democratic is a matter of more debate. City hall wins grudging respect from some critics even as they point to its problems. For example:

> Overall the city has been well served by its politicians, although some of the bureaucrats a level or two down from the mayor are a joke. They're old-style Irish pols—you know, pompous and inefficient—and some of them take the

bottle with them not only to the office but when they go out on inspection. (interview)

On the other hand, we cited earlier a minority activist who provided another perspective when s/he called the city "Spring-gate—you know, like Watergate" (interview).

Despite Springfield's high levels of "civic idealism" and "political confidence," as shown in Chapter Three, there are still many people who believe that the machine still functions, if somewhat less smoothly than before. But several political veterans commented that "politics aren't what they used to be," and one implied an inadvertent widening of access in the following remark:

> In recent years, there's been a breaking down of party discipline. You just can't deliver people like you used to. The days of controlling votes are gone. (interview)

Although there is a distinction between the electoral processes and the processes of administrative control, the two are certainly correlated, shaping both power and access.

One major opening in access to Springfield's political leadership occurred during the major civic crisis of the 1960s and 1970s, when a precipitous downturn in the city's downtown economy forced the city's political elite to reach out to economic leaders for help. The downturn undercut the control of the Irish Democratic politicians who ran the city administration; the results of their attempts at change are the gist of Chapter Three. According to some observers, the politicians may have ceded too much in the process. One critic spoke for many in describing the mayor as a "mole in the political infrastructure who takes his orders from [the newspaper publisher]" (interview). Meanwhile, there have been more recent strains from the standpoint of business. In the following interview, one of the city's leading executives ruminated on both politics as usual and the problems that had begun to mount within it:

> Politics here is really based on ethnic ties. Everyone knows that the people who control this city are the Irish and the Italians. Are they Catholics? Yes, but that's not the big thing. For example, we called [a candidate] early in the game and gave our support for mayor. It's not a matter of great talent or competence. It's just that the Irish community was solidly in line, so we gave a fund-raiser and talked to other businesses about doing the same. After all, we wanted to be with a winner. . . . The cooperation between city hall and the business community has been good for a long time, but recently I've begun to sense a change. The business group is pretty small relative to the population, at least when compared to other cities. The core is getting tired

of having people look to them all the time for project money, political endorsements, and fund-raisers. It's the same people all the time, and the load's getting heavy. (interview)

Business leaders were getting tired in part because political elites had turned to them repeatedly for the funds to ward off political challenges. For example, city hall raised money from local businesses to develop both the shelter for the homeless and the school health clinic. In the former case it was a way of avoiding the obligations and political control that state money (and the local activists who controlled it) represented; in the latter situation, local funds circumvented potential confrontations with local pro-life groups that would accompany outside foundation resources. Thus, Springfield's elite was preserving its control of power against attempts to widen access for others.

Generally, ties between politics and business included few links to religion. It is true that many of the new economic leaders were now Catholic, but theirs was a new Catholicism that did not involve obeisance to the bishop or the need to bring him along into the new power base. Although there were ample symbolic occasions in which politicians basked in their religion as well as their ethnicity, neither "*the* Church" nor the churches were often invited to participate in the everyday wielding of routine power. The line between business and politics was far more blurred than that between sacred and secular, and far less likely to incite public political controversy. Even in the midst of the occasional crisis—or perhaps because religious activists were at the center of several such crises—religion had become a suspect presence more often indulged than obeyed.

Clearly broad variation in the access to power is a fundamental factor in helping to control the influence of such politically marginal institutions as religion. But power is a multifaceted concept, as our explorations in Chapter Five demonstrated. In particular, several dimensions of power are related specifically to questions of access. For example, consider the ideologically loaded distinction between *democratic* versus *nondemocratic* power. The distinction refers generally to issues involving political means rather than ends, since it is possible to imagine a "democratic" majority closing access to dissenting minorities as well as a "democratically" elected elite that then is insulated from general accountability. As we noted in our case studies, religion's formal and informal prohibitions from participation in the processes of electoral democracy often leaves religious organizations with little recourse but to try for access through nonconventional routes and strategies.

But a concern with democracy raises a somewhat different political issue at the level of the organization rather than the community. This concerns the relation between an organization's internal and external politics. There is no question that most religious institutions have become internally more democratic in recent years, especially as greater influence and participation has been extended to women and minority groups, and less arbitrary power is invested in ecclesiastical authority. But it is possible that this surge in internal democracy may result in declining external effectiveness. Precisely because of the decline of religious authority and the difficulty of mobilizing an increasingly active and diverse constituency, many religious institutions have become less politically united in either ends or means.

As a result, they are also less effective in the sort of behind-the-scenes politicking that characterized earlier epochs of urban politics as well as our three contemporary case studies of religious influence in Springfield. Although the city's Catholic Church is by no means as committed to such diversity as some other denominations, even Catholicism has been affected by these trends. The declining influence of conventional churches in general has left most political battles to special religious interest groups with small cadres of like-minded activists. These groups, often feeling shut out of the corridors of both sacred and secular power, must seek to compensate through resolve what they lack in resources.

Some cynics may charge that the increasing democracy and diversity of religious organizations may be partly responsible for religion's loss of community prestige. An organization may lose some clout and command once some of its internal authority is dispersed to former subservients. This may be all the more likely in Springfield, given its overall conservatism on such issues and its conservative political elite. After all, such processes tend to make organizations such as churches less similar to the upper echelons of business and politics.

Meanwhile, still another closely related distinction involves the classic *elite* versus *pluralist*, noted briefly in our discussion of differentiation. A staple of the continuing debate over community power more generally, it really masks two distinctions, one concerning the hierarchy of control (elite versus mass) and the other concerning the span of control (monistic versus pluralistic). Thus, even in a highly differentiated structure, particular segments can be controlled by very strict elites; conversely, even in a nondifferentiated and monistic context, all power may accrue to the masses. The finer shadings and scholarly traditions supporting one side or another of this debate are featured in many other studies, and need not concern us further here (cf. Waste 1986). Since the time has past when religion defined and constituted the community's elite, its influence in secular affairs depends upon either cultivating the favor of the elite or minimizing the influence of the elite. Again, Springfield illustrates both options, although its Catholic Church has begun to see diminishing returns from the former and could soon join other religious groups in seeking the latter.

Two further related distinctions also help to clarify the conditions of religious power in the secular sphere. One involves *primary* versus *secondary* power. Primary power is essentially the subject of the classic power definitions; that is, the ability to seize and carry though a political transaction despite obstacles. Secondary power, on the other hand, refers to the ancillary capacity to alter and adjust policies without controlling their central thrust. A related distinction concerns *positive* versus *negative* power. If the former involves the ability to produce change, the latter entails the capacity to veto change or significantly alter its direction. In general, negative power is more common and easier to mount than positive power. In fact, the greater prevalence of negative power has led some to suggest that our biggest national problem with respect to power is not too much, but too little: not elites but a power vacuum. In any government—whether in Washington or in Springfield—checks and balances can become stalemated.

The opposition to sex education in the Springfield schools provides a clear illustration of secondary-negative power. Here a small group of activists were able to paralyze the city's officialdom even though their opposition to abortion and contraception had become a minority view in the community. Playing upon the insecurities of politicians caught in the midst of a changing sexual, religious, and political culture, they were able to force officials to back down in their pursuit of outside funding for a curriculum that would confront directly both AIDS and teenage pregnancies. While there is some evidence that the city's economic elite is forming a new coalition to produce the desired change, the matter is still far from resolved.

Variations in Issues and Issue Definition

So far we have seen how religious influence hangs in the balance of variations in both community context and the patterned access to power. But of course, power is not a disembodied, abstract concept. It is a tool or resource used by social actors in pursuit of interests embedded within particular and concrete issues. Thus a third and final political contingency concerns the nature of the issues themselves.

Consider, for example, the elemental difference between *dominant* versus *minority* issues. We mean this less in terms of numbers represented and more in terms of respect conferred. Dominant positions are widely legitimated and enjoy a perception of being in everyone's interests, or somehow inherent in the order of things. On the other hand, positions that clearly benefit a visible minority, or are perceived as lead-

ing to divisive consequences for the community, must struggle for legitimation and sponsoring power wielders.

It is tempting to think of dominant interests as unproblematic. They are
so consensual that the exercise of power seems unnecessary to their resolution, and without obstacles and open conflict, how can one speak of
power at all? But as we noted in Chapter Five, the notion of power has
been expanded to include not just decisionmaking itself but the prior
processes that form the background of the decisions and the subsequent
difficulties of implementing and rationalizing them. In the climate of
agreement that surrounds dominant positions, the exercise of power is
considerably smoothed and enhanced—to the place where power holders
can deny that it is being exercised at all.

We have made much of Springfield's tendency to approximate consensus by keeping dominant issues in the public arena and minority issues
outside of it. It is not surprising that most of the principal religious groups
have participated in that tendency; indeed, virtually all of the city's larger
and more established religious groups have become reluctant to champion
a community cause that is not dominantly legitimate. And only a few—
most recently illustrated by the city's Catholic Church's stand on abortion—have risked trying to convert public opinion to their own position.
It is worth pausing to recapitulate the gains and losses of that strategy.

One of the major threads of this work is the way Springfield's Catholicism has changed over the past century and a half, and especially since
World War II. Once a source of community division in its own right, the
Church was seen by members and opponents alike as an embattled minority led by an authoritative ecclesiastical hierarchy and often an authoritarian bishop. But gradually this began to give way to a new position for
Catholics in the community, one that involved shifts from working class to
middle class, minority to majority, and outsider to insider within the city's
power enclaves. This was accompanied by changes in the Church itself.
The current bishop has frequently been described as more of a pastoral
leader than an autocrat, one who refrains from hurling pronouncements
but works instead on his "public relations" both within the Church and
within the city at large, whose consensual core has become his target.
There is little question of the bishop's social standing, and he has frequent
contact with the mayor. A chancery official commented appreciatively on
the "attentiveness of the media, especially coming from Boston. We jump
when they call, and they get the message out" (interview). Moreover, as
one political aide put it:

> Believe me, the bishop and the mayor don't have to look each other's phone
> numbers up in the book. Besides, they sit side by side at the head table of
> some dinner or another at least once a week (interview).

Even so, the chancery's pursuit of power through community consensus-building has been frustrating. Quite apart from the difficulty of orchestrating the community at large, it has been increasingly difficult to avoid cacophony within the Church itself. In fact, members of both the chancery staff and the mayor's office commented independently on the problem:

> Well, Catholic diversity is a part of the whole changing society, and we're having to adjust to it, even if it does involve a loss of the sense of sin. (interview)

> There's no question that he [the bishop] doesn't have the power that bishops once had. Diversity has really hit the Catholic Church and its ability to mobilize people. (interview)

All of this is apparent with respect to our three case studies. While it is true that the bishop supported the objectives of each of the contending religious movements, he left it to the more marginal religious activists to push the positions to the point of political confrontation. But if the activists appreciated the bishop's background support, few saw themselves as carrying his water.

All three of the episodes involved minority rather than dominant issues, although the one (i.e., homelessness) in which the challengers were most successful in shaping the outcome was the one in which there was at least a basic consensus over objectives, if not procedures. This case underscores the difference between those issues around which a consensus already exists and those issues for which power is deployed to actively shape a consensus—or at least the semblance of one. It clearly makes a difference whether one is simply representing a minority faction, or is pushing a minority perspective to the point where it disturbs the flow of routine politics.

While consensus makes politics more comforting and more convenient, many power seekers have no hope of achieving it and therefore follow the time-honored strategy of relying on uncivil activism. Sometimes purposely divisive, their techniques depend more on pressure than persuasion—whether through moral appeals, legal means, political threats, or personal embarrassment. Indeed, political challengers on behalf of minority positions are often uneasy with establishments of any sort and suspicious of any arrangements that smack of cooptation. Minority issues are more apt to surface in social movements than in major civic institutions, and are more apt to remain at that level.

A second content-related distinction that helps to account for religious influence—or the lack of it—involves *public* versus *private* issues. A fundamental attribute of power is being able to control whether issues become public or private. This does not happen automatically; it is the result of various groups' efforts to define the issue in the way that serves them best. Politicians, as representatives of public institutions, frequently have vested interests in seeing controversial matters relegated to the private sphere where no publicly controversial or publicly accountable decisions need be made. Some private institutions, including religious groups, are eager to comply with this, for they are apt to lose influence over issues that lose their private character. Many would prefer to enact a more "indirect" model of power whereby members convert the lessons learned in weekly services into their own individual political actions. This allows the institution to maintain some control over private issues while at the same time joining the dominant ethos on public issues.

One measure of the importance of the public-private distinction is the frequency with which public positions are at odds with private views. While this is neither universal among nor restricted to politicians, we have seen several instances in which Springfield's political figures have been caught in this squeeze. A number confided that their private views on abortion and contraception were considerably more liberal than their public stance. Our survey results indicated that there were also many others in the community who shared an uneasiness about "going public" with a more permissive position, including members of the clergy from virtually all faiths.

Nor were questions of sexuality the only ones to irritate the public-private membrane. Each of our other two religious-political conflicts concerned similar problems. There were many citizens who would have preferred to regard homelessness and all other matters of personal disadvantagement as private failings left to private coping. Much the same was true of the ravaged black neighborhood economy, and here a number of Springfielders no doubt felt that the city's elite had succeeded in establishing a laissez-faire world of private enterprise that should be free from public pressure to act altruistically.

In each of our case studies, a key resource and strategy for the activists challenging city hall was precisely the capacity to make such private issues public. This was as true of the advocates for the homeless as it was for the Covenant or the pro-life groups that consistently threatened to publicly expose politicians for their lack of support. In each instance, once an issue became public, it became a movement resource and was subject to very different political dynamics involving a moral discourse whose volatility placed virtually every politician in harm's way. This was not simply a matter of a private-public transformation; it also depended on the activists' making sure that issues, once public, were not to be treated as matters of mere administrative routine. The activists made it clear that political officials were not to be trusted to conduct business as usual and to fold these issues into their normal agendas (cf. Habermas 1968; Back 1986). There were major value commitments at stake, and the challengers pushed for widespread community concern and debate.

This brings us to a final distinction among issues and their associated politics; namely, *cultural* versus *structural*. By now, this distinction should be familiar as one of our major conceptual motifs in a project that began with a concern over church and state, expanded to religion and power, and then broadened yet again to culture and structure. To reprise our discussion in Chapter Five, whereas structural power involves the conventional structures on which conventional politics depend—that is, votes, budgets, personnel decisions, and strategic coalitions—cultural power invokes such cultural resources as symbols, ideologies, moral appeals, and altered meanings. Put more metaphorically, whereas structural power involves the basic political edifice, cultural power includes the shifting soil of beliefs, values, meanings, and legitimacy on which any political structure ultimately rests.

Most political officials prefer to remain hunkered within shelters of structural issues, structurally constructed. But most challengers and activists have an interest in definining the issues more culturally so that they can be dealt with in less conventional political fashion. The redefinition is not easy. As we have just seen, breaking away from politics-as-usual may require coercion and justification in making public what many citizens would prefer to keep private (cf. Raymond Williams 1977; Huntington 1981).

But if there is a shift to an agenda amenable to cultural power, this can have echoing implications throughout the political process. Once cultural issues surface to become openly contested, all bets are off. Suddenly politicians are themselves forced to play cultural roles by invoking new rhetoric and forging new alliances. As the focus moves outside of city hall to the city at large, new pressures mount from new adversaries and new constituents, all interacting on a far wider stage. Once embroiled in a wider cultural dispute, large cities may come to resemble small towns; differentiated institutions may close ranks and behave as if they were undifferentiated settings; and formerly closed corridors of power may be forced open.

All of this is especially significant for religion. Presumably the religious establishment has greater moral credibility than most community institutions and is therefore in a favorable position to use moral appeals in leading cultural debate. But there are structural risks in playing the cultural game, especially if it involves a controversial issue at the high-stakes table of community politics. Many religious groups and leaders shrink from the possible loss of members, dollars, and community standing. At the same time, religion has no monopoly on cultural power. Any outsiders seeking leverage over civic politics are apt to find it an inviting alternative to the insiders' structural base. But once a political agenda becomes culturally redefined, it is subject to far broader interpretations than may have been originally intended. As the relevant expertise shifts from the arbiters of practicality to the custodians of principle, both the source and form of power may change. Although cultural victories must ultimately be translated back into structural terms to be secured, structural patterns themselves may be transformed in the process.

And yet the difference between structural and cultural issues also lends itself to hypocrisy. At one level, every successful politician is adept at cloaking structural priorities in cultural guise, and this ideological process frequently entails using cultural style to mask structural substance—or its absence. This is a common critical motif in virtually every city; in Springfield, it is represented in the following comment from a black clergyman:

> The city emphasizes more style over substance. Its basic politics are conservative and stress consensus at all costs—at least on the surface. (interview)

Not a few politicians were cynical about deploying religion as part of their cultural facade, whether endorsing a Jewish menorah on the city's Court Square during the holiday season to stymie the "liberal" constitutionalists who could not protest for fear of seeming anti-Semitic, or approving an annual city prayer breakfast as "good political fodder for my supporters and political contributors" (interviews). Sometimes there is a division of labor between those politicians who attend to structure and those who cultivate appearances. One respondent quoted a longtime city politician on how he fit into the scene: "This city is run by fifteen guys with a conscience, and I'm their hatchet man" (interview).

Finally, even religious groups may employ a style at odds with their substance. Several clergy were described as making more of their symbolic appearances on civic occasions than their actual civic influence would justify. Several described themselves in similar terms, noting somewhat apologetically their faithful appearance at the prayer breakfasts.

But, of course, cultural power also involves something deeper. It has the potential to legitimate or delegitimate political arguments or actors, to keep some issues public and to keep others out of the public eye altogether, and to frame the terms with which issues are discussed when they become public. Clearly these are capabilities as important to incumbents as to challengers, to power brokers as to power skeptics. Indeed, this is yet another reason why political outsiders have an interest in defining issues in cultural terms; it is often the first step in substituting new cultural understandings for ones that have become so routine as to become part of the political structure itself.

In each of our three instances of conflict, religious protagonists mounted a cultural offensive against city hall. The outside activists challenged the established political agenda and the inside politicians'own priorities. They converted management decisions into moral issues. But only religion's efforts on behalf of the homeless appear to have produced a clear-cut victory. At least in the short run, the lid on sex education in the schools has remained largely secure, and advances in black-neighborhood development have been more symbolic than even a cultural offensive would approve. As these developments imply, simply declaring a cultural battle does not guarantee winning the political war. If cultural power offers opportunities for religion, opportunities can be ignored or squandered. Religion itself does not exhaust the ranks of the culturally competent and morally engaged, and on occasion religious advocates may even meet their match in politicians, some of whom hope to float to victory themselves on a rising cultural tide.

AN "ABRIDGING" OF FAITHS?

Now that we have considered some nonreligious factors in the relation between religion and power, let us deal with some variations in religion itself. Earlier we described a series of master motifs of Western history, including the concept of social differentiation. Another candidate for the same laurels is the term *secularization*. Put simply, secularization involves the double entendre in the title of this book, an "abridging of faith." Secularization describes the process by which the sacred gives way to the secular—a process that involves demystification and disenchantment with respect to religion's "meaning" dimension, and disengagement and displacement concerning religious "belonging." At whatever point, otherworldly ideas and objects once set apart for special veneration come to seem more ordinary. As a result, they are forced to compete with this-worldly claims on this-worldly terms, and their power is altered in both kind and degree (cf. Berger 1967; Tsacchen 1991).

Basically a straightforward concept, secularization is rendered complex by its many referents and levels. Although we shall be concerned here with its implications for the decline of conventional religion, secularization may apply to other manifestations of the sacred, including aspects of culture that have no overt religious form. Moreover, in addition to referring to the changing experiences of individuals, secularization may apply to organizations, communities, or larger cultures (cf. Dobbelaere 1985)—in what follows we sift Springfield through each of these four levels. Finally, while secularization in any one of the above areas or levels tends to be accompanied by secularization in others, it is dangerous to assume that the process applies either totally across the board or consistently through time. Indeed, secularization is often linked dialectically with its opposite, "sacralization." Trends in one direction frequently provoke countermovements toward the other, as conceptions of the sacred undergo continual change and redefinition.

Individual Secularization in Springfield

A recent "letter to the editor" of the city's daily newspaper responded to the expressed concern of several clergy that sports events scheduled during the Sunday "hour of worship" have contributed to the city's overall decline in church attendance:

> If they haven't realized it by now, the days of a full house at services are a thing of the past, in all faiths. A few times a year during certain holidays, attendance increases. [But] today's younger and more affluent worshippers won't attend services out of fear, guilt, family obligation, or respect for the clergy. They are turned off by long and untimely sermons, by the way they are treated by the clergy, and very often by the lay leadership, who often have an attitude of superiority over the congregants.
>
> As for passing any legislation rescheduling athletic and, or, other events so they won't conflict with hours of worship, this would, no doubt, backfire. We are all granted freedom of worship . . . to attend how, where, and when we choose, if at all.
>
> One final thought: Does the fact that fund-raising, including legalized Bingo games, are held within the walls of some houses of worship bother any of you? (*Union-News*, March 27, 1990)

The letter's author had been emboldened by the newspaper's similar editorial several weeks earlier (*Union-News*, March 10, 1990). Both the letter and the editorial seemed in accord with the community's recent trends in religious worship. That is, religious attendance had declined steadily since the 1950s, and this was at least partly because religion itself was less salient in the lives of individuals.

The theme has been embroidered variously by our respondents. By the mid-1980s, the decline in membership, attendance, and participation in the old Yankee Protestant churches had been going on for several decades and was no longer worth puzzling over or remarking upon. Now there is a growing concern about the soft underbelly of evangelical Protantism, despite its recent growth. As one evangelical pastor put it:

> A lot of Evangelicals have moved from the back tracks to Main Street. We've really risen into the middle class. But even though we're better off financially, we may not be religiously. It's kind of watered down commitment to the church. After all, folks have their boats and their places on the Cape to keep up. There's also been a loss of the pastor's authority and a change in style. Everyone seems to be doing his own thing. (interview)

This is an important reminder that secularization as a long-term trend offers few exemptions. Evangelicals may both start and end the process considerably to the right of the religious mainstream, but the process affects them nonetheless.

But, of course, it is the Catholics who are at the center of every religious analysis in Springfield, including secularization. Many of our respondents elaborated the point. Indeed, one Episcopal priest discussed the Catholic change in terms of the same upward mobility applied to the Evangelicals above, and a Catholic sister noted one of the predictable consequences:

> There's just too much change for the Catholic Church to deal with. As the lay people are more mobile, they get more moderate. They've made it, and they look around and say, "Hey, I don't feel oppressed." They just don't participate in the church as much or in the same way as before. (interview)

> Catholics are beginning to vote with their feet. They move from one church to another where they like what's happening more, and more and more they just leave parish life altogether. (interview)

In fact, many older Catholics have joined many older liberal Protestants in a nostalgic fondness for the past—albeit quite different pasts in each case. According to one member of the chancery staff, some priests have made a point of reminding their reminiscing laity of "the bad as well as the good, and making sure that there is some negative nostalgia too" (interview).

In the best social science tradition, we would use our questionnaire data to subject these insights to rigorous empirical scrutiny. Alas, this would be asking too much of an instrument designed for a different purpose. We included no questions precisely on the point, and it is difficult to test any hypothesis concerning change with data collected at a single point in time. For example, we can show that, compared to non-Catholics, Catholics come more often from "highly religious" homes (29 percent versus 18 percent), attend church more frequently (60 percent attend once a week or more, versus 42 percent), are more likely to have most or all of their closest friends involved in religion (59 percent versus 47 percent), but are no more likely to say that religious beliefs are "very important in their personal life" (53 percent each). This last pattern is partially belied by a further finding that, again compared to non-Catholics, Catholics are more likely to report that both their church teachings *and* their private religious beliefs were "very influential" in shaping their attitudes toward abortion (43 percent versus 26 percent, and 55 percent versus 41 percent, respectively).

As interesting—and perhaps as predictable—as these patterns are, they tell us very little about secularization itself because they do not address the issues across time. And yet the last comparison concerning influences over abortion attitudes does yield two implicit clues. First, we asked an identical question concerning attitudes toward "welfare aid to the disadvantaged and shelter for the homeless," and the influence of both religious beliefs and church teachings declined considerably for the entire sample (to 29 percent overall for church teachings and to 38 percent for private religious beliefs). When we asked a third question about how the respondents voted in the 1984 Reagan-Mondale presidential election, the percentages plummeted further across the sample (to only 3 percent citing the influence of church teachings and 13 percent citing private religious beliefs). Clearly some issues are more subject to church and religious influence than others, and it is hardly surprising that abortion should outrank welfare aid in this respect, while both eclipse a vote in a general election. Insofar as religion ever affected *all* issues in Springfield but now only influences a select few, this is an indication that secularization has in fact occurred among Springfield's citizens.

Meanwhile, a second indication resides in the same findings; namely, in the consistently greater influence of personal religious beliefs compared to formal church teachings. This is evidence of the "privatization" of religion, as church members are no longer so beholden to church authority for their personal convictions. For many scholars, privatization and secularization have become virtually synonymous. While this takes their affinity too far, there is no question that the two stand in close relation.

Finally, there is one other clue to individual secularization that should be introduced—and then immediately qualified. The questionnaire did probe one variable that relates specifically to time in asking the respondent's *age*. If religion is declining over time, then presumably it should be weaker among the young than the old. Looking specifically at Catholics, this is the general tendency for virtually every one of the religious measures noted above; that is, religiousness of home, church attendance, proportion of close friends involved in religion, importance of religious beliefs in the respondent's personal life, and the influence of church teachings and private religious convictions in the respondent's attitudes toward social issues. And yet we have not included the actual percentages here for two reasons. First, they are cumbersome, but second and more important, they may be deceptive.

One puzzle in the pattern is that it applies much less consistently to Springfield's non-Catholics. This underscores our earlier point that secularization does not apply equally across the board, and it is possible that many non-Catholics experienced their major secularizing pattern several decades earlier. For example, liberal Protestants and Jews are no longer going through the process in the same dramatic way as Catholics, while most Evangelicals and black Protestants have not yet begun the process in a way that shows up empirically.

And yet a second caution applies to inferences from age data generally. Using information on age alone collected at only one point in time, it is virtually impossible to know whether the distinctive attributes of youth are due to long-term historical trends such as secularization, to the distinctive experiences of this particular youthful group, or to the qualities of youth in every generation. In fact, the relationship between age and religious involvement is commonly curvilinear or U-shaped. Neither the old nor the young are as religiously active as the middle-aged, who see religion as especially important to their families and their children. Interestingly enough, this pattern gives religion one possible advantage in influencing community politics. Since a church's most active parishioners are at an age when they are also the community's most active citizens and consistent voters, they provide a possible bridge between church and state. However, we noted earlier the precarious basis of such an "indirect" religious influence in civic affairs. Its impact is not only uncertain but also by no means unreciprocated. Just as these parishioners may carry the sacred message into the secular sphere, so may they bring secular concerns and priorities back into the religious inner sanctum.

As important as the question of individual secularization is in Springfield, others have assessed it better elsewhere (cf. Castelli and Gremillion 1987; D'Antonio, et. al. 1989). We have so far covered only one level at which secularization may occur. While it is true that most scholarly analyses stress this individual level, and many are restricted to it, it would be irresponsible to skip over the organizational, community, and cultural aspects of secularization. They give the concept more depth but also more complexity.

Organizational Secularization

Obviously any secularization that occurs among individuals has implications for religious organizations, but it is not altogether clear how these are realized. Is there a "normal" sequence of individual secularization by which a decline occurs first in the "meaning" dimensions of religious belief or in the "belonging" aspects of church and synagogue participation? Certainly it is possible to imagine both nonactive believers and nonbelieving church participants. Presumably, these tendencies are conditioned by the denominational context. If so, it is perhaps reasonable to expect that, given the strong emphasis on churchly participation among Catholics, attendance will decline more slowly than some of the more private beliefs surrounding it. On the other hand, Protestantism and Judaism may be increasingly divided between those fervent remnants who continue with

the traditional theological beliefs, and those who tend to treat their
churches and synagogues as more secular points of community together-
ness. This is part of the distinction between conservative and liberal Protestantism, and between Orthodox and Reform Judaism. Catholicism itself may begin to reflect such differences, at least informally.

But such speculation takes us beyond the immediate case. Just as secularization can affect individuals, it can also affect organizations—in this
instance religious organizations, ranging from broad denominations to
local churches and synagogues (Roof and McKinney 1987). Springfield is
hardly exempt from the process. Much of Chapter Two's history of the city
and its religious dimension can be read as a study in secularization. Over
the past three and a half centuries, Springfield's churches have undergone
a series of changes that might be construed as declines in traditional religion. We doubt that any local observers peering back over the city's seventeenth, eighteenth, or nineteenth centuries, respectively, were moved
to cite an *increase* in religious conviction and involvement over the previous one hundred years. Certainly that is not the message to be conveyed
at the end of the twentieth century.

As early as 1910, Springfield's churches showed signs of adapting to
their secular context. In that year, Trinity Methodist Church proclaimed
itself the city's first "institutional" church, featuring an extensive recrea-
tional program, with a swimming pool to be shared with the public schools
(*Springfield Republican*, May 21, 1910). Of course, many Protestant
churches followed this trend in what some have termed an "edifice complex." But by the 1920s, Springfield Protestantism was aware that something was amiss and called in the renowned religious sociologist, H. Paul
Douglass, for an extensive survey and eventually a blistering report on the
lassitude that had come to characterize local Protestant recruitment efforts. But by then the city was in the midst of a critical demographic transition toward Catholicism, a transition that prefigured much of the change
to follow as the century continued.

In the 1960s, Eugene G. Carper performed another study of the city's
Protestant churches, ostensibly in the Douglass tradition. Among other
things, he urged considerable congregational consolidation:

> In terms of pastors' time alone, the closing of 55 Protestant churches could
> mean that 55 pastors would not have to prepare a Sunday morning sermon—
> an aggregate savings of 660 hours/per week. (Carper, *The Springfield Study*,
> joint publication of the Springfield Council of Churches and the Department
> of Research, Massachusetts Council of Churches, February, 1969, p. 79)

Of course, the criterion itself speaks of secularization, and of what organizational analysts term "goal displacement," or the tendency to lose
sight of basic objectives while allowing means to become ends in their own

right. Because of the otherworldly nature of many religious objectives, churches are especially vulnerable to such this-worldly stress.

By the 1960s, Catholicism had begun its own organizational secularization (cf. Greeley 1981b, 1985; McNamara 1985; Ruether 1987). This involved a downturn in the numbers so important to the Church—those attending Mass, those in parochial schools, and the ranks of local priests and sisters. These declines were both cause and consequence of other changes. Attendance at Mass continued to erode even after Saturday evening services were instituted in 1970. Thomas Day's quasi-whimsical *Why Catholics Can't Sing* (1990) relates such trends to the secularization of American church music, as a guitar and a cantor have replaced the exalted and exalting tradition of the polyphonic motet. And according to one local priest:

> Divorce and remarrying have caused a lot of controversy and caused a lot of people to stay away from church. On the other hand, it's also given hope to a lot of people. In fact, a lot have been brought back into the Church by the recent practice of granting more annulments. (interview)

Several ecclesiastical officials commented on what might be called a "declericalization" of key church positions and functions as a response not only to clergy shortages but also a desire to open up the Church to the community. Mercy Hospital's wards were no longer dominated by the "free labor" provided by the Sisters of Providence, and its board of directors had not only seen priests replaced by laity but Catholics give way to non-Catholics. Prior to World War II, all seventy-two of the teaching stations at Cathedral High School were manned by priests or the religious; by the late 1980s, only a handful remained. Indeed, although several observers commented that children were sent to parochial schools to discharge their parents' religious obligations, the parochial schools were experiencing their own goal displacement, as providing education began to eclipse instilling religious beliefs as their primary goal. Tuition was instituted in 1975—and raised in 1977.

But perhaps the most important indication of organizational secularization concerned the relation between the laity and Church authority. Consider the following remarks by a high-ranking member of the chancery staff, a parish priest, and a prominent lay member, respectively:

> In the past, it was "Yes, Bishop." Now it's "Why, Bishop?" People are more educated, and they try to penetrate into the reasons behind the teachings and the pronouncements. (interview)

> The people in the pews aren't passive listeners anymore. They know more about many administrative problems than the clergy do, and they sure aren't just obedient voters on economic issues. In fact, the whole relationship has changed. (interview)

The Catholic tradition of education used to be, "Don't think; believe." But that's pretty well changed now. The Church has to lead with a much gentler pull on the string, because otherwise the string will break. (interview)

Actually, describing the Church's problem as one of an overly probing and challenging laity may be an optimistic gloss. Even more disturbing than the parishioners who ask too many questions are the increasingly diffident who ask none at all. Still, it is clear that the problem of authority has become a major issue for Catholicism worldwide. While it is customary to argue that Vatican II opened the floodgates of questioning and criticism in the early 1960s, this important occasion may have been as much an effect as the cause. There is little doubt that what Seidler and Meyer (1989) have termed the new Catholic pattern of "contested accommodation" would have arisen without it.

In the long run, changes overtaking Catholicism today bear a ghostly resemblance to the changes set in motion among Protestant churches at the time of the Reformation, almost half a millenium ago. A number of our interviewees concurred that a kind of "Protestantization" was underway in the Springfield diocese. The burgeoning crisis of authority is part of that process, along with increasing emphasis on such secularizing values as individual freedom, intellectual inquiry, political diversity, and democratic procedures. It is a testament to the genius of the Catholic Church that it was able to keep such pressures under ecclesiastical control for so long. However, their growing intractability, especially in areas such as Western Europe and the United States, is itself a commentary on the shifting social basis of Catholicism. The same social processes that began to dominate so many Protestant denominations much earlier have now become a reality within Catholicism. As but one example, membership mobility from the working class into the middle class may involve losses as well as gains from the standpoint of a church as an organization.

In addition to long-run "Protestantization" in the abstract, there is a shorter-term version of the process that is more concrete. Precisely as Catholicism has become more established in communities like Springfield, it has attracted increasing numbers of Protestants, as well as refugees from other faiths—many involved in the rising number of interfaith marriages. This pattern may help to explain why the bishop has become more receptive to ecumenical dialogue and has agreed to host interfaith services. It may also account for why the diocesan cathedral can begin a standard Sunday Mass with the rousing processional "A Mighty Fortress Is Our God," once the anthem of the Reformation itself.

But at the level of membership movement, there is also considerable "Catholicizing" of the city's old-line Yankee Protestant redoubts. The senior pastor of one of Springfield's most prominent downtown Protestant churches was himself raised as a Catholic. The minister of yet another liberal Protestant bulwark estimates that more than one fourth of his current parishioners are either former—or continuing—Catholics. The highest proportion is among young participants, including many involved in mixed marriages and a number of Hispanic families eager to remove their children from both the Catholicism and the Pentecostalism of the ghetto, although, according to one respondent, "unfortunately, blacks are just not welcome" (interview). As one pastor put it:

> Some Protestant churches not only provide a kind of mobility experience but also a sort of intellectual stimulation in their sermons. In fact, a lot of Catholics tell me they go to Mass early in the mornings and then come home and listen to a Protestant service on the radio just to get the sermons—and their parents and grandparents used to do the same thing. Maybe some of these people find the Protestant service a kind of decompression stage between traditional Catholicism, on the one hand, and a more secular sort of intellectual freedom, on the other. (interview)

But it is not just the Catholics who are changing. The Protestant pastor above indicated that his congregation is shifting away from some of its sacred rituals to provide wider appeal. For example, it is even now considering a return from individual communion cups to a common chalice. For this particular denomination, the individual cups once symbolized the "individualism" so basic to the sixteenth-century emergence of Protestantism itself.

Community Secularization

Because this is an overarching topic of the book as a whole, and another summary would be superfluous, we need not tarry long here. However, it is worth stressing again that one of the reasons why we undertook this study was that so little attention had been given to religion at the community level. Since all four levels of religion and secularization have a measure of independence, one can imagine various combinations of persistence, decline, and resurgence within the individual, organizational, community, and cultural spheres. At the same time, what goes on at any given level should ordinarily be related to what goes on elsewhere.

It is not hard to describe a typical process of community secularization. Originally, a community is dominated by a single, undifferentiated churchly presence. Gradually, this broad "theocratic" model succumbs both to the rise of secular authority and to a new religious pluralism. In the process, religious authority is relativized and loses much of its absolute character. Moreover, the city is increasingly divided into a series of coexisting religious communities, each partly unto itself with its own schools, hospitals, merchants, professionals, and even political

practices—a structure known as "pillarization" in religiously divided
countries such as Belgium and the Netherlands (cf. Dobbelaere 1989).
Finally, even this structure begins to dissolve. As religions of every stripe
are left on the civic margins, denominational differences begin to lose
their urgency. As a response to this "marginalization," a new ecumenism
develops both as a form of broad mutual defense and as a factor in religion's occasional offensive sallies into the political fray.

Certainly this three-stage sequence from theocracy through pillarization to marginalization can be seen in the long stretch of Springfield's
history, beginning with its early Congregationalist theocracy, moving
through its stage of Protestant, Catholic, and even Jewish pillarization,
and ending in its current situation of an increasingly ecumenical marginalization. After all, ecumenism was a characteristic of each of our three case
studies of religious influence. At the same time, there is ample evidence
of attempts by religious leaders to cooperate in retaining and regaining
credibility within the city as a whole. Here religious symbols take on special importance, whether the holiday menorah on Court Square initiated
by Hassidic Jews, the mayor's annual "prayer breakfast" begun by evangelical Protestants, or the shifting of the city's major political ceremonies
to the Catholic diocesan cathedral, St. Michael's.

There is a tendency now to downplay religion and religious differences.
According to an administrator at Mercy Hospital, "The day is past when
we can just be a Catholic hospital for the Catholic population (interview)."
And as a longtime Protestant pastor noted:

> As Catholics have moved up in the community, they have become board
> members in a lot of places where before they weren't welcome at all—for
> example, in the local Protestant colleges. But, you know, now the question of
> a person's religion or whether someone is Catholic is just no longer asked.
> (interview)

In one sense, this is a major victory for religion and religious toleration.
In another sense, it is another sign of decline. In previous years, one
didn't ask about religion because one knew the answer already. Now one
doesn't ask because one doesn't care. Generally speaking, every religion
has gained community acceptance at the price of any one religion's political dominance (cf. Demerath and Williams 1992).

Cultural Secularization

We have used the term "culture" frequently, generally in juxtaposition
with "structure," as in the difference between ideals, symbols, and beliefs, on the one hand, and formal organizational, political, and economic
networks, on the other. Here again, secularization in one is apt to be

accompanied by secularization in the other—but not always. In fact, there is an ambiguity concerning the sequence of cultural versus structural secularization that parallels the previous puzzle concerning secularization in the "meaning" and "belonging" facets of religion for the individual (cf. Bell 1976). This is not surprising, because the two distinctions are reflections of each other at different levels.

Overall, secularization tends to occur more slowly in the realm of culture than structure. Culture is generally more resistant to change than specific structural arrangements, and it is not surprising that traditional cultural motifs should have a staying power that often goes beyond their immediate pertinence. In fact, nostalgia might be defined as the pining for cultural forms that are no longer structurally realistic or appropriate, and without the kind of nostalgic observances occasioned by holidays and other special moments, many religious groups would be in even worse condition than they are. One example of how religion may fare differently at the cultural level and the structural level is that of American liberal Protestantism. In structural terms, there is no question that its churches are suffering decline. But in cultural terms, there is also no question that Protestantism has won a great victory—both within the churches and in society at large—on behalf of the very values mentioned earlier such as freedom, tolerance, intellectual inquiry, and democracy. In fact, the two developments are linked by a diabolical irony. The very values at the heart of the Protestant cultural victory were the same values largely responsible for its structural decline. What was emancipating at one level was self-defeating at another. No organization, church or otherwise, can mobilize and sustain a membership that is encouraged to follow its own druthers rather than submit to the call of commitment and authority.

As various religious groups contribute to the larger culture of a pluralistic society, they produce a kind of national amalgam known as "civil religion." The concept has been subject to intensive exegesis and wide dispute, to which we have contributed elsewhere (Demerath and Williams 1985; Williams and Demerath 1991). Here we want only to point out that this national canopy may have its local manifestations. In contrast to the "civil religion," we have used the notion of "civic" religion to refer to that sense of shared religious convictions that spans a single city or municipality.

There are certainly indications of a civic religion in Springfield. This includes not only the shibboleths of a common Judeo-Christian legacy but an array of other convictions and commitments that have become consensually sacred—notions distilled from our constitutional and capitalistic heritage. Indeed, it is precisely the symbols and meanings associated with this level of civic religion that is appealed to by those religious activists concerned with homelessness, black neighborhood development, and matters of abortion and contraception. It is at this level of discourse and dispute that the broadest battles of city politics are joined (cf. Beckford 1989).

And yet secularization may affect civic as well as civil religion. Symbols may become divorced from substance, and religious ideas may gradually begin to lose their relevance and their urgency. While individuals, organizations, and the community as a whole may all share a reluctance to jettison these beliefs and ideals, rhetorical commitments may lose their compelling salience. There is even evidence of this in Springfield, though it is much less talked about in a city that continues to prize the forms of religion, if not always its traditional functions.

Secularization and Sacralization

So far we may seem to have provided a one-sided portrayal of religious tendencies. In developing the case for secularization, we have neglected its opposite, "sacralization." In the process, we have neglected some obvious instances of sacralization within Springfield itself. All three of our case studies of religious activism would appear to qualify insofar as each involved a sacred intrusion into the secular realm. Certainly the city has a variety of religious groups whose persistent vitality is a sacralizing testament; these include both white and black conservative Protestants, Hispanic Pentecostals, and pockets of continuing—even surging—spirituality within the established religious communities, whether Catholic, Protestant, or Jewish. In fact, just as there is evidence of secularization at the individual, organizational, community, and cultural levels, so is there evidence of sacralization at each level—albeit to a lesser extent.

Since the two concepts move in opposite directions, evidence for one would appear to be evidence against the other. This, at least, is the way the two are generally presented. Even worse, arguments on behalf of one as a universal trend are trumped by anecdotes on behalf of the other as a critical negative test. Thus, broad theories of secularization have recently been under siege by those who cite such American counterexamples as the rise of religious cults, the Moral Majority, and the electronic church, not to mention the rich variety of religious "fundamentalisms" around the world, including Jewish, Christian, Islamic, Hindu, and Sikh.

But there is a spuriousness to this battle, and appearances may be deceiving for several reasons. First, while there is no question that traditional religion endures and prospers in some quarters, one must be careful not to confuse the few with the many, or the exception with the rule. In almost every context, including Springfield, these are minority movements rather than majority tendencies. Second, even for the conservative religious minority there is considerable question as to the movement's "religious" significance. Without doubting the deep-seated spirituality of many adherents, there are those for whom religious conservatism serves as a surrogate for more secular concerns, whether traditional family values and political concerns or the need for communal belonging and solidarity. It is not always easy to relate symbols to substance, or sacred to secular. The sectarian spirit often affords wide moral legitimacy for more secular agendas, and insofar as religion may be a proxy rather than a primary end in itself, the analyst must beware (cf. Demerath 1991). Third, secularization itself may be misconstrued. Rather than moving from the sacred heights into a meaningless abyss, it often involves a transition between two different conceptions of the sacred.

In fact, here is another instance in which seeming opposites have a dialectical linkage. On the one hand, a traditional religion that refuses to adapt to a changing context may become an anachronism increasingly irrelevant to its members. From this perspective, at least some degree of secularization is a precondition for religious vitality rather than its enemy (Luhmann 1984). On the other hand, secularization that goes too far can provoke a sacralizing response. Thus, the religious "sect" is a self-conscious reaction to a parent "church" that is perceived as betraying basic moral or doctrinal tenets.

These latter two examples suggest the pertinence of the special form of dialectic we have called "temporal." If either tendency is in long-range ascendancy, the other is apt to occur as a short-run response. There are few examples of long-range sacralization today, but to say that the United States—or the West in general—is undergoing a long-range and culturally dominant process of secularization is not to deny important short-range sacralizing responses; for example, the action of Springfield's own "right-to-life" activists in opposition to abortion and sex education. Ironically these responses are often far more concerted and strident than the long-run trend they oppose. As a result, they tend to claim not only headlines but in some cases a temporary political advantage as well. Desperate to oppose a tide that is running against them, activists are far more likely than secularizationists to take on the shrill tone and extreme tactics of the true believer, as all three of our case studies confirm.

Finally, both secularization and sacralization "set limits" for each other (Stark and Bainbridge 1985). As we have already noted, religious institutions cannot afford to cleave permanently to their most traditional forms. It is no surprise that America's (and Springfield's) conservative religions of today reflect considerable change when compared to their predecessors of one hundred, fifty, or even twenty-five years ago. But secularization also has its limits. In perhaps all too sociological terms, every society needs a sense of the sacred to provide the elemental faith and ritual that give it coherence and cohesion. This is the fundamental insight of Emile Durkheim (1912), though it is important to note that the sacred need not involve conventional religion, or even "civil religion." In the same way, every individual presumably requires a sacred cultural core of commit-ments and priorities as a source of meaning and guidance, though again it need not be religious in the colloquial sense. In Durkheim's terms, secu-larization that goes too far can result in "anomie" (or social confusion and normative upheaval) at any of our four levels.

Much of the foregoing may appear to be a purely theoretical rumination on religion in the abstract. But all of these dialectical permutations of sectarianism and secularization find concrete manifestations in Spring-field. What is more, they have important implications for the relations between church and state and between religion and power in Springfield's political scene. In fact, it is here that the confrontation between them strikes sparks. In patterns of religious change, it is frequently the political extensions of religious doctrine that are first affected by trends of both secularization and sacralization. Insofar as middle-class Springfield Catho-lics have become more secularized, this is most readily apparent in their reluctance to take political positions on matters such as abortion and birth control, which are currently losing their sacred salience. Conversely, in-sofar as Springfield's conservative religionists have undergone a sacred recrudescence, this is especially conspicuous in their insistence on forcing the same issues into the secular political arena.

EPILOGUE

This last chapter has been an attempt to both summarize our Springfield involvement and relinquish that involvement. Somehow it seems appro-priate that perhaps the tersest summary comes not from us but from one of our interviewees, a veteran Catholic school administrator who had a personal hand in much of Springfield's recent history and was moved to reflect upon it:

> I guess the real irony is that Catholics got power just when it was no longer fashionable for a religious group to have power. (interview)

So much for at least a penultimate word.

Throughout this book, we have tried to "bridge the gap" to a set of broader issues at work in broader contexts. But disengagement is difficult. As the appendix to follow explains, it is hard to know when to end a book that concerns a past bleeding into the present. Basically our research ended in 1988, though we have maintained some local contacts and have continued to read the local newspaper. Several more recent develop-ments are especially worth noting as the study ends.

In 1989, the city's longtime congressman retired and was replaced by the sitting mayor, who won two years later in a bitter Irish versus Italian reelection battle against his own predecessor as mayor. Meanwhile, the new mayor was Springfield's first woman in the office. But this election was less a triumph of gender than one more example of ethnic politics-as-usual. A practicing lawyer, she was from an old Hungry Hill family, had put in her time in lesser posts to win her way to the front of the Irish queue, had received the overwhelming support of the business community, and had won handily over her Italian male rival in the primary before sweeping the general election with no significant opposition. However, toward the end of only her first term in office, she announced her retirement. The city has now begun to give desultory attention to a new mayoral race, this one between two men, one Scotch-Irish and the other Italian. In the midst of such ethnic competition, perhaps Springfield's most startling recent political occurence involved allegations that the city's longtime Irish district attorney had inappropriately intervened in the trials and sentencing of several convicted Italian mafiosi. The real news here was of an enduring Irish-Italian friendship forged on the handball courts of the local Young Men's Christian Association—courts that the district attorney himself described as "mobbed."

Meanwhile, Springfield faces a major fiscal crisis. The city has experienced a precipitous and traumatic drop in outside financial assistance. This began with the federal budget slashes of the Reagan administration, but it was exacerbated by a national recession that surfaced first in Massachusetts, where it was accompanied by a cross-fire of recriminations, a virtual political paralysis, and signs of a possible unraveling of the state's loosely woven fabric of ethnic, class, and religious differences. All of this led in turn to the election of a "no new tax" Republican governor, William Weld, who has presided over massive reductions in public spending, including aid on which cities had grown critically dependent. Springfield itself has now suffered through major cuts of municipal services and employees, cuts whose toll on the mayor were no doubt largely responsible for her decision not to seek reelection.

Springfield's downtown area has begun to show some of the signs of its earlier distress in the 1960s—vacant space, broken windows, and a sometimes eerie silence in buildings that now bear mocking witness to the enthusiasm of the high-rolling, high-rising downtown revitalization of the 1980s. Springfield Central has once again begun to rally to the cause. However, this time it will lack the participation and the capital of one of the city's most meteoric businesses, Monarch Capital, which has now plummeted to the depths of bankruptcy even more quickly than it once soared to the heights of the city's skyline.

In all of this, religion continues its roles as sideline observer and occasional participant. The recent retirement of Bishop McGuire marks the end of another diocesan era. However, this has been another winter of concern for the homeless. Although a small refurbished shopping plaza has just reopened in Mason Square, prospects appear bleak for further assistance to black neighborhoods. Opponents of abortion continue their weekly protests at a local abortion clinic, sometimes chaining themselves to the building and forcing the police to arrest them. Greater reductions in the public school budget will almost certainly lead to yet another post-ponement of sex education, and it is likely that the city's School Commit-tee will spurn the funds for free condom distribution made available in a startling decision by the state Board of Education. In sum, neither Spring-field's religion nor its politics seem on the threshold of transformation or epiphany.

That rel. is drawn upon as a cultural resource does not give it cultural power/authority. Soc. affects way rel. gets used.

APPENDIX A

A METHODOLOGICAL POSTSCRIPT

MORE THAN twenty years ago, the first author of this book was commissioned to examine the methodological problems inherent in analyzing religious change. After a lengthy review of historical, literary, and demographic sources, his conclusion was a sigh of despair: "Ask any question and our response is likely to be a contemplative silence, a scholarly scowl, and finally a long list of methodological conundrums leading to that ultimate conclusion, 'It all depends' " (Demerath 1968, p. 349).

This appendix elaborates the point for the Springfield study. We realize that it is customary to register such caveats at the outset of a monograph, but we were reluctant to either bore or alienate the reader at such an early stage. Moreover, we wanted to say a little more than is appropriate in an introduction, and we felt that some of the issues are best understood only after gaining deeper familiarity with the research. As a multimethod study, this was also a multiproblem study, and we want to comment on difficulties encountered with our questionnaire survey, our interviews with community citizens, and our use of demographic and historical materials. Some of the difficulties are standard fare for the methods at issue. But others are more specific to our particular challenge of making sense of a controversial relationship between two areas that can each be controversial in its own right: religion and politics. The challenge is even more daunting when the study involves contemporary events and personages in a middle-sized city where the maintenance of collective and individual reputations is not only crucial but often precarious.

QUESTIONNAIRE QUALMS

As reproduced in Appendix B to follow, the questionnaire comprises standard items on the respondent's personal background, family situation, socioeconomic status, religion, and ethnicity. It also includes a series of batteries concerning perceptions of the city itself and its religious and political affairs; attitudes toward a number of church-state issues that have received attention in the nation's courts and media; and specific judg-

A version of this appendix was presented to the Society for the Scientific Study of Religion in Louisville, Kentucky, October 1987, under the title "Richness vs. Rigor: Contending with History in a Community Study."

ments concerning the three issues of community controversy that we have isolated for special analysis; that is, abortion and sex education, city-provided care for the homeless, and economic development of a dominantly black neighborhood.

Given such riches, the survey might have played a far more prominent role in the study than it actually did. In fact, one can imagine a book developed entirely from the questionnaire and revolving around a succession of complex analyses presented in tabular and graphic form. In contrast, we have minimized such quantitative trappings and, if anything, deemphasized the questionnaire study. Why?

A lack of positivistic faith is not a major reason. Indeed, in the strict nineteenth-century sense of "positivism," almost no one we know qualifies, but in the current colloquial sense of the term, almost everyone does. That is, it is hard now to swallow assumptions about the inherent rationality of the social world and its actors, but it is routine to pursue empirical data for theoretical testing. Actually we have more faith in quantitative methods than most publishers have in their readers' quantitative tolerance. As a result, we have tried to compromise. While the text does include a few simple tables, we have avoided complicated statistical presentations and sought wherever possible to bootleg numerical results into prose summaries.

At the same time, we also have some doubts about the survey data on which most of these statistics depend. The problems are not so much with the instrument itself, although inevitably there are a few questions we would now word differently, and others we wish we had included. The real difficulty lies with the quality of the sample. Although the sample was small to begin with because of our limited budget, there is nothing inherently wrong with smallness itself in the sampling business. In general, one would prefer a small sample that is well drawn and well responded to rather than a large sample that is poorly designed or results in a low response rate.

Alas, while our small sample was well-enough drawn, it was plagued by a response paucity. As noted in Chapter One, only 47 percent or 256 members of our general sample filled out the questionnaire and returned it—and this was after three follow-up mailings (see Appendix B) and a phone call reminder. This also reflects the deletion of several sample members who were deceased, too ill to respond, or had moved to addresses unknown to the postal service. In the case below, we even deleted a questionnaire that had been filled out by the wrong person:

> This questionnaire was sent to my husband. However, he felt it was too much
> to ask him to spend a few minutes helping someone out, so I filled it out

instead. I tried to convince him to answer the questions himself, but when he decides to be stubborn, pigheaded, close-minded, and a FLAMING JERK, there's really no talking him out of it.

Recall that, in addition to using a general sample, we also sent the questionnaire to three "elite" samples. One might expect these groups to respond at a higher rate in view of their higher educational levels and greater overall sophistication. Surprisingly enough, however, their response rates tended to be slightly lower, perhaps because of special concerns over being identified. Thus, public school teachers and administrators responded at a rate of 43 percent; the political elite (drawn from lists of ward chairs, former City Council and School Committee members, and all City Commission members appointed by the current mayor) returned at a rate of just over 44 percent; and the economic subsample (generated from a roster of CEOs of companies with over 150 employees, plus business people on the mailing list of the city's downtown development organization) responded at just under 38 percent. The religious sample (Catholic priests and sisters drawn from diocesan records, and Protestant and Jewish clergy taken from the mailing list of the local Council of Churches) had an overall return of 45 percent, with Catholics at 49 percent and the others at just over 40 percent.

Whenever one is faced with low response rates, one must confront the possibility that the reasons are not random and that the results provide a biased reflection of the population at issue. While that is difficult to check conclusively, our respondents appear to have provided a good representation of Springfield's overall population in terms of social class, ethnicity, religious identification, and political party affiliation, with two major exceptions. First, Hispanics now constitute some 10 percent of the city's population but composed only 3 percent of our sample; second, Republicans now make up 11 percent of the registered electorate but accounted for 16 percent of our respondents. Clearly our general sample was slightly skewed toward middle-class whites. But this should not preclude reasonable inferences about the city's political culture, especially since the sample may represent the politically engaged portion of the population better than the population as a whole. Even so, there is sufficient variation in responses for even the most controversial items to sustain analysis and ward off any suggestion of an artificial consensus.

Questionnaire response rates hang in the balance of a number of factors, including the complexity of the items, the credibility of the investigators, and the subject matter itself. No doubt our survey had deficiencies on each of the former counts, but we suspect the subject matter raised the most problems. Even the respondents that did comply seemed especially concerned over our interest in religion, and many were suspicious about our sponsorship and funding. Here are several examples of scrawled comments in the margins or at the end of questionnaires:

> It was stated in the first paragraph that this questionnaire was about "some issues concerning the city of Sporingfield." However, I feel that [it] has definite religious overtones and appears to be someone's personal religious crusade.

> I found this most interesting to work through. The big question in my mind: who is behind this??? Who is paying for the obvious expense. . . ? Is it city hall, the Mayor, Springfield Central, a fundamentalist group, or whomever?

> I guess I belong to that small group of educated but perhaps naive minority WASP population that finds this all rather irrelevant.

> [This is] like somebody studying the national impact of dirty lyrics in rock music. Well, anyways, I hope you are interested enough in your project to be doing this survey without some research grant.

> I do not believe in over-education because it takes away your common sense and wisdom. . . . Where does the money come from for this questionnaire?

A great many respondents were complimentary about the questionnaire and asked for a copy of "its results." Oh, that such surveys are as easily tabulated and compactly catalogued as this suggests. At the other extreme were those respondents who found the exercise threatening. In some cases, this was no doubt because it assumed some knowledge that they didn't have, or requested an attitude that was still unformulated. No amount of reassurance could placate those who saw it as an examination, perhaps because we used our professorial titles and university letterhead as a way of reinforcing our scholarly bona fides and guarantees of anonymity. Overall, however, we are convinced that it was our concern with religion and the controversies surrounding church and state that proved the single most formidable obstacle. But then this applied to our remaining methods as well.

KICKING OVER THE TRACES—OR LACK OF THEM

If scholarship concerning religion can be generally faulted for its "softness," part of the problem lies with religion itself. It is hardly a phenomenon easily amenable to concrete objectivity and dispassionate rigor, and some of its aspects are particularly elusive. For instance, in the United States, students of the separation of church and state are "hoist on their own petard." In what some scholars have argued is an overly pious act of constitutional reverence, the U.S. Census has been so careful to observe church-state separation as to eschew any full enumeration of individuals' religion since 1890. And because the federal census now collects no information on religion per se, state and municipal agencies have followed suit—again to preserve the sanctity of separation.

Despite the lack of current data, we would ordinarily leap at the prospect of using the 1890 census as a centennial benchmark. But, alas, most of those records were destroyed by a Washington fire long ago. Other census data from earlier periods tend to be spotty in their coverage and poorly mobilized. This is also true of the last U.S. "Current Population Survey" to deal specifically with religion in 1936. While it provides a potentially interesting fifty-year comparison point, it was not a full enumeration, and its limited sampling frame yielded very little data for cities the size of Springfield.

As one final example of the difficulties with historical demographics, consider the Special Report of the U.S. Census on "Religious Bodies" published in 1906 but based on data collected in 1900—not from individuals but from the churches themselves. According to those tallies, turn-of-the-century Springfield had a total of 39,941 church communicants. Of these, 12,526 were members of Protestant churches and 26,840 were Roman Catholic. Of course, there is no doubt that this was a period of intense growth for Catholicism in Springfield, as we saw in Chapter Two. Still, the finding that Catholics outnumbered Protestants more than two to one strains credulity. It may more accurately reflect the tendency of the Catholic churches to report all parish members of whatever age, whereas the Protestants at that time generally excluded children from their totals. This alone could account for a substantial portion of the difference between the two communities.

The U.S. Census's next report on religious bodies in 1936 illuminates this possible difference. Whereas 25 percent of Springfield's reported Catholics were under age 13 in 1930, this described only 3.6 percent of Congregationalists and 2.8 percent of Methodists, though 16.9 percent of Episcopalians. Indeed as Demerath argued in 1968, much of the apparent growth of Protestant church membership over the first half of the twentieth century was due to various denominations bowing to the practice of Catholics and others and beginning to include children in their own counts. This occurred unevenly as theological definitions of membership gave way to the pressure of competing more favorably in the battle of church statistics.

Church membership statistics have long been infamous for their lack of reliability. And as denominational switching has become more prevalent, the numbers have become increasingly precarious, particularly when they are fifty years old and more. Several of Springfield's once prominent Congregational churches have merged or disbanded, often without a single repository for their surviving records. As another problem, inferring religious identification from the ethnic data available in the census masks one of the most interesting trends in Springfield's current religious landscape: the defection of minorities—primarily Hispanics—to Pentecostal Protestantism even as they remain nominal Catholics. One Assembly of God pastor cautioned us that, of the roughly 1,500 people who consider his church their spiritual home, only 750 or so are actually enrolled members.

One somewhat embarrassing consequence of all of this comes in response to the frequent question, "Just how many Catholics are there in Springfield today?" The fact is we don't really know. While one can compute estimates based on, say, constant proportions of ethnic groups, it may be that the constants themselves have changed over time. Moreover, even the very term "Catholic" now means different things to different people. Although there is certainly a plurality—and perhaps a majority—of nominal Catholics in Springfield (that is,, those who were raised in families associated with the Catholic Church or express Catholicism as their general religious affiliation), we all know that there is many a slip twixt the cup and the lip. Baptized Catholics have strayed from the faith in radically different directions. Some are virtually secular in their apostasy; others retain their Catholic identification while attending Sunday services in local Protestant churches, including those whom we have already noted among Hispanic Pentecostals.

We have already described some of the problems of inferring religion from ethnicity. But as a sidenote, it should be noted that even the census data on ethnicity itself pose difficulties. Before 1980, the federal census categorized persons, and their parents, as either native or foreign-born. No one whose parents were born in the United States is recorded as having any particular ethnic background. This means that ethnic self-identification, and ethnic group numbers, are consistently underrepresented. There was a question on the pre-1980 form concerning the respondent's "mother tongue," but that is little help in Springfield, where the first ethnic and religious tension was between Yankee Protestants and Irish Catholics. Thus, for historical periods when ethnicity and religion were more closely allied than they are now, our ability to identify ethnicity is greatly hampered.

The problem of collecting hard data on religion arises in other ways too. For reasons we well respect, very few public institutions collect data on the religious backgrounds or practices of their clientele. This applies to hospitals, schools, election commissions, and so forth. This frustrates the scholar even as it benefits the citizen. And as still another case, consider the question of church property value. In trying to get a sense of the changing role of different religious denominations in a city, one could do worse than seek out the computerized economic data yielded by tax valuations. But, here too, there is a hook. Because churches are tax exempt for their religious property, there is little motivation for tax assessors to spend much time in updating religious assets over time. The result is a set of comparative figures that are more alluring than accurate. Thus, in Springfield, the total assessments for all religious groups is astonishingly low. Between the citywide assessments in 1960 and 1983, the value of church holdings in both land and buildings increased by less than 5 percent. Although these data do give us a sense of the relative worth of various religious groups and possible past differential assessments between them, they provide little comparison with the city in general and no firm measure of growth over the past quarter century.

Finally, religion's special status interferes in subtler ways. Clergy are accorded special dispensations as saints among sinners, and we suspect a tendency for this halo effect to both constrain and filter the responses of informants, interviewees, and questionnaire respondents. People invoke different perspectives for priests, rabbis, and ministers. Asking political questions about religious leaders can sometimes produce either reflexive support or embarrassed discomfort. It is far easier for most persons to imagine the mayor attending religious services than the bishop wielding political power. This even applies to estimating the influence of whole religious groups. Our questionnaire includes an item in an agree-disagree format worded as follows: "Catholics are likely to have more influence around City Hall than non-Catholics." As we noted in Chapter One, several of our pretest respondents used the same phrase in reaction, namely: "I wouldn't touch that question with a ten-foot pole." Indeed, not even our items concerning the role of organized crime made more people uncomfortable.

And yet we do not want to overstress this syndrome. By and large, we suspect respondents of today are far more open than their forebears in assessing the pros and cons of religion's community presence. Overall, we have learned far more from talking to people than from seeking data behind their backs. In fact, a chief frustration of this research was the difficulty of finding sufficient rigor in support of the enormous richness produced by our interviews. Many of the problems here have less to do with religion itself than with the context in which it and we have been operating.

Data Collection and Contamination in Small Cities and Quasi-Bureaucracies

Most sociologists who "use" history rely on data sets that have already been compiled, cleaned, and often computerized. National data have frequently stood the test of national scholarly scrutiny. They are generally recognized as a national resource and are often surrounded by a community of potential users who are zealous in warding off methodological errors and political incursions. Alas, this is rarely the case in other contexts. As a rule of thumb, the smaller the social unit, the poorer the social data—or at least the less heed paid to the importance of maintaining good data for posterity's sake. While Springfield is certainly larger than most of America's towns and cities, it is still small by the standards of both researchers and residents, one of whom captured its middling size this way: "You know what people look like, but you don't know what they're cooking" (*Boston Globe*, July 10, 1989).

The basic problem is that historical data are rarely disinterested. Their chances of survival are not random, and may well be inversely related to their scholarly richness. The difficulty is compounded when the local reputations of organizations and individuals frequently rise and fall on the basis of the images they project, whether in the form of quantitative measures of performance or qualitative remarks for the record. Indeed, individuals are often far more on the line in cities like Springfield than in larger metropolitan, state, or federal settings. Smaller cities are less developed in their institutional growth, and their organizations are less complex, hence less insulating for their individual members. In larger and more convoluted settings, major decisions and processes are often played out impersonally between bureaucratic structures. But in smaller and simpler locales, quasi-bureaucracies leave individuals more exposed and more tied to others through personal networks that span institutional sectors.

Thus, in Springfield, church-state relations are often read as mayor-bishop relations, and the individuals involved are well aware of the implications. No doubt this happens to a degree in Boston, New York, or Washington as well, but there institutions take precedence over individuals, and large organizations generally leave paper trails of good records for posterity. This is very much in keeping with the Weberian bureaucratic ideal-type and a considerable blessing for historical scholarship. Moreover, because individuals are more often seen as transient occupants of enduring organizational roles in these larger settings, they find it easier to step outside the roles and speak candidly about various events and personages. Even if off the record and not for attribution, this too is a major boon to scholarly understanding.

In contrast, consider several examples of loss of information in Springfield. The first involves the archives of the Catholic Diocese of Western Massachusetts, which has been located in Springfield since 1879. Virtually no archival materials have been turned over to the city's small but well-tended library, despite the librarian's continuing efforts. This may be largely because of diocesan anxiety over the uses to which such materials might be put. Indeed, it is possible that because of such anxiety, few such materials have been preserved. According to one respondent, a bishop who took office in the 1950s reported that his predecessor "must have kept his furnace burning for days" while destroying archival materials, for the cupboard was absolutely bare.

Or consider the minutes of the city's School Committee meetings. In some ways, this is Springfield's most sensitive barometer of community opinion and dispute, and service on the committee has served as the first step up the political ladder for the vast majority of persons entering Springfield politics over the last half-century. (It is amazing how many newly minted lawyers return to town unmarried and childless but with a "great interest in the city's schools.") It is true that committee minutes are kept on file and stored chronologically. However, it is also true that these minutes are bare bones at best, since there is a well-known tendency for major discussion and decisions to occur outside of the committee's formal meetings. And perhaps even more damaging to the historical record, every committee member has an opportunity to edit his or her own statements before the minutes are filed. Once again the problems of personal reputation tend to take precedence over good organizational recordkeeping. A kind of political paranoia pervades the city atmosphere as opponents know each other all too well.

The minutes of the other forum of the city's public decisionmaking, the City Council, are equally sketchy. Although city councillors are not permitted to edit the proceedings, the written transcript merely records motions, seconds, and votes; verbatim debate is missing altogether. Thus perfunctory zoning changes, streetlight authorizations, and resolutions congratulating successful high school sports teams are thoroughly enmeshed with the hottest political topics of the day. And should a religious group be caught up in a controversy due to city hall decisions, we would need to know all about it *before* going to the minutes. The references are all listed by order numbers, agenda numbers, or specific street address. Neither School Committee nor City Council minutes have indexes.

This last point speaks to another part of the problem: there is a lack of both interest and resources for maintaining good access even to poor data. Here the best example may be city and county court records. It would seem natural for anyone interested in changing patterns of church-state relations to look for trends in locally litigated cases that involve community religious conflict and conflict between religious bodies and the city. One could imagine a content analysis of such court decisions over the years and a possible table presenting the amount of local religious conflict experienced by decade. Unfortunately, the task would require many person-months of file burrowing. While federal and state court records are at least crudely indexed for easy access, this is not the case at the county or city level, where the files are only organized chronologically. Since religion is likely to be only a small needle in this large haystack, we decided not to pursue the search.

Of course, newspaper files are a critical resource for any historical study, and in one sense we were uncommonly lucky there. Springfield has a rich journalistic heritage extending well back to the first half of the nineteenth century. We spent many hours going through clipping files organized by topic headings, and we also consulted the city library's own index of its newspaper holdings on microfilm. But despite the librarians' resolve and hard work, they simply do not have the capacity for indexing and clipping on a suitably systematic basis. Indeed, it was common for us to find stories begun without endings, conflicts alluded to without denouement, and nuggets mined but never polished. Further, the deterioration of newsprint has meant that many sources from the early part of the century have literally become "historical dustbins." Still the library's newspaper file rewarded the time we invested in it perhaps more than any other single historical source.

SEDUCTIONS BY THE QUICK FIX

As all of the foregoing suggests, scholars working at a local level must generally create data rather than discover them. We are not the first to find that history does not write itself, and we have developed great admiration for historians whose elegant writing is a gloss on the decidedly inelegant mucking about in archival ratholes in search of incremental epiphanies. We have done our own share of "truth construction," only to find that the resulting structures can be precarious.

For example, any study of church-state relations in New England is inevitably a study of mainline Protestant decline and the growth of Catholicism. Earlier we reviewed the problems of extracting religious conclusions from census tables. Still, it is possible to develop basic time lines not only through demographic data but also through the changing representations of different religious groups in positions of political and economic power. Thus, as we noted in the text itself, if the tipping point for a Catholic demographic plurality was in the 1920s, it did not occur until the 1950s among political office holders, and it has only occurred in the 1980s in the executive ranks of major banking and business firms. But the implications of this trend are far from straightforward.

The problem is not so much the reliability of this Protestant-to-Catholic trajectory, but rather its meaning. Certainly it seems unambiguous that Springfield has moved from a seventeenth-century Congregationalist bastion to a late-twentieth-century Catholic principality. On the basis of numbers alone, the city appears thoroughly dominated by the Catholic Church, and by extension, its ecclesiastical authorities, particularly the bishop. It is not hard to imagine the networks of power and the direction of influence. But are things as simple as this scenario would suggest? Not according to other information collected simultaneously. As we have seen, it makes an enormous difference that, as Catholics have become more numerous and more potent in the political economy, they have also become more middle-class and more eager to be at the core of a community consensus rather than antagonists of community conflict. Further, the relationship between Catholic laity and clergy has changed considerably. No longer does the bishop have broad lay support for aggressive community politicking from a partisan Catholic standpoint. Whether because he senses this or because his personality is different from his predecessor's, the current bishop has fashioned his role accordingly. In fact, the most influential person in Springfield today may well be Jewish: the publisher of The Springfield Newspapers, Inc.

At least that is what most of our one hundred–odd interviews would suggest, including those with the bishop, the mayor, and the publisher. And yet it is possible that some of the city's political marginals are correct in charging that behind this facade of democratic essentialism, the mayor is still taking orders from the bishop—though a few allege that the orders run in the opposite direction. Here it is difficult to find hard data of any sort. The advent of the telephone has meant the loss of paper trails, and messages put on paper are meant as often to cover tracks as to leave them. Fortunately, we had access through interviews with the figures themselves, but as we shall discuss momentarily, interviews pose their own problems of trust and reliability.

Meanwhile, another example also suggests the wisdom of looking gift numbers in the mouth. Quite apart from what has happened to the demography of Springfield's Catholic community in recent years, it is clear that the mainline Protestants continue in long-term decline, while their evangelical brethren are only a small local minority in spite of the movement's national prominence. This suggests that Protestant power has eroded. And yet once again, the issue is more complicated. WASPs (White Anglo-Saxon Protestants) continue to exercise disproportionate economic influence through their holdings and roles in Springfield's business institutions. The Evangelicals' influence also belies these numbers, especially on matters relating to abortion and sexuality, where at least a small group of Evangelicals has been more Catholic than the bishop. A number of liberal Protestant clergy have said that they feel much more comfortable around Catholic priests than their evangelical Protestant counterparts. On the other hand, one evangelical pastor estimated that 60 to 75 percent of his Sunday attenders were nonmember Catholics.

Clearly power is not a matter of numbers alone, and the relationship between church and state is more complicated than a sheer electoral tally.

In fact, the real political decisions in Springfield are only rarely subject to electoral vote. Since 1960 when the city adopted a nonpartisan political model, elections have rarely turned on substantive issues. The real decision is more who will run than who will be elected, and slates tend to be controlled by the insiders in a somewhat oligarchical fashion. A comment we have heard (and reported) more than once about mayoral contests is, "It's an anointment, not an election." And yet politicians know full well that the legitimacy of the system depends upon its remaining within the consensual middle ground of community sentiment. In fact, as we noted in Chapter Seven, there is now some danger that even Catholic politicians may be overly cautious in estimating the traditionalism of their Catholic constituencies. Although no politician has yet been voted out of office for being too traditional on issues such as abortion and contraception, this has at least become imaginable.

Through all of these nuances, we have been served well by our interviews with past and present leaders. As we described them in Chapter One, these interviews ranged from forty-five minutes to two and one-half hours and were only semistructured so that they might range widely and probe deeply. Rather than taping the interviews at the expense of rapport, we chose instead to have one of us take copious notes. We explained that we would not quote for attribution and that the goal of the scholar is somewhat different from that of the investigative journalist. By and large, our interviewees were friendly and forthcoming, despite some understandable initial reservations.

However, it is far from clear how "history" would be different if the historian had interview access to the principal actors of antiquity. Of course, every methodology has its vulnerability, and since we are using multiple methods, we may be multiply at risk. It is hardly a revelation that interviews are fraught with bias. This is particularly the case when one is trying to reconstruct a historical past on the basis of present testimony with respondents whose images and interests hang in the balance. The biases of retrospectivity are well known and fundamentally are only special cases of the bias that lurks whenever individuals are consulted for their judgment concerning the world around them. However, there are some special problems in asking people about historical events. The further those events have receded into the past, the greater the risk of bias, selectivity, and reconstruction, and the less the chances of obtaining independent corroboration. Though some respondents will simply say they don't remember, others may have conveniently forgotten, and still others may seek to construct a scene that never occurred.

Then there is the problem of becoming a respondent's agent. Occasionally we felt as if respondents were describing people and events in ways calculated to affect our public portrayal. Clearly one must be careful about accepting allegations of political corruption, financial payoffs, behind-the-scenes religious influence, or, for example, charges that the parents of parochial schools have been encouraged to substitute tax-deductible donations to the Church for school tuition payments. Some of these episodes can be checked out, but others—especially when they concern past behavior for which no records exist—cannot. While it is sometimes justifiable to report the charges as such, and with no names attached, it is sometimes prudent to eschew the matter altogether.

How then does one distinguish between a historiographic sow's ear and silk purse? How does one tell whether the quick fix is more an invitation to scholarly corruption or the basis of an elegantly simple and penetrating insight? Of course, final judgment rests with the whole picture, both methodologically and theoretically. One must be able to tell a story that is maximally consistent with all of one's sources and makes maximal sense within one's theoretical perspective. But this can lead to the corresponding danger of imposing a theoretical filter on empirical data. Indeed, theory is itself another source of the unduly quick fix. The phenomena of religion and community power are awash with theoretical models, ranging from secularization to religious revival and from pluralism to elitism. Clearly one cannot simply opt for one model as the basis of data collection and interpretive choice. Just as a study often benefits by being multimethod, there are also advantages to being multitheoried—especially when it may lead to a new perspective as a synthesis of the old. This requires both rigor and richness at a theoretical as well as a methodological level.

WRITING A COMMUNITY HISTORY: MAKING FRIENDS OR INFLUENCING PEOPLE?

Springfield has recently been the subject of two very good studies of its seventeenth- and nineteenth-century past, both using quite straightforward historical techniques and archival sources (Innes 1983; Frisch 1972). On occasion, we have envied these authors for data that seemed relatively finite, episodes for which there are no competing interpretations, and subjects who do not talk back. Indeed, if the ultimate test of conventional historical scholarship is whether it tells the historians themselves anything new, we must satisfy an additional criterion; namely, our ability to say something that seems both new and true to the citizens themselves.

Relatively few historians face the problem of describing a living population that will have reactions in response. Where history is used to provide context and momentum for analysis of a contemporary situation, problems begin to mount. This may be one reason for the tradition of anonymity that long dominated sociological community studies; namely, "Middletown,"

"Yankee City," and so on. At one level, of course, this tradition was designed to spare the subjects. At quite a different level, it seeks to spare the authors from the subjects. This has not always been successful; perhaps the most notable incident was the hanging in effigy of Arthur Vidich at a Fourth of July parade in his research site of "Springdale" (see Vidich and Bensman 1968). Townspeople felt that promises of anonymity were broken since they could easily identify compatriots through the aliases provided by the authors.

More recently, however, the style has changed, and sociologists have become more brazen in identifying their study sites. This is part of a broader chest-baring and declaring of one's values and biases; it is also part of a new ethical sensitivity to the rights of respondents. Thus, respondents have a right to know what a study is about and a right to see the results that involve them. Although there are exceptions for studies that would be impossible without some degree of dissimulation, honesty is generally the best policy.

These principles are sometimes easier to agree with in the abstract than to apply in practice. Were we to describe our study as an assessment of church-state compliance and violation, many respondents would see it as a gun at their temple. How much easier (and no less truthful) to describe our interests as the changing role of religion in the community. In addition, there are persisting canons that allow us to engage in some degree of truth retention if only for the sake of the subjects themselves. Unlike many investigative reporters, social scientists are not expected to provide the actual names of their subjects, and many have risked judicial contempt proceedings and imprisonment in order to stand behind the pledges of anonymity given to their interviewees. Certainly we feel strongly about that, but at what point should we leave off the naming of names and begin to use pseudonyms as proxies?

Over the course of this project, we considered a variety of pseudonyms for Springfield itself—some so general as to be vapid (e.g., "multi-city"); some so specific as to belie deception itself (e.g., names related to the city's once-critical economic function as a federal armory and its role as the birthplace of basketball and the site of its Hall of Fame). But none of these deceptions offers much protection; the people we are most likely to offend will learn about the book anyway; many others will never know. Accordingly, while we did not use "Springfield" in the title, we made no effort to camouflage it in the text. However, there are many references equivalent to journalism's infamous "highly placed sources." This seemed the least we could offer respondents who were generous even as they were vulnerable.

In all of this, we take perverse comfort in the realization that sociology tends to bore and befuddle people long before it provokes them. Insofar as the book offers more jargon than prose, we will at least have put some distance between ourselves and our subjects. And although Springfield is only a medium-sized city, it offers more anonymity to its residents than the truly small towns that have occupied so many sociologists in the "community studies" tradition.

And yet one hopes that the book will have some resonance within Springfield. After all, while our scholarly colleagues will be the most important judges of the project's merits and shortcomings, the city's residents are significant arbiters too. We have no illusions of knowing more about any single sector of the community than its chief participants. However, in bringing together a more diverse set of perspectives and a wider range of information than most individuals command, the book may lead to new insights, or at least a reconsideration of the old.

THE SPRINGFIELD QUESTIONNAIRE AND FOLLOW-UP APPEALS TO SAMPLE RESPONDENTS

 UNIVERSITY OF MASSACHUSETTS AT AMHERST   Department of Sociology

Thompson Hall
Amherst, MA 01003
(413) 545-0577

Dear Springfield area resident:

The enclosed is not a prize give-away, a sales pitch, or an attempt to get your opinion of some new product. Rather, it is a brief questionnaire about some issues concerning the city of Springfield.

We think you will agree that the issues are important and interesting. What you help us to learn about Springfield will help us to understand other American cities and what is happening in the nation overall.

Since this is not a test, there are no right or wrong answers. However, we are vitally interested in your personal views and perceptions. Even though you may not feel like an "expert," your opinions matter greatly.

In fact, you will be responsible not just for yourself but for thousands of others like you. Any time a person is selected as part of a small random sample like this one, the response becomes all the more important in representing a segment of the larger population. Of course, your individual responses will not be reported in any way. The identifying number is soley for internal office use.

For all of these reasons, we hope that we can count on you to fill out the questionnaire and return it in the stamped envelope as soon as possible. If you have any questions beforehand, feel free to call us collect at 413-545-0577. If you have comments or suggestions afterwards, by all means add them in the space provided at the end.

With deep appreciation for your assistance.

APPENDIX B

Springfield Survey

1) First here are a series of statements to which we would like your personal reaction. Use either pen or pencil to circle your responses on the scales to the right. People will have different opinions on each, but remember, there are no right or wrong answers.

Strongly Agree	Agree	Agree Somewhat	Disagree Somewhat	Disagree	Strongly Disagree
SA	A	AS	DS	D	SD
6	5	4	3	2	1

	SA	A	AS	DS	D	SD
a) In Springfield, people from different backgrounds basically get along as equals.	6	5	4	3	2	1
b) The problems of this city seem beyond the control of the city government.	6	5	4	3	2	1
c) A minority religious group should be able to practice its rituals and beliefs even if it offends the religion of the majority.	6	5	4	3	2	1
d) Springfield's city government is basically honest and free of corruption.	6	5	4	3	2	1
e) It is proper to have religious prayers in the city's public events.	6	5	4	3	2	1
f) Almost every major decision made in city government reflects the influence of a small group of people behind the scenes.	6	5	4	3	2	1
g) Religious groups should keep separate from what goes on in city politics and city hall.	6	5	4	3	2	1
h) With so many groups in Springfield, the city is not a real community.	6	5	4	3	2	1
i) A city's public agencies (e.g., hospitals, welfare offices) should not have policies which are opposed by the city's religious majority.	6	5	4	3	2	1
j) The city's School Committee should not include parents whose children are enrolled in private or parochial schools.	6	5	4	3	2	1
k) Catholics are likely to have more influence around City Hall than non-Catholics.	6	5	4	3	2	1
l) Local community issues and news stories are not very interesting to me.	6	5	4	3	2	1
m) All things considered, Springfield is an ideal community in which to live.	6	5	4	3	2	1
n) The separation of church and state is a good idea.	6	5	4	3	2	1
o) U.S. Supreme Court decisions are more and more out of touch with the views of the people.	6	5	4	3	2	1
p) City authorities should strictly control the efforts of religious cults to recruit and convert young people.	6	5	4	3	2	1
q) Nowadays the Federal Government is too influenced by religious groups and their leaders.	6	5	4	3	2	1
r) U.S. Government policies have greatly limited the freedom of religion in our country today.	6	5	4	3	2	1

2) There are many types of groups represented in the Springfield area. How would you rate the following in terms of their **current influence** in the community? (Again, circle your responses to the right.)

	A Great Deal of Influence	Moderate Influence	A Little Influence	No Influence
Irish Catholics	4	3	2	1
Jews	4	3	2	1
Blacks	4	3	2	1
Italian Catholics	4	3	2	1
Born-Again Christians	4	3	2	1
Hispanics	4	3	2	1
Protestants (e.g. Congregationalist, Episcopalian, Methodist)	4	3	2	1
Organized Crime	4	3	2	1
Suburban Residents	4	3	2	1

3) a) If there were a proposal in Springfield **to raise property taxes,** how influential would each of the following persons/groups be in affecting the outcome? (Please assume that each of the groups would be interested enough to try.)

	Great Influence	Moderate Influence	Some Influence	A Little Influence	No Influence
City Council	5	4	3	2	1
Downtown business community	5	4	3	2	1
Springfield newspapers	5	4	3	2	1
Protestant ministers	5	4	3	2	1
Mayor's Office	5	4	3	2	1
Roman Catholic clergy	5	4	3	2	1
School Committee	5	4	3	2	1
Jewish community leaders	5	4	3	2	1
Local neighborhood councils	5	4	3	2	1
General public opinion	5	4	3	2	1

b) If a local cable television company wanted to **add an X-rated pornographic channel,** how influential would each of the following persons/groups be in affecting the outcome?

	Great Influence	Moderate Influence	Some Influence	A Little Influence	No Influence
City Council	5	4	3	2	1
Downtown business community	5	4	3	2	1
Springfield newspapers	5	4	3	2	1
Protestant ministers	5	4	3	2	1
Mayor's Office	5	4	3	2	1
Roman Catholic clergy	5	4	3	2	1
School Committee	5	4	3	2	1
Jewish community leaders	5	4	3	2	1
Local neighborhood councils	5	4	3	2	1
General public opinion	5	4	3	2	1

4) Any city has limited resources. What priority should the city give to each of the following activities?

	Extremely Important	Important	Desirable	Not a Priority
a) downtown business development	4	3	2	1
b) city care for the homeless	4	3	2	1
c) reducing crime	4	3	2	1
d) responding to the needs of the poor and disadvantaged	4	3	2	1
e) improved maintenance of city streets and parks	4	3	2	1
f) development of Winchester Square area	4	3	2	1
g) improving the public schools	4	3	2	1
h) responding to the needs of minorities such as Blacks and Hispanics	4	3	2	1

5) Below are a number of possible practices which might occur in the community. **Whether you agree or disagree with the practices themselves**, indicate your feelings about whether they **should be allowed** to occur. (For example, you might personally oppose Communists but strongly support their right to have a public rally; in this case you would circle "5" to the right of item "p")

	Should definitely be legal	Should probably be legal	Not Sure	Should probably be illegal	Should definitely be illegal
a) exempting persons from wartime military service because of deep personal convictions.	5	4	3	2	1
b) parents educating their children at home for religious reasons.	5	4	3	2	1
c) beginning City Council meetings with a prayer.	5	4	3	2	1
d) allowing student religious groups to meet in a public high school.	5	4	3	2	1
e) allowing a critically ill patient to refuse medical treatment for religious reasons.	5	4	3	2	1
f) clergy using their pulpits to support particular political candidates.	5	4	3	2	1
g) atheists teaching in the public schools.	5	4	3	2	1
h) groups using drugs as part of their religious rituals.	5	4	3	2	1
i) organized prayer in the public schools.	5	4	3	2	1
j) students refusing to salute the flag or recite the pledge of allegiance for religious reasons.	5	4	3	2	1
k) teaching the Bible's version of Creation in public school science classes.	5	4	3	2	1
l) a Christmas nativity scene on city property during the holiday season.	5	4	3	2	1
m) a program of sex education in a public junior high school.	5	4	3	2	1
n) religious groups not paying taxes on their church properties.	5	4	3	2	1
o) allowing a book against religion and the churches to be available in the public library.	5	4	3	2	1
p) a Communist political rally in a public park.	5	4	3	2	1
q) state certification of religious (or parochial) school teachers.	5	4	3	2	1
r) hospitals or clinics performing abortions.	5	4	3	2	1

6) Now we would like you to evaluate several possible actions in the schools. Indicate your response to each on the scale as follows:

Strongly Support	Support	Moderately Support	Moderately Oppose	Oppose	Strongly Oppose
SS	**S**	**MS**	**MO**	**O**	**SO**
6	5	4	3	2	1

a) Thinking of a **public** junior high school, how do you feel about the following kinds of activities?

	SS	**S**	**MS**	**MO**	**O**	**SO**
1) A school teacher leading prayers at the beginning of the school day.	6	5	4	3	2	1
2) A moment of silence at the beginning of each day.	6	5	4	3	2	1
3) Prayers led by local clergy from different faiths.	6	5	4	3	2	1
4) Classroom instruction about various religious faiths.	6	5	4	3	2	1
5) A moment of silent prayer at the beginning of the day.	6	5	4	3	2	1
6) A coach leading prayer before an athletic contest.	6	5	4	3	2	1
7) Religious music as part of the school's holiday assembly.	6	5	4	3	2	1

b) Now thinking about religious or **parochial** schools, how would you feel about giving the following kinds of **public** or state assistance to such schools?

	SS	**S**	**MS**	**MO**	**O**	**SO**
1) Enough support so that parents do not have to pay extra for children to attend a religious school.	6	5	4	3	2	1
2) Textbooks for all non-religious subjects.	6	5	4	3	2	1
3) Public school experts to teach special subjects in parochial schools.	6	5	4	3	2	1
4) Bussing for student transportation to and from school.	6	5	4	3	2	1
5) Access to public school facilities where needed (e.g., labs, gyms, classrooms, etc.)	6	5	4	3	2	1
6) Tuition tax credits for parents of children in private or parochial schools.	6	5	4	3	2	1

Supplemental Sheet for Public School Teachers

6c) The public schools are very important to Springfield. Accordingly, we have drawn a special sample of public school employees for several additional questions. As before, your answers will be confidential and anonymous.

   a) Overall, how important is religion as an issue in your school? (check one)

   _____1) very important — it surfaces frequently in one form or another.
   _____2) important — it comes up fairly often in one form or another.
   _____3) not very important — it emerges only occasionally.
   _____4) unimportant — it never really comes up at all.

   b) How often, if at all, have any religious groups (of students, parents or outsiders) held meetings in your school in the past year? (check one)

   _____1) 5 or more occasions.
   _____2) 1 - 4 occasions.
   _____3) none to my knowledge.

   c) How often do any of the following occur in your own classroom? (check one for each item)

	Daily	Monthly	Several Times Yearly	Never
1) moment of silent prayer				
2) moment of silence				
3) spoken prayer				
4) religious festivities (e.g., Christmas carols or displays)				
5) religious training				
6) teaching about religion				

   d) How many other teachers in your school do you think engage in these activities at least somewhat? (check one for each item)

	All or Most	About Half	A Few	None
1) moment of silent prayer				
2) moment of silence				
3) spoken prayer				
4) religious festivities (e.g., Christmas carols or displays)				
5) religious training				
6) teaching about religion				

   e) If you ever observe a moment of silence in your own classroom, approximately what precentage of your students respond as follows?

   1) noisy indifference   _____ %
   2) bored resignation   _____ %
   3) respectful contemplation _____ %
   4) prayerful meditation   _____ %
                                100%

   f) Finally, we are interested in sharing between public schools and private religious or parochial schools. This might include facilities, resources (e.g., textbooks), teaching expertise or teachers. Apart from bussing and Title I remedial teaching, how much sharing would you say occurs in the school system as you know it? (check one)

   _____1) A great deal.
   _____2) A substantial amount.
   _____3) Not very much.
   _____4) None that I am aware of.

7) Abortion is an issue that has become a matter of wide discussion. How much influence has each of the following had in **shaping your attitudes** toward abortion?

	Very Influential	Moderately Influential	Somewhat Influential	Not at all Influential
1) Information gained from radio or TV.	4	3	2	1
2) My own religious beliefs.	4	3	2	1
3) My private humanitarian convictions.	4	3	2	1
4) Church teachings.	4	3	2	1
5) Positions of political leaders.	4	3	2	1
6) The views of close friends or relatives.	4	3	2	1
7) Positions of experts and scientists.	4	3	2	1

b) Now think about your feelings concerning **welfare aid to the disadvantaged and shelter for the homeless**. How influential have the following been?

	Very Influential	Moderately Influential	Somewhat Influential	Not at all Influential
1) Information gained from radio or TV.	4	3	2	1
2) My own religious beliefs.	4	3	2	1
3) My private humanitarian convictions.	4	3	2	1
4) Church teachings.	4	3	2	1
5) Positions of political leaders.	4	3	2	1
6) The views of close friends or relatives.	4	3	2	1
7) Positions of experts and scientists.	4	3	2	1

c) How much influence did each of the following have on your vote in the **1984 Reagan-Mondale Presidential election?**

	Very Influential	Moderately Influential	Somewhat Influential	Not at all Influential
1) Information gained from radio or TV.	4	3	2	1
2) My own religious beliefs.	4	3	2	1
3) My private humanitarian convictions.	4	3	2	1
4) Church teachings.	4	3	2	1
5) Positions of political leaders.	4	3	2	1
6) The views of close friends or relatives.	4	3	2	1
7) Positions of experts and scientists.	4	3	2	1

8) Now we would like to ask a few questions about yourself and your family.

   a) What is your current age? _____

   b) Are you: 1. male   2. female   (circle one)

   c) What is your current family status?   (circle one)

      1. single
      2. married
      3. unmarried, but living together
      4. separated
      5. divorced
      6. widowed

   d) How many children do you have; and what are their ages?

      # _____   ages: _____

   e) If you have school age children, what type of school have they attended? (Circle as many as apply.)

      1. public schools
      2. private, religious or parochial
      3. private, non-religious
      4. other: _____

   f) What types of schools did **you** attend when growing up? (Circle as many as apply.)

      1. public schools
      2. private, religious or parochial
      3. private, non-religious
      4. other: _____

   g) If your children attend public schools, indicate whether they have experienced any of the following by checking the appropriate category for each:

	Yes	Don't Think So	Don't Know
1. spoken prayer in a public school.			
2. silent prayer in the school.			
3. teaching the Bible's version of Creation.			
4. participating in student religious group during school hours.			
5. feeling uncomfortable about some school program or activity for religious reasons.			

9) What is your present **occupation**? Please check the space to the left. If more than one, check your primary job. If there is another major wage earner in your household, also check his or her occupation.

Yours	Other Wage Earner		
_____	_____	1)	Owner of Business or Industrial firm
_____	_____	2)	Top Management of business or agency (e.g. President, VP, etc.)
_____	_____	3)	Professional (e.g. Doctor, Lawyer, Engineer, Accountant)
_____	_____	4)	Service Professional (e.g. Teacher, Social Worker, Counselor)
_____	_____	5)	Middle Management (e.g. Division Chief or Supervisor)
_____	_____	6)	Sales Work
_____	_____	7)	Clerical Work (e.g. Secretary, Receptionist, Retail Counter Work)
_____	_____	8)	Foreman or Skilled Crafts (e.g. Carpenter, Plumber)
_____	_____	9)	Manual Work, Semi-Skilled (e.g. Factory Line, Mechanic)
_____	_____	10)	Laborer, no training required
_____	_____	11)	Operator (trucks, heavy equipment)
_____	_____	12)	Farmer
_____	_____	13)	Military (rank _____)
_____	_____	14)	Unemployed
_____	_____	15)	Student
_____	_____	16)	Homemaker
_____	_____	17)	Retired (was a _____)
_____	_____	18)	Other (_____)

10) a) What is your current **household** income?   (circle one)

1. less than $10,000
2. $10,000 to $14,999
3. $15,000 to $19,999
4. $20,000 to $24,999
5. $25,000 to $29,999

6. $30,000 to $34,999
7. $35,000 to $39,999
8. $40,000 to $49,999
9. $50,000 to $74,999
10. $75,000 and above

b) Circle the highest level of **schooling** you have completed.

| Elementary | Junior High | High School | College | Graduate Study |

1 2 3 4 5 6 / 7 8 9 / 10 11 12 / 13 14 15 16 / 17 18 19 20 21 and up

c) If you were asked to use one of these four names for your **social class**, which one describes you best. (circle one)

1. lower class
2. working class
3. middle class
4. upper class

d) How long have you lived in this area?   (number of years) _____

e) What do you consider your primary ethnic background? _____
    (e.g., Black, French, Irish, Italian, Jewish, Puerto Rican, etc.)

11) Do you have a religious preference?   (circle one)

a) 1. Roman Catholic
    2. Jewish (check one: Conservative _____; Orthodox _____; Reform _____)
    3. Protestant (write in denomination _____)
    4. Other (write in _____)
    5. None

b) How important are religious beliefs in your personal life?   (circle one)

    1. Very Important   3. Not Very Important
    2. Fairly Important   4. Not At All Important

c) How often do you attend religious services?   (circle one)

    1. More than once a week.   5. Several times a year.
    2. About once a week.   6. Once a year or less.
    3. Once every several weeks.   7. Never.
    4. About once a month.

d) Think for a moment of your half-dozen closest friends. How many of them attend a church or synagogue on
    a regular basis?   (circle one)

    1. All
    2. Most
    3. Some
    4. None

e) Would you say you have been "born again" or have had a born-again religious experience?   (circle one)

    1. Yes
    2. No
    3. Not Sure

f) How would you describe the religiousness of your home when you were growing up?   (circle one)

    1. Highly Religious
    2. Moderately Religious
    3. Somewhat Religious
    4. Not Very Religious
    5. Not At All Religious

12) a) How would you describe your **political** views?   (circle one number)

Radical		Liberal	Moderate		Conservative		Very Conservative	
1	2	3	4	5	6	7	8	9

b) How would you identify your party preference?   (circle one)

1. Democratic   3. independent   5. none
2. Republican   4. other (write in:_____)

c) For whom did you vote in the last Presidential Election?   (circle one)

1. Reagan   3. other
2. Mondale   4. did not vote

13) All things considered -- job, family, friends, style of life, etc. — how would you evaluate your life today when compared with the following: (circle one for each item)

	Much Better	Somewhat Better	About Equal	Somewhat Worse	Much Worse
a) Compared to what I **expected** ten years ago, my life is...	5	4	3	2	1
b) Compared to what a person like me **deserves**, my life is...	5	4	3	2	1
c) Compared to what I would anticipate **for my children**, my life is...	5	4	3	2	1

This ends the questionnaire. However, if you have questions, comments, or suggestions, by all means add them here:

Thank you very much for your help. Put the completed questionnaire in the stamped envelope provided and mail it as soon as possible.

Appeals to Sample Respondents

Follow-up #1:

Recently you received a questionnaire concerning a number of issues facing Springfield. If you have already completed it and mailed it back, this is to thank you once again. If you have not yet done so, this is to remind you of its importance.

It is hard to be persuasive with a postcard. However, we will keep trying because your response is so critical to the study. In fact, if we don't hear from you soon, we shall send you another copy of the questionnaire itself in case you have misplaced the original. Needless to say, this is an expense we would like to avoid, just as you no doubt would like to avoid us bugging you further.

With deep appreciation for your patience and your help.

Follow-up #2:

Just in case you mislaid our earlier questionnaire, here is another one. If you had decided not to fill it out, won't you please reconsider? We realize it is a chore for you, but your response is absolutely critical for us.

It is worth repeating that there are no right or wrong answers; that your responses will be strictly confidential, and that the study has no hidden motives or sponsors. We have no ties to any individuals, agencies, or organizations in Springfield, and we are conducting the study solely on our own initiative. It is pure social science research designed to increase understanding of some important issues facing cities like Springfield and the country as a whole.

Again, we greatly need your help. We promise not to betray your effort and your trust.

Follow-up #3:

Yes, we are persistent. Every one of our questionnaires means a lot to our research. Even if there are a few questions you feel you cannot answer, we would sure appreciate your responses to the rest.

Because some information is better than none, our next step will be to call you and ask a few questions over the phone. Needless to say, we would like to avoid bugging you this way. Since you no doubt would like to avoid it too, why not take just a few minutes to complete the questionnaire and send it back? As the saying goes: "pretty please?"

Again, our thanks,

STATISTICAL ADDENDA

Instead of burdening the text with overly complicated statistical details of our questionnaire analysis, we have collected several of the most important here. The following reports on three principal topics. First, our development of several aggregate indexes to measure a series of important variables. Second, the interrelations among these indexes. Third, a series of regression analyses of Springfielders attitudes toward the legality of abortion.

INDEX CONSTRUCTION

In various chapters of this book we have used several indexes that measure either attitude or behavior sets. Here we present the logic and details of the index constructions. Indexes are constructed by combining separate attitudinal or behavioral measures. The resulting aggregate scale is designed to reveal a commonality underlying the separate individual measures. Not only does this offer protection from the vagaries that can undermine the reliability and validity of any one measure, but it is a way of tapping several dimensions of a multidimensional concept.

The items composing an index should obviously be related both theoretically and empirically. That is, there should be an a priori reason to expect the responses to several individual measures to be similar—they should share a theoretical logic. And then, of course, the responses should be related in fact as evidenced by the data. This can be measured by statistics such as Pearson correlation coefficients or a factor analysis. In constructing our indexes we used both sets of statistics as a method of balancing the possible weaknesses of each method alone. For items to be included in an index, they should be neither statistically unrelated, nor too highly related, since the latter would indicate that they risk redundancy.

In Table C.1 are the Pearson r correlation coefficients for questions designed to tap attitudes concerning the proper relationship between religion and government. We expected two sets of attitudes to cohere: one covering issues in which public or government-sponsored religious displays/rituals were considered legitimate; the other covering issues in which an individual's or a group's right to religious expression was considered protected from government regulation.

Two clear attitude sets emerge from these items. First, we took prayer at public events, city council meetings, and public schools, the teaching of creationism, and a Christmas crèche, and combined them to form an index. All have significant relationships at the .001 level with coefficients

TABLE C.1

Correlations Concerning the Proper Relation between Religion and Government
(General Population Sample, N = 231–254)

	1 Proper Prayer at Public Events	2 Prayer at City Council Meetings	3 Crèche on City Property	4 Prayer in Public Schools	5 Teach Creationism	6 Avoid Military Service	7 Educate Children at Home	8 Refuse Medical Treatment	9 Students Refuse to Salute Flag	
	1.000	.600**	.422**	.588**	.424**	-.036	-.035	-.051	-.177*	1
		1.000	.397**	.563**	.382**	-.025	.072	.013	-.093	2
			1.000	.543**	.382**	-.180*	-.046	-.147	-.255**	3
				1.000	.491**	-.098	-.017	-.118	-.248**	4
					1.000	.023	.125	-.043	-.109	5
						1.000	.335**	.249**	.377**	6
							1.000	.294**	.078	7
								1.000	.331**	8
									1.000	9

* $p < .01$ ** $p < .001$

Approaching Springfield—and its bridges—from the south.

ranging from .382 to .600. We called this the Nonestablishment Index, since the items represent government-sponsored religious events, or practices that have an implied sponsorship given their connection with public events. In general they are practices similar to those in cases in which the Supreme Court has ruled that the "establishment" clause of the religion portions of the First Amendment are applicable.

The second groups of items—refusal of medical treatment, military service, home education, and refusal to salute the flag—were combined into a Free Exercise Index, since they pertain to issues in which an individual or group is allowed to ignore certain obligations due to its religious beliefs. Cases of this type have produced Supreme Court decisions involving the "free exercise" clause. Of the four items included here, "flag salute" is the least tidy, since it fails to be significantly related to one item in its own index, but is related to two items in the Nonestablishment Index. However, we left it in the Free Exercise Index because of its clear substantive meaning in this context. Interestingly, because our survey was in the field before the politics of flag burning became controversial in 1988, that was not a distorting factor. Clearly the flag is a powerful symbol that can override otherwise "consistent" attitudes. Finally, it is worth noting that, unlike Table 4.1 in Chapter Four, these two indexes do not measure the extent to which our respondents agreed with the Supreme Court in judging whether these practices should be legal or illegal; instead, we are concerned here with the extent to which they believed either "establishment" practices or "free exercise" liberties should be more broadly legitimate. See Table C.1.

Meanwhile, a third set of items concerning religion and politics also coheres. These questions in Table C.2 are less concerned with the proper relationship between governmental and religious practices than they are with the involvement of religious organizations in partisan and electoral politics. They reflect the common understanding that the United States has a "separation of church and state" even though those words are not a part of any of the nation's ruling documents, and are more often a description of a normative ideal than historical reality.

We included these three items in a correlation matrix with the items forming the two previous indexes described above. The first two, religious groups staying separate from city politics and clergy not endorsing candidates, emerged as a separate cluster. However, the third—approval of the "separation of church and state" as a general *idea*—did not have as clear a pattern of correlation. This may be due to the widespread agreement with the wording of the item: "The separation of church and state is a good idea." There was relatively little variation in the responses, leading us to believe that this is such a generally accepted normative statement that it fails to touch on important related issues of religion and politics. Further, when included in a factor analysis, it was the weakest variable in the index. As a result, we omitted it from the Separation Index. See Table C.2.

TABLE C.2
Items Concerning Broad Separation of Religion and Politics
(General Population Sample, $N = 236$)

1 Religious Groups Stay Separate from City Politics	2 Clergy Should Not Use Pulpit for Candidate Endorsements	3 Separation of Church and State Good	
1.000	.375**	.342**	1
	1.000	.049	2
		1.000	3

** $p < .001$

Table C.3 contains items that ask for respondents' attitudes toward Springfield, as a community, as a place to live, and with regard to the quality of local government. Here we expected two indexes to emerge: one that contained attitudes toward Springfield as a community; the other that revealed a sense of the honesty and efficacy of Springfield's city gov-

TABLE C.3
Items Bearing on Civic Idealism
(General Population Sample, $N = 236$)

Items	Equals	Community	Ideal	Control	Honest/ Free	Behind- Scenes Influence
People get along as equals	1.000	.340**	.331**	.298**	.400**	.257**
Springfield is real community		1.000	.302**	.380**	.315**	.279**
Springfield is ideal place to live			1.000	.314**	.391**	.253**
City problems beyond control of city government				1.000	.363**	.235**
City government honest/free of corruption					1.000	.439**
Every city government decision reflects behind-scenes influence						1.000

* $p < .01$ ** $p < .001$

ernment. Alas, the resulting statistics were not so clear. The correlation coefficients vary consistently among all six items; when entered into a factor analysis (Table C.6), only one factor emerged. But we believe there are solid conceptual reasons to keep the two attitude sets separate, even as we note the clear, positive relationship between attitudes toward the community and attitudes toward the city government. Therefore, we used items "equals," "community," and "ideal," to form the Civic Idealism Index; and "control," "honest," and "behind scenes," to form the Political Confidence Index. See Table C.3. Correlation matrixes separating the two item sets in Table C.4 show reasonable coherence for each index, with a strong correlation between them (r = .577). See Table C.4.

TABLE C.4
Matrices for Indexes of Civic Idealism and Political Confidence

	Civic Idealism Index Items (N = 241)		
	People in Springfield Get Along as Equals	*Even with Different Groups, Springfield is Real Community*	*Springfield is Ideal Place to Live*
People in Springfield get along as equals	1.000	.307**	.340**
Even with different groups, Springfield is real community		1.000	.282**
Springfield is ideal place to live			1.000

	Political Confidence Index Items (N = 247)		
	Problems of City Beyond Control of City Government	*City Government Honest/Free of Corruption*	*Every City Government Decision Reflects Behind-Scenes Influence*
Problems of city beyond control of city government	1.000	.314**	.234**
City government honest/ free of corruption		1.000	.404**
Every city government decision reflects behind-scenes influence			1.000

** $p < .001$

As one last measure, we combined several items to form a Personal Religiosity Index. Though this index combines both attitudinal and behavioral measures, the strong correlations among the items makes the index defensible. It combines a measure of meaning (beliefs), participation (attendance), and a sense of belonging (friends). See Table C.5.

As a check on the possibility of spurious correlations in the tables already mentioned here, we submitted the items to a factor analysis. The factors that emerged in Table C.6 reveal the strength of the constructed indexes. We began by dumping all of the individual items listed above into one factor analysis. Five factors emerged, identical to the indexes just described (remembering that the Civic Idealism and Political Confidence indexes were grouped as one). Deletion of any group of items decreased the number of factors generated, giving us a fairly confident indication that the data support our decision to combine these many items into indexes. See Table C.6.

Finally, Table C.7 is the correlation matrix for all six of the indexes we constructed. In general the indexes are not significantly related, and the only exception difficult to explain is the negative correlation between the Separationist and Free Exercise indexes ($r = -.286$). One would think that, as support for the separation of religion and politics increases, support for religious expression unrestrained by government would also increase. Clearly this is not the case. While a full discussion of this seeming anomaly is out of place here, the correlation does lead to some intriguing questions concerning how the population of Springfield defines such important cultural categories as "religion," "politics," and "separation." See Table C.7.

TABLE C.5
Items Composing an Index of Personal Religiosity
($N = 240$)

Item	Importance of Religious Beliefs	Attendance at Religious Services	Number of Friends Attending Regularly
Importance of religious beliefs	1.000	.557**	.294**
Attendance at religious services		1.000	.427**
Number of friends attending regularly			1.000

** $p < .001$

TABLE C.6
Rotated Factor Matrix, Using General Population Sample

Variable	1	2	3	4	5
	\multicolumn{5}{Factor}				
(Nonestablishment Index)					
Prayer—city council	.75				
Prayer—public schools	.80				
Prayer—city public events	.75				
Creation story in public schools	.70				
Crèche on city property	.68				
(Idealism and Confidence Indexes)					
People get along as equals		.66			
City is ideal place to live		.63			
Springfield is a real community		.65			
City problems beyond government control		.61			
Small groups make decisions behind scenes		.61			
City government is basically honest		.71			
(Personal Religiosity Index)					
Attendance at religious services			.79		
Importance of religious beliefs			.77		
Number of friends who attend			.66		
(Free Exercise Index)					
Refusal of military service				.77	
Educate children at home				.62	
Refusal of medical treatment				.65	
Students refusal to salute flag				.57	
(Separationist Index)					
Religion to be kept separate from city hall and politics					.79
Clergy using pulpit for political endorsements					.75
Eigenvalue:	3.67	2.55	2.20	1.60	1.09
Percentage of variance explained:	18.40	12.80	11.00	8.00	5.50

Total percentage of variance explained: 55.60

TABLE C.7
Pearson *r* Correlation Coefficients among Constructed Indexes
(General Population Sample, *N* = 226–238)

	Nonestab-lishment	Free Exercise	Separa-tionist	Civic Idealism	Political Confidence	Personal Religiosity
Nonestablishment	1.000					
Free Exercise	−.140	1.000				
Separationist	−.058	−.286**	1.000			
Civic Idealism	.100	−.011	−.069	1.000		
Political Confidence	.115	.082	−.118	.577**	1.000	
Personal Religiosity	.348**	−.120	−.203**	.103	.029	1.000

** *p* <.001

MEASURING ATTITUDES TOWARD ABORTION

Springfield's version of the abortion debate demonstrates a typical diversity, both in its public expression and in the private attitudes of its citizens. In Chapter Seven, we discussed the public issue in the context of the relationships between religion and various local political processes. Here we want to explore some of the citizenry's private attitudes in more detail.

As we saw in Chapter Seven, our survey showed that a majority of Springfield's population favored the continued legality of abortion, although the sentiment was by no means unanimous. The question occurred within a battery asking whether a series of practices should be legal or illegal. This particular entry involved "hospitals or clinics performing abortions." The item was intentionally general. Eschewing the litany of contingencies that complicate the issue for policy purposes, our objective was simply to obtain a sense of the respondent's overall perspective. The respondents were offered five possible response categories: (1) definitely legal, (2) probably legal, (3) definitely illegal, (4) probably illegal, and (5) not sure.

To briefly recapitulate the findings reported in Chapter Seven, just over 55 percent of our general population sample answered that abortion should either "definitely" or "probably" be legal, compared to one third who answered "definitely" or "probably" illegal. Further, "definitely legal" responses outweighed "definitely illegal" responses 34 percent to 25 percent. But what was more telling was the variety within religious communities. Unfortunately, our sample of Protestants was too small to yield a reliable measure of the difference between religious liberals and conservatives, and it was somewhat compounded by race since most of the conservative Protestants were black Baptists. However, it is worth noting that, overall, Springfield's Catholics were even more varied than its Protestants on the issue.

Seventy-five percent of Protestants favored legality compared to 19 percent taking an illegal position. On the other hand, Catholics were more evenly split and skewed slightly toward legality. Forty-six percent of Catholics answered that abortion should definitely or probably be legal, whereas only 40 percent answered definitely or probably illegal; the percentages in the extreme categories were roughly equal—25 percent answering definitely legal and 27 percent answering definitely illegal. Finally, some 14 percent of our Catholic respondents remained "not sure" on the issue, as compared to only 6 percent of the Protestants. Given the continued clarity of the official Catholic position, the large number of "not sure" responses is interesting. It seems unlikely that these persons were unaware of the Church's position. This may instead indicate a state of transition out of the institution, a dimension of secularization.

To examine these attitudes toward abortion further, we performed a series of regression analyses along several lines. Regression is a statistical technique for looking at a group of possible explanatory factors (independent variables) and assessing the impact of each in turn while "holding the others constant." In what follows we shall report on several groups of factors purporting to account for attitudes toward the legality of abortion (the dependent variable).

Table C.8 is the regression equation for the general population sample that resulted after several prior analyses. We began with an equation that included a variety of independent variables, including the Personal Religiosity Index (PRI), the extent of Conservative Political Views, the respon-

TABLE C.8
Four Possible Explanations of Attitudes Favoring Abortion Legality
(General Population Sample, $N = 251$)

Variable	B	Beta	Significant T
Influence of Church Teachings	−.643	−.487	.000
Status	.052	.145	.011
Personal Religiosity Index	−.065	−.119	.085
Conservative Political Views	−.109	−.096	.089

Equation: R^2: .365
Adjusted R^2: .352
Significant F: .000

dent's estimate of the Influence of Church Teachings on his or her moral judgments, Status (education plus income), Age, and whether or not the respondent was a Catholic. Interestingly, neither Age nor Catholicism reached statistical significance; hence, both were dropped. Conservative Political Views and the Personal Religiosity Index were only marginally significant statistically, but they contribute to the overall strength of the equation. We had some concern that the high correlation between Influence of Church Teachings and the PRI meant that both could not be significant in the same equation. Therefore we ran the analysis with the PRI alone, while deleting the Church Teachings item. Without reporting the resulting equation here, suffice it to say that it was much weaker, predicting only 16 percent less of the overall variance.

The R^2 indicates the percentage of the variation in the dependent variable "predicted" by the equation. The *Betas* are standardized coefficients that indicate the relative contribution of each independent variable in "predicting" variation in the dependent variable. The T score is the statistical significance of the variable's relationship to the dependent variable, while the F statistic measures the significance of the overall equation. Thus, as the influence of church teachings, the PRI, and conservative political views increase, the likelihood of support for legal abortions decreases. On the other hand, support for legality increases with rising status (education and income). The overall equation explains just over 35 percent of the variation in attitudes toward the legality of abortion. With only four independent variables, that is quite respectable.

Although Catholicism was not a significant variable in the equation (see Table C.8), Catholic and non-Catholic differences were important in much of our research on Springfield, and we expected them to have some influence on abortion. Thus, we explored the Catholic/non-Catholic difference further. For example, while increased education is moderately correlated with abortion legality for non-Catholics ($r = .26$; $p<.01$), there is no correlation among Catholics ($r = .08$; n.s.). Also, age has opposite relations among respondents in the two groups: among Catholics, increasing age is negatively correlated with abortion legality ($r = -.25$; $p<.01$); for non-Catholics the relationship is of similar strength but in the opposite direction ($r = .26$; $p<.01$). While the latter correlation is something of a surprise, it may well reflect young conservative Protestants who are sympathetic to pro-life positions.

Table C.9 presents regression analyses for the general population sample separated into Catholic and non-Catholic groups (the latter including those who claimed no religious preference). Both initial equations contained the same independent variables: Influence of Church Teachings, the PRI, Political Views, Status, and Age. Note that different factors are better predictors for the two different groups. For Catholics, Influence of Church Teachings was the best independent variable by far; for non-Catholics, Age and Status were also significant. Overall, the Personal Religiosity Index was not as strong as a predictor. Again we substituted the PRI for Church Teachings and came up with equations explaining 10 percent less of the variance.

Thus, for our Catholic respondents, the influence of their Church's teachings on the abortion question was the strongest independent variable; as the Church's teachings increased in importance to the respondent, he or she was less likely to favor the legality of abortion. Increases in status produced slight increases in attitudes favoring legality; the PRI had only a slight negative effect. Among non-Catholics, Influence of Church Teachings was also strong and in a negative direction. However, both Age and Status (no doubt due to education's strength in non-Catholic's attitudes) had significant positive effects on attitudes toward abortion legality. Neither Conservative Political Views nor the PRI achieved statistical significance. See Table C.9.

Commentators on American religion have often noted the strength of its associational qualities of participation. That is, frequent attendance at religious services is an important dimension in American religion. We also found church attendance to be the strongest variable of the items that

TABLE C.9
Regressions on Abortion Legality for Catholics and Non-Catholics

Catholics (General Population Sample, N = 144)			
Variable	B	Beta	Significant T
Influence of Church Teachings	−.670	−.485	.000
Status	.050	.144	.052
Personal Religiosity Index	−.097	−.158	.068

Equation: R^2: .375
        Adjusted R^2: .359
        Significant F: .000

Non-Catholics (General Population Sample, N = 107)			
Variable	B	Beta	Significant T
Influence of Church Teachings	−.679	−.509	.000
Age	.023	.272	.002
Status	.089	.255	.004

Equation: R^2: .363
        Adjusted R^2: .342
        Significant F: .000

composed our Personal Religiosity Index: attendance, importance of religious beliefs, number of religious friends. Table C.10 explores these influences on abortion attitudes more fully by reporting separate regression analyses for respondents who were "active" attenders (several times per month or more) versus those who were "less active" (several times per year or less). Again, the equations for both groups began with the same independent variables: Influence of Church Teachings, Conservative Political Views, Status, and Catholicism (as a "dummy variable"; i.e., simply *yes* or *no*).

For the active attenders, Catholicism did not warrant inclusion in the final equation. The Influence of Church Teachings was the best predictor, and Status was also strong. The overall equation, while statistically significant, was not as strong as those reported above, explaining about 28 percent of the variance in attitudes toward legality. For the less active attenders, it is interesting that only the Influence of Church Teachings was statistically significant. While both Catholicism and Status contributed to the overall strength of the equation, neither reached significance on its own. We can only speculate as to why this should be the case, but the continued clarity of the Catholic Church and many conservative Prot-

TABLE C.10
Regressions on Abortion for Active and Less Active Church Attenders

Active Attenders (General Population Sample, $N = 146$)			
Variable	B	Beta	*Significant* T
Influence of Church Teachings	−.722	−.489	.000
Status	.072	.193	.017
Conservative Political Views	−.208	−.163	.044

Equation: R^2: .297
          Adjusted R^2: .278
          Significant F: .000

Less Active Attenders (General Population Sample, $N = 102$)			
Variable	B	Beta	*Significant* T
Influence of Church Teachings	−.688	−.541	.000
Catholicism (dummy variable)	.291	.105	.258
Status	.033	.113	.209
Conservative Political Views	−.068	−.080	.383

Equation: R^2: .299
          Adjusted R^2: .268
          Significant F: .000

estant churches on abortion is no doubt a factor. Even people who are not regular attenders know those "official" positions and are influenced by them. See Table C.10.

Our questionnaire samples also included a representation of Springfield's political and economic elites. Since the crux of our analysis of abortion in Springfield's politics concerned the interaction between activists and members of the city's political establishment, we examined the attitudes of the political-economic elite in more detail here.

In response to our question concerning their private views on the legality of abortion, almost 70 percent were favorable, with only 21 percent in either the definitely or probably illegal categories, and another 10 percent not sure. Perhaps predictably, the political leaders were somewhat more conservative than the economic. Thirty percent of the political elite, as opposed to 14 percent of the economic elite, felt that abortion should be illegal. This may be partly because the political leaders were closer to the popular pulse and partly because they included a higher proportion of Catholics in their ranks: 55 percent as opposed to 44 percent among the economic elite. Even among Catholic members of the entire political-economic elite sample, a majority favored legality (52 percent, as compared to 36 percent answering illegal), but it is worth noting that 88 percent of the non-Catholic elites chose legality (as distinct from actually approving the practice).

Table C.11 presents the final regression equation for our political and economic elite sample. The initial equation contained the same independent variables used in the analysis of the general population sample: Influence of Church Teachings, the PRI, Status, Age, Conservative Political Views, and Catholicism. Status, Age, and the PRI all failed to achieve statistical significance. Unlike the general sample, however, elite identification as Catholic did have a significant effect on attitudes toward abortion's legality; not surprisingly, Conservative Political views also played a

TABLE C.11
Basic Abortion Regression for Combined Political-Economic Elite
$(N = 69)$

Variable	B	Beta	Significant T
Influence of Church Teachings	−.733	−.601	.000
Catholicism	−.630	−.225	.025
Conservative Political Views	−.168	−.158	.079

Equation: R^2: .542
Adjusted R^2: .518
Significant F: .000

more substantial role. Finally, although the political-economic elite sample was distinctly more favorable to the legality of abortion than was the general sample, within the elite itself the distinction between Catholics and non-Catholics was clearly important. See Table C.11.

The strength of both Church Teachings and Catholicism in Table C.11 warrant further examination. Accordingly, Table C.12 presents regression equations for both Catholic and non-Catholic members of the political-economic elite. While the equation was stronger for Catholics, the Influence of Church Teachings was the only predictor variable achieving significance; Status, Age, the PRI, and Political Views were all dropped. For the non-Catholic elites, Conservative Political Views were significant and had a negative effect on favoring legality. Although the PRI was of only marginal significance, dropping it hurts the strength of the overall equation. Interestingly, it had a positive effect on the dependent variable for non-Catholic elites; that is, here greater personal religiousness was associated with a slight increase in the favoring of legality. See Table C.12.

Chapter Four reported that personal religiosity among the political-economic elites was strongly related to support for publicly sanctioned religious displays. This is obviously not as dramatic or as statistically significant concerning the legality of abortion. Among those elites reporting regular weekly attendance at religious services, 62 percent responded with an answer favoring legality. And among those responding that their

TABLE C.12

Regressions on Abortion for Catholic vs. Non-Catholic Political-Economic Elite

	Catholic Political-Economic Elite		
Variable	B	Beta	Significant T
Influence of Church Teachings	−.990	−.736	.000

Equation: R^2: .538
          Adjusted R^2: .525
          Significant F: .000

	Non-Catholic Elite		
Variable	B	Beta	Significant T
Influence of Church Teachings	−.533	−.541	.002
Conservative Political Views	−.265	−.398	.012
Personal Religiosity Index	.255	.198	.228

Equation: R^2: .400
          Adjusted R^2: .336
          Significant F: .002

religious beliefs were "very important" to them, 61 percent answered either definitely or probably legal. It is true that the majorities favoring legality were even more substantial among elites who were less religious in either attendance or belief, but even Catholic elite members who were active religious participants had a pro-choice majority. Indeed, by some measures, elite respondents who were *less active* in their faith were at least as conservative in their attitudes toward abortion as more active respondents.

Regression analyses for the political-economic elite, divided between frequent and less frequent religious service attenders, are included in Table C.13. Note that the overall equation was stronger for the *less* active factions, as was the influence of church teaching on their attitudes toward abortion. Also, while Catholicism was a stronger predictor for the active faction, Conservative Political Views was a stronger variable in the equation for less active respondents. Overall, personal religiosity itself did not appreciably effect the political and economic elites' attitudes in this area. See Table C.13.

In sum, while Springfield's population generally favored the continued legality of abortion, our more detailed analysis specified several factors that contributed to opposing legality rather than favoring it. The most

TABLE C.13
Regressions for Active vs. Less Active Attenders among Political-Economic Elite

	Religiously Active Elite		
Variable	B	Beta	*Significant* T
Influence of Church Teachings	−.627	−.474	.005
Catholicism (dummy variable)	−1.067	−.323	.045
Conservative Political Views	−.255	−.205	.162

Equation: R^2: .475
Adjusted R^2: .414
Significant F: .001

	Religiously Less Active Elite		
Variable	B	Beta	*Significant* T
Influence of Church Teachings	−.813	−.721	.000
Conservative Political Views	−.122	−.160	.186
Catholicism (dummy variable)	−.217	−.101	.427

Equation: R^2: .600
Adjusted R^2: .559
Significant F: .000

important of these was the influence of one's church's teaching on the subject. The more one was influenced by his or her church in forming an opinion, the more likely that opinion was to oppose legality. Increased social status—reflected here as a combination of higher income and education—was the only variable to consistently have positive effects on attitudes toward legality. Personal religious practices were much less significant than church teachings, and for the general sample, Catholic status was not a major independent variable. Both of those findings surprised us. However, we were certainly not surprised that, for those persons still influenced by their church and its teachings, abortion remained anathema.

For the political-economic elite, the story was somewhat different. Catholic identification was more important, as was political viewpoint. Both of those findings, and their inverse relations to legality, are easily interpreted. Status was less important, perhaps due to the generally higher status of the elite members of the sample. Overall, the equations for the elite sample were not as strong, perhaps reflecting the higher support for abortion legality found in the marginals. Thus, among the elite a religiously pluralist position seems to have been more common; abortion as a practice may not have been approved, but there was tolerance for its legality.

In general, the picture of Springfield as a "Catholic" city whose residents overwhelming oppose abortion due to their personal religious commitments needs serious revision.

BIBLIOGRAPHY

Aiken, Michael, and Paul E. Mott, eds. (1970). *The Structure of Community Power*. New York: Random House.

Alford, Robert R., and Roger Friedland (1985). *Powers of Theory*. Cambridge: Cambridge University Press.

Almond, Gabriel, and Sidney Verba (1965). *The Civic Culture*. Boston: Little, Brown and Company.

———. (1980). *The Civic Culture Revisited*. Boston: Little, Brown and Company.

Bachrach, Peter, and Morton S. Baratz (1962). "The Two Faces of Power." *American Political Science Review*, 56:947–952.

Back, Kurt W. (1986). "Why Is Abortion a Public Issue? The Role of Professional Control." *Politics and Society* 15:197–206.

Baltzell, E. Digby (1964). *The Protestant Establishment: Aristocracy and Caste in America*. New York: Random House.

———. (1979). *Puritan Boston and Quaker Philadelphia: Two Protestant Ethics and the Spirit of Class Authority and Leadership*. Boston: Beacon Press.

Banfield, Edward C., and James Q. Wilson (1963). *City Politics*. Cambridge: Harvard University Press and MIT Press.

Bauer, Frank, Jr. (1975). *At the Crossroads: Springfield, Massachusetts, 1636–1975*. Springfield, Mass.: U.S.A. Bicentennial Committee of Springfield, Inc.

Beckford, James A. (1983). "The Restoration of 'Power' to the Sociology of Religion." *Sociological Analysis* 44: 11–32.

———. (1989). *Religion and Advanced Industrial Society*. London: Unwin Hyman.

Bell, Daniel (1976). *The Cultural Contradictions of Capitalism*. New York: Basic Books.

Bellah, Robert N. (1967). "Civil Religion in America." *Daedalus* 96:1–21.

Bellah, Robert N., and Phillip E. Hammond (1980). *Varieties of Civil Religion*. New York: Harper and Row.

Bellah, Robert N., Richard Madsen, William M. Sullivan, Ann Swidler, and Steven M. Tipton (1985). *Habits of the Heart*. Berkeley: University of California Press.

Berger, Peter (1967). *The Sacred Canopy*. New York: Doubleday Anchor.

Blau, Peter M. (1964). *Exchange and Power in Social Life*. New York: John Wiley.

Bresnahan, Daniel (1971). "The Springfield Plan in Retrospect." Ed.D. dissertation, Teachers College, Columbia University.

Burnham, Walter Dean (1981). "The 1980 Earthquake: Realignment, Reaction, or What?" in *The Hidden Election*, T. Ferguson and J. Rogers, eds. New York: Pantheon.

Burns, Kathryne A. (1976a). "The French and French-Canadian Community," in *Springfield's Ethnic Heritage*. Springfield, Mass.: U.S.A. Bicentennial Committee of Springfield, Inc.

──────. (1976b). "The Irish Community," in *Springfield's Ethnic Heritage*. Springfield, Mass.: U.S.A. Bicentennial Committee of Springfield, Inc.

Campbell, Ernest Q., and Thomas F. Pettigrew (1959). "Racial and Moral Crisis: The Role of Little Rock Ministers." *American Journal of Sociology* 64:509–516.

Caplow, Theodore, Howard M. Bahr, and Bruce A. Chadwick (1983). *All Faithful People*. Minneapolis: University of Minnesota Press.

Castelli, Jim and Joseph Gremillion (1987). *The Emerging Parish: The Notre Dame Study of Catholic Life Since Vatican II*. San Francisco: Harper and Row.

Catabia, Ronald (1979). "Citizen Participation on Community Development Block Grant Neighborhood Councils, Community Development Funding, and Organizational Density." M.A. thesis, Springfield College, Springfield, Mass.

Chatto, Clarence, and Alice Halligan (1945). *The Story of the Springfield Plan*. New York: Barnes and Noble.

Clark, Christopher (1990). *The Roots of Rural Capitalism: Western Massachusetts (1780–1860)*. Ithaca: Cornell University Press.

Clark, Terry Nichols, and Lorna Ferguson (1983). *City Money: Politcal Processes, Fiscal Strain and Retrenchment*. New York: Columbia University Press.

Clarke, Christopher R. (1964). "The Secularization of Public Education." M.A. thesis, School of Education, American International College, Springfield, Mass.

Clegg, Stewart (1975). *Power, Rule and Domination*. London: Routledge and Kegan Paul.

Clough, Donald P. (1955). "A Study of the Socio-Economic and Ethnic Characteristics of the Area Adjacent to Springfield College, Census Tracts 17 and 18." M.S. thesis, Springfield College, Springfield, Mass.

Coulter, Philip B. (1968). "Public Opinion and Urban Redevelopment in Springfield." Springfield, Mass.: Springfield Redevelopment Authority.

Curran, Mary Doyle (1948 [1986]). *The Parish and the Hill*. New York: Feminist Press.

Dahl, Robert A. (1957). "The Concept of Power." *Behavioral Science* 2:201–205.

D'Antonio, William, James Davidson, Dean Hoge, and Ruth Wallace (1989). *American Catholic Laity in a Changing Church*. Kansas City, Mo.: Sheed and Ward.

──────. (1961). *Who Governs?* New Haven: Yale University Press.

Day, Thomas (1990). *Why Catholics Can't Sing*. New York: Crossroad Press.

Demerath, N. J., III (1968). "Trends and Anti-Trends in Religious Change," in *Indicators of Social Change*, Wilbert E. Moore and Eleanor Sheldon, eds., New York: Russell Sage Foundation.

────── (1991). "Religious Capital and Capital Religions: Cross-Cultural and Non-Legal Factors in the Separation of Church and State." *Daedalus* 120:21–40.

Demerath, N. J., III, and Rhys H. Williams (1984). "Separation of Church and State? A Mythical Past and Uncertain Future." *Society* 21:3–10.

────── (1985). "Civil Religion in an Uncivil Society." *Annals* 480:154–166.

────── (1992). "Secularization in a Community Context: Tensions of Religion and Politics in a New England City." *Journal for the Scientific Study of Religion*, vol. 31, no. 6. (See also Williams and Demerath.)

Devine, Donald (1972). *The Political Culture of the United States: The Influence of Member Values on Regime Maintenance*. Boston: Little, Brown and Company.

Dexter, Lewis A. (1970). *Elite and Specialized Interviewing*. Evanston, Ill.: Northwestern University Press.

Dobbelaere, Karl (1985). "Secularization Theories and Sociological Paradigms." *Sociological Analysis* 46: 377–387.

——— (1987). "The Evolutionary Differentiation Between Society and Interaction," in *The Micro-Macro Link*, J. Alexander, et. al., eds. Berkeley: University of California Press.

——— (1989). "The Secularization of Society? Some Methodological Suggestions," in *Secularization and Fundamentalism Reconsidered*, Jeffrey K. Hadden and Anson Shupe, eds. New York: Paragon House.

Dolan, Jay P. (1983). *The Immigrant Church*. Notre Dame, Ind.: University of Notre Dame Press.

Dolbeare, Kenneth M., and Phillip E. Hammond (1971). *The School Prayer Decisions: From Court Policy to Local Practice*. Chicago: University of Chicago Press.

Domhoff, G. William (1978). *Who Really Rules?* Santa Monica, Calif.: Goodyear Publishing Company.

———. (1983). *Who Rules America Now?* New York: Simon and Schuster.

———. (1986). "The Growth Machine and the Power Elite: A Challenge to Pluralists and Marxists Alike," in *Community Power*, R. Waste, ed. Beverly Hills, Calif.: Sage.

Domhoff, G. William, ed. (1980). *Power Structure Research*. Beverly Hills, Calif.: Sage.

Douglass, H. Paul (1926). *The Springfield Church Study*. New York: George H. Doran.

Dunn, Charles, W., ed. (1984). *American Political Theology*. New York: Praeger Publishers.

Durkheim, Emile (1912 [1965]). *The Elementary Forms of the Religious Life*. New York: Free Press.

Earle, John R., Dean D. Knudsen, and Donald W. Shriver, Jr. (1976). *Spindles and Spires: A Restudy of Religion and Social Change in Gastonia*. Atlanta: John Knox Press.

Eisinger, Peter K. (1980). *The Politics of Displacement: Racial and Ethnic Transition in Three American Cities*. New York: Academic Press.

Finke, Roger, and Rodney Stark (1990). *The Churching of America, 1776–1990*. New Brunswick, N.J.: Rutgers University Press.

Friedland, Roger, and Donald Palmer (1984). "Park Place and Main Street: Business and the Urban Power Structure." *Annual Review of Sociology* 10:393–460.

Frisch, Michael H. (1972). *Town into City: Springfield, MA, and the Meaning of Community, 1840–1880*. Cambridge: Harvard University Press.

———. (1987). "Town into City," in *Springfield, 1636–1986*, M. Konig and M. Kaufman, eds. Springfield, Mass.: Library and Museum Association.

Gamson, William A. (1968). *Power and Discontent*. Homewood, Ill.: Dorsey Press.

——— (1990). *The Strategy of Social Protest*. 2d ed. Belmont, Calif.: Wadsworth Publishing Company.

Gans, Herbert J. (1962). *The Urban Villagers: Group and Class in the Life of Italian-Americans*. New York: Free Press.

Garvey, Richard C. (1987). "Twentieth Century Springfield," in *Springfield, 1636–1986*, M. Konig and M. Kaufman, eds. Springfield, Mass.: Library and Museums Association.

Geertz, Clifford (1973). *The Interpretation of Cultures*. New York: Basic Books.

Gelin, James A. (1984). *Starting Over: The Formation of the Jewish Community of Springfield, Massachusetts, 1840–1905*. Lanham, Md.: University Press of America, Inc.

Glock, Charles Y., Benjamin B. Ringer, and Earl R. Babbie (1967). *To Comfort and to Challenge*. Berkeley: University of California Press.

Greeley, Andrew (1981a). *The Irish Americans*. New York: Harper and Row.

———— (1981b). *The Religious Imagination*. New York: Sadlier Press.

———— (1985). *American Catholics Since the Council: An Unauthorized Report*. Chicago: Thomas More.

Green, Mason A. (1888). *Springfield, 1636–1886: History of Town and City*. Springfield, Mass.: C. A. Nichols and Company.

Guth, James L. (1983a). "The New Christian Right," in *The New Christian Right*, R. Liebman and R. Wuthnow, eds. New York: Aldine.

————. (1983b). "Southern Baptist Clergy: Vanguard of the Christian Right?" in *The New Christian Right*, R. Liebman and R. Wuthnow, eds. New York: Aldine.

Habermas, Jurgen (1968). "Science and Technology as Ideology," in *Towards a Rational Society*. Boston: Beacon Press.

————. (1975). *Legitimation Crises*. Trans. by Thomas McCarthy. London: Heinemann Press.

Hackett, David G. (1990). *The Rude Hand of Innovation: Religion and Social Order in Albany, N.Y., 1776–1836*. New York: Oxford University Press.

Hadden, Jeffrey K. (1969). *The Gathering Storm in the Churches*. Garden City, N.Y.: Doubleday.

Hadden, Jeffrey K., and Anson Shupe, eds. (1989). *Secularization and Fundamentalism Reconsidered*. New York: Paragon House.

Hanna, Mary T. (1979). *Catholics and American Politics*. Cambridge: Harvard University Press.

Hartford, William (1989). *Working People of Holyoke*. New Brunswick, N.J.: Rutgers University Press.

Himmelstein, Jerome L. (1986). "The Social Basis of Antifeminism: Religious Networks and Culture," *Journal for the Scientific Study of Religion* 25:1–15.

Holstead, Roland E. (1982). *The Differential Response of Protestant Church Polities to Racial Change in an Urban Area*. Ph.D. dissertation, Department of Sociology, University of Connecticut, Storrs.

Hunter, Floyd (1953). *Community Power Structure*. Chapel Hill: University of North Carolina Press.

Huntington, Samuel P. (1981). *American Politics: The Promise of Disharmony*. Cambridge, Mass.: Belknap Press.

Innes, Stephen (1983). *Labor in a New Land*. Princeton: Princeton University Press.

————. (1987). "Distinguished and Obscure Men," in *Springfield, 1636–1986,* M. Konig and M. Kaufman, eds. Springfield, Mass.: Library and Museums Association.

Jackson, Kenneth T. (1967). *The Ku Klux Klan in the City, 1915–1930.* New York: Oxford University Press.

Jenkins, J. Craig (1983). "Resource Mobilization Theory and the Study of Social Movements." *Annual Review of Sociology* 9:527–553.

Johnson, Mary B. (1990). An Empirical Test of American Attitudes Towards the "Consistent Ethic of Life." M.A. thesis. Department of Sociology, University of Massachusetts, Amherst.

Kaynor, Edward (1962). "Citizen Participation in Government." M.A. thesis, University of Massachusetts, Amherst.

Konig, Michael F. (1986). *A Study in Leadership: Springfield and Its Mayors, 1945 to the Present.* Westfield, Mass.: Institute for Massachusetts Studies.

Ladd, Everett Carll, Jr. (1972). *Ideology in America.* New York: W. W. Norton and Company.

Lenski, Gerhard (1961). *The Religious Factor.* Garden City, N.Y.: Doubleday.

Lucas, Paul R. (1976). *Valley of Discord: Church and Society along the Connecticut River, 1636–1725.* Hanover, N.H.: University Press of New England.

Luhmann, Niklas (1984). *Religious Dogmatics and the Evolution of Societies.* New York: Edwin Mellen Press.

Lukas, J. Anthony (1986). *Common Ground.* New York: Vintage Books.

Luker, Kristin (1984). *Abortion and the Politics of Motherhood.* Berkeley: University of California Press.

Lukes, Steven (1974). *Power: A Radical View.* London: Macmillan.

Lynd, Robert S., and Helen Merrell Lynd (1929). *Middletown.* New York: Harcourt and Brace.

————. (1937). *Middletown in Transition.* New York: Harcourt and Brace.

Mannheim, Karl (1936). *Ideology and Utopia.* New York: Harcourt and Brace.

Martin, John Frederick (1991). Profits in the Wilderness: Entrepreneurship and the Founding of New England Towns. Chapel Hill: University of North Carolina Press.

McAdam, Doug (1983). "Tactical Innovation and the Pace of Insurgency." *American Sociological Review* 48:735–754.

McCarthy, John D., and Mayer N. Zald (1977). "Resource Mobilization and Social Movements: A Partial Theory." *American Journal of Sociology,* 82:1212–1241.

McClosky, Herbert, and Alida Brill (1983). *The Dimensions of Tolerance.* New York: Russell Sage Foundation.

McGuire, Meredith B. (1983). "Discovering Religious Power." *Sociological Analysis* 44:1–10.

McLoughlin, William G. (1971). *New England Dissent, 1630–1833. The Baptists and the Separation of Church and State.* Cambridge: Harvard University Press.

McNamara, Patrick H. (1969). "Priests, Protests, and Poverty Intervention." *Social Science Quarterly* 50:695–702.

———— (1985). "American Catholicism in the Mid-Eighties." *The Annals* 480:63–74.

Miller, Perry (1939). *The New England Mind.* 2 vols. Cambridge: Harvard University Press.

Mills, C. Wright (1956). *The Power Elite.* New York: Oxford University Press.

Molotch, Harvey (1976). "The City as a Growth Machine: Toward a Political Economy of Place." *American Journal of Sociology* 82:309–333.

Morgan, Edmund (1963). *Visible Saints: The History of a Puritan Idea.* New York: New York University Press.

Nichols, J. Bruce (1988). *The Uneasy Alliance: Religion, Refugee Work, and U.S. Foreign Policy.* New York: Oxford University Press.

Nobles, Gregory H. (1983). *Divisions Throughout the Whole: Politics and Society in Hampshire County, Ma., 1740–1775.* New York: Cambridge University Press.

Page, Charles H. (1952). "Bureaucracy and the Liberal Church." *Review of Religion* 16:137–150.

Platt, Gerald M., and Rhys H. Williams (1988). "Religion, Ideology, and Electoral Politics." *Society* 25:38–45.

Polsby, Nelson W. (1963). *Community Power and Political Theory.* New Haven: Yale University Press.

Pope, Liston (1942). *Millhands and Preachers.* New Haven: Yale University Press.

Quinley, Harold E. (1974). *The Prophetic Clergy: Social Activism Among Protestant Ministers.* New York: John Wiley.

Reichley, A. James (1985). *Religion in American Public Life.* Washington, D.C.: Brookings Institution.

Robbins, Thomas (1987). "Church-State Tension in the United States," in *Church-State Relations: Tensions and Transitions*, Thomas Robbins and Dick Anthony, eds., pp. 67–75. New Brunswick, N.J.: Transaction Books.

Roof, Wade Clark, and William McKinney (1987). *American Mainline Religion: Its Changing Shape and Future.* New Brunswick, N.J.: Rutgers University Press.

Roozen, David A., William McKinney, and Jackson W. Carroll (1984). *Varieties of Religious Presence: Mission in Public Life.* New York: Pilgrim Press.

Rose, Arnold M. (1967). *The Power Structure.* London: Oxford University Press.

Rosenzweig, Roy (1983). *Eight Hours for What We Will.* New York: Cambridge University Press.

Rossi, Peter H. (1970). "Power and Community Structure," in *The Structure of Community Power*, M. Aiken and P. Mott, eds. New York: Random House.

Ruether, Rosemary Radford (1987). *Contemporary Roman Catholicism: Crises and Challenges.* Kansas City, Mo.: Sheed and Ward.

Ryan, Dennis P. (1983). *Beyond the Ballot Box: A Social History of the Boston Irish, 1845–1917.* Amherst: University of Massachusetts Press.

Ryan, William (1971). *Blaming the Victim.* New York: Random House.

Scott, Jacqueline, and Howard Schuman (1988). "Attitude Strength and Social Action in the Abortion Dispute." *American Sociological Review* 53:785–793.

Seidler, John, and Katherine Meyer (1989). *Conflict and Change in the Catholic Church.* New Brunswick, N.J.: Rutgers University Press.

Selvin, Hanan C., and Warren O. Hagstrom (1960). "Determinants of Support for Civil Liberties." *British Journal of Sociology* 11:51–73.

Simmel, Georg (1903 [1950]). "The Role of the Stranger," in *The Sociology of Georg Simmel*, Kurt Wolff, ed. Glencoe, Ill.: Free Press.

Snow, David A., E. Burke Rochford, Jr., Steven K. Worden, and Robert D. Benford (1986). "Frame Alignment Processes, Micromobilization, and Movement Participation." *American Sociological Review* 51:464–481.

Stark, Rodney and William Bainbridge (1985). *The Future of Religion*. Berkeley: University of California Press.

Stone, Clarence N. (1976). *Economic Growth and Neighborhood Discontent*. Chapel Hill: University of North Carolina Press.

——— (1980). "Systemic Power in Community Decision Making: A Restatement of Stratification Theory." *American Political Science Review* 74:978–990.

Sullivan, Robert E., and James M. O'Toole, eds. (1985). *Catholic Boston: Studies in Religion and Community, 1870–1970*. Boston: Roman Catholic Diocesan Archives.

Sullivan, Winnifred F. (1987). "Religion and Law in the United States: 1870 to the Present," in John F. Wilson, ed. *Church and State in America*, vol. 2. New York: Greenwood Press.

Swidler, Ann (1986). "Culture in Action: Symbols and Strategies." *American Sociological Review* 51:273–286.

Tawney, R. H. (1926). *Religion and the Rise of Capitalism*. New York: Harcourt, Brace and Co.

Tocqueville, Alexis de (1848 [1969]). *Democracy in America*. New York: Harper and Row.

Tsacchen, Olivier (1991). "The Secularization Paradigm: A Systematization." *Journal for the Scientific Study of Religion* 30:395–415.

Underwood, Kenneth W. (1957). *Protestant and Catholic*. Boston: Beacon Press.

Van Moorseven, Hen C., and Ger Van der Tan. (1978). *Written Constitutions: A Computer Study*. Dobbs Ferry, N.Y.: Oceana Publishers.

Varenne, Herve (1977). *Americans Together: Structured Diversity in a Midwestern Town*. New York: Columbia University Teachers College Press.

Vidich, Arthur J., and Joseph Bensman (1968). *Small Town in Mass Society*. Revised edition. Princeton: Princeton University Press.

Warner, W. Lloyd, ed. (1963). *Yankee City*. Abridged edition. New Haven: Yale University Press.

Waste, Robert J., ed. (1986). *Community Power: Directions for Future Research*. Beverly Hills, Calif.: Sage.

Weber, Max (1905 [1946]). "The Protestant Sects and the Spirit of Capitalism," in *From Max Weber*, H. H. Gerth and C. W. Mills, eds. New York: Oxford University Press.

———. (1905 [1958]). *The Protestant Ethic and the Spirit of Capitalism*. New York: Scribner's.

Whitt, J. Allen (1982). *Urban Elites and Mass Transportation*. Princeton: Princeton University Press.

Williams, Raymond (1977). *Marxism and Literature*. Oxford: Oxford University Press.

Williams, Rhys H., and N. J. Demerath III (1991). "Religion and Political Process in an American City." *American Sociological Review* 56:417–431.

Wilson, John F. (1979). *Public Religion in American Culture*. Philadelphia: Temple University Press.

—— ed. (1987). *Church and State in America*, vols. 1 and 2. Westport, Conn.: Greenwood Press.

Wood, James R., and Mayer N. Zald (1966). "Aspects of Racial Integration in the Methodist Church: Sources of Resistance to Organizational Policy." *Social Forces* 45:255–265.

Wood, Michael, and Michael Hughes (1984). "The Moral Basis of Moral Reform: Status Discontent vs. Culture and Socialization as Explanations of Anti-Pornography Social Movement Adherence." *American Sociological Review* 49:86–99.

Wright, James D. (1976). *Dissent of the Governed*. New York: Academic Press.

Wrong, Dennis (1980). *Power*. New York: Harper Colophon Books.

Wuthnow, Robert (1988). *The Restructuring of American Religion*. Princeton: Princeton University Press.

Zurcher, Louis A., and R. George Kirkpatrick (1976). *Citizens for Decency: Antipornography Crusades as Status Defense*. Austin: University of Texas Press.

INDEX

Abington Township v. *Schmepp*, 110

abortion, 5, 102, 214–215, 269; attitudes toward, 217–220, 233–236, 288, 338–346; and hospitals, 132, 135, 216, 221, 231; and local activist groups, 224–227; as political issue, 92, 127 128, 134–135, 221–224, 229–230, 233, 236–238, 240, 246–248, 250, 260, 268, 280–283. *See also* sexuality

African-Americans, 12, 51, 59, 123, 273; churches of, 119, 134, 198; clergy, 187–190, 195, 204, 211–212; in local history, 178, 181–182; and politics, 79, 88, 90, 119, 134, 176–177, 182–183, 194–195; social differences among, 182, 186–187, 196, 204, 209–210

Baptists, xvi, 27–32, 40, 50, 146, 180

Bishop (Catholic): and abortion issue, 135–136, 220–223, 232, 245, 247; political style of, 71–72, 85–86, 127–128, 136–139, 158, 163, 188, 220–223, 232, 237, 243, 245, 262–263, 281–282, 313. *See also* Catholicism; clergy; religion

Catholicism (Roman): attitudes toward abortion, 215–220, 338–345; attitudes toward church-state issues, 101–102, 106; discrimination against, 34, 41–42, 52; ecclesiastical authority in, 46, 50, 52–54, 70–72, 137–138, 153, 177, 188, 261, 263, 281–282, 292–293, 295, 312–313; as established religion, 7, 95–96, 121, 140, 256, 258, 260, 295, 312; ethnicity within, 177–179, 294; and homeless issue, 152, 163; local growth of, 39–56, 107, 312; mobility within, 71–72, 178, 281–282, 294–295, 299, 313; numbers of, 307–308; politics and power of, 7, 46–47, 98, 118–119, 121, 127, 136, 162, 221, 238–239, 245, 256, 273, 279, 299; and public schools, 115, 122–123, 125, 131; and secularization, 261, 278, 288–293, 297, 299; Spring-

field diocese of, 3, 43–44, 310–311. *See also* Bishop, religion

church-state relations: in American history, xiii, 3, 107, 255; attitudes toward, 100–103, 106, 109, 257–258, 331, 333, 336–338; and the Constitution, 4, 6, 22, 31, 96, 103; in local politics, 97, 111, 135–137, 140, 159, 255–258; and Massachusetts' law and politics, xvi, 27–29, 31, 110, 112–113, 125–128, 133, 137, 222, 255, 273; scholarship on, xiii, 5–6; U.S. Supreme Court cases on, 5, 29, 97, 99, 102, 109–110, 114, 124, 139, 159–160, 214, 260

cities: crises in, 58–59; dynamics of, 9–10, 60, 92, 94–95, 165, 171, 270–272, 309–311, 316–317; growth of, 32, 52; urban renewal and, 59, 78, 181

city government: attitudes toward, 82–84, 145, 183–184, 185, 192, 277; bureaucracies in, 92, 200, 275–276, 309–311; and churches, 134, 137, 151, 155, 159–160; and city services, 119, 121, 132, 155; and economic development, 78–81, 193; and hospitals, 132, 135, 241–242, 244; relations with state government, 149, 152, 155, 194, 272–273; structure of, 59–64, 137, 185, 199, 201, 273–274, 314. *See also* political culture; politics

Civil Liberties Union of Massachusetts, 112, 120, 256; and abortion issues, 135–136, 233; and religion in schools, 125–127, 129

clergy: attitudes toward abortion, 219–220; attitudes toward church-state issues, 101, 125; attitudes toward government, 84–85, 146, 184–185; attitudes toward sex education, 240; and community influence, 86–87, 108, 153, 158, 309; differences among, 225, 266–267; and political activism, 127, 148–149, 151–153, 156–157, 161, 187–190, 195–199, 203–204, 208–212, 246, 265, 285

Native Americans, 23, 26, 40

newspapers, 39, 73–75, 312; Catholic, 44–
45, 49, 107, 111, 131; and economic development, 73–75, 200, 202–203, 212;
and homeless issue, 143, 148, 153; and
politics, 62, 68, 73–74, 85–87, 195–196,
204, 274, 277, 313; and sexuality issues,
135, 229, 231–232, 240. *See also* elites

organized crime, 90, 176; and Catholic
Church, 71, 89–90; and city government/
politics, 88–90, 111, 300

parochial schools, 5, 93, 102, 122, 124, 292;
and city government, 129–130; enrollment in, 123, 131, 292; public aid to, 106,
108–109, 121–131, 134, 222, 235; relations with state regulators, 120, 124, 130–
131; sex education in, 239–240. *See also*
Catholicism; public schools

pluralism, 12, 45, 167–168; religious, 9, 27,
45, 107, 220, 255, 266, 279, 295

political culture: and civic morality, 136,
234–235, 237–238, 241, 243, 246, 248,
269, 280; and civic religion, 82–84, 134,
141–142, 185, 212, 271, 274–277, 285,
296–297, 334–338; and confrontation,
154, 194, 203–204, 208, 210–211, 213,
227, 230–232, 237, 246, 282; and consensus, 94, 100, 158, 162, 191–193, 196, 198,
200, 214, 237–238, 258, 274–275, 277,
281–282, 296, 314; interpersonal relations
in, 93–94, 271, 310–311; issue defiinition
in, 193, 268; and moral legitimacy,
164, 206–210, 212–213, 233, 238, 265,
268, 276, 284, 286, 298; "neighborhood"
in, 185, 192, 199, 212; and political
leadership, 234, 236, 251–252; "public/
private" dynamic in, 169, 191, 217, 230,
235, 237, 260, 268–269, 282–284; and religion, 97–100, 114, 133–134, 137–139,
146, 153, 157, 164, 188–189, 191, 263,
274–275, 281, 298, 305–306; and symbolism, 134, 170–171, 189, 194, 206–207,
222, 263, 268. *See also* politics; power;
religion

politics: and city elections, 52–53, 55–56,
60–61, 63–66, 194, 197, 201, 228–229,
236, 273–274; context of, 92, 269–275;
and economic planning, 79 81; and

ethnoracial differences, 52, 59, 62, 84–
85, 88, 180, 183, 197–198, 204–205, 208–
209, 213, 230, 264; issue-specific, 264,
267, 269; perceptions of power in, 85–90;
and social change, 249–250, 252–253. *See
also* city government; political culture;
power

power, 90–94; and access, 269, 375–280;
cultural, 9, 95, 164, 169–172, 206, 213,
215, 230, 233, 237, 252, 276, 282–286,
313; definition and nature of, 90, 167–
170, 278–281; and issues, 280–281, 283,
285–286; structural, 9, 95, 167–168, 171,
276–277, 284–285. *See also* city government; elites; politics

Protestantism (mainline), 7, 11, 162, 225;
African-American, 178, 185, 187, 218,
290; attitudes of, 85, 101, 218; and business elite, 74–75, 313; decline of, 12, 35–
38, 53, 57, 68, 77, 146–147, 256–257, 262,
291, 296, 312; as established religion, 4–
5, 22, 24, 32, 107–108, 110; and politics,
68, 88, 119–120, 147; and secularization,
287, 289–291, 293–294, 296–297. *See also*
religion

public schools, 5, 39–40, 56, 72, 78, 102,
123, 239, 251; attitudes toward, 114–117,
131, 145; and busing, 123–124, 179;
health clinic in, 238, 244–248, 252–253,
264; and relations with parochial schools,
124–131; and religion, 72, 105–106, 109–
117, 125–126, 129; sex education in, 240–
243, 245, 280; "Springfield Plan" in, 108,
130, 238; and state regulators, 115, 257,
273. *See also* city government; parochial
schools; politics

Puritanism, 23–24, 28

Quakers, 27, 29, 40, 180

religion: and city services, 117, 121, 134;
"civil," 21, 82, 112, 133–134, 180, 296,
299; holiday symbols of, 97–99, 102, 104;
organizational structures in, 38, 166, 182,
187, 198, 209, 213, 219–220, 225, 265–
267, 278–279, 290–291; and political identification, 47, 50–51, 55–56, 93, 157; as
political resource, 95, 158, 161, 163–164,
166, 170–171, 189–190, 193, 208–209,
211–213, 233, 268, 266, 276, 278, 284–